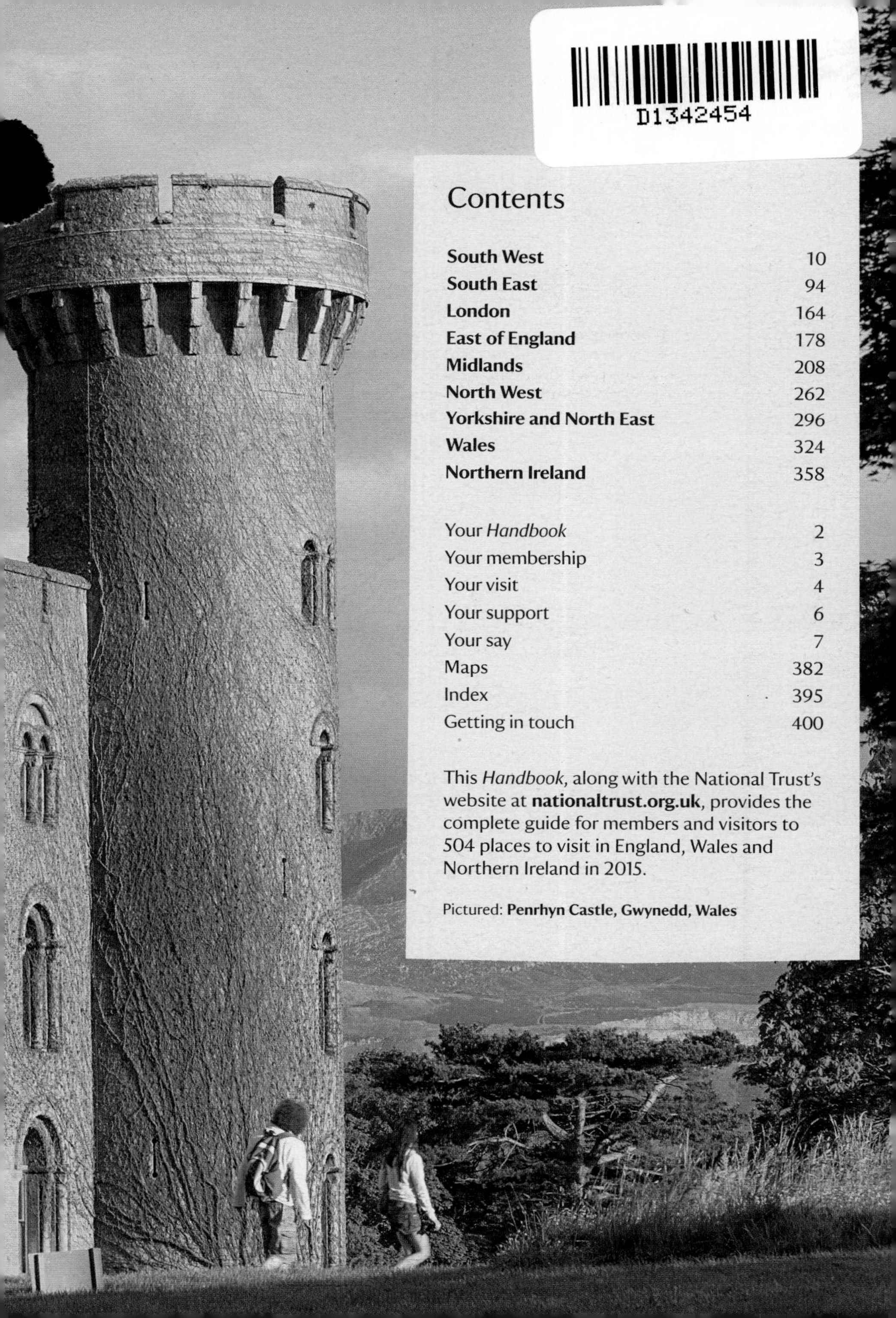

Contents

This *Handbook*, along with the National Trust's website at **nationaltrust.org.uk**, provides the complete guide for members and visitors to 504 places to visit in England, Wales and Northern Ireland in 2015.

Pictured: **Penrhyn Castle, Gwynedd, Wales**

Your *Handbook*

Handbook

Use it to plan your visits

app

Search in your app store for 'National Trust'

Website

A handy place to visit first: nationaltrust.org.uk

Getting here **guide**

A useful supplement is available on request (see panel opposite)

Your *Handbook* is just one way to make the most of your visits.

To help you find your way around this book, we've arranged individual places into geographical areas, then ordered them alphabetically. You can get a general feel for an area's coast and countryside, and then for each place within that area.

Maps

For easy reference, we've grouped all the maps together at the back of your *Handbook* (see pages 382 to 394). They show all the places we mention.

Opening arrangements

We'd like you to have enough time to enjoy your visit to the full. **Please be aware that last entry is 30 minutes before the time shown on the property tables.**

Occasionally we have to change opening arrangements at short notice because of a special event or something unexpected such as dangerous weather conditions. Wherever possible, we do try to publicise any closures. You can check on our website or with the place you are visiting. To make sure of opening times, check on the day if possible.
If you would like extra copies of this *Handbook*, they're available to buy, while stocks last.

Example place		M	T	W	T	F	S	S
House								
11 Feb–4 Nov	11–5	M	T	W	T	F	S	S
5 Nov–28 Nov	11–5	M	T	W	·	·	S	S
1 Dec–9 Dec	10:30–4:30	M	T	W	T	F	S	S
Garden, shop and tea-room								
11 Feb–30 Mar	10–5	M	T	W	T	F	S	S
31 Mar–30 Sep	10–6	M	T	W	T	F	S	S
1 Oct–4 Nov	10–5	M	T	W	T	F	S	S
5 Nov–28 Nov	10–5	M	T	W	·	·	S	S
1 Dec–9 Dec	10–4:30	M	T	W	T	F	S	S

Last entry to house and tea-room 20 minutes before closing. 7 December: open to 7.

Black type indicates that the place or facility is **open** on these days.

A grey dot indicates that the place or facility is **closed** on these days.

Special notes or important information regarding opening.

Your membership

Your membership not only gives you access to places you love and ones you've yet to discover, it also helps care for the 500+ places listed in this *Handbook*. It means that together we can make sure they're always there for everyone to enjoy. That couldn't happen without you – thank you so much.

With this year's membership card you can explore the places we look after as often as you like.

Membership of the National Trust gives you free parking in Trust car parks and free entry to most of the places we look after during normal opening times and under normal opening arrangements.

Membership cards are not transferable.

If your card is lost or stolen, please contact the Supporter Services Centre on 0344 800 1895. A temporary card can be sent quickly to a holiday address or emailed to you.

Visiting other organisations

The National Trust is part of an international family of like-minded organisations sharing a passion for caring for heritage and nature. As a member, you can enjoy visiting special places cared for by 14 other National Trusts around the world for free on production of a current membership card – including Scotland, Australia, New Zealand, Canada and Italy. There's a full list on our website or available from the Supporter Services Centre.

The National Trust for Scotland (NTS) looks after special places in Scotland. As a National Trust member you are entitled to visit NTS properties in Scotland free of charge. Don't forget to take your latest membership card with you.

Entry to places owned by the Trust but maintained and administered by English Heritage or Cadw (Welsh Government's historic environment service) is free to members of the Trust, English Heritage and Cadw. These places are listed in the *Handbook*.

Getting here guide

We want you to have a safe and pleasant journey to each of our properties. So to help, we've included a grid reference under each property entry, allowing you to locate the place you want to visit on the maps at the back of your *Handbook*. Where appropriate we have also included Sat Nav details.

You'll also find up-to-date details of how to get to us in the *Getting here* guide, which you can request by calling 0344 800 1895 or visit our website **nationaltrust.org.uk/gettinghere2015**

Here's where you can also get more help to plan your journey:

Transport Direct: **transportdirect.info**

Sustrans: **sustrans.org.uk** or telephone 0117 929 0888.

National Rail Enquiries: **nationalrail.co.uk** or call 08457 48 49 50.

Traveline: **traveline.info** or call 0871 200 2233.

For taxis from railway stations see **traintaxi.co.uk**

Public transport in Northern Ireland: **translink.co.uk** or call 028 9066 6630.

Your visit

What you pay

As a member you can enjoy free entry virtually everywhere as often as you like. Sometimes there may be a charge to cover extra costs involved: at some places we manage in partnership; on special event days; for guided tours; to access certain areas or additional facilities. At the few places where this is the case, we make this clear in the note at the end of the description.

For accurate up-to-date admission prices head to **nationaltrust.org.uk** or call our Supporter Services team on 0344 800 1895.

Children

Under-fives go free, and there's a reduced admission price for five to sixteen-year-olds (typically 50 per cent). Seventeen-year-olds and over pay the adult price. Unaccompanied children are admitted at the Trust's discretion. Discounted prices apply to families in most cases and there's a range of family-friendly facilities (see 'Making the most of your day' in each entry or the 'Useful information for families' section opposite).

Group visits

Please book all group visits in advance with your destination. Discounts are usually available for groups of 15 plus. Travel trade information is at **nationaltrust.org.uk/groups**, telephone 0844 800 2329 or email **traveltrade@nationaltrust.org.uk**

Booking in advance

At some smaller places such as Mr Straw's House, you'll need to book in advance. Sometimes timed tickets are issued to everyone – including members – especially on busy days. Check our website for more information.

Safety

We want you to enjoy exploring and discovering new places, which is why we take your safety very seriously. We have practical advice for planning your visit, what to wear and bring, on our website.

Dogs

Whether the family pet or your trusted guide, your dog is welcome at the National Trust. Where possible, we provide fresh water, exercise areas and shady spaces in car parks – so no need to leave your dog in a hot car.

Well-behaved dogs are welcome at most coast and countryside places, but please observe local notices – particularly at sensitive times of year. Dogs should be kept on a short lead when crossing fields between 1 March and 31 July, and always when near grazing animals. In some areas, particularly beaches, there may be restrictions, usually seasonal.

To help others enjoy the places we look after, please clear up dog mess and dispose of it responsibly, taking it away with you where dog-waste bins aren't provided.

Eating and shopping

Did you know that the money you spend in our shops, restaurants, tea-rooms and coffee shops looks after special places? Your next cup of tea and slice of Victoria sponge could help go towards the cost of repaving a footpath or restoring a tapestry.

Our shops stock a wide range of merchandise, much of it exclusive to the National Trust. You can also shop online at **shop.nationaltrust.org.uk**

Access

The symbols inside the front cover indicate the access and facilities at each place. Please ring before your visit in case a particular provision needs to be booked.

Carers or essential companions of disabled visitors enjoy free entry on request.

An Admit One card can be issued to make this easier, call 01793 817634 or email enquiries@nationaltrust.org.uk

Useful information for families

All our restaurants and cafés have high chairs, children's menus and colouring sheets. Most places have baby-changing and baby-feeding areas – some also have parent and baby rooms. At some of the historic places we look after we might ask you to leave your pushchair at the entrance, but we do have front-carrying slings for smaller babies and hip-seat carriers or reins for toddlers, which you're very welcome to borrow. We welcome baby back-carriers wherever we can, although it may not always be possible where space is limited and at very busy times.

We have lots of ways to make visiting with children fun and enjoyable. As well as special children and family events throughout the year, we have guides, trails and quizzes, as well as our Tracker Packs – child-size backpacks complete with activity sheets and bug-hunting kit. Tracker Packs are free to borrow – at some places a small deposit may be required. Many sites have discovery rooms and play areas and there is plenty of space to play in gardens and parkland.

Sometimes we might restrict access to certain areas because birds are nesting or because we have wildlife there that needs a bit of peace and quiet. But there's always a helpful volunteer or member of staff on hand to tell you all you need to know.

Photography

You are very welcome to take pictures during your visits. When indoors please don't use a flash or a tripod, as it can disturb other people. All pictures taken at indoor sites are at the discretion of the Property/General Manager. Prior permission from the owners of loan items may also need to be acquired. Mobile phones with built-in cameras can also be used without flash.

At most places special arrangements can be made for interested amateurs to take interior photographs outside normal opening hours. Requests need to be made in writing to the place you'd like to go, giving your address. We're not able to offer this everywhere and there may be an admission charge (including National Trust members).

All requests for commercial, non-editorial filming and photography need to go through our Broadcast and Media Manager, who can be contacted on 020 7824 7128.

Your support

Supporting our work

As a charity we rely on the financial support of our members and donors to look after the special places in our care. You can help us by making a donation. From supporting one of our appeals to leaving a legacy in your Will, you can make a difference to the places that you love. Please visit our website **nationaltrust.org.uk/getinvolved/donate/waysofgiving** or contact the Supporter Services Centre for details. Thank you to everyone who supports us so generously.

Volunteering

Helping out at a National Trust place as a volunteer is a great way to discover more about a place that means something to you, and share your interest with others. As a charity we completely depend on our volunteers to look after the coastline, countryside, historic buildings and gardens in our care. To find out how you could get involved, head to **nationaltrust.org.uk/get-involved/volunteer**

Supporter groups

You can also help us and have fun at the same time by joining a Supporter Group. Our Centres/Friends groups enjoy talks, holidays, social events and days out while raising funds, and our National Trust Volunteer groups get stuck in with practical outdoor tasks. Discover more at **nationaltrust.org.uk/get-involved/volunteer/ways-to-volunteer/supporter-groups**

Events

Meet our conservationists at our 'Conservation in Action' events. Learn more about our work with a 'behind-the-scenes tour' of a garden or house, or attend a lecture lunch. Enjoy wildflower walks and live summer concerts, living history events and countryside open days, open-air theatre productions, craft fairs and carol concerts.

For what's happening at a place near you, visit **nationaltrust.org.uk/visit/whats-on/events**

Heritage Lottery Fund

Using money raised through the National Lottery, the Heritage Lottery Fund (HLF) sustains and transforms a wide range of heritage for present and future generations to take part in, learn from and enjoy.

The HLF has awarded grants totalling £100 million to the National Trust in the last 20 years. It has supported many of the Trust's most important projects, including Tyntesfield, the Giant's Causeway, Knole and Castle Drogo.

If you would like to find out more please visit **hlf.org.uk**

heritage lottery fund
LOTTERY FUNDED

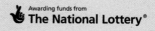

Awarding funds from
The National Lottery®

The Royal Oak Foundation

Through the generous support of its members and donors across the US, Royal Oak makes grants to the Trust. Royal Oak members enjoy free entry to National Trust places, and lectures and tours in the US. For more information please visit **royal-oak.org**

Your say

Annual General Meeting

Our Annual General Meeting (AGM) each autumn is an opportunity for you to meet our Trustees and staff, ask questions and contribute to debates. Most importantly, you can exercise your right to vote on both resolutions and elections to our Council.

You can also vote online and watch the live AGM webcast. There will be more details in the autumn magazine and on our website **nationaltrust.org.uk/agm**

Governance

A guide to the Trust's governance arrangements is available on our website **nationaltrust.org.uk/about-us** and on request from The Secretary.

Our Annual Report and Financial Statements are available online at **nationaltrust.org.uk/annualreport** and on request from **annualreport@nationaltrust.org.uk**

Privacy Policy

The National Trust's Privacy Policy sets out the ways in which we process personal data. The full Privacy Policy is available on our website **nationaltrust.org.uk** The National Trust makes every effort to comply with the principles of the Data Protection Act 1998.

Use made of personal information

Personal information provided to the National Trust via our website, membership forms, fundraising responses, emails and telephone calls will be used for the purposes outlined at the time of collection or registration in accordance with the preferences you express.

By providing personal data to the National Trust you consent to the processing of such data by the National Trust as described in the full Privacy Policy. You can alter your preferences as explained in the following paragraph.

Verifying, updating and amending your personal information

If, at any time, you want to verify, update or amend your personal data or preferences please write to:

National Trust,
Supporter Services Centre,
PO Box 574,
Manvers,
Rotherham,
S63 3FH.

Verification, updating or amendment of personal data will take place within 28 days of receipt of your request.

If subsequently you make a data protection instruction to the National Trust, which contradicts a previous instruction (or instructions), then the Trust will follow your most recent instruction.

Subject access requests

You have the right to ask us, in writing, for a copy of all the personal data held about you (a 'subject access request').

There's a payment fee of £10. To access your personal data held by the National Trust, please apply in writing to:
The Data Protection Officer,
National Trust,
Heelis, Kemble Drive,
Swindon,
Wiltshire,
SN2 2NA.

Map 1

South West

Kynance Cove, Cornwall

Outdoors in the South West

The ultimate holiday peninsula, for locals and visitors, blessed with a spectacular variety of landscapes, seascapes and natural wonders for you to explore and enjoy.

Baggy Point

near Croyde, North Devon

Map (1) E5 1939

Baggy Point is the impressive headland at Croyde, once owned by the Hyde family and overlooking one of the best surfing beaches in the South West. Huge coastal views, great walks and opportunities to climb, surf and coasteer make it a must-do destination for anyone visiting North Devon. **Note**: toilets (not National Trust) on main beach slipway, 500 yards from Trust car park.

Eating and shopping: Sandleigh tea-room, garden and shop (tenant-run) serving drinks and food grown in the walled garden. New open-air covered seating area overlooking garden. Tea-room is next to car park, close to beach slipway. Car park kiosk serving cold drinks and snacks.

Thrift on the cliff edge at Baggy Point, North Devon

Making the most of your day: free children's activity pack (to borrow). Walks leaflets available from car park kiosk. Arlington Court and the National Carriage Museum is nearby. **Dogs**: welcome on leads (except for seasonal ban on Croyde Beach from May to September).

Access:
Sat Nav: use EX33 1PA. **Parking**: car park in Moor Lane, Croyde.

Finding out more: 01271 870555 or baggypoint@nationaltrust.org.uk

Baggy Point
Car park is usually manned March to November and at busy periods, and locked at dusk.

Brean Down

North Somerset coast

Map (1) H4 1954

One of Somerset's most striking coastal landmarks: a dramatic limestone promontory jutting out into the Bristol Channel. You can relax on the beach at the foot of the down or take a walk along this spectacular 'natural pier' to the Palmerston fort, which provides a unique insight into Brean's past. **Note**: steep climbs and cliffs; please stay on main paths. Tide comes in quickly.

Eating and shopping: Cove Café serving cooked breakfast, lunch or tea and cakes. Shop selling ice-cream, buckets and spades and beach games.

Making the most of your day: fort with gun magazines (open most weekends). Welcome beach hut. Wild Wednesdays for children during school holidays. Downloadable circular walk. **Dogs**: welcome on leads.

Access: **Building**
Sat Nav: use TA8 2RS. **Parking**: at the beach.

Finding out more: 01278 751874 or breandown@nationaltrust.org.uk

Brean Down
Café (01278 751897) and shop opening hours vary according to weather.

The Palmerston fort on the tip of Brean Down, Somerset, was built in the 1860s to protect the Bristol Channel

Brownstone and Coleton Camp

between Dart Estuary and Brixham, Devon

Map (1) G9 1981

Rugged and captivating stretch of coast east of the Dart Estuary, with cliffs, beaches and traditional farmland. From Trust car parks you can easily reach the coast path for great walking and superb views. Close to Brownstone car park is one of the few remaining Second World War gun batteries. **Note**: public toilets at nearby Kingswear, or at the Trust's Coleton Fishacre (when open).

Eating and shopping: café at nearby Coleton Fishacre offering tea and homemade cakes or a hearty lunch.

Making the most of your day: spectacular views of the coast. Peregrines, seals and dolphins can be spotted from the coast path. The Froward Point area is known for its rare flora. **Dogs**: on leads near livestock and on cliff paths.

Access:
Sat Nav: use TQ6 0EH for Brownstone; TQ6 0EQ Coleton Camp; TQ6 0EF Mansands and Scabbacombe. **Parking**: at Brownstone (for Froward Point and Brownstone Battery), Coleton Camp, Mansands (for Woodhuish and Mansands Beach) and Scabbacombe.

Finding out more: 01803 753010 or coletoncamp@nationaltrust.org.uk

Cheddar Gorge

The Mendips, Somerset

Map (1) I4 1910

At almost 400 feet deep and three miles long, Cheddar is England's largest gorge. It was formed during successive Ice Ages, when glacial meltwater carved into the limestone, creating steep cliffs. The gorge is a haven for wildlife and contains many rare plants, including the Cheddar pink. **Note**: terrain is steep away from the road. Caves and car parks privately owned (charge including members).

Eating and shopping: gift shop and information centre.

Making the most of your day: 4-mile circular gorge walk (details from shop and information centre) and Strawberry Line (NCN26) cycle route to Cheddar. **Dogs**: welcome on leads in shop and gorge.

Access:
Sat Nav: use BS27 3QE. **Parking**: pay and display car parks on both sides of gorge, not National Trust (charge including members).

Finding out more: 01278 751874 or cheddargorge@nationaltrust.org.uk

Cheddar Gorge		M	T	W	T	F	S	S
Information centre and shop								
14 Mar–19 Jul	11–5	M	T	W	·	F	S	S
20 Jul–6 Sep	11–5	M	T	W	T	F	S	S
7 Sep–1 Nov	11–5	M	T	W	·	F	S	S

Also open Bank Holidays.

The Castle Folly at Fyne Court, Somerset

Fyne Court

near Bridgwater, Somerset

Map (1) H5 1967

A hidden Somerset gem in the Quantock Hills. While the house (the former home of amateur scientist Andrew Crosse) no longer stands, the site, within woods and meadows, is simply beautiful. A great place for splashing in streams, building dens, discovering ruins and following trails. Information room in courtyard.

Eating and shopping: Courtyard tea-room serving light lunches, cream teas and cakes. Bags of charcoal for sale in tea-room.

Making the most of your day: events, including open-air theatre, Wild Wednesdays for families in school holidays and free Thursday tours of the grounds in the summer. Three walking trails and a children's play trail. **Dogs**: welcome on leads.

Access: **Grounds**
Sat Nav: use TA5 2EQ. **Parking**: on site.

Finding out more: 01643 862452 or fynecourt@nationaltrust.org.uk

Fyne Court		M	T	W	T	F	S	S
Estate								
Open all year		**M**	**T**	**W**	**T**	**F**	**S**	**S**
Tea-room								
21 Mar–1 Nov	10:30–4*	**M**	**T**	**W**	**T**	**F**	**S**	**S**

*Extended opening hours in the school holidays. Opening times vary according to weather conditions.

Glastonbury Tor

near Glastonbury, Somerset

Map (1) I5 1933

Iconic tor, topped by a 15th-century tower offering spectacular views of the Somerset Levels, Dorset and Wiltshire. **Note**: sorry no toilet. For Sat Nav use BA6 8YA for nearest car park, not National Trust (charge including members).

Finding out more: 01278 751874 or glastonburytor@nationaltrust.org.uk

Leigh Woods

Bristol

Map (1) I4 1909

Beautiful haven on Bristol's doorstep, with diverse woodland and wonderful views of Avon Gorge and the suspension bridge. Excellent network of paths, including a 1¾-mile easy-access trail, links to the National Cycle Network and new 'Yer Tiz' off-road cycle trail. **Note**: sorry no toilet.

Eating and shopping: picnics welcome.

Making the most of your day: natural play area. Permanent orienteering course (map available from office). **Dogs**: welcome (but be aware of cattle).

Access: [icon]
Sat Nav: use BS8 3PL for North Road entrance; BS8 3QB for Leigh Woods car park.
Parking: limited. Either on site (not National Trust) or on North Road (off A369).

Finding out more: 0117 973 1645 or leighwoods@nationaltrust.org.uk

Little Dartmouth

near Dartmouth, Devon

Map (1) G9 1970

Coastal woods, cliffs and coves west of Dartmouth, with views over the Dart Estuary and Start Bay. In spring and summer the coastal paths are ablaze with colour from wild flowers, and if you walk to Gallants Bower you'll discover a Civil War Royalist encampment and panoramic views over Dartmouth. **Note**: toilets at Dartmouth Castle (not National Trust).

Eating and shopping: picnics welcome. Café at Dartmouth Castle (not National Trust).

Making the most of your day: downloadable 4-mile circular walk. Dartmouth Castle nearby (not National Trust).

Access: [icon]
Sat Nav: use TQ6 0JP.
Parking: at Little Dartmouth.

Finding out more: 01752 346585 or littledartmouth@nationaltrust.org.uk

Parke

near Bovey Tracey, Devon

Map (1) G7 1974

Set on the south-eastern edge of Dartmoor, this tranquil country park contains numerous delights. Riverside paths follow the course of the Bovey, as it meanders through woodlands and meadows rich in plant and wildlife. There is also a medieval weir and orchard with historic apple trees.

Eating and shopping: Home Farm Café (not National Trust).

Making the most of your day: orienteering trails and geocaching. Events and apple days. Self-guided woodland trails and quizzes. **Dogs**: on leads where stock grazing.

Access: [icons] **Countryside** [icon]
Sat Nav: use TQ13 9JQ. **Parking**: on site.

Finding out more: 01626 834748 or parke@nationaltrust.org.uk

Parke		M	T	W	T	F	S	S
Parkland, woodland and walks								
Open all year	Dawn–dusk	M	T	W	T	F	S	S
Home Farm Café								
Open all year	10–5*	M	T	W	T	F	S	S

*Café: closes at 4 in winter. Late-night opening summer weekends.

At the foot of the Dewerstone in the Plym Valley, Devon

Plymbridge Woods and Plym Valley

near Plymouth, Devon

Map (1) F8 1968

The wooded valley of the River Plym creates a 'green bridge' from Plymouth to the heights of Dartmoor. At its lower end, Plymbridge is the starting point for cycle trails and walks, discovering birdlife and industrial ruins. The upper valley climbs through rocky crags to open onto the high moors.

Eating and shopping: mobile refreshment van in Plymbridge car park (weekends). Riverside picnic spots.

Making the most of your day: old railway line cycle path and wooded mountain-bike trail. Peregrine falcons to spot from viaduct (spring). Paddling and swimming in the river. Geocaching, den-building, downloadable Tracker Packs, orienteering and events.
Dogs: welcome under control.

Access:
Sat Nav: use PL7 4SR for Plymbridge; PL7 5HD Shaugh Prior; PL7 5EH Cadover Bridge.
Parking: at Plymbridge, Shaugh Prior and Cadover Bridge.

Finding out more: 01752 341377 or plymvalley@nationaltrust.org.uk

Purbeck Countryside

near Corfe Castle, Dorset

Map (1) K7 1976

A world in miniature – heaths, hills, cliffs and coast ready to be explored on foot or by bike.

Finding out more: 01929 450002 or purbeck@nationaltrust.org.uk

Salcombe to Hope Cove

near Salcombe, Devon

Map (1) F9 1938

This spectacular stretch of coast west of the Salcombe Estuary includes the headlands of Bolt Head and Bolt Tail and secluded sandy beaches. The majestic ragged cliffs have claimed countless ships over the centuries. There is an easy-access route at Bolberry Down and a family trail at East Soar. **Note**: sorry no toilet.

Eating and shopping: Walkers' Hut café (tenant-run) at East Soar serving hot drinks and homemade cakes. Nearby Overbeck's offering crab sandwiches and cream teas with sea views.

Making the most of your day: downloadable walks and Salcombe Estuary canoe map guides. Canoe hire available through Singing Paddles (not National Trust). **Dogs**: welcome on leads where animals grazing.

Access:
Sat Nav: use TQ7 3DY for Bolberry Down and TQ7 3DR for East Soar. **Parking**: at East Soar, Bolberry Down, Snapes Point and Hope Cove (not National Trust).

Finding out more: 01752 346585. 01548 561904 (Walkers' Hut) or salcombe@nationaltrust.org.uk

Salcombe to Hope Cove

For opening times of the Walkers' Hut, telephone 01548 561904.

South Milton Sands

Thurlestone, near Kingsbridge, Devon

Map 1 F9 1980

This popular beach – a long sweep of golden sand and rock pools – edges a sheltered bay of crystal-clear water and looks out to the iconic Thurlestone Rock offshore. The nearby wetland is home to many bird species and is an ideal place to spot rare migratory visitors.

Eating and shopping: Beach House café (concession) serving refreshments and lunches (locally caught fish).

Making the most of your day: great for swimming (RNLI lifeguard in summer). Wetsuits, as well as windsurf and paddle boards for hire. The South West Coast Path offers great walks. **Dogs**: welcome on coast path and beach.

Access: Café
Sat Nav: use TQ7 3JY. **Parking**: behind beach.

Finding out more: 01752 346585 or southmiltonsands@nationaltrust.org.uk

South Milton Sands

Beach café seasonal opening (call 01548 561144 for details).

Stonehenge Landscape

near Amesbury, Wiltshire

Map 1 K5 1927

The National Trust cares for 827 hectares (2,100 acres) of downland within the Stonehenge World Heritage Site. The landscape is studded with ancient monuments and contains a diverse range of wildlife. The visitor shuttle from the English Heritage visitor centre includes an optional stop at Fargo woodland (National Trust). **Note**: English Heritage manages stone circle, visitor centre and shuttle (Trust members free), booking essential. Pay and display car park (English Heritage-run) free to Trust members, booking essential to guarantee a space.

Eating and shopping: café and shop at visitor centre (not National Trust).

Making the most of your day: guided walks and family activities throughout the year. **Dogs**: welcome on leads and under close control. Assistance dogs only at stone circle.

Access:
Parking: at visitor centre (English Heritage), free to Trust members displaying Trust sticker. Booking essential to guarantee space. Limited parking at Woodhenge.

Finding out more: 01980 664780 or stonehenge@nationaltrust.org.uk

Studland Beach

Studland, near Swanage, Dorset

Map (1) K7 1982

Glorious slice of Purbeck coastline with a 4-mile stretch of golden, sandy beach, gently shelving bathing waters and views of Old Harry Rocks and the Isle of Wight. Includes the most popular naturist beach in Britain. The heathland behind the beach is a haven for native wildlife and features all six British reptiles. Designated trails through the sand dunes and woodlands allow for exploration and spotting of deer, insects and bird life as well as numerous wild flowers. Studland was the inspiration for Toytown in Enid Blyton's *Noddy*. **Note**: toilets at Shell Bay, Knoll Beach and Middle Beach; also South Beach (not National Trust).

Eating and shopping: seaside café with spectacular views of Old Harry Rocks serving fresh, locally sourced food (inside and outside seating). Log burner in winter. Knoll Beach shop sells seaside-themed goods, including buckets and spades, swimwear and local gifts.

Making the most of your day: year-round events, including geocaching, wildlife-themed guided walks, slacklining, beach volleyball, food events and Discovery Centre for private hire. Watersports. Coastal change interpretation hut. **Dogs**: restrictions apply 1 May to 30 September.

Access: **Grounds**
Sat Nav: use BH19 3AH for Knoll Beach.
Parking: at Shell Bay (7 to 9); South Beach (9 to 11); Knoll Beach and Middle Beach (9 to 8, or dusk if earlier).

Finding out more: 01929 450500 or studlandbeach@nationaltrust.org.uk

Studland Beach		M	T	W	T	F	S	S
Shop and café								
1 Jan–28 Mar	10–4	M	T	W	T	F	S	S
29 Mar–28 Jun	9:30–5*	M	T	W	T	F	S	S
29 Jun–6 Sep	9–6	M	T	W	T	F	S	S
7 Sep–24 Oct	9:30–5*	M	T	W	T	F	S	S
25 Oct–31 Dec	10–4	M	T	W	T	F	S	S

*Shop and café open one hour later at weekends. Shop and café opening hours may be longer in fine weather and shorter in poor. Shop and café closed 5 March and 25 December.

Wembury

near Wembury village, Plymouth, Devon

Map (1) F9 1939

A great beach, and more: some of the best rock pools in the country, good surfing, masses of wildlife and views of a distinctive island – the Great Mewstone. Starting point for lovely inland and coastal walks to Wembury Woods and the Yealm Estuary, as well as around Wembury Point. **Note**: toilet (not National Trust).

Eating and shopping: Old Mill Café serving coffees, homemade cakes, soups, pasties and ice-cream, as well as beach shop selling everything from spades and wetsuits to windbreaks (both concessions). Pub in Noss Mayo (not National Trust), a walk and ferry ride away.

Making the most of your day: rock-pooling at Marine Centre, surfing, kayaking and snorkelling. **Dogs**: welcome on coast path all year, and on beach 1 October to 30 April.

Access: [icons] Café [icon] Marine Centre [icon]
Beach [icon]
Sat Nav: use PL9 0HP.
Parking: just above beach.

Finding out more: 01752 346585.
01752 862538 (Marine Centre) or
wembury@nationaltrust.org.uk

Wembury
For details of the Old Mill Café seasonal opening, telephone 01752 863280.

Cornish Coast

It's all about the coast, laden with memories of childhood holidays: sandy beaches, harbours and secret coves, cafés on the water's edge, breathtaking clifftop paths.

Boscastle

near Camelford, Cornwall

Map (1) D7 [icons] 1955

The Trust cares for much of the land in and around the harbour village of Boscastle, including the cliffs of Penally Point and Willapark, which guard the sinuous harbour entrance; Forrabury Stitches, high above the village and divided into ancient 'stitchmeal' cultivation plots; and the lovely Valency Valley running inland. **Note**: toilet by main car park (not National Trust).

Eating and shopping: café with courtyard seating (free wi-fi), shop and visitor centre.

Making the most of your day: children's quiz/ trail. Coasteering available nearby. Holiday cottages. Combine with a visit to Tintagel Old Post Office, just a few miles along the coast.
Dogs: welcome on walks and in café courtyard.

Access: [icons] Grounds [icon]
Sat Nav: use PL35 0HD. **Parking**: 100 yards, pay and display, not National Trust (charge including members).

Finding out more: 01840 250010 or
boscastle@nationaltrust.org.uk

Boscastle		M	T	W	T	F	S	S
Shop, café and visitor centre								
1 Jan–28 Feb	10:30–4	M	T	W	T	F	S	S
1 Mar–2 Aug	10–5	M	T	W	T	F	S	S
3 Aug–4 Sep	10–5:30	M	T	W	T	F	S	S
5 Sep–1 Nov	10–5	M	T	W	T	F	S	S
2 Nov–31 Dec*	10:30–4	M	T	W	T	F	S	S

*Closed 25 and 26 December.

Bude to Morwenstow

North coast, Cornwall

Map (1) D6 [icons] 1960

Here is one of Cornwall's wildest corners. Glorious beaches, perfect for rock-pooling or surfing, are backed by sheer and twisted cliffs. Exhilarating coastal walks along the clifftops, and intriguing local characters to discover, such as Parson Hawker, the vicar of Morwenstow, and the Grenville family of Stowe. **Note**: seasonal toilets at Sandymouth and Duckpool.

Sandymouth near Bude, Cornwall, is a popular surf beach

Eating and shopping: café at Sandymouth (concession) open seasonally. The Rectory Tea-rooms at Morwenstow (tenant-run). Pubs, shops and cafés in Kilkhampton and Bude (none National Trust).

Making the most of your day: surf school at Sandymouth. Rock-pooling at all beaches. Hawker's Hut made of driftwood, on the coast path at Morwenstow. **Dogs**: welcome under control everywhere, including beaches.

Access: **Coast and beach**
Sat Nav: for Northcott Mouth use EX23 9EE; Sandymouth EX23 9HW; Duckpool EX23 9JN; Morwenstow EX23 9SR.
Parking: at Northcott Mouth, Sandymouth, Duckpool and Morwenstow.

Finding out more: 01208 863046 or bude@nationaltrust.org.uk

Bude to Morwenstow
Café at Sandymouth open seasonally (01288 354286). Rectory Tea-rooms at Morwenstow (01288 331251).

Cape Cornwall

near St Just, Land's End Peninsula, Cornwall

Map (1) A9 1987

Known as the connoisseurs' Land's End, the distinctive headland of Cape Cornwall is part of a wild and rugged landscape, rich in tin-mining history and part of the Cornish Mining World Heritage Site. Views to Longships Lighthouse and Isles of Scilly. Sea-birds, including puffins, nest on the Brisons rocks. **Note**: narrow lanes, unsuitable for caravans. Seasonal toilets at Cape Cornwall.

Eating and shopping: from Easter to end October, mobile snack van in Cape Cornwall car park offering tea, coffee, sandwiches and homemade cake. Nearby St Just has several shops, stores, pubs and a post office (none National Trust).

Making the most of your day: perfect beach for rock-pooling and wild swimming. Local crab and lobster fishermen still use Priest's Cove. Coast path goes by Ballowall Barrow and the Coastwatch hut. **Dogs**: welcome, but under control near livestock.

Access:
Sat Nav: use TR19 7NN for Cape Cornwall car park, and TR19 7QQ for Botallack Count House car park. **Parking**: at Cape Cornwall, Porth Nanven (Cot Valley), Ballowall and Botallack Count House.

Finding out more: 01736 791543 or capecornwall@nationaltrust.org.uk

Carne and Pendower

near Veryan, Cornwall

Map ① C9 1961

Two of the best beaches on the lovely Roseland peninsula: fine stretches of sand and rock pools, popular with families. Walks along the coast and inland will reveal the area's wildlife – great for butterflies in summer and birds in winter – and history, from the Bronze Age to the Cold War. **Note**: seasonal toilets in both car parks.

Eating and shopping: seasonal ice-cream van at Carne. The renowned Hidden Hut (tenant-run) is not far away at Porthcurnick Beach.

Making the most of your day: the beaches are ideal for bathing and rock-pooling. A path leads inland to Carne Beacon, one of Britain's largest Bronze Age barrows. Downloadable walking trails cover the wider area. **Dogs**: seasonal dog restrictions on beaches (under control near livestock).

Access:
Sat Nav: for Carne use TR2 5PF and Pendower TR2 5LW. **Parking**: on site.

Finding out more: 01872 580553 or carne@nationaltrust.org.uk

Carnewas at Bedruthan

near Padstow, Cornwall

Map ① C8 1930

This is one of the most popular destinations on the Cornish coast. Spectacular clifftop views stretch across Bedruthan Beach (not National Trust). The Trust has rebuilt the steep cliff staircase to the beach, but visitors need to be aware of the risk of being cut off by the tide. **Note**: unsafe to bathe at any time. Toilet not always available.

Eating and shopping: Trust shop and café (concession) with clifftop tea-garden. Picnic area.

Making the most of your day: children's quiz/trail, walks leaflet and information panel. Play area. Bunkhouse and holiday cottages. Why not combine with a visit to nearby Trerice? **Dogs**: welcome.

Access: **Car park and clifftop**
Sat Nav: use PL27 7UW. **Parking**: on site.

Finding out more: 01637 860563 or carnewas@nationaltrust.org.uk

Carnewas at Bedruthan		M	T	W	T	F	S	S
Shop								
14 Feb–22 Feb	11–4	M	T	W	T	F	S	S
28 Feb–8 Mar	11–4	·	·	·	·	·	S	S
14 Mar–1 Nov	10:30–5	M	T	W	T	F	S	S
Café								
14 Feb–27 Mar	11–4	M	T	W	T	F	S	S
28 Mar–1 Nov	10:30–5	M	T	W	T	F	S	S
26 Dec–31 Dec	11–4	M	T	W	T	·	S	S

Cliff staircase closed from 2 November to mid-February.
Telephone 01637 860701 to confirm café opening times in winter.

Godrevy

near Hayle, Cornwall

Map ① B9 1939

Long sandy beaches on St Ives Bay with wildlife-rich cliffs and walks. Godrevy café in dunes (concession). **Note**: unstable cliffs and incoming tides. Toilets open main season only. Parking limited around wet weather and busy times. For Sat Nav use TR27 5ED.

Finding out more: 01872 552412 or godrevy@nationaltrust.org.uk

Holywell and Crantock

near Newquay, Cornwall

Map (1) C8 1951

Close to Newquay, this feels like a different Cornwall: two classic north coast beaches with expanses of golden sand, great for sandcastles and surfing. Footpaths inland and around the coast invite you to discover wildlife-rich dunes and sandy grassland, a quiet estuary, cliffs carpeted with wild flowers, unspoilt coves and caves. **Note**: toilets at Crantock open seasonally.

Eating and shopping: refreshments available nearby at Holywell, Crantock, Cubert and West Pentire. Fern Pit café (not National Trust), across the Gannel Estuary from Crantock beach, is accessible by ferryboat at high tide during main season or by footbridge at low tide.

Making the most of your day: surf schools and board hire at Crantock and Holywell. Rock-pooling at Holywell. Seals and rare butterflies. Summer wild flowers at West Pentire to discover. **Dogs**: welcome under control everywhere, including beaches.

Access:
Sat Nav: use TR8 5RN for Crantock, TR8 5PF for Holywell and TR8 5QS for Treago Mill.
Parking: at Crantock (height restriction barrier when unmanned), Holywell and Treago Mill for Polly Joke Beach (also known as Porth Joke).

Finding out more: 01208 863046 or holywellandcrantock@nationaltrust.org.uk

Holywell Bay: a classic north Cornish beach

Power-kiting above Lantic Bay in Cornwall

Lantic Bay and Lansallos

between Polperro and Polruan, Cornwall

Map (1) D9 1936

East of Fowey, a long stretch of unspoilt coast much loved by walkers, rich in wild flowers and birds. Car parks at Lantic Bay, Lantivet Bay and Lansallos, with footpaths linking to the coast path, make great starting points to discover the sandy beaches and smaller rocky coves. **Note**: toilets at Lantivet Bay car park.

Eating and shopping: this is a remote and undeveloped coast, perfect for picnics. Nearest shops and pubs in Polruan, Pelynt, Bodinnick and Polperro (none National Trust).

Making the most of your day: downloadable walking trails. Play trails at Lansallos and Lantic Bay car parks. Great stretch of coast for kite-flying, paddling and bathing. Trust-run campsite at Lansallos, and several holiday cottages nearby. **Dogs**: welcome, under close control around livestock.

Access:
Sat Nav: use PL13 2PX for Lansallos and PL23 1NP for Lantivet Bay and Lantic Bay.
Parking: at Lansallos, Lantivet Bay and Lantic Bay.

Finding out more: 01726 870146 or lanticbay@nationaltrust.org.uk

Lizard Point and Kynance Cove

The Lizard peninsula, near Helston, Cornwall

Map (1) C10 1935

Lizard Point, mainland Britain's most southerly point, offers dramatic coastal walks, wild flowers and interesting geological features. Two miles north lies Kynance Cove, considered one of the most beautiful beaches in the world. The Lizard Wireless Station museum at nearby Bass Point is open regularly celebrating Marconi's historic technological experiments. **Note**: Kynance car-park toilets closed during winter; beach can be completely covered at high tide.

Eating and shopping: café at Kynance Cove (March to October), café at Lizard Point (open all year) – both concessions.

Making the most of your day: Cornish choughs and seals can be seen from the Wildlife Watchpoint (spring and summer). To make the most of Kynance beach, visit at low tide. **Dogs**: seasonal day-time dog bans on some beaches, including Kynance.

Access: **Lizard Wireless Station** **Lizard Point**
Sat Nav: use TR12 7NU for Lizard Point; TR12 7PJ Kynance. **Parking**: at Lizard Point and Kynance.

Finding out more: 01326 561407. 01326 291174 (Rangers/Wireless station) or lizard@nationaltrust.org.uk

The Lizard
Telephone for opening times of the Lizard Wireless Station.

Mullion Cove and Poldhu Cove

The Lizard peninsula, near Helston, Cornwall

Map (1) C10 1945

Mullion Cove is home to a historic working harbour, with turquoise calm water in the summer and towering Atlantic waves in the winter. Nearby Poldhu is a family-friendly sandy beach with dunes. The Marconi Centre celebrates Poldhu as the site of the first transatlantic wireless signal. **Note**: car park and toilets not National Trust. National Trust campsite at Teneriffe Farm, Mullion.

Eating and shopping: seasonal café at Mullion Cove during summer. Cafés, shops and pub in Mullion village and café at Poldhu beach open all year (none National Trust).

Making the most of your day: kayaks for hire at Mullion Harbour for exploring hidden bays and caves. Surf school at Poldhu offering lessons for all the family. Fascinating wildlife and excellent walking at Predannack.
Dogs: welcome, except for seasonal day-time dog ban on Poldhu beach.

Access: **Mullion harbour**
Sat Nav: use TR12 7BU for Poldhu; TR12 7EP for Mullion Cove; TR12 7EZ for Teneriffe Farm Campsite and Predannack Wollas. **Parking**: at Mullion Cove and Poldhu (neither National Trust).

Finding out more: 01326 291174 or mullioncove@nationaltrust.org.uk

The beach at Poldhu Cove on The Lizard, Cornwall

Penrose

near Helston, Cornwall

Map ① B10 1974

Home to Loe Pool, Cornwall's largest lake, Penrose is a mix of woods, farmland, parkland, cliffs and beaches: a great place to explore. There are 16 miles of bridleways and footpaths, including a trail around the pool and many coast path links. At Gunwalloe, a medieval church divides two beaches.

Eating and shopping: Stables Café with parkland views. Picnics welcome in the neighbouring walled garden.

Making the most of your day: you can hire a bike at Porthleven, try the easy-access route from Helston to the café, or pick a downloadable trail to follow. Free *Outdoors Guide* and maps available. **Dogs**: welcome (seasonal dog ban at Gunwalloe Church Cove).

Access: **Gunwalloe beach** **Stables/parkland**
Sat Nav: use TR13 0RD for Penrose Hill and TR12 7QE for Gunwalloe. **Parking**: around Loe Pool (Penrose Hill for Stables Café), and at Gunwalloe.

Finding out more: 01326 558423 or penroseestate@nationaltrust.org.uk

Penrose		M	T	W	T	F	S	S
Stables Café								
3 Jan–29 Mar	10–4:30	·	·	·	·	·	S	S
3 Apr–30 Oct	10–4:30	M	T	W	T	F	S	S
31 Oct–20 Dec	10–4:30	·	·	·	·	·	S	S

Polzeath to Port Quin

near Wadebridge, Cornwall

Map ① D7 1936

An outstanding stretch of unspoilt coast. Port Quin and Port Gaverne were once busy fishing ports. The headlands of Pentire and the Rumps have spectacular views and wild flowers. Lundy Bay is at the foot of a secluded valley filled with wildlife, while Pentireglaze Haven's sandy beach offers great rock-pooling. **Note**: nearest toilets in Polzeath village (not National Trust).

Eating and shopping: pubs, cafés and shops in Polzeath village (not National Trust).

Making the most of your day: seals, rare bats, corn buntings and puffins to spot. Well-preserved Iron Age ramparts on the Rumps (above). Quirky Doyden Castle is a Trust holiday cottage. Sea kayaking and coasteering available. **Dogs**: welcome under control. Seasonal dog ban on Polzeath beach (including Pentireglaze Haven).

Access: **Coast and beach**
Sat Nav: use PL29 3SU for Port Quin; PL27 6QY Pentireglaze and Pentire Farm; PL27 6QZ Lundy Bay. **Parking**: at Port Quin, Pentire Farm, Lead Mines (Pentireglaze) and Lundy Bay. Also at Polzeath (not National Trust).

Finding out more: 01208 863046 or portquin@nationaltrust.org.uk

Porthcurno

near Penzance, Land's End peninsula, Cornwall

Map (1) B10 1994

Soft, white shell beach with popular freshwater stream, surrounded by turquoise seas. Great for watching birds, basking sharks and dolphins. **Note**: for Sat Nav use TR19 6JU. Car parking and toilet charges (including members).

Finding out more: 01736 791543 or porthcurno@nationaltrust.org.uk

St Agnes and Chapel Porth

near Truro, Cornwall

Map (1) C9 1956

This breathtaking coastal landscape is a walkers' paradise, with sweeping expanses of rare coastal heath – dazzling purple and yellow in late summer – huge skies and views, an ancient beacon site and dramatic mine ruins. There is a popular surf beach that becomes a vast expanse of sand at low tide. **Note**: seasonal toilets at Chapel Porth.

Eating and shopping: Chapel Porth Beach café open daily in summer and most winter weekends (01872 552487). Picnics welcome.

Making the most of your day: footpaths help you explore the landscape. World Heritage Site mine buildings at Wheal Coates and Trevellas and the legend of Giant Bolster to discover. **Dogs**: welcome everywhere, except on Chapel Porth Beach from Easter Sunday to 30 September inclusive.

Access:
Sat Nav: use TR5 0NS for Chapel Porth; TR5 0NT Wheal Coates; TR4 8BZ Towan Cross; TR5 0NU St Agnes Head. **Parking**: At Wheal Coates, St Agnes Head, St Agnes Beacon, Towan Cross and Chapel Porth (very busy in summer).

Finding out more: 01872 552412 or chapelporth@nationaltrust.org.uk

St Anthony Head and Porth

near St Mawes, Cornwall

Map (1) C9 1959

This remote peninsula on the south coast of Cornwall is a hidden treasure. The combination of cliffs, creeks, headlands, woods and lovely beaches, linked by many miles of footpaths, gives a fantastic variety of walking routes. Pick your route to suit your mood, or the weather that day.

Eating and shopping: many wonderful spots for picnicking. Seasonal pop-up tea-room at Porth. Not far away is Porthcurnick, where you'll find the renowned Hidden Hut beach café (tenant-run).

Making the most of your day: historic military remains on St Anthony Head, and a bird hide for spotting peregrines. Quiet sandy Towan Beach close to Porth. **Dogs**: welcome (under control near livestock).

Access:
Sat Nav: use TR2 5HA for St Anthony and TR2 5EX for Porth. **Parking**: at St Anthony Head and Porth.

Finding out more: 01872 580553 or stanthonyhead@nationaltrust.org.uk

The Cotswolds

One of the most English of landscapes, the Cotswold Hills form a patchwork quilt of woods, winding river valleys, flower-filled meadows and commons and picturesque villages of honey-coloured limestone.

Crickley Hill

Birdlip, Gloucestershire

Map (1) K2 1935

Sitting high on the Cotswold escarpment with views towards the Welsh hills, the hill overlooks Gloucester and Cheltenham. **Note**: partly owned and managed by Gloucestershire County Council, including car park and visitor centre. For Sat Nav use GL4 8JY. Parking charges (including members).

Finding out more: 01452 814213 or crickleyhill@nationaltrust.org.uk

Haresfield Beacon

near Stroud, Gloucestershire

Map (1) J2 1931

Prominently positioned on three spurs of the Cotswold escarpment. Views across the Severn Estuary towards the Forest of Dean and Brecon Beacons. The wildlife is some of the best in the Cotswolds and there's a wealth of archaeological features, including long and round barrows, a hill fort and cross dyke. **Note**: Cotswold Way National Trail runs through estate.

Eating and shopping: pubs in Randwick and Haresfield (not National Trust). Ice-cream vendor in Shortwood car park (not Trust) on sunny days. Picnics welcome.

Making the most of your day: wildlife, from bluebells to butterflies, to spot, as well as superb veteran beech trees on the slopes of Shortwood. Great place to fly a kite and watch buzzards and kestrels. **Dogs**: welcome but please keep on a lead if there is livestock grazing.

Access:
Sat Nav: use GL6 6PP for Shortwood car park.
Parking: at Shortwood.

Finding out more: 01452 814213 or haresfieldbeacon@nationaltrust.org.uk

Minchinhampton and Rodborough Commons

near Stroud, Gloucestershire

Map (1) J2/3 1913

Sunrise at Minchinhampton Common, Gloucestershire

These historic Cotswold commons, traditionally grazed, are famed for rare flowers and butterflies, prehistoric remains and far-reaching views. Minchinhampton Common contains a nationally important complex of Neolithic and Bronze Age burial mounds, while the limestone grasslands of Rodborough Common have abundant wild flowers, including the rare pasqueflower and many different varieties of orchids.

Eating and shopping: many great picnic spots (no picnic tables). The historic Winstones ice-cream factory is on Rodborough Common and ice-cream vans are usually found in the reservoir car park in summer. Several pubs around the edge of both commons (none National Trust).

Making the most of your day: the commons are great places to walk, picnic, spot butterflies or fly a kite, and there are regular events throughout the year. Downloadable Rodborough Common butterfly walk available. **Dogs**: welcome everywhere (under close control near livestock).

Access:
Sat Nav: use GL5 5BJ for Minchinhampton; GL5 5BP Rodborough. **Parking**: at Reservoir car park on Minchinhampton Common; Rodborough Fort car park on Rodborough Common.

Finding out more: 01452 814213 or minchinhampton@nationaltrust.org.uk

Woodchester Park

Nympsfield, near Stroud, Gloucestershire

Map (1) J3 1994

This tranquil wooded valley contains a 'lost landscape': remains of an 18th- and 19th-century landscape park with a chain of five lakes. The restoration of this landscape is an ongoing project. Waymarked trails (steep in places) lead through picturesque scenery, passing an unfinished Victorian mansion. **Note**: mansion managed by Woodchester Mansion Trust. Toilet not always available. Mansion not National Trust, admission charges apply (including members).

Making the most of your day: waymarked trails through valley. **Dogs**: under close control, on leads where requested.

Access: **Grounds**
Sat Nav: use GL10 3TS. **Parking**: pay and display for non-members, accessible from Nympsfield road, 300 yards from B4066 junction.

Finding out more: 01452 814213 or woodchesterpark@nationaltrust.org.uk

Woodchester Park	
Open every day all year	Dawn–dusk

Exmoor

Where moorland meets the sea: a National Park with high moorland, ancient woods, rushing river valleys, remote farms and cliffs plunging into the Bristol Channel.

Heddon Valley

near Parracombe, between Lynton and Combe Martin, North Devon

Map (1) F5 1963

The dramatic West Exmoor coast, favourite landscape of the Romantic poets, offers not only the Heddon Valley, but also Woody Bay and the Hangman Hills to explore. There are spectacular coastal and woodland walks, and a car park, shop and information centre in the Heddon Valley.

Eating and shopping: shop selling walking equipment and clothing, maps, postcards, local products, books and ice-cream.

Making the most of your day: all-terrain children's buggies and an all-terrain mobility scooter available to hire from shop. Barbecues free to borrow. **Dogs**: welcome.

Access: **Countryside**
Sat Nav: use EX31 4PY. **Parking**: opposite shop.

Finding out more: 01598 763402 or heddonvalley@nationaltrust.org.uk

Heddon Valley		M	T	W	T	F	S	S
Shop								
14 Mar–2 Apr	10:30–4:30	M	T	W	T	F	S	S
3 Apr–30 Sep	10:30–5	M	T	W	T	F	S	S
1 Oct–1 Nov	10:30–4:30	M	T	W	T	F	S	S

Holnicote Estate

near Minehead, Somerset

Map (1) G5 1944

Set within Exmoor National Park, Holnicote was part of the Acland bequest, one of the largest estates donated to the National Trust. There are 20 square miles of spectacular landscape to explore, with five pretty villages and vast tracts of moorland, including Dunkery Beacon, Somerset's highest point. Ancient Horner Wood has many species of bat, fungi and lichen. With more than 150 miles of paths, including the South West Coast Path (below), this is a fantastic area for walking, horse-riding, cycling and orienteering. Wildlife highlights include red deer, Exmoor ponies and the heath fritillary butterfly.
Note: toilets at Bossington and Horner car parks; also at Selworthy (not National Trust).

Eating and shopping: Periwinkle tea-room on Selworthy Green serves light lunches or cream teas. Shop selling gifts and information on exploring the estate. Barbecues welcome in picnic field at Bossington car park.

Making the most of your day: Selworthy and Webber's Post orienteering trails. Downloadable walks or walk packs available from shop. Wild Wednesdays for children during school holidays. **Dogs**: welcome on leads.

Access: Grounds
Sat Nav: use TA24 8TP for Selworthy; TA24 8HY Horner Wood; TA24 8HF Bossington.
Parking: at Selworthy, Horner, Webber's Post, Bossington, Allerford, Dunkery and North Hill.

Finding out more: 01643 862452 or holnicote@nationaltrust.org.uk

Holnicote Estate		M	T	W	T	F	S	S
Tea-room								
21 Mar–26 Jul	10:30–5	·	T	W	T	F	S	S
27 Jul–6 Sep	10:30–5	M	T	W	T	F	S	S
8 Sep–1 Nov	10:30–5	·	T	W	T	F	S	S
Shop								
21 Mar–1 Nov	12–5	·	·	W	T	F	S	S

Open Bank Holiday Mondays. Shop open Tuesdays in summer holidays. Opening hours vary according to weather conditions. Estate office open Monday to Friday, 8:30 to 5.

Watersmeet		M	T	W	T	F	S	S
Tea-room and tea-garden								
14 Feb–22 Feb	11–3	M	T	W	T	F	S	S
14 Mar–2 Apr	10:30–4:30*	M	T	W	T	F	S	S
3 Apr–30 Sep	10:30–5*	M	T	W	T	F	S	S
1 Oct–1 Nov	10:30–4:30*	M	T	W	T	F	S	S

*Shop opens 30 minutes after tea-room and tea-garden from 14 March.

Watersmeet

near Lynmouth, North Devon

Map (1) F5 1955

This area, where the lush valleys of the East Lyn and Hoar Oak Water tumble together, is a haven for wildlife and offers excellent walking. At the heart sits Watersmeet House (above right), a 19th-century fishing lodge, which is now a tea-garden, shop and information point. **Note**: deep gorge with steep walk down to house.

Eating and shopping: tea-garden serving hot and cold food and drinks in a magnificent wooded setting. Shop selling Exmoor produce and gifts, walking gear and maps.

Making the most of your day: Exmoor Spotter chart for families and *Exmoor Coast of Devon* walks leaflet available. **Dogs**: allowed on leads in tea-garden.

Access: Building Grounds
Sat Nav: use EX35 6NT. **Parking**: pay and display (not National Trust) on Watersmeet Road; steep walk down to house. Trust car parks nearby at Combe Park and Countisbury.

Finding out more: 01598 752648 or watersmeet@nationaltrust.org.uk

Jurassic Coast

England's first natural World Heritage Site: 95 miles of Dorset/Devon coastline, a thrilling geological 'walk through time' spanning 185 million years of Earth's history.

Branscombe

near Seaton, Devon

Map (1) H7 1965

Nestling in a valley that reaches down to the sea on East Devon's dramatic Jurassic Coast, the village of Branscombe is surrounded by picturesque countryside with miles of tranquil walking through woodland, farmland and beach. Charming thatched houses, forge and restored watermill add to the timeless magic of the place. **Note**: nearest toilets at information point, village hall and beach car park.

Eating and shopping: Old Bakery tea-room (concession) serving homemade soups, ploughman's, sandwiches and cream teas (seasonal opening). Quality ironwork on sale from the Old Forge.

Making the most of your day: trail (graded as easy) winding up from the beach to the village, passing Manor Mill, Old Bakery and forge. The beach is great for swimming and picnics. **Dogs**: welcome on leads in the Old Bakery garden, orchard and wider countryside.

Access: Building Mill Grounds
Sat Nav: use EX12 3DB. **Parking**: next to Old Forge, limited spaces. Also village hall and beach car parks (neither National Trust).

Finding out more: 01752 346585 or branscombe@nationaltrust.org.uk

Branscombe		M	T	W	T	F	S	S
Manor Mill								
29 Mar–28 Jun	2–5	·	·	·	·	·	·	**S**
1 Jul–26 Aug	2–5	·	·	**W**	·	·	·	**S**
30 Aug–1 Nov	2–5	·	·	·	·	·	·	**S**
Old Forge								
Open all year	10–5*	**M**	**T**	**W**	**T**	**F**	**S**	**S**

*Telephone 01297 680481 to confirm forge opening times. For the Old Bakery tea-room opening, telephone 01297 680333.

Burton Bradstock

near Bridport, Dorset

Map (1) I7 1973

One of the main gateways to Dorset's Jurassic Coast, with easy access to spectacular sandstone cliffs and miles of unspoilt beaches. Family-friendly Hive Beach is part of Chesil Bank – the largest shingle ridge in the world. Nearby, Burton Cliff glows bright gold in the sunlight.

Eating and shopping: tenant-run Hive Beach Café on Chesil Bank serving local seafood.

Making the most of your day: events through the year, some especially for families. Paddling, swimming and outdoor activities. Circular and clifftop walks. Hive Beach popular for diving and angling. **Dogs**: welcome. Dog-free zone on Hive Beach 1 June to 30 September.

Access:
Sat Nav: use DT6 4RF. **Parking**: on site.

Finding out more: 01297 489481 or burtonbradstock@nationaltrust.org.uk

Golden Cap

near Bridport, Dorset

Map (1) I7 1961

Spectacular countryside estate on the Jurassic Coast – England's only natural World Heritage Site. The great rocky shoulder of Golden Cap is the south coast's highest point, with breathtaking views (below). Stonebarrow Hill is a good starting point for discovering the 25 miles of footpaths around the estate.

Eating and shopping: small volunteer-run shop and information centre, with toilets and bunkhouse, in the old radar station at Stonebarrow car park, Charmouth.

Making the most of your day: play trail on Langdon Hill. Smugglers' trail on Stonebarrow Hill. Family activities and events all year. Charmouth Beach for fossils and traces of 185 million years of Earth's history. **Dogs**: welcome.

Access:
Sat Nav: for Stonebarrow use DT6 6RA and Langdon Hill DT6 6EP. **Parking**: at Stonebarrow Hill and Langdon Hill.

Finding out more: 01297 489481 or goldencap@nationaltrust.org.uk

Golden Cap
Stonebarrow shop and information centre open seasonally.

Ringstead Bay

Dorset coast, near Weymouth

Map (1) J7 1949

This quiet, unspoilt stretch of the Jurassic Coast in West Dorset is like the seaside of childhood memories: a perfect sweep of shingle beach with rock pools inviting you to explore, backed by farmland and cliffs covered with flowers and butterflies. The seawater is incredibly clear and safe for bathing.

Eating and shopping: picnics welcome at the Trust car park at the top of the hill, with its views of the Jurassic Coast World Heritage Site. Shop and café at the beach car park (not National Trust).

Making the most of your day: spectacular views of the bay and across to the Isle of Portland to enjoy. Why not walk out to the chalk headland of White Nothe?
Dogs: welcome everywhere, especially on the South West Coast Path.

Access:
Sat Nav: use DT2 8NQ for Southdown.
Parking: on the clifftop farmland at Southdown Farm, and at beach car park (not National Trust).

Finding out more: 01297 489481 or ringsteadbay@nationaltrust.org.uk

Additional coastal and countryside car parks in the South West

Cornwall

Duckpool	SS	202 117
Sandymouth	SS	203 100
Northcott Mouth	SS	204 084
Strangles Beach	SX	134 952
Glebe Cliff, Tintagel	SX	050 884
Lundy Bay	SW	953 796
Pentireglaze	SW	942 799
Park Head	SW	853 707
Treago Mill (Polly Joke)	SW	778 601
St Agnes Beacon	SW	704 503
Wheal Coates	SW	703 500
Reskajeage Downs	SW	623 430
Derrick Cove	SW	620 429
Fishing Cove	SW	599 427
Trencrom	SW	517 359
Carn Galver	SW	422 364
Botallack	SW	366 334
Cot Valley	SW	358 308
Chyvarloe	SW	653 235
Gunwalloe	SW	660 207
Predannack	SW	669 162
Poltesco	SW	725 157
Bosveal (Durgan)	SW	775 276
Nare Head	SW	922 379
Penare (Dodman)	SW	998 404
Lamledra (Vault Beach)	SW	011 411
Coombe Farm	SX	110 512
Lantivet Bay	SX	157 517
Hendersick	SX	236 520

Devon

Countisbury	SS	747 497
Combe Park	SS	740 477
Woody Bay	SS	676 486
Trentishoe Down	SS	635 480
Torrs Walk, Ilfracombe	SS	512 476
Hartland:		
Brownsham	SS	285 259
Exmansworthy	SS	271 266
and East Titchberry	SS	244 270
Stoke	SX	558 466
Ringmore	SX	649 457
East Soar	SX	713 376
Snapes Point	SX	739 404
Prawle Point	SX	775 354
Scabbacombe	SX	912 523
Man Sands	SX	913 531
Salcombe Hill	SY	148 889
Cadover Bridge	SX	533 636
Shaugh Prior	SX	554 645
Dunsland	SS	410 053
Fingle Bridge	SX	743 899
Steps Bridge	SX	804 884
Hembury Woods	SX	730 680
Holne Woods	SX	713 707
Danes Wood	SX	969 990
Ellerhayes	SS	975 011
Ashclyst Forest Gate	SX	999 995

Dorset

Cogden	SY	503 883
Stonebarrow Hill	SY	383 933
Langdon Hill	SY	413 931
Lambert's Castle	SY	366 988
Spyway	SY	998 782
Acton	SY	988 785
Dean Hill Viewpoint	SZ	006 818

Gloucestershire

Haresfield: Cripplegate	SO	832 086
and Ash Lane	SO	824 066
Mayhill	SO	691 221
Dover's Hill	SP	136 395

Somerset

Sand Point	ST	330 660
Wellington Monument	ST	143 167
Staple Plain, Quantock Hills	ST	116 410
Holford	ST	154 410
Blackdown Hills and Quarts Moor	ST	151 169
King's Wood, Mendip Hills	ST	421 560
Ivy Thorn, Polden Hills	ST	480 345
Walton Hill, Polden Hills	ST	466 350

Wiltshire

Whitesheet Hill	ST	797 349
Win Green Hill	ST	925 206
Overton Hill	SU	118 681
Pepperbox Hill	SU	211 247
Cley Hill	ST	838 449

A collection of 18th-century curiosities, including many shells, in the Library bookcase at A la Ronde, Devon

A la Ronde

Exmouth, Devon EX8 5BD

Map (1) G7 1991

When you come and see this quirky 16-sided house and hear its fascinating stories, you enter another world. Home to creative cousins Jane and Mary Parminter, whose imaginations ran wild in its design and decoration, every nook and cranny displays objects and mementoes from their travels and collections. The rooms are full of surprises. Even some of the walls have been decorated with a wide variety of feathers, shells and pictures made of seaweed and sand. The magical and fragile shell-encrusted gallery, said to contain nearly 25,000 shells, can be viewed via a 360-degree touch-screen virtual tour. **Note**: small and delicate rooms.

Eating and shopping: shop selling gifts, local produce and artwork, plants and ice-cream. Licensed tea-room (concession) with open-air seating and sea views. Orchard picnic area. Second-hand book sales.

Making the most of your day: **Indoors** Events, workshops and exhibitions. School holiday craft activities. Self-guided themed tours and house family trail. **Outdoors** Nature-spotter sheets. **Dogs**: welcome on leads in grounds. Complimentary dog bags and biscuits from shop.

Access:
House **Grounds**
Parking: on site.

Finding out more: 01395 265514 or alaronde@nationaltrust.org.uk

A la Ronde		M	T	W	T	F	S	S
31 Jan–1 Nov	11–5	**M**	**T**	**W**	**T**	**F**	**S**	**S**

Grounds and shop open 30 minutes earlier and close 30 minutes later. Tea-room opens 30 minutes earlier; last orders at 5 and closes as shop and grounds. Last admission to house at 4.

For other ways to get involved go to nationaltrust.org.uk/get-involved/volunteer

Antony

Torpoint, Cornwall PL11 2QA

Map (1) E8 1961

Still the family home of the Carew Poles after hundreds of years, this beautiful early 18th-century house has fine collections of paintings, furniture and textiles. The landscape garden offers sweeping views to the River Lynher and includes a formal garden with topiary, a knot garden and sculptures.
Note: members admitted free to Woodland Garden (not National Trust) only when house is open.

Eating and shopping: self-service tea-room offering light lunches and afternoon tea. Picnics welcome in the grounds. Gift shop with souvenirs, plants and local produce. Small second-hand bookshop.

Making the most of your day: **Indoors** Quizzes and trails. **Outdoors** Garden and family events. Modern sculpture throughout garden and Woodland Garden. Games and croquet on lawn. Quizzes and trails.
Dogs: assistance dogs only.

Access: **House** **Grounds**
Parking: 250 yards.

Finding out more: 01752 812191 or antony@nationaltrust.org.uk

Antony		M	T	W	T	F	S	S
Garden, shop and tea-room								
1 Apr–28 May	12–5*	·	T	W	T	·	·	·
2 Jun–30 Aug	12–5*	·	T	W	T	·	·	S
1 Sep–29 Oct	12–5*	·	T	W	T	·	·	·
Woodland Garden (not National Trust)								
1 Mar–31 Oct	11–5:30	·	T	W	T	·	S	S

*House opens at 1. Timed ticket entry to house.
Also open Good Friday and Easter Sunday, Sundays 3 and 24 May and Bank Holiday Mondays.

Antony, Cornwall, rises above the morning mist

Arlington Court and the National Trust Carriage Museum

Arlington, near Barnstaple, Devon EX31 4LP

Map (1) F5 1949

Hidden in the lichen-draped landscape of North Devon, Arlington surprises and delights. The house's starkly classical exterior cloaks what lies inside – the passion of 11 generations of the Chichester family. Rosalie, last of the line, remained single and pursued with dedication her many interests, including collecting shells, ships, pewter and more to create her own museum. The stable block now houses a nationally important display of carriages used to ferry passengers from first cry to last breath, via grand state occasions. The garden, restored to Victorian glory, bursts with colour; the conservatory's exotic plantings reflect the family's world travels.

Eating and shopping: tea-room serving meals made with produce grown in the walled garden, when available (reduced menu November to March). Shop selling gifts and produce. Arlington chutney, grown on site and cooked by an award-winning producer, is a speciality.

Making the most of your day: **Indoors** School holiday activities and craft workshops. Activity sheets. Interactive museum displays. Spy on the bats in the attic. **Outdoors** Ranger skills workshops and holiday activities. Woodland play areas. Walks. **Dogs**: welcome on leads in garden, Carriage Museum and wider estate.

Access:
House **Museum** **Grounds**
Sat Nav: from South Molton, don't turn left into unmarked lane (deliveries only).
Parking: 150 yards.

Finding out more: 01271 850296 or arlingtoncourt@nationaltrust.org.uk

Arlington Court		M	T	W	T	F	S	S
14 Feb–22 Feb	11–4	M	T	W	T	F	S	S
14 Mar–1 Nov	11–5*	M	T	W	T	F	S	S
7 Nov–20 Dec	11–4	·	·	·	·	·	S	S

Reduced access to house and Carriage Museum in February, November and December. *Garden, shop and tea-room open 10:30. Grounds open dawn to dusk, all year.

Ashleworth Tithe Barn

Ashleworth, Gloucestershire GL19 4JA

Map (1) J2 1956

Barn, with immense stone-tiled roof, picturesquely situated close to the River Severn. **Note**: sorry no toilet.

Finding out more: 01452 814213 or ashleworth@nationaltrust.org.uk

A typically elegant interior at Arlington Court, Devon: the home of the National Trust Carriage Museum

Some places are easy to get to on foot or by public transport. See page 3

The ancient standing stones at Avebury, Wiltshire, make up the largest prehistoric stone circle in the world

Avebury

near Marlborough, Wiltshire

Map (1) K4 1943

At Avebury, the world's largest prehistoric stone circle partially encompasses a pretty village. Millionaire archaeologist Alexander Keiller excavated here in the 1930s, and there is a museum bearing his name. Arranged in two parts, the Alexander Keiller Museum is divided into the Stables, displaying archaeological treasures from across the World Heritage Site, and the Barn, a 17th-century threshing barn housing interactive displays and children's activities that reveal the story of this ancient landscape. Avebury Manor, on the edge of the village, was transformed in a partnership between the National Trust and the BBC, creating a hands-on experience that celebrates and reflects the lives of the people who once lived here. **Note**: English Heritage holds guardianship of Avebury Stone Circle (owned and managed by the National Trust).

Eating and shopping: Circles Café and the Manor tea-room. Shop selling local gifts, including Avebury honey and books on the archaeology and mythology of the area.

Making the most of your day: **Indoors** Specialist talks and guided tours of the manor. Family activities in museum and events during holidays. **Outdoors** Guided tours of the stone circle all year. Talks and guided tours of the landscape. Hunt for the golden hare at Easter or for witches' cats at Hallowe'en.
Dogs: assistance dogs only in house, garden and café. Elsewhere dogs on leads welcome.

Access:
Buildings **Grounds**
Sat Nav: use SN8 1RD. **Parking**: 300 yards. Please do not park on village streets.

Finding out more: 01672 539250 or avebury@nationaltrust.org.uk.
National Trust Estate Office, High Street, Avebury, Wiltshire SN8 1RF

Avebury		M	T	W	T	F	S	S
Stone circle								
Open all year	Dawn–dusk	**M**	**T**	**W**	**T**	**F**	**S**	**S**
Manor house and garden								
14 Feb–28 Mar	11–4	**M**	**T**	**W**	**T**	**F**	**S**	**S**
29 Mar–31 Oct*	11–5	**M**	**T**	**W**	**T**	**F**	**S**	**S**
1 Nov–27 Dec	11–4	·	·	·	**T**	**F**	**S**	**S**
Museum								
1 Jan–28 Mar	10–4	**M**	**T**	**W**	**T**	**F**	**S**	**S**
29 Mar–31 Oct	10–6	**M**	**T**	**W**	**T**	**F**	**S**	**S**
1 Nov–31 Dec	10–4	**M**	**T**	**W**	**T**	**F**	**S**	**S**

*Manor closed 20 to 22 June. Shop and café open every day. Last entry to manor one hour before closing; timed tickets to manor during peak times, available on arrival and online. In winter, part of garden and museum may be closed. Everything closes at dusk if earlier. All except stone circle closed 24 and 25 December.

Standing stone at Avebury, Wiltshire (above), and the manor house (below)

 Please display your current sticker for free parking

Barrington Court in Somerset: attractive Strode House

Barrington Court

Barrington, near Ilminster, Somerset TA19 0NQ

Map (1) 16 1907

Colonel Lyle, whose family firm became part of Tate & Lyle, rescued the partially derelict 16th-century Court House in the 1920s, surrounding it with a productive estate. A keen collector of architectural salvage, Colonel Lyle filled the house with his collection of panelling, fireplaces and staircases. Empty of furniture, the house is full of atmospheric echoes of the past. The walled White Garden, Rose and Iris Garden and Lily Garden were influenced by Gertrude Jekyll, with playing fountains, vibrant colours and intoxicating scents. The original kitchen garden supplies the restaurant and continues the Lyle family's vision of self-sufficiency. **Note**: independently run artisan workshops (opening times vary).

Eating and shopping: Beagles Café serving light refreshments. Strode Dining Room offering tea, homemade cakes and main meals with ingredients often grown in the kitchen garden. Children's menu available. Gift shop selling gifts, plants and award-winning cider and apple juice. Second-hand bookshop.

Making the most of your day: **Indoors** House trails and seasonal events. Activities in artisans' workshops. **Outdoors** Trails and tours. Seasonal events, including Easter Egg hunts. Holiday cottage in Strode House.
Dogs: assistance dogs only in formal garden.

Access: **Building**
Grounds
Sat Nav: misdirects visitors to rear entrance – follow brown signs from Barrington village.
Parking: 200 yards.

Finding out more: 01460 241938 or barringtoncourt@nationaltrust.org.uk

Barrington Court		M	T	W	T	F	S	S
3 Jan–15 Feb	10:30–3	·	·	·	·	·	**S**	**S**
16 Feb–1 Nov	10:30–5	**M**	**T**	**W**	**T**	**F**	**S**	**S**
7 Nov–27 Dec	10:30–3	·	·	·	·	·	**S**	**S**

Bath Assembly Rooms

Bennett Street, Bath, Somerset BA1 2QH

Map (1) J4 1931

The Assembly Rooms were at the heart of fashionable Georgian society. The Fashion Museum is on the lower ground floor. **Note**: limited visitor access during functions. The Fashion Museum is run by Bath and North East Somerset Council. Entry charge for The Fashion Museum (including members).

Finding out more: 01225 477789 or bathassemblyrooms@nationaltrust.org.uk

Blaise Hamlet

Henbury, Bristol BS10 7QY

Map (1) I3 1943

Delightful hamlet of nine picturesque cottages, designed by John Nash in 1809 for Blaise Estate pensioners. **Note**: access to green only; cottages not open. Sorry no toilet.

Finding out more: 01275 461900 or blaisehamlet@nationaltrust.org.uk

Bradley

Totnes Road, Newton Abbot, Devon TQ12 6BN

Map (1) G8 1938

Unspoilt and fascinating medieval manor house, still a relaxed family home, in a green haven among riverside meadows and woodland. Many charming original features, such as the medieval cat hole and gargoyles. The quiet and peaceful chapel was licensed for services in 1428. **Note**: sorry no toilet. Parking from 10.30 on open days.

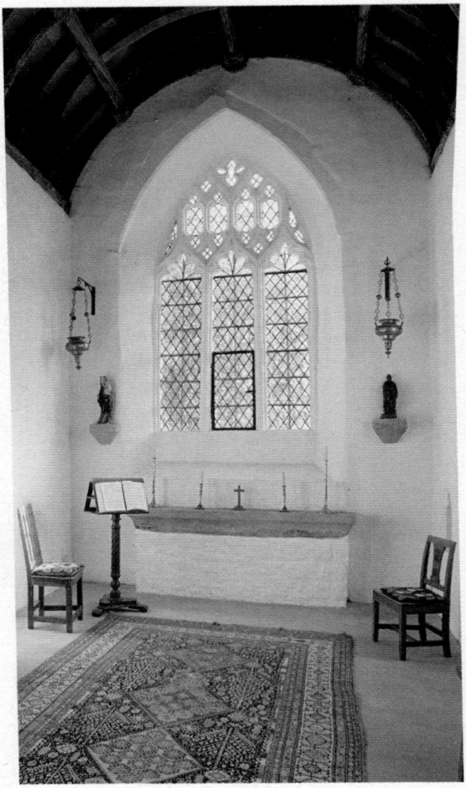

The quiet and peaceful chapel at Bradley, Devon

Eating and shopping: table-top shop selling honey, souvenirs, gifts and postcards.

Making the most of your day: open-air theatre and countryside craft events. Walks in surrounding countryside. For a truly medieval experience, visit nearby Compton Castle. **Dogs**: welcome in meadows and woodland. Assistance dogs only in garden and house.

Access: **Building**
Grounds
Sat Nav: TQ12 1LX directs to gate lodge (follow driveway for parking). **Parking**: in meadow. For designated parking call 01626 354513.

Finding out more: 01803 661907 or bradley@nationaltrust.org.uk

Bradley		M	T	W	T	F	S	S
1 Apr–30 Sep	11–5	·	**T**	**W**	**T**	·	·	·

Brownsea Island

Poole Harbour, Poole, Dorset BH13 7EE

Map ① K7 1962

The perfect day's adventure, this island wildlife sanctuary is easy to get to but feels like another world from the moment you step ashore. The island sits in the middle of Poole Harbour, with dramatic views to the Purbeck Hills. Thriving natural habitats, including woodland, heathland and a lagoon, have created havens for wildlife, such as the red squirrel and a huge variety of birds. The island is rich in history too. It is the birthplace of the Scouting and Guiding movement, and there are the remains of daffodil farming, pottery works and the village of Maryland to explore. **Note**: half-hourly boat service from 10 (not National Trust). No public access to castle. Small entry fee to Dorset Wildlife Trust area (including members).

Eating and shopping: coffee bar, Villano Café and self-service at the Outdoor Centre. Mobile ice-cream unit (peak periods). Gift shop selling Brownsea Island outdoors range, local produce, souvenirs and ice-cream. Scout and Guide trading post sells memorabilia.

Making the most of your day: family activities, tree-climbing trails, Tracker Packs and natural play area. Events. Walks and talks. Open-air theatre. Outdoor and visitor centres. Introductory walks and buggy tours for less-mobile visitors (booking advised). **Dogs**: assistance dogs only.

A rare red squirrel (above) on Brownsea Island (below) in Poole Harbour, Dorset

Access: **Building** **Grounds**

Sat Nav: for Sandbanks Jetty use BH13 7QJ; for Poole Quay BH15 1HP. **Parking**: near Sandbanks and Poole Quay, not National Trust (charge including members).

Finding out more: 01202 707744 or brownseaisland@nationaltrust.org.uk

Brownsea Island		M	T	W	T	F	S	S
Hourly boat service from Poole Quay and Sandbanks*								
7 Feb–15 Mar	10–4	·	·	·	·	·	**S**	**S**
Full boat service from Poole Quay and Sandbanks								
21 Mar–1 Nov	10–5	**M**	**T**	**W**	**T**	**F**	**S**	**S**

Shop and Villano Café open until last boat. *Special weekend openings: boats leave every 60 minutes from Poole and Sandbanks; shop, café and visitor centre will all be open.

Buckland Abbey, Garden and Estate

Yelverton, Devon PL20 6EY

Map (1) E8 1948

Hundreds of years ago, Cistercian monks chose this tranquil valley as the perfect spot in which to worship, farm their estate and trade. The Abbey, later converted into a house, today combines furnished rooms with museum galleries bringing to life the story of how seafaring adventurers Sir Richard Grenville and Sir Francis Drake changed the shape of Buckland Abbey and the fate of England. Outdoors, the Cider House Garden includes a walled kitchen garden and wild garden; there are community growing areas, orchards and the impressive Great Barn, as well as woodland walks with far-reaching views and late spring bluebells. **Note**: Abbey interior presented in association with Plymouth City Museum.

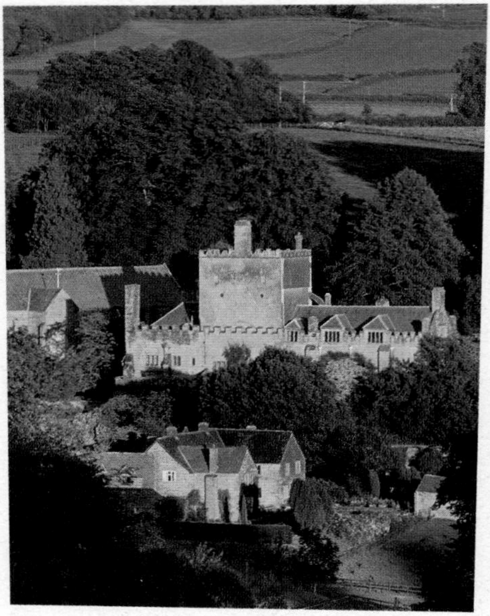

Eating and shopping: Ox Yard Restaurant serves freshly cooked local produce, often using ingredients grown in the kitchen garden. Picnics welcome in grounds. Shop selling gifts and plants. Gallery and second-hand bookshop. Holiday cottage.

Making the most of your day: **Indoors** New 'Rembrandt Revealed' exhibition. **Outdoors** Willow Patch natural play area and zip wire for younger visitors. Year-round events, estate walks and trails. **Dogs**: welcome on designated walks (map available from reception).

Access:
Abbey **Reception**
Grounds
Sat Nav: do not use. **Parking**: 150 yards.

Finding out more: 01822 853607 or bucklandabbey@nationaltrust.org.uk

Buckland Abbey		M	T	W	T	F	S	S
14 Feb–6 Mar	11–4*	M	T	W	T	F	S	S
7 Mar–1 Nov	10:30–5:30*	M	T	W	T	F	S	S
7 Nov–29 Nov	11–4*	·	·	·	·	·	S	S
1 Dec–20 Dec	11–4*	M	T	W	T	F	S	S

*Abbey opens 30 minutes after estate and closes 30 minutes earlier.

Discovering the lovely garden (left) at Buckland Abbey in Devon (above)

Castle Drogo

Drewsteignton, near Exeter, Devon EX6 6PB

Map (1) F7 1974

This year, the ground-breaking project to make Castle Drogo watertight – for the first time in its life – enters a new phase. This is conservation on a grand scale, and from the moment you arrive it's obvious that this is a very different visit. Lutyens's famous castle is covered by scaffolding and wrapped to protect it from the elements. Inside, rooms are redisplayed – you will see elements of the collection brought together in creative ways, and darkened spaces brought to life revealing new aspects of Drogo's remarkable story. A special viewing platform enables you to watch the craftsmanship of the stonemasons. **Note**: access may be restricted or changed due to building works. Restrictions apply to viewing platform.

Eating and shopping: licensed café with extra open-air seating, specialising in seasonal menus and venison from the Drogo Estate. Picnics welcome in garden and grounds. Shop showcasing local beers, preserves, gifts and plants inspired by Castle Drogo's history and garden.

Work is underway to make Castle Drogo, Devon, watertight. This is truly conservation on a grand scale

Making the most of your day: **Indoors** Specialised guided tours, family trails and quizzes. **Outdoors** Lutyens-designed terraced garden. Croquet. Walks through Teign Gorge and nearby Fingle Woods, offering 27 miles of newly re-opened footpaths. **Dogs**: welcome on leads in grounds and wider estate. Assistance dogs only in formal garden.

Access:
Building **Grounds**
Sat Nav: for Fingle Bridge car park use EX6 6PW; for Steps Bridge car park EX6 7EG.
Parking: 400 yards. Additional car parks at Fingle Bridge (for Fingle Woods) and Steps Bridge in Teign Valley.

Finding out more: 01647 433306 or castledrogo@nationaltrust.org.uk

Castle Drogo		M	T	W	T	F	S	S
Estate								
Open all year	Dawn–dusk	M	T	W	T	F	S	S
Garden, visitor centre, café and shop								
1 Jan–8 Mar	11–4	M	T	W	T	F	S	S
9 Mar–1 Nov	9:30–5:30	M	T	W	T	F	S	S
2 Nov–31 Dec	11–4	M	T	W	T	F	S	S
Castle and project viewing platform*								
9 Mar–1 Nov	11–5	M	T	W	T	F	S	S
7 Nov–20 Dec	11–4	·	·	·	·	·	S	S

Garden, visitor centre, café and shop closed 24 to 26 December. During restoration project the visitor route may change. *Last entry for the castle and viewing platform 30 minutes before closing (opening of the project viewing platform is subject to weather conditions).

The mosaics at Chedworth Roman Villa, Gloucestershire: one of the grandest Roman villas in the country

Chedworth Roman Villa

Yanworth, near Cheltenham, Gloucestershire GL54 3LJ

Map (1) K2 1924

One of the grandest Roman villas in the country, rediscovered by Victorians 150 years ago. Leading the way in archaeology and conservation, the site has now embarked on an exciting five-year summer excavations programme. A new conservation building, opened in 2012, provides better-than-ever access to extensive mosaic floors, hypocaust systems and bathhouse rooms. The refurbished museum houses a range of finds and artefacts from the Villa, collected by keen Victorian antiquarians. The tranquil setting, within a wonderfully rich wildlife haven, provides an opportunity to wander among the Roman ruins while enjoying idyllic rural views.

Eating and shopping: café serving sandwiches, cakes, snacks, hot and cold drinks and ice-cream. Shop offering Roman-themed souvenirs, books and games, as well as seasonal plants and gifts.

Making the most of your day: **Indoors** Updated guidebook and audio guides. Activities, including Roman dressing-up for children. Costumed interpreters and living history events. **Outdoors** Family activities and trails (weekends and school holidays). **Dogs**: assistance dogs only.

Access: **Reception** **West Range** **Grounds**
Parking: on lane at entrance, plus woodland overflow (March to October).

Finding out more: 01242 890256 or chedworth@nationaltrust.org.uk

Chedworth Roman Villa		M	T	W	T	F	S	S
14 Feb–28 Mar	10–4	M	T	W	T	F	S	S
29 Mar–24 Oct	10–5	M	T	W	T	F	S	S
25 Oct–29 Nov	10–4	M	T	W	T	F	S	S

Clevedon Court

Tickenham Road, Clevedon,
North Somerset BS21 6QU

Map (1) I4 1961

Home to the lords of the manor of Clevedon for centuries, the core of the house is a remarkable survival, featuring rare domestic architecture from the medieval period. The house was bought by Abraham Elton in 1709 and it is still the much-loved family home of his descendants today. **Note**: the Elton family opens Clevedon Court for the National Trust.

Eating and shopping: kiosk serving cream teas and soft drinks.

Making the most of your day: extensive collection of Elton Ware pottery, Nailsea glass and prints of industrial archaeology. Family guide and children's quiz/trail.
Dogs: assistance dogs only.

Access: **Building** **Grounds**
Parking: 50 yards (unsuitable for trailer or motor caravans). Alternative parking 100 yards east of entrance in cul-de-sac.

Finding out more: 01275 872257 or clevedoncourt@nationaltrust.org.uk

Clevedon Court		M	T	W	T	F	S	S
1 Apr–30 Sep	2–5	·	·	**W**	**T**	·	·	**S**

Car park open 1:15. House entry by timed ticket, not bookable. Open Bank Holiday Mondays.

Clevedon Court, North Somerset: remarkable survival

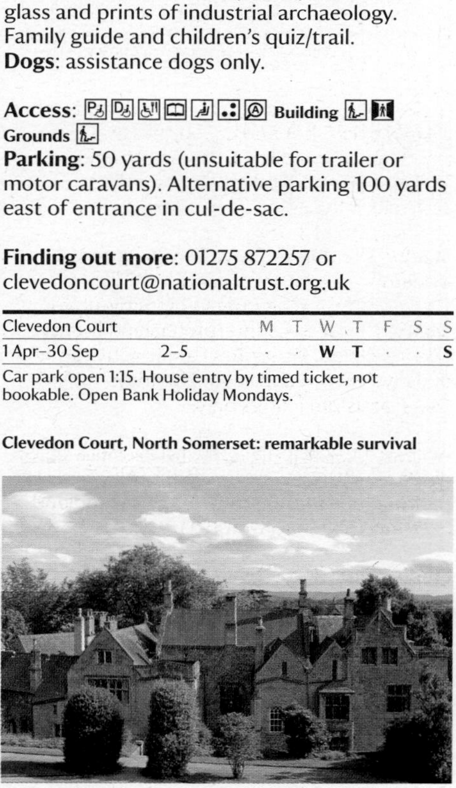

The music room at Clouds Hill in Dorset

Clouds Hill

Wareham, Dorset BH20 7NQ

Map (1) J7 1937

The rooms of this tiny, isolated cottage reveal the reflective, private and complex personality of T. E. Lawrence: 'Lawrence of Arabia'. They remain much as he left them in 1935, a peaceful refuge from both military life and his celebrity status. The motorbike shed contains an exhibition about his life. **Note**: sorry no toilet.

Eating and shopping: shop selling books, gifts and Lawrence memorabilia.

Making the most of your day: Max Gate and Hardy's Cottage – the Dorchester homes of writer Thomas Hardy, friend of T. E. Lawrence – are nearby. Why not combine your visits?
Dogs: welcome on leads in grounds only.

Access: **Building** **Grounds**
Parking: on site.

Finding out more: 01929 405616 or cloudshill@nationaltrust.org.uk

Clouds Hill		M	T	W	T	F	S	S
11 Mar–25 Oct	11–5	·	·	**W**	**T**	**F**	**S**	**S**
28 Oct–1 Nov	11–4	·	·	**W**	**T**	**F**	**S**	**S**

Open Bank Holiday Mondays. No electric light, so last admission at dusk.

Coleridge Cottage

35 Lime Street, Nether Stowey, Bridgwater, Somerset TA5 1NQ

Map (1) H5 [1909]

A visit to the award-winning former home of Samuel Taylor Coleridge offers the opportunity to immerse oneself in the sights, sounds and smells of an 18th-century cottage. Coleridge's poetry is brought to life in this simple house, the birthplace of the literary Romantic Movement, and its garden.

Eating and shopping: light refreshments in the tea-room; shop selling gifts reflecting Coleridge's life and work.

Making the most of your day: **Indoors** Regular events, special tours. Family activities and trails. Chance to get hands-on in the kitchen. **Outdoors** You can hear poetry in the garden and draw water from the well.

Access: **Building** **Garden**
Parking: in pub or village car parks (neither National Trust).

Finding out more: 01278 732662 (Infoline). 01643 821314 or coleridgecottage@nationaltrust.org.uk

Coleridge Cottage		M	T	W	T	F	S	S
7 Mar–1 Nov	11–5	M	·	·	T	F	S	S
5 Dec–20 Dec	11–3	·	·	·	·	·	S	S

Coleton Fishacre

Brownstone Road, Kingswear, Devon TQ6 0EQ

Map (1) G9 [1982]

This evocative 1920s Arts and Crafts-style house, with its elegant Art Deco interiors, perfectly encapsulates the spirit of the Jazz Age. The former country home of the D'Oyly Carte family, it has a light, joyful atmosphere and inspiring views. You can glimpse life 'upstairs and downstairs' and try on 1920s clothing in the popular handling room. In the garden, paths weave through glades and past tranquil ponds and rare tender plants from New Zealand and South Africa; many exotic plants thrive beneath the tree canopy. You can also walk down to the coastal viewpoint through the valley garden.

Eating and shopping: 1920s-inspired Café Coleton and Art Deco-inspired shop selling china, music, gifts, souvenir guides and plants seen in this RHS-accredited garden.

Making the most of your day: daily guided garden walks from Easter, led by a member of the garden team. Events, including theatre in the garden and monthly jazz club. Family trails and seasonal activities. **Dogs**: welcome on leads around garden perimeter and outside Café Coleton (map available from reception).

Access: [access symbols] **Building** [symbols]
Grounds [symbols]
Parking: 20 yards from reception; overflow parking 150 yards.

Finding out more: 01803 842382 or coletonfishacre@nationaltrust.org.uk

Coleton Fishacre		M	T	W	T	F	S	S
14 Feb–1 Nov	10:30–5	**M**	**T**	**W**	**T**	**F**	**S**	**S**
7 Nov–20 Dec	11–4	·	·	·	·	·	**S**	**S**
27 Dec–31 Dec	11–4	**M**	**T**	**W**	**T**	·	·	**S**

Simple Coleridge Cottage, Somerset (opposite); cocktail hour, 1920s style, at Coleton Fishacre, Devon (below); medieval Compton Castle, Devon (bottom right)

Compton Castle

Marldon, Paignton, Devon TQ3 1TA

Map (1) G8 [symbols] 1951

A rare survivor, this medieval fortress with high curtain walls, towers and two portcullis gates, set in a landscape of rolling hills and orchards, is a bewitching mixture of romance and history. Home for nearly 600 years to the Gilbert family, including Sir Humphrey Gilbert, half-brother to Sir Walter Ralegh. **Note**: hall, sub-solar, solar, medieval kitchen, scullery, guard room and chapel open. Credit cards not accepted.

Eating and shopping: Castle Barton restaurant (not National Trust) opposite. Table-top shop selling souvenirs, gifts, souvenir guides and postcards. Picnics welcome in the orchard.

Making the most of your day: history and squirrel trails for children. New 1½-mile circular footpath, accessible from opposite the castle. **Dogs**: welcome in the orchard. Assistance dogs only in castle and garden.

Access: [symbols] **Building** [symbols] **Grounds** [symbols]
Parking: on site. Additional parking at Castle Barton opposite entrance, 100 yards.

Finding out more: 01803 661906 or comptoncastle@nationaltrust.org.uk

Compton Castle		M	T	W	T	F	S	S
1 Apr–29 Oct	10:30–4:30	·	**T**	**W**	**T**	·	·	·

Open Bank Holiday Mondays: 6 April, 4 May, 25 May and 31 August.

Every corner of romantic Corfe Castle in Dorset has a tale to tell

Corfe Castle

Wareham, Dorset BH20 5EZ

Map (1) K7 1982

One of Britain's most iconic and evocative survivors of the English Civil War, the castle was partially demolished in 1646 by the Parliamentarians. A favourite haunt for adults and children alike, the romantic ruins, with their breathtaking views across Purbeck, are totally captivating. There are 1,000 years of history as a royal palace and fortress to discover and, with fallen walls and secret places, 'murder holes' and arrow loops, every corner has a tale to tell of treachery and treason. More recently, a wide variety of wildlife has made its home here. **Note**: steep, uneven slopes; steps; sudden drops. All/parts of castle may close in high winds.

Eating and shopping: 18th-century tea-room serving cream teas. Summer garden with unrivalled castle views and an open log fire in winter. Shop in village square, offering products ranging from pocket-money treats to luxury locally made gifts. Visitor centre at the car park.

Making the most of your day: daily family trail. Monthly themed events, with activities every weekend and all school holidays April to September. Highlights include medieval archery, falconry, re-enactments, open-air theatre and cinema. **Dogs**: welcome on short leads.

Access: **Grounds**
Parking: 800 yards (uphill walk). Norden park and ride (½ mile) and West Street in village, neither National Trust (charge including members).

Finding out more: 01929 481294 (ticket office). 01929 480921 (shop). 01929 481332 (tea-room) or corfecastle@nationaltrust.org.uk

Corfe Castle		M	T	W	T	F	S	S
Castle, shop and tea-room								
1 Jan–28 Feb	10–4	**M**	**T**	**W**	**T**	**F**	**S**	**S**
1 Mar–31 Mar	10–5	**M**	**T**	**W**	**T**	**F**	**S**	**S**
1 Apr–30 Sep*	10–6	**M**	**T**	**W**	**T**	**F**	**S**	**S**
1 Oct–31 Oct	10–5	**M**	**T**	**W**	**T**	**F**	**S**	**S**
1 Nov–31 Dec	10–4	**M**	**T**	**W**	**T**	**F**	**S**	**S**

*Shop and tea-room close at 5:30. Tea-room closed for refurbishment 5 to 9 January. Shop closed 6 January. Castle, shop and tea-room: closed 5 March and 25 to 26 December.

Cotehele

St Dominick, near Saltash, Cornwall PL12 6TA

Map 1 E8 1947

The Edgcumbes built their rambling granite and slate-stone home high above the River Tamar, and it remained in their family for nearly 600 years. Time has stood still here. The Hall, with its ancient timber roof and displays of weaponry, and the warren of tapestry-clad rooms beyond have changed little since Tudor times. The 5-hectare (12-acre) garden features historic daffodils, terraces, ponds and orchards with 150 local apple varieties. The Valley Garden, with medieval stewpond and dovecote, leads to Cotehele Quay – thriving in Victorian times – where you'll find 1899 Tamar sailing barge *Shamrock*, lime kilns and the Discovery Centre. **Note**: the house has no electricity so feel free to bring a torch.

Eating and shopping: restaurant near house serving hot lunches and cakes. Tea-room on quay offering light lunches, cakes and cream teas. Gift shop and plant centre. Art and craft gallery featuring West Country artists. Second-hand bookshop. Eight holiday cottages. Picnic area.

Making the most of your day: **Indoors** 'Around the World' theme highlighting international influences in the house, garden and restaurants. First World War exhibition featuring local memories. **Outdoors** Play area. Year-round events and walks. **Dogs**: welcome throughout estate. Assistance dogs only in formal garden.

Access:
Building **Grounds**
Sat Nav: ignore from Tavistock, follow brown signs. **Parking**: at house and on quay.

Finding out more: 01579 351346 (office). 01579 352711 (Barn Restaurant). 01579 352713 (shop) or cotehele@nationaltrust.org.uk

Cotehele		M	T	W	T	F	S	S
House								
14 Mar–1 Nov	11–4	M	T	W	T	F	S	S
2 Nov–31 Dec*	11–4	M	T	W	T	F	S	S
Garden and estate								
Open all year	Dawn–dusk	M	T	W	T	F	S	S
The Edgcumbe tea-room								
3 Jan–13 Mar	11–4	M	T	W	T	F	S	S
Barn Restaurant, The Edgcumbe, shop, plant sales, gallery								
14 Feb–13 Mar	11–4	M	T	W	T	F	S	S
14 Mar–1 Nov	11–5	M	T	W	T	F	S	S
2 Nov–31 Dec	11–4	M	T	W	T	F	S	S

*Hall of house and Christmas garland only. Everything closed 25 and 26 December, except garden and estate.
Barn Restaurant opens 10:30 in main season.

Time seems to have stood still at Cotehele, Cornwall

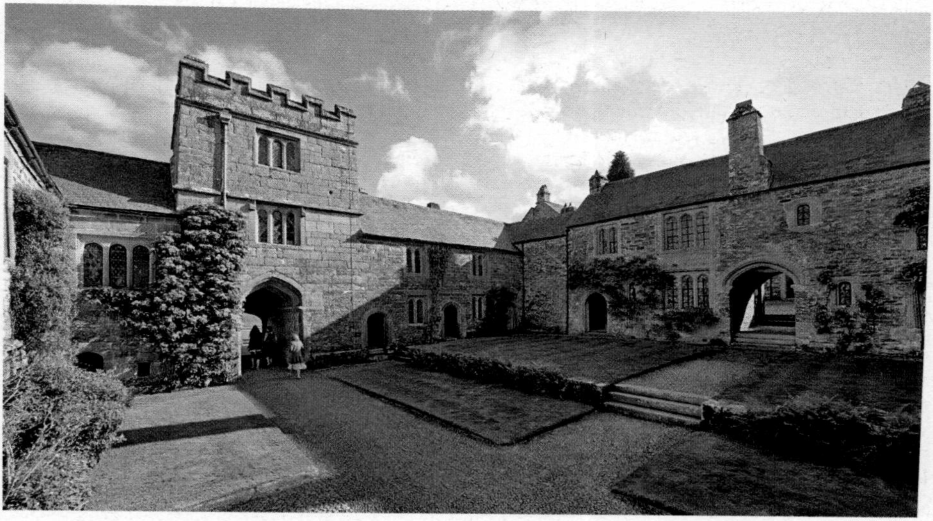

Cotehele Mill

St Dominick, near Saltash, Cornwall PL12 6TA

Map (1) E8 1947

A peaceful walk alongside the Morden stream from Cotehele Quay takes you to the restored 19th-century Cotehele Mill (below). On Thursdays and Sundays you can watch corn being ground into flour. Traditional woodworker and potter, as well as re-created wheelwright's, saddler's and blacksmith's workshops. Look out for baking days. **Note**: nearest toilets and parking at Cotehele Quay.

Eating and shopping: Cotehele flour, apple juice and chutney, gifts and ice-creams for sale. The Edgcumbe tea-room at nearby Cotehele Quay serves light lunches and cream teas. Pasties available from the kiosk on the quay. Picnics welcome in meadow.

Making the most of your day: **Indoors** Events, including milling and bakery demonstrations plus dress-up days. Opportunity to mill grain at the hand quern. Interpretation boards. **Outdoors** Family trails. Two holiday cottages. **Dogs**: welcome, but assistance dogs only in bakery and mill.

Access: **Building** **Grounds**
Parking: by arrangement only. Shuttlebus from Cotehele House.

Finding out more: 01579 350606 (mill). 01579 351346 (Cotehele) or cotehele@nationaltrust.org.uk

Cotehele Mill		M	T	W	T	F	S	S
14 Mar–30 Sep	11–5	M	T	W	T	F	S	S
1 Oct–1 Nov	11–4:30	M	T	W	T	F	S	S

The Courts Garden

Holt, near Bradford on Avon, Wiltshire BA14 6RR

Map (1) J4 1943

This curious English country garden is a hidden gem. Garden rooms of different styles, shaped by the vision of past owners and gardeners, reveal themselves at every turn. Featuring herbaceous borders, quirky topiary, a peaceful water garden (above) and arboretum, there is also a kitchen garden and naturally planted spring bulbs.

Eating and shopping: seasonal produce grown in the kitchen garden for sale, as well as a small selection of gifts and guidebooks. Sales from the second-hand bookshop support conservation work. Rose Garden tea-room serving lunch and afternoon tea. Picnics welcome in the arboretum.

Making the most of your day: trails and a hidden wildlife garden for young explorers. Keen gardeners can pick up tips from the friendly team. **Dogs**: assistance dogs only.

Access: **Garden**
Parking: 80 yards in village hall car park (not National Trust). Follow signs for overflow parking. Please avoid parking on village streets.

Finding out more: 01225 782875 or courtsgarden@nationaltrust.org.uk

The Courts Garden		M	T	W	T	F	S	S
Garden and tea-room								
1 Feb–1 Mar	11–5:30*	·	·	·	·	·	S	S
2 Mar–1 Nov	11–5:30*	M	T	·	T	F	S	S

Tea-room last orders 4:45. *Garden closed at dusk in winter if earlier. Garden access out of season by appointment only.

Some places are easy to get to on foot or by public transport. See page 3

Dinton Park and Philipps House

Dinton, Salisbury, Wiltshire SP3 5HH

Map (1) K5 1943

Neo-Grecian house in a tranquil park, designed by Jeffry Wyatville for William Wyndham in 1820. **Note**: sorry no toilet. Park is open daily all year. For house opening arrangements visit website or telephone.

Finding out more: 01672 538014 or sw.customerenquiries@nationaltrust.org.uk

Dunster Castle

Dunster, near Minehead, Somerset TA24 6SL

Map (1) G5 1976

Dramatically sited on top of a wooded hill, a castle has existed here since at least Norman times. Its impressive medieval gatehouse and ruined tower are a reminder of its turbulent history. The castle that you see today, owned by the Luttrell family for over 600 years, became an elegant country home during the 19th century. The terraced garden displays varieties of Mediterranean and subtropical plants, while the tranquil riverside wooded garden below, with its natural play area, leads to the historic working watermill. There are panoramic views over the Bristol Channel and surrounding countryside from the castle and grounds.

Eating and shopping: 17th-century stables shop selling local and regional gifts and guidebooks. Light refreshments available at the Camellia House. Riverside tea-room and shop selling stoneground flour at Dunster Working Watermill. Places to eat and drink in Dunster village (not National Trust).

Impressive Dunster Castle, Somerset (top) became an elegant country home during the 19th century (above)

Making the most of your day: Indoors Interactive exhibitions and 'Chapters' bring Dunster Castle's stories to life. Tours of the Victorian kitchens and behind the scenes. **Outdoors** Events, including open-air theatre and re-enactments, many costumed. **Dogs**: welcome in parkland and garden on short leads.

Access: Castle
Stables **Grounds**
Parking: 300 yards. Enter from A39.

Finding out more: 01643 823004 (Infoline).
01643 821314 or
dunstercastle@nationaltrust.org.uk

Dunster Castle		M	T	W	T	F	S	S
Castle								
7 Mar–1 Nov	11–5*	M	T	W	T	F	S	S
Garden, park and shop								
7 Mar–1 Nov	10–5	M	T	W	T	F	S	S
2 Nov–31 Dec	11–4	M	T	W	T	F	S	·

*Last entry to castle 45 minutes before closing.
'Dunster by Candlelight': castle open 4 to 9, Friday 4 and Saturday 5 December. Shop also open 1 January and then weekends only in January; closed 25 and 26 December.

Fully operating Dunster Working Watermill in Somerset

Dunster Working Watermill

Mill Lane, Dunster, near Minehead,
Somerset TA24 6SW

Map (1) G5 1976

A fully operating 18th-century double-overshot watermill, built on the site of a mill mentioned in the Domesday survey of 1086.
Note: admission to watermill inclusive with a Dunster Castle garden ticket.

Finding out more: 01643 821759 (mill).
01643 821314 (Dunster Castle) or
dunstercastle@nationaltrust.org.uk

Dyrham Park

Dyrham, near Bath,
South Gloucestershire SN14 8ER

Map (1) J4 1961

Now is your chance to see Dyrham as you have never seen it before, as the roof of this 17th-century mansion is removed and replaced. You can look behind the scenes in our open stores, discover more about the building of Dyrham in the project exhibition and then step back in time with our sensory journey through William Blathwayt's world. From May you'll be able to see the works up-close with roof-top scaffolding tours. Outdoors, the 110-hectare (270-acre) park provides plenty of space for exploration, as well as far-reaching views towards the Welsh hills. In May, the lost terraces of William Blathwayt will re-open alongside the formal garden and will be the perfect place for a stroll. **Note**: re-roofing project may cause disruption.

 Please display your current sticker for free parking

Eating and shopping: tea-room serving lunch, cakes and refreshments. Courtyard and garden kiosks (with outdoor seating) offering drinks, ice-cream and snacks on summer and busy days. Shop selling plants, books, local products and crafts. Indoor and outdoor picnic tables in the Old Lodge.

Making the most of your day: **Indoors** Events and activities all year, including meet-the-expert conservation days and behind-the-scenes tours. **Outdoors** Guided tours of the park and garden. New family trail through the park, with natural play zones and fun things to find along the way. Children can play at Old Lodge or borrow a Tracker Pack to help explore nature. The Cotswold Way passes Dyrham, for walking further afield. Nearby Prior Park Landscape Garden offers great views and access to the Bath Skyline, where you can enjoy a six-mile circular walk encompassing beautiful woodlands, meadows and historic features. **Dogs**: welcome in car park only (exercise area at far end).

Deer at Dyrham Park, South Gloucestershire (below) and 'View down a Corridor' by van Hoogstraten (right)

Access: **House** **Grounds**

Sat Nav: use SN14 8HY and enter via A46.
Parking: 20 yards from visitor centre.

Finding out more: 0117 937 2501 or dyrhampark@nationaltrust.org.uk

Dyrham Park		M	T	W	T	F	S	S
Project experience								
7 Mar–20 Dec	11–5	**M**	**T**	**W**	**T**	**F**	**S**	**S**
Roof-top tours*								
9 May–20 Dec	10–5	**M**	**T**	**W**	**T**	**F**	**S**	**S**
Garden, shop and tea-room								
14 Feb–20 Dec	10–5	**M**	**T**	**W**	**T**	**F**	**S**	**S**
Park								
Open all year**	10–5	**M**	**T**	**W**	**T**	**F**	**S**	**S**

Last admission one hour before closing. Closes dusk if earlier than 5. *Weather dependent. Whole place closed until 1 on 9 and 23 September, 4, 11, 18 and 25 November, 2 and 9 December. **Except 25 December.

East Pool Mine

Pool, near Redruth, Cornwall TR15 3NP

Map (1) C9 1967

East Pool celebrates the extraordinary lives of the people who worked at the very heart of the Cornish Mining World Heritage Site. With two great beam engines, preserved in their towering engine houses, this is a great place for all the family to discover the dramatic story of Cornish mining.

Eating and shopping: small shop selling gifts, including local minerals, mining and Cornish history books, plus hot drinks.

Making the most of your day: **Indoors** Hands-on exhibits and working models. **Outdoors** Family activities and trails. Free guided tours. Trevithick Cottage, home of the celebrated Cornish engineer Richard Trevithick, is nearby at Penponds. **Dogs**: welcome in outdoor areas.

Michell's engine house at East Pool Mine in Cornwall

Access: Taylor's Engine House Michell's Engine House Grounds **Sat Nav**: use TR15 3NH. For Trevithick Cottage use TR14 0QG. **Parking**: parking in Morrisons superstore (far end). Also at Michell's Engine House, off A3047.

Finding out more: 01209 315027 or eastpool@nationaltrust.org.uk. Trevithick Road, Pool, Cornwall TR15 3NP

East Pool Mine		M	T	W	T	F	S	S
East Pool Mine and Taylor's Engine House								
17 Mar–31 Oct	10:30–5	·	T	W	T	F	S	·
Michell's Engine House								
17 Mar–31 Oct	12–4	·	T	W	T	F	S	·

Open Bank Holiday Mondays and Bank Holiday Sundays (March to October), and for booked visits November to February. Trevithick Cottage opening hours vary, please contact East Pool Mine for details.

Finch Foundry

Sticklepath, Okehampton, Devon EX20 2NW

Map (1) F7 1994

The foundry was a family-run business producing a range of tools for South West industries, including farming and mining, in the 19th century. The huge waterwheels and tilt hammer spring into action during regular demonstrations. Outside is a delightful cottage garden with Tom Pearse's summerhouse (Widecombe Fair fame). **Note**: narrow entrance to car park – height restrictions.

Working the forge at Finch Foundry, Devon

Eating and shopping: small tea-room serving snacks, cakes, tea and coffee. Small gift shop.

Making the most of your day: **Indoors** Family activities, stories, demonstrations and tours of machinery. Live blacksmithing event on St Clement's Day (21 November). **Outdoors** Great starting point for moorland walks.
Dogs: welcome in all areas except tea-room.

Access: Foundry Grounds
Parking: on site.

Finding out more: 01837 840046 or finchfoundry@nationaltrust.org.uk

Finch Foundry		M	T	W	T	F	S	S
14 Mar–1 Nov	11–5	M	T	W	T	F	S	S

Demonstrations of the working machinery throughout the day. Foundry and shop open for St Clement's Day, 21 November (patron saint of blacksmiths).

Glendurgan Garden

Mawnan Smith, near Falmouth, Cornwall TR11 5JZ

Map (1) C9 1962

Glendurgan Garden was described by its creators, the Quakers Alfred and Sarah Fox, as a 'small peace [sic] of heaven on earth'. Visitors can find out why it proved to be just this for the Foxes and their 12 children by exploring Glendurgan's three valleys, running down to the sheltered beach at Durgan on the Helford River. There is a puzzling maze, created by Alfred and Sarah to entertain the family. You can enjoy camellias, magnolias and primroses in early spring, then rhododendrons and bluebells in May, followed by the exotic greens of summer and dramatic autumn colour.

Eating and shopping: tea-house (concession) serving homemade cakes, soups, sandwiches, jacket potatoes, salads and daily changing specials. Ice-cream on sale at the beach in good weather. Shop and plant centre.

Making the most of your day: Durgan Beach on Helford River. Durgan Fish Cellar provides local information and children's activities (open in good weather). **Dogs**: assistance dogs only in garden. Walks in surrounding countryside (details available at Glendurgan).

Glendurgan Garden, Cornwall: the perplexing maze

Access: Garden entrance
Parking: on site.

Finding out more: 01326 252020 or glendurgan@nationaltrust.org.uk

Glendurgan Garden		M	T	W	T	F	S	S
14 Feb–31 Jul	10:30–5:30	·	T	W	T	F	S	S
1 Aug–31 Aug	10:30–5:30	M	T	W	T	F	S	S
1 Sep–1 Nov	10:30–5:30	·	T	W	T	F	S	S

Garden closes dusk if earlier. Open Bank Holiday Mondays.

Godolphin

Godolphin Cross, Helston, Cornwall TR13 9RE

Map (1) B9 2000

Hidden away in shaded woodland, Godolphin escaped modernisation and contemporary fashions. The granite-faced terraces and sunken lawns of the Side Garden have seen little change since the 16th century, and Victorian farm buildings tell the story of Godolphin as a tenant farm. Once home to a bustling and prosperous tin mine, and now part of the Cornish Mining World Heritage Site, the estate is rich in archaeology, rare plants and wildlife. Godolphin Hill provides panoramic views from coast to coast. The house is a Trust holiday home, so you can stay here and experience the splendour that mining riches bought.
Note: house open to public on limited dates between holiday lets (check before visiting).

Eating and shopping: small tea-room in the Piggery serving tea, coffee, sandwiches, cakes and ice-cream. Range of gifts and souvenirs, including local artwork. Blankets available to borrow from the Piggery for picnics in the orchard, garden or estate.

Godolphin, Cornwall: magnificent magnolia (below) and farm buildings on the estate (above)

Making the most of your day: free guided tours. Family trails, walks booklet. Gardener's potting shed has information on flora and fauna. Programme of events and activities throughout the year. Trengwainton Garden nearby. **Dogs**: welcome outdoors on short leads.

Access: **House**
Garden
Parking: 300 yards.

Finding out more: 01736 763194 or godolphin@nationaltrust.org.uk

Godolphin		M	T	W	T	F	S	S
Estate								
Open all year		M	T	W	T	F	S	S
Garden and outbuildings								
1 Jan–31 Jan	10–4	M	T	W	T	F	S	S
1 Feb–1 Nov	10–5	M	T	W	T	F	S	S
2 Nov–31 Dec*	10–4	M	T	W	T	F	S	S
House								
7 Feb–12 Feb	10–5	M	T	W	T	·	S	S
7 Mar–12 Mar	10–5	M	T	W	T	·	S	S
4 Apr–9 Apr	10–5	M	T	W	T	·	S	S
2 May–7 May	10–5	M	T	W	T	·	S	S
6 Jun–11 Jun	10–5	M	T	W	T	·	S	S
4 Jul–9 Jul	10–5	M	T	W	T	·	S	S
5 Sep–10 Sep	10–5	M	T	W	T	·	S	S
3 Oct–8 Oct	10–5	M	T	W	T	·	S	S
28 Nov–13 Dec	10–4	M	T	W	T	F	S	S

*Closed 24 and 25 December.

Great Chalfield Manor and Garden

near Melksham, Wiltshire SN12 8NH

Map (1) J4 1943

A monkey, soldiers and griffins adorn the rooftops of this moated medieval manor, looking over the terraces of the romantic garden with topiary houses, rose garden and spring-fed fish-pond. The manor reflects the style and grandeur of the past. All is lovingly looked after by the Floyd family. **Note**: home to the donor family tenants, who manage it for the National Trust. Members attending annual plant fair before normal opening times pay for admission.

Eating and shopping: guidebooks, postcards and plants for sale. You can help yourself to tea and coffee in the Motor House for a small donation.

Making the most of your day: visits to the house are by guided tour. There are also barns, meadows, gatehouse and a beautiful parish church. Maps for a cross-country walk to The Courts Garden are available. **Dogs**: assistance dogs only.

Access: **Manor** **Garden**

Parking: 100 yards, on grass verge outside manor gates.

Finding out more: 01225 782239 or greatchalfieldmanor@nationaltrust.org.uk

Great Chalfield		M	T	W	T	F	S	S
Manor								
1 Apr–29 Oct	Tour*	·	**T**	**W**	**T**	·	·	**S**
Garden								
1 Apr–29 Oct	11–5	·	**T**	**W**	**T**	·	·	·
5 Apr–25 Oct	2–5	·	·	·	·	·	·	**S**

*Admission to manor house by 45-minute guided tour only (places limited, not bookable). Tuesday, Wednesday and Thursday at 11, 12, 2, 3 and 4; Sunday at 2, 3 and 4. Additional timed manor tickets may be available Sundays and other busy days. Group visits welcome Friday and Saturday (not Bank Holidays) by written arrangement with donor family tenant, Mrs Robert Floyd (charge including members).

The medieval moated Great Chalfield Manor, Wiltshire, is surrounded by a romantic garden

Greenway

Greenway Road, Galmpton, near Brixham, Devon TQ5 0ES

Map (1) G8 2000

Take a glimpse into the lives of the famous and much-loved author Agatha Christie and her family. Their relaxed, atmospheric holiday home is set in the 1950s when the family would spend time here. The family were great collectors and the house is filled with archaeology, Tunbridgeware, silver, porcelain and books. There is a large and romantic woodland garden, with restored vinery and peach house, which drifts down the hillside towards the sparkling Dart Estuary and the boathouse. Please consider 'green ways' to get here: ferry (shuttle service available from quay), vintage bus, steam train, cycling or walking. **Note**: booking essential for car parking. Steam train halt approximately ½ mile away (walk through woodland).

Greenway, Devon, inside and out (below and above)

Eating and shopping: licensed Barn Café serving lunches, cakes and cream teas. Tack-room for takeaway options open at peak times. Agatha Christie-inspired shop selling books, DVDs, music, local food, gifts, plants and souvenir guides.

Making the most of your day: guided garden tours. Events including twilight tours, garden workshops and theatre in the garden. Family croquet, clock golf, trails and quizzes. Arrive on Barnaby, the 1950s vintage bus. **Dogs**: welcome in garden on leads (tethering rings available in courtyard). Dog bin at reception.

Access:
Buildings **Garden**
Parking: spaces must be booked (telephone infoline or visit website) – same-day booking possible by telephone. No parking on Greenway Road or Galmpton.

Finding out more: 01803 842382 (Infoline). 01803 882811 (ferry and vintage bus). 01803 555872 (steam train) or greenway@nationaltrust.org.uk

Greenway		M	T	W	T	F	S	S
7 Mar–29 Mar	10:30–5	·	·	W	T	F	S	S
31 Mar–5 Apr	10:30–5	·	T	W	T	F	S	S
6 Apr–12 Apr	10:30–5	M	·	W	T	F	S	S
15 Apr–26 Jul	10:30–5	·	·	W	T	F	S	S
28 Jul–6 Sep	10:30–5	·	T	W	T	F	S	S
9 Sep–1 Nov	10:30–5	·	·	W	T	F	S	S
5 Dec–20 Dec	11–4	·	·	·	·	·	S	S
27 Dec–31 Dec	11–4	M	T	W	T	·	·	S

Open Bank Holiday Mondays 6 April, 4 May, 25 May and 31 August.

 Why not share your pictures with us? #nationaltrust

Hailes Abbey

near Winchcombe, Cheltenham,
Gloucestershire GL54 5PB

Map (1) K1 1937

Once a Cistercian abbey, founded in 1246 by Richard of Cornwall. Pilgrims visited and financed 'the Holy Blood of Hailes'.
Note: financed, managed and maintained by English Heritage (0117 975 0700).

Finding out more: 01242 602398 or hailesabbey@nationaltrust.org.uk

Hardy's Cottage

Higher Bockhampton, near Dorchester,
Dorset DT2 8QJ

Map (1) J7 1948

The writer Thomas Hardy was born and grew up in this cottage, and wrote his early novels *Under the Greenwood Tree* and *Far from the Madding Crowd* here. Visitors can enjoy its homely atmosphere and savour a taste of the world Hardy captured in his novels and poetry.
Note: nearest toilet at visitor centre (near car park).

Eating and shopping: Thomas Hardy's books for sale, postcards and small gifts.

Making the most of your day: new visitor centre open for this year. Why not combine your visit with a trip to Max Gate, Hardy's later home in Dorchester, just a couple of miles away? **Dogs**: welcome on leads in garden only.

Access: **Building** **Grounds**
Parking: 700 yards (not National Trust).

Made simply of cob and thatch, Hardy's Cottage in Dorset provides a taste of the world Thomas Hardy captured in his novels

Finding out more: 01305 262366 or hardyscottage@nationaltrust.org.uk

Hardy's Cottage		M	T	W	T	F	S	S
11 Mar–1 Nov	11–5	·	·	**W**	**T**	**F**	**S**	**S**

Open Bank Holiday Mondays. Closes at dusk if earlier.

Heelis

Kemble Drive, Swindon, Wiltshire SN2 2NA

Map (1) K3 2005

The Trust's award-winning central office is a remarkable example of an innovative and sustainable building.

Finding out more: 01793 817575 or heelis@nationaltrust.org.uk

The intricately designed Arts and Crafts garden at Hidcote in Gloucestershire is famed throughout the world

Hidcote

Hidcote Bartrim, near Chipping Campden, Gloucestershire GL55 6LR

Map (1) L1 1948

This world-famous Arts and Crafts garden nestles in a north Cotswolds hamlet. Created by the talented and wealthy American horticulturist Major Lawrence Johnston, Hidcote's colourful and intricately designed outdoor 'rooms' are full of surprises, which change in harmony with the seasons. Many of the unusual plants found growing in the garden were collected from Johnston's plant-hunting trips to faraway places. Wandering through the maze of narrow paved pathways you come across secret gardens, unexpected views and plants that burst with colour. The Wilderness with its secluded stretch of tall trees is just right for a picnic.

Eating and shopping: Barn Café, plus Winthrop's Café and conservatory. Largest Trust plant centre. Shop selling exclusive Hidcote souvenirs.

Making the most of your day: daily introductory talks. Exclusive evening Head Gardener tours and open-air theatre events. Themed family activities and workshops.
Dogs: assistance dogs only.

Access:
Visitor reception **Grounds**
Parking: 100 yards.

Finding out more: 01386 438333 or hidcote@nationaltrust.org.uk

Hidcote		M	T	W	T	F	S	S
14 Feb–1 Mar	11–4	·	·	·	·	·	**S**	**S**
2 Mar–4 Oct	10–6	**M**	**T**	**W**	**T**	**F**	**S**	**S**
5 Oct–1 Nov	10–5	**M**	**T**	**W**	**T**	**F**	**S**	**S**
7 Nov–20 Dec	11–4	·	·	·	·	·	**S**	**S**

Last admission to garden one hour before closing. Barn Café closed during November and December.

Killerton

Broadclyst, Exeter, Devon EX5 3LE

Map (1) G6 1944

Would you give away your family home for your political beliefs? Sir Richard Acland did just this with his estate, which includes 20 farms and 250 cottages and is one of the largest in the Trust. Killerton House, built in 1779, brings to life generations of Aclands, one of Devon's oldest families. More a family home than a grand house, it is a place you can imagine living in. Killerton houses a large collection of historic and contemporary fashion; this year's exhibition – 'The F Word: the Changing Language of Fashion' – charts innovation in dress. One of Killerton's highlights is the garden, created by Veitch. It is beautiful year-round, with rhododendrons, magnolias, unusual trees, flower borders, sweeping lawns and countryside views.

Killerton, Devon: a blaze of agapanthus (below) and a detail of an 1810 silk dress (above) from this year's exhibition of historic fashion

Eating and shopping: large shop selling award-winning Killerton cider, chutney, flour and honey, plus wide range of local gifts, food and books. Second-hand bookshop. Well-stocked plant centre. Food and drink available in the Killerton Kitchen, Stables Café and Thirsty Dragon kiosk. Picnics welcome.

Making the most of your day: **Indoors** To get in the Killerton mood you can play the piano, browse in the library or dress up in replica costumes. **Outdoors** The secret paths in the garden allow you to discover the Bear's House, champion trees and extinct volcano. Events, including summer plays, Easter Egg hunts, Killerton at Christmas, Apple weekend, car shows and more. Family trails with wonderful views, cycle tracks and orienteering trails allow you to explore the wider estate. Ashclyst Forest, a short drive away, offers waymarked woodland paths and butterfly glades.
Dogs: welcome on leads in park and on estate walks.

Access:
House **Grounds**
Sat Nav: postcode leads to house, so follow brown signs to main car park. For Ashclyst Forest use EX5 3DT. **Parking**: main car park 280 yards. Additional smaller car parks, including Ashclyst Forest Gate, Ellerhayes Bridge, Dane's Wood.

Finding out more: 01392 881345 or killerton@nationaltrust.org.uk

Killerton		M	T	W	T	F	S	S
House and Killerton Kitchen restaurant								
14 Feb–22 Mar	11–4	**M**	**T**	**W**	**T**	**F**	**S**	**S**
23 Mar–1 Nov	11–5	**M**	**T**	**W**	**T**	**F**	**S**	**S**
21 Nov–31 Dec*	11–4	**M**	**T**	**W**	**T**	**F**	**S**	**S**
Chapel, garden, Stables Café, shop and plant centre								
1 Jan–22 Mar	11–4	**M**	**T**	**W**	**T**	**F**	**S**	**S**
23 Mar–31 Dec**	10–5:30	**M**	**T**	**W**	**T**	**F**	**S**	**S**
Park								
Open all year	8–7	**M**	**T**	**W**	**T**	**F**	**S**	**S**

*Special Christmas opening 21 November to 3 January 2016 (house closed 24, 25 and 26 December).
**Closed 25 December. Garden and park open daily until 7 or dusk if earlier.

Browsing in the library at Killerton, Devon

Entry is still possible at most places up to 30 minutes before closing

Killerton Estate: Budlake Post Office (above left) and Marker's (above) in Devon

Killerton Estate: Budlake Post Office, Marker's and Clyston Mill

Killerton Estate, Broadclyst, Devon

Map (1) G7 1944

You can get a feel for life on the wider estate by searching out Marker's, a modified medieval hall-house with unusual painted screen; the picturesque working watermill at nearby Clyston; and Budlake, a thatched cottage that once served as the village post office, with a pretty cottage garden. **Note**: nearest toilets by Broadclyst car park.

Eating and shopping: Clyston flour available at the mill or at the large gift shop at Killerton. Wide range of food and drink on offer at Killerton in the Killerton Kitchen, Stables Café or Thirsty Dragon kiosk.

Making the most of your day: unusual and quirky things to spot, from the red telephone box and two-seated privy at Budlake. Flour ground at Clyston. Map available at Killerton. **Dogs**: on leads at Budlake and Clyston Mill. Assistance dogs only at Marker's.

Access: **Marker's** **Clyston**
Parking: for Marker's and Clyston use Broadclyst village car park.

Finding out more: 01392 881345 or killerton@nationaltrust.org.uk

Killerton Estate		M	T	W	T	F	S	S
28 Mar–1 Nov	1–5	**M**	**T**	**W**	·	·	**S**	**S**

King John's Hunting Lodge

The Square, Axbridge, Somerset BS26 2AP

Map (1) I4 1968

This early Tudor timber-framed wool merchant's house (*circa* 1500) provides a fascinating insight into local history. **Note**: run as a local history museum by Axbridge and District Museum Trust. Entry charges (including members).

Finding out more: 01934 732012 or kingjohns@nationaltrust.org.uk

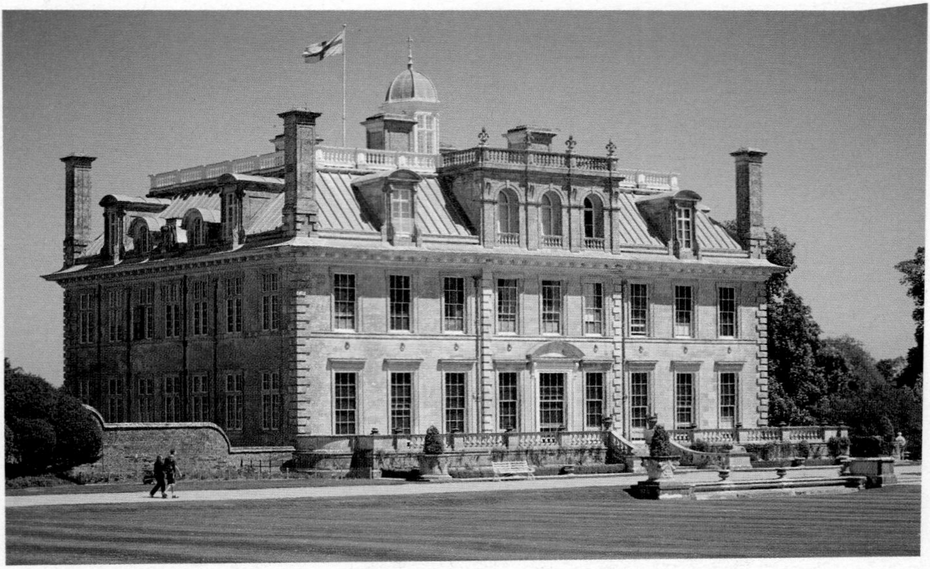

An Italian palace in the heart of Dorset, magnificent Kingston Lacy (above) boasts sumptuous interiors (right), as well as a wonderful garden, estate, park and woodland (opposite bottom)

Kingston Lacy

Wimborne Minster, Dorset BH21 4EA

Map (1) K7 1982

The 'exiled collector' William John Bankes transformed his family home to create an Italian palace in the heart of Dorset. The Bankes family's desire to surround themselves with only the finest art and sculpture is reflected through the lavish interiors he created. Today you can discover an internationally acclaimed art collection, including paintings by Rubens, Titian and Tintoretto, exquisite carvings and the largest private collection of Egyptian artefacts in the UK. There's even more to explore outside, across sweeping lawns, through the Japanese Garden, to the kitchen garden, currently being restored to its Edwardian heyday. The woodland and parkland walks are wonderful whatever the season – keep an eye open for Kingston Lacy's fine herd of Red Ruby Devon cattle.

Eating and shopping: prize-winning scones, beef from the Kingston Lacy Red Ruby Devon herd in the stableyard café. Regional and local foods and wines, plants, high-quality gifts and souvenirs for sale in the old kitchen shop.

Making the most of your day: seasonal spectacles of winter snowdrops, spring bluebells, summer flowers and autumn colour to enjoy. You can relax in a deckchair on the lawn or explore the kitchen garden. Restoration work continues on the glasshouses and visitors can pick up tips from our garden volunteers. Families can discover the wooden play areas and tick off another of the '50 things'. Seasonal events all year, including Easter, Hallowe'en and Christmas. Across the estate there are excellent walks and trails, including a riverside walk at Eye Bridge and the Iron Age hill fort of Badbury Rings, home to 14 varieties of orchid. **Dogs**: welcome on leads in restaurant courtyard, park and woodlands.

Access:
Building **Grounds**
Sat Nav: unreliable, follow B3082 to main entrance. Use DT11 9JL for Badbury Rings; BH21 4EL for Eye Bridge. **Parking**: on site or at Eye Bridge, Pamphill Green and Badbury Rings (where there is a charge on point-to-point race days, including members).

Some places are easy to get to on foot or by public transport. See page 3

Finding out more: 01202 883402 or kingstonlacy@nationaltrust.org.uk

Kingston Lacy		M	T	W	T	F	S	S
House								
7 Mar–1 Nov*	11–5	**M**	**T**	**W**	**T**	**F**	**S**	**S**
2 Nov–26 Nov	Tour	**M**	**T**	**W**	**T**	**F**	**S**	**S**
27 Nov–23 Dec	11–6	**M**	**T**	**W**	**T**	**F**	**S**	**S**
26 Dec–31 Dec**	11–3	**M**	**T**	**W**	**T**	·	**S**	**S**
Garden, park, shop and restaurant								
1 Jan–6 Mar	10:30–4	**M**	**T**	**W**	**T**	**F**	**S**	**S**
7 Mar–1 Nov	10:30–6	**M**	**T**	**W**	**T**	**F**	**S**	**S**
2 Nov–26 Nov	10:30–4	**M**	**T**	**W**	**T**	**F**	**S**	**S**
27 Nov–23 Dec	10:30–7	**M**	**T**	**W**	**T**	**F**	**S**	**S**
26 Dec–31 Dec	10:30–4	**M**	**T**	**W**	**T**	·	**S**	**S**

*Guided tours Monday and Tuesday. **Open for exhibition only. Timed tickets may operate on busy days. Last admission to house one hour before closing. Shop and restaurant close 30 minutes before garden. Closed 24 and 25 December.

The fabulous Gothic façade of Knightshayes in Devon

Knightshayes

Bolham, Tiverton, Devon EX16 7RQ

Map (1) G6 1972

One of the South West's finest and the only existing 'garden in a wood', Knightshayes' garden is a masterpiece of architectural planting. As well as showcasing every continent's most beautiful, unusual discoveries, there are hidden glades and views across the Exe Valley. The Gothic house is a rare example of the genius of William Burges, whose opulent designs inspire extremes of opinion. The restored walled garden combines productivity, using traditional techniques, with aesthetic appeal. It's one of the best examples of a Victorian kitchen garden in the country.

Eating and shopping: Stables Café serving hot meals, made using ingredients from the kitchen garden, also soups, sandwiches, cakes and drinks. Conservatory Tea-room serving snacks, cakes, ice-cream and drinks. Picnics welcome. Well-stocked shop and plant centre, with plants from the Knightshayes collection.

Making the most of your day: **Indoors** Newly opened kitchens to explore. Traditional Victorian Christmas. **Outdoors** Garden tours. Play area. Events, including outdoor music in the summer and Christmas illuminations.
Dogs: welcome on leads in parkland and woods; in formal garden, November to February only.

Access:
House **Stables** **Gardens**
Sat Nav: do not use, follow brown signs on nearing Tiverton/Bolham. **Parking**: on site.

Finding out more: 01884 254665 or knightshayes@nationaltrust.org.uk

Knightshayes		M	T	W	T	F	S	S
House, garden, shop, plant centre and café*								
1 Jan–1 Mar	10–4	M	T	W	T	F	S	S
2 Mar–1 Nov	10–5	M	T	W	T	F	S	S
2 Nov–31 Dec	10–4	M	T	W	T	F	S	S
Parkland and woodland								
Open all year	Dawn–dusk	M	T	W	T	F	S	S

*House opens 11. Selected rooms open in the winter. Late-night opening until 8, 31 October and 4, 5, 11, 12, 18 and 19 December. Whole place closed 24 and 25 December. Mid-Devon Show Saturday 25 July: open as usual but expect delays.

 Please display your current sticker for free parking

Lacock Abbey, Fox Talbot Museum and Village

Lacock, near Chippenham, Wiltshire SN15 2LG

Map (1) K4 1944

You can see why Ela of Salisbury chose this spot for her abbey in 1232: nestled alongside the River Avon in a rolling Wiltshire landscape, Lacock invites you to stay. The Abbey bears testament to a legacy of more than 800 years of past owners with sophisticated taste, who sensitively turned it from a nunnery into a quirky family home, furnished with well-loved mementoes and furniture. Seasonal colour can be discovered in the wooded grounds, botanic garden, greenhouse and orchard. The museum celebrates William Henry Fox Talbot, who created the first photographic negative and established this as a birthplace of photography. Lacock has a homely feel, and the village with its timber-framed cottages is to this day a bustling community. **Note**: during the winter, the first-floor furnished rooms of the Abbey are open at weekends only.

Eating and shopping: lots of places to eat and drink in Lacock village, including The Stables tea-room. Three National Trust shops and a variety of other retail options (including a second-hand bookshop at the Abbey) make Lacock a great place for shopping.

Making the most of your day: **Indoors** The Abbey offers two distinct experiences: peaceful ground-floor monastic cloisters and first-floor furnished rooms. The museum provides an insight into the history of photography which appeals to all ages and includes changing exhibitions. In 2015 the birthplace of photography story is brought to life through exciting displays in the Abbey and museum. **Outdoors** The level grounds are great for picnics and walks. For families there are outdoor play features and changing trails. Special events cater for all interests and ages. Lacock is also a famous filming location and its appearances include *Harry Potter, Cranford* and *Pride and Prejudice*. **Dogs**: welcome in Abbey grounds from 1 November to 31 March.

Access:
Abbey **Museum**
Grounds
Sat Nav: can direct down one-way street. Set to Hither Way, Lacock, for car park.
Parking: 220 yards. No visitor parking on village streets.

Finding out more: 01249 730459 or lacockabbey@nationaltrust.org.uk

Lacock Abbey		M	T	W	T	F	S	S
Abbey cloisters and grounds, museum, tea-room, shops*								
2 Jan–13 Feb	11–4	**M**	**T**	**W**	**T**	**F**	**S**	**S**
14 Feb–1 Nov	10:30–5:30	**M**	**T**	**W**	**T**	**F**	**S**	**S**
2 Nov–31 Dec	11–4	**M**	**T**	**W**	**T**	**F**	**S**	**S**
Abbey rooms (first floor)**								
3 Jan–8 Feb	Tour	·	·	·	·	·	**S**	**S**
14 Feb–1 Nov	11–5	**M**	**T**	**W**	**T**	**F**	**S**	**S**
7 Nov–13 Dec	12–4	·	·	·	·	·	**S**	**S**
Village								
Open all year		**M**	**T**	**W**	**T**	**F**	**S**	**S**

Last admission to Abbey 45 minutes before closing. *Shops and tea-room open at 10 in main season; in winter, tea-room opens from 10:30 and cloisters and grounds may close at dusk; all closed 25 and 26 December, except tea-room open on 26 December. **Great Hall in Abbey rooms open for Christmas 19, 20 and 27 December (12 to 4). Village businesses open and close at various times.

Lacock, Wiltshire: the Abbey (bottom) sits at the edge of the attractive village (below)

Lanhydrock

Bodmin, Cornwall PL30 5AD

Map (1) D8 1953

The home of the Victorian Agar-Robartes family, the house appears as if they have just popped out for tea. There are more than 50 rooms to explore and it's easy to see the contrasts between the servants' life 'downstairs' and the elegant family rooms. The extensive garden is full of colour all year and there is plenty to discover across the estate, from ancient woodlands to tranquil riverside paths. There are off-road cycle trails, with special trails for families and novice riders, and you can even hire a bike from us.

Lanhydrock, Cornwall: walking towards the extensive house (above) and the Long Gallery (below)

Eating and shopping: Victorian Servants' Hall restaurant, the Stables snack bar and the Park Café. Shop selling local foods and gifts. Second-hand bookshop, plant centre and cycle hire.

Making the most of your day: **Indoors** There is a remarkable ceiling in the Long Gallery, Victorian servants' quarters and extensive kitchens to explore. **Outdoors** Garden tours, walks through the woodland, park and riverside paths, as well as a magnificent collection of magnolias, which flower all through spring. Children will love the new adventure playground and family-friendly off-road cycle trails (map available).
Dogs: dog-friendly walks throughout estate (assistance dogs only in garden).

Access:
House **Grounds**
Sat Nav: use PL30 4AB (1 Double Lodges).
Parking: 600 yards.

Finding out more: 01208 265950 or lanhydrock@nationaltrust.org.uk

Lanhydrock		M	T	W	T	F	S	S
House								
1 Mar–31 Oct	11–5:30	**M**	**T**	**W**	**T**	**F**	**S**	**S**
1 Nov–29 Nov*	11–4	·	·	·	·	·	**S**	**S**
1 Dec–31 Dec*	11–4	**M**	**T**	**W**	**T**	**F**	**S**	**S**
Garden								
14 Feb–31 Dec	10–6	**M**	**T**	**W**	**T**	**F**	**S**	**S**
Estate and cycle trails								
Open all year	Dawn–dusk	**M**	**T**	**W**	**T**	**F**	**S**	**S**
Refreshments and cycle hire								
1 Jan–28 Feb	10–4	**M**	**T**	**W**	**T**	**F**	**S**	**S**
1 Mar–1 Nov	10–5:30**	**M**	**T**	**W**	**T**	**F**	**S**	**S**
2 Nov–31 Dec	10–4	**M**	**T**	**W**	**T**	**F**	**S**	**S**
Shop								
14 Feb–31 Dec	11–5:30†	**M**	**T**	**W**	**T**	**F**	**S**	**S**

*Selected rooms only. **Cycle hire 9:30 to 5. †Shop closes at 4 in February, November and December. Plant centre and second-hand bookshop open daily 1 March to 1 November. House, shop and refreshments close at 5 in March and October. Closed 25 December.

The 17th-century gatehouse at Lanhydrock in Cornwall

Lawrence House

9 Castle Street, Launceston, Cornwall PL15 8BA

Map (1) E7 1964

This Georgian town house, now a museum, hosts special exhibitions. Large display of costumes and a children's toy room.
Note: leased to Launceston Town Council.

Finding out more: 01566 773277 or lawrencehouse@nationaltrust.org.uk

Levant Mine and Beam Engine

Trewellard, Pendeen, near St Just, Cornwall TR19 7SX

Map (1) A9 1967

High on the cliffs overlooking the Atlantic, Levant was one of Cornwall's champion mines for over 100 years. Men and boys tunnelled deep under the sea while women and girls laboured on the surface. Today Levant is a great base from which to explore the industry that shaped Cornwall. **Note**: exposed clifftop location, uneven ground.

Eating and shopping: light refreshments available, including hot and cold drinks, ice-cream and pasties. Small shop selling books, minerals, souvenirs and postcards.

Making the most of your day: **Indoors** Daily running of the restored steam-driven beam engine and guided tours. Tunnel to the man-engine shaft. Rock-breaking and mineral-washing area. **Outdoors** Easy clifftop walks to Geevor and Botallack. **Dogs**: welcome on leads.

Access:
Reception **Engine house**
Grounds
Parking: 328 yards.

Finding out more: 01736 786156 or levant@nationaltrust.org.uk

Levant Beam Engine		M	T	W	T	F	S	S
9 Jan–13 Mar	10:30–4	·	·	·	·	F	·	·
15 Mar–1 Nov	10:30–5	M	T	W	T	F	·	S
6 Nov–11 Dec	10:30–4	·	·	·	·	F	·	·

Engine steaming from 11.

Levant Mine, Cornwall, is built on cliffs overlooking the Atlantic Ocean

Little Clarendon

Dinton, Salisbury, Wiltshire SP3 5DZ

Map (1) K5 1940

Late 15th-century stone house with curious 20th-century chapel. **Note**: sorry no toilet.

Finding out more: 01747 873250 or littleclarendon@nationaltrust.org.uk

Lodge Park and Sherborne Estate

Aldsworth, near Cheltenham, Gloucestershire GL54 3PP

Map (1) K/L2 1983

Within the tranquil Sherborne Park Estate sits England's only surviving 17th-century deer-coursing grandstand. Enchanting Lodge Park was built in 1634 to satisfy John 'Crump' Dutton's love of gambling and entertaining. Now a place to explore, discover, picnic and play. Don't miss the dramatic views from the roof. **Note**: toilet at Lodge Park only.

Eating and shopping: light refreshments and plants for sale at Lodge Park's courtyard café on open days. Tea-room in Sherborne village (not National Trust).

Making the most of your day: living history, family events, children's quizzes and colouring, croquet, historic shepherd's hut, woodland play trail and beautiful walks in Bridgeman landscape at Lodge Park. Country walks across the wider estate. **Dogs**: on leads in Lodge Park grounds; under control across the estate.

Access: **Building**
Parking: on site for Lodge Park. For Sherborne Estate use Ewe Pen Barn car park or Water Meadows (off A40 towards Sherborne).

The grandstand at Lodge Park in Gloucestershire

Finding out more: 01451 844130 or lodgepark@nationaltrust.org.uk

Lodge Park and Sherborne Estate		M	T	W	T	F	S	S
Lodge Park								
6 Mar–8 Nov	11–4	·	·	·	·	**F**	**S**	**S**
Sherborne Estate								
Open all year	Dawn–dusk	**M**	**T**	**W**	**T**	**F**	**S**	**S**

Lodge Park opens Bank Holiday Mondays and occasionally closes for weddings and private functions (telephone to confirm opening times). Extended opening hours on event days.

Loughwood Meeting House

Dalwood, Axminster, Devon EX13 7DU

Map (1) H7 1969

Atmospheric 17th-century thatched Baptist meeting house dug into the hillside; open daily all year. **Note**: sorry no toilet.

Finding out more: 01752 346585 or loughwood@nationaltrust.org.uk

Lundy

Bristol Channel, Devon

Map (1) D5 1969

Undisturbed by cars, this wildlife-rich island, designated the first Marine Conservation Area, encompasses a small village with an inn, Victorian church and the 13th-century Marisco Castle. **Note**: financed, administered and maintained by the Landmark Trust. Ferry from Bideford or Ilfracombe. MS *Oldenburg* fares (including members), discounts available.

Eating and shopping: tavern serving hot and cold food and drinks. Shop selling souvenirs, Lundy stamps, snacks and ice-creams.

Making the most of your day: diving, walking, letterboxing, bird and wildlife-watching. Holiday cottages (not National Trust). **Dogs**: assistance dogs only.

Access: **Building** **Grounds**
Sat Nav: use EX34 9EQ for Ilfracombe; EX39 2EY Bideford. **Parking**: at Bideford and Ilfracombe, not National Trust (charge including members).

Finding out more: 01271 863636 or lundy@nationaltrust.org.uk. The Lundy Shore Office, The Quay, Bideford, Devon EX39 2LY

Lundy

MS *Oldenburg* sails from Bideford or Ilfracombe up to four times a week from the end of March until the end of October carrying both day and staying passengers. A helicopter service operates from Hartland Point from November to mid-March, Mondays and Fridays only, for staying visitors.

Lydford Gorge

Lydford, near Tavistock, Devon EX20 4BH

Map (1) F7 1947

This dramatic legend-rich river gorge (the deepest in the South West) offers a variety of adventurous walks. The gorge provides a truly breathtaking experience: around every corner the River Lyd plunges, tumbles, swirls and gently meanders as it travels through the steep-sided, oak-wooded valley. There are amazing features carved out by the water over thousands of years, from the 30-metre Whitelady Waterfall to the turbulent pothole called the Devil's Cauldron. Throughout the seasons there is an abundance of wildlife and plants to see, from woodland birds to wild garlic in the spring and fungi in the autumn. **Note**: rugged terrain, vertical drops.

Eating and shopping: shop selling gifts, books, outdoor clothing and footwear. Two tea-rooms serving soup, sandwiches, cream teas, cakes and local ice-cream. Takeaway drinks and food available.

Making the most of your day: family events, wildlife-themed and bushcraft activities, children's play area, bird hide. **Dogs**: welcome on leads.

Dramatic legend-rich Lydford Gorge in Devon

Access:
Buildings Gorge
Parking: on site.

Finding out more: 01822 820320 or lydfordgorge@nationaltrust.org.uk

Lydford Gorge		M	T	W	T	F	S	S
Gorge, shop and both tea-rooms								
7 Mar–4 Oct	10–5*	**M**	**T**	**W**	**T**	**F**	**S**	**S**
5 Oct–1 Nov	10–4*	**M**	**T**	**W**	**T**	**F**	**S**	**S**
Gorge, shop, waterfall tea-room								
7 Nov–27 Dec**	11–3:30	·	·	·	·	·	**S**	**S**

*Waterfall tea-room opens at 11; closing time dependent on the weather. **Only short walk to waterfall open: other gorge paths closed due to weather conditions and maintenance work. Short walk to waterfall also open during daylight hours in January and February. Closed 26 December.

Lytes Cary Manor

near Somerton, Somerset TA11 7HU

Map (1) 15 1949

This intimate medieval manor house, with its beautiful Arts and Crafts-inspired garden, was originally the family home of the Elizabethan herbalist Henry Lyte. After years of neglect Lytes Cary was lovingly restored in the 20th century by Sir Walter Jenner and is arranged as it was in his time. A stroll around the garden rooms, divided by high yew hedges, reveals collections of topiary (including the 12 Apostles), sensuous herbaceous borders and manicured lawns. A visit to this harmonious manor is wonderfully relaxing and uplifting.

Eating and shopping: small tea-room offering light refreshments. Picnic tables in the courtyard. Shop selling gifts, garden accessories and plants. Second-hand books available.

The Whitelady Waterfall at Lydford Gorge, Devon (opposite), and lovingly restored Lytes Cary Manor in Somerset (above left and right)

Making the most of your day: tranquil walks on the wider estate and children's outdoor natural play area. Community allotments are bursting with creative and colourful designs. West wing is available as a holiday rental. **Dogs**: welcome on leads on estate walks only.

Access: **Building** **Grounds**
Parking: 40 yards.

Finding out more: 01458 224471 or lytescarymanor@nationaltrust.org.uk

Lytes Cary Manor		M	T	W	T	F	S	S
House								
2 Mar–1 Nov	11–5	**M**	**T**	**W**	**T**	**F**	**S**	**S**
Garden, parkland, refreshments and shop								
2 Mar–1 Nov	10:30–5	**M**	**T**	**W**	**T**	**F**	**S**	**S**
Estate walks								
Open all year	Dawn–dusk	**M**	**T**	**W**	**T**	**F**	**S**	**S**

Limited access to garden on frosty and wet days.

Market Hall

High Street, Chipping Campden, Gloucestershire GL55 6AJ

Map (1) K1 1942

Outstanding building, constructed nearly 400 years ago to give shelter to market traders. **Note**: nearest toilet in town centre.

Finding out more: 01386 438333 or markethall@nationaltrust.org.uk

Max Gate

Alington Avenue, Dorchester, Dorset DT1 2AB

Map (1) J7 1940

Max Gate, home to Dorset's most famous author and poet, Thomas Hardy, was designed by the writer himself in 1885. This atmospheric Victorian house is where Hardy wrote some of his most famous novels, including *Tess of the d'Urbervilles* and *Jude the Obscure*, as well as most of his poetry.

Eating and shopping: Thomas Hardy's books, souvenirs and small gifts on sale. Tea, coffee and cakes available.

Making the most of your day: Hardy's Cottage, the thatched cottage in which the writer was born, is just a couple of miles away. **Dogs**: welcome on leads in garden only.

Access: **Building** **Garden**
Sat Nav: unreliable, look for signs from A352.
Parking: 50 yards, limited (not National Trust).

Finding out more: 01305 262538 or maxgate@nationaltrust.org.uk

Max Gate		M	T	W	T	F	S	S
11 Mar–1 Nov	11–5	·	·	W	T	F	S	S

Open Bank Holiday Mondays. Closes at dusk if earlier.

Victorian Max Gate in Dorset: designed by Thomas Hardy

The library in tranquil Mompesson House in Wiltshire

Mompesson House

The Close, Salisbury, Wiltshire SP1 2EL

Map (1) K5 1952

When walking into the celebrated Cathedral Close in Salisbury, visitors step back into a past world, and on entering Mompesson House, featured in the award-winning film *Sense and Sensibility*, the feeling of leaving the modern world behind deepens. The tranquil atmosphere is enhanced by the magnificent plasterwork, fine period furniture and graceful oak staircase, which are the main features of this perfectly proportioned Queen Anne house. In addition, the Turnbull collection of 18th-century drinking glasses is of national importance. The delightful walled garden has a pergola and traditionally planted herbaceous borders.

Eating and shopping: tea-room serving locally baked scones and cakes, light lunches and teas. National Trust shop only 60 yards away. Turnbull Glass Collection catalogue for sale.

For other ways to get involved go to nationaltrust.org.uk/get-involved/volunteer

Making the most of your day: regular croquet sessions on the lawn and occasional live music, including Northumbrian Pipers.
Dogs: assistance dogs only.

Access: [access symbols] **Building** [symbols]
Grounds [symbols]
Parking: 260 yards in city centre, not National Trust (charge including members).

Finding out more: 01722 420980 (Infoline). 01722 335659 or mompessonhouse@nationaltrust.org.uk

Mompesson House		M	T	W	T	F	S	S
14 Mar–1 Nov	11–5	M	T	W	·	·	S	S

Open Good Friday.

Montacute House

Montacute, Somerset TA15 6XP

Map (1) 16 [symbols] 1931

Built in golden Ham stone, Montacute House commands a central position in the picturesque village sharing its name and is a beacon of Elizabethan pomp and style. Inside are oak-panelled rooms, tapestries, samplers and a 52-metre Long Gallery displaying over 50 period portraits, in a long-term partnership with the National Portrait Gallery. The surrounding clipped lawns, wobbly hedges, hidden paths and parkland all entice exploration. Edward Phelips – a wealthy, ambitious lawyer and Member of Parliament – built this grand mansion to advertise his lofty position and success. Over 400 years later, does this Elizabethan masterpiece still have the power to impress?.

Eating and shopping: café serving a variety of homemade seasonal lunches and tempting cakes to be enjoyed inside or out. Gift shop and plant sales. Monthly farmers' markets all year, 10 to 2.

The sun catches the golden stone of Elizabethan Montacute House, Somerset

Making the most of your day: **Indoors** National Portrait Gallery exhibition 'Pictured and Seen'. **Outdoors** Regular 'Tudor Welcome' garden tours and seasonal events. Family trails and swings. Tintinhull Garden and Barrington Court nearby. **Dogs**: welcome in garden on short leads (on gravel paths only).

Access: **Building** **Grounds**
Parking: on site.

Finding out more: 01935 823289 or montacute@nationaltrust.org.uk

Montacute House		M	T	W	T	F	S	S
House								
2 Mar–1 Nov	11–4:30	**M**	**T**	**W**	**T**	**F**	**S**	**S**
7 Nov–27 Dec*	12–3	·	·	·	·	·	**S**	**S**
Garden, parkland, café and shop								
1 Jan–28 Feb	11–4	·	·	**W**	**T**	**F**	**S**	**S**
1 Mar–1 Nov	10–5	**M**	**T**	**W**	**T**	**F**	**S**	**S**
4 Nov–31 Dec	11–4	·	·	**W**	**T**	**F**	**S**	**S**

*Some rooms may not be open. Whole place closed for essential maintenance 26 to 30 January, and closed 24 and 25 December.

Fountain at Montacute House, Somerset

Newark Park

Ozleworth, Wotton-under-Edge, Gloucestershire GL12 7PZ

Map (1) J3 1949

You can always expect the unexpected at Newark Park, which overlooks the splendid Ozleworth Valley. From Tudor beginnings to dramatic rescue by a 20th-century Texan, Newark has a wonderful quirky character and eclectic collections. The garden and estate provide space to play and contemplate, with new discoveries at every turn. **Note**: toilets in car park (accessible toilet only at house).

Eating and shopping: shop in visitor reception selling souvenirs and gifts. New café in garden serving light lunches, cakes and hot drinks with outdoor seating and some indoor seating in the house.

View from the Garden Hall at Newark Park, Gloucestershire

Some places are easy to get to on foot or by public transport. See page 3

Making the most of your day: waymarked walks and geocaching on the estate. Children's Tracker Pack available. Garden games and croquet on the lawn. Peacocks to keep you company. **Dogs**: welcome on leads (livestock grazing).

Access: Building Grounds
Sat Nav: only works from north, follow brown signs from Wotton-under-Edge and A46 from south. **Parking**: 100 yards.

Finding out more: 01793 817666 (Infoline). 01453 842644 or newarkpark@nationaltrust.org.uk

Newark Park		M	T	W	T	F	S	S
18 Feb–1 Mar	11–4	·	·	W	T	F	S	S
4 Mar–1 Nov	11–5	·	·	W	T	F	S	S
5 Dec–13 Dec	11–4	·	·	·	·	·	S	S

Open Bank Holidays. Closes dusk if earlier.

Overbeck's

Sharpitor, Salcombe, Devon TQ8 8LW

Map (1) F9 1937

Tucked away on the cliffs above Salcombe is this hidden paradise: a subtropical garden (right), bursting with colour, filled with exotic and rare plants and surprises round every corner, which surrounds the seaside home of scientist and inventor Otto Overbeck. The garden's views over the estuary and coast are truly breathtaking. Inside, among Otto's eclectic collections – glimpses of a bygone age – are his 'Rejuvenator', once believed to cure all ills, and the melodious giant music box called a polyphon (you can choose a disc to play). Generations of children return to discover the secret room and Fred the friendly ghost. **Note**: entrance path and grounds are very steep in places.

Eating and shopping: licensed tea-room serving cream teas and light lunches (crab sandwiches a speciality) – terrace with sea views. Shop selling local produce, books, plants and gifts, such as 'First Flight', a statuette inspired by the bronze girl in the garden.

Making the most of your day: **Indoors** Activities, including art workshops. Tours and trails – themes include music, cooking and history. Children's quizzes and trails. **Outdoors** Walks and trails. Guided and self-guided tours. Statue garden. **Dogs**: allowed in reception area and on coastal walks.

Access: Building Grounds
Sat Nav: follow brown signs through Malborough. **Parking**: limited at top of drive and approach lane. Additional parking at East Soar (1 mile walk along coast path).

Finding out more: 01548 842893 or overbecks@nationaltrust.org.uk

Overbeck's		M	T	W	T	F	S	S
14 Feb–1 Nov	11–5	M	T	W	T	F	S	S

Tea-room open until 4:45.

Priest's House, Muchelney

Muchelney, Langport, Somerset TA10 0DQ

Map (1) I6 1911

Medieval hall-house, built in 1308.
Note: private home, but open 15 March to 27 September, Sunday and Monday, 2 to 5. Sorry no toilets.

Finding out more: 01458 253771 or priestshouse@nationaltrust.org.uk

Prior Park Landscape Garden

Ralph Allen Drive, Bath, Somerset BA2 5AH

Map (1) J4 1993

Two views of Prior Park Landscape Garden in Somerset

This magical landscape garden, perched on a hillside overlooking Bath, was created between 1735 and 1764 by Ralph Allen, a local entrepreneur. The garden is being restored to appear much as it did at the time of Allen's death in 1764. Here you can discover Ralph Allen's story and why Prior Park is unlike many other gardens. Although there are few flowers and no formal beds, winding paths will lead you to hidden retreats, a grotto, views over Georgian Bath, cascades, tranquil lakes and an elegant Palladian Bridge – one of only four in the world. **Note**: house not accessible. Steep slopes, steps and uneven paths.

Eating and shopping: Tea Shed by the lakes serving light snacks, cakes and refreshments (please note outdoor seating only, in tea garden). Small shop selling outdoor-related products and pocket-money gifts.

Making the most of your day: events and activities all year. Free guided tours and seasonal trails. Natural play area. The Bath Skyline 6-mile circular walk is just minutes from the garden. **Dogs**: welcome on short leads.

Access: **Grounds**
Parking: for disabled visitors only. Car parks in city centre, 1 mile (steep, uphill walk). Frequent bus services from bus station, Abbey and Manvers Street (by bus station).

Finding out more: 01225 833422 or priorpark@nationaltrust.org.uk

Prior Park Landscape Garden		M	T	W	T	F	S	S
3 Jan–31 Jan	10–4	·	·	·	·	·	S	S
1 Feb–1 Nov	10–5:30	M	T	W	T	F	S	S
7 Nov–27 Dec	10–4	·	·	·	·	·	S	S

Last admission one hour before closing. Closes dusk if earlier than 5:30. Tea Shed: check opening times.

Some places are easy to get to on foot or by public transport. See page 3

St Michael's Mount

Marazion, Cornwall TR17 0HS

Map (1) B9 1954

This iconic rocky island, crowned by a medieval church and castle, is home to the St Aubyn family and a 30-strong community of islanders. Visitors can immerse themselves in history at the Mount, where the architecture dates back to the 12th century, and legends – such as that of Jack the Giant Killer – abound. There is a subtropical terraced garden and spectacular views of Mount's Bay and the Lizard from the castle battlements. If the tide is in, you can take an evocative boat trip to the island or, at low tide, walk across the ancient causeway from Marazion. **Note**: steep climb to the castle up uneven, cobbled, historic pathway. St Aubyn Estates/National Trust partnership. Members have to pay for parking and for boat trips to Mount at high tide.

Eating and shopping: Island Café (licensed) serving Cornish pasties, sandwiches and cream teas. Sail Loft Restaurant (licensed) serving Newlyn fish, daily specials, cream teas and homemade cakes. Island Shop and Courtyard Shop selling local contemporary gifts, Cornish produce, jewellery, bags, arts and crafts.

Making the most of your day: **Indoors** Children's quiz. Events, exhibitions. Guided tours (by arrangement). You can find out more by asking our knowledgeable room guides. Sunday church services (Whitsun to September). **Outdoors** Garden trail for children. **Dogs**: assistance dogs only in castle and garden.

Access: **Castle** **Village**
Parking: numerous spaces in Marazion, opposite St Michael's Mount, not National Trust (charge including members).

Finding out more: 01736 710265. 01736 710507 (Estate Office) or stmichaelsmount@nationaltrust.org.uk stmichaelsmount.co.uk. Estate Office, King's Road, Marazion, Cornwall TR17 0EL

St Michael's Mount		M	T	W	T	F	S	S
Castle								
15 Mar–28 Jun	10:30–5	M	T	W	T	F	·	S
29 Jun–31 Aug	10:30–5:30	M	T	W	T	F	·	S
1 Sep–1 Nov	10:30–5	M	T	W	T	F	·	S
Garden								
20 Apr–1 Jul	10:30–5	M	T	W	T	F	·	·
2 Jul–28 Aug	10:30–5:30	·	·	·	T	F	·	·
3 Sep–25 Sep	10:30–5	·	·	·	T	F	·	·

Last admission 45 minutes before castle closes (enough time should be allowed for travel from the mainland). Castle winter opening, call Estate Office for details.

Magical St Michael's Mount, Cornwall, is crowned by a medieval church and castle

The Staircase Hall at Saltram, Devon, gives a taste of the magnificent decoration throughout this elegant Georgian house

Saltram

Plympton, Plymouth, Devon PL7 1UH

Map (1) F8 1957

Standing high above the River Plym with magnificent views across the estuary, Saltram's 202 hectares (500 acres) of rolling landscape parkland now provide wooded walks and open space for rest and play on Plymouth's outskirts. Saltram House was home to the Parker family from 1743 and reflects the family's increasingly prominent lifestyle during the Georgian period. Its magnificent decoration and original contents include Robert Adam's Neo-classical Saloon, original Chinese wallpapers, 18th-century Oriental, European and English ceramics and a superb country-house library. Outside, there's a tranquil garden, with 18th-century orangery and follies, to explore. After wandering along scented pathways and the magnificent lime avenue, why not treat yourself to afternoon tea in the new Chapel Gallery and tea-room?

Eating and shopping: Park Café serving meals, drinks, snacks and ice-cream. The Chapel tea-room offering light lunches and afternoon tea with waitress service. Shop selling seasonal gifts, local food, books and plants. The Chapel Gallery sells locally made arts and crafts.

Making the most of your day: **Indoors** Dressing up, guided tours, themed trails, conservation in action and the 2015 curatorial exhibition highlights our impressive collection of ceramics. **Outdoors** The park (open all year) is ideal for anyone wanting a stroll with the dog, a run, cycle or simply to feed the ducks. Activities and events, including open-air theatre, family activities, guided walks and tours throughout the year. Why not book our outdoor classroom for a Forest School session or a child's birthday? Seasonal trails can be found in the garden leading along myriad pathways. **Dogs**: welcome in the park (identified on- and off-lead areas).

Access: **House** **Grounds**
Sat Nav: enter Merafield Road not postcode.
Parking: 50 yards.

Saltram: the Garden Room (above) and grounds (below)

Finding out more: 01752 333500 or saltram@nationaltrust.org.uk

Saltram		M	T	W	T	F	S	S
House								
28 Feb–1 Nov	11–4:30*	M	T	W	T	F	S	S
House: West Wing								
14 Feb–22 Feb	11–3:30	·	·	·	·	·	S	S
2 Nov–31 Dec	11–3:30	M	T	W	T	F	S	S
Garden, Park Café and shop								
1 Jan–27 Feb	10–4	M	T	W	T	F	S	S
28 Feb–1 Nov	10–5	M	T	W	T	F	S	S
2 Nov–31 Dec	10–4	M	T	W	T	F	S	S
Chapel Gallery and Tea-room								
28 Feb–1 Nov	1–5	M	T	W	T	F	S	S
7 Nov–20 Dec	1–4**	·	·	·	·	·	S	S
Park								
Open all year	Dawn–dusk	M	T	W	T	F	S	S

*West Wing family and domestic rooms only 11 to 12; whole house from 12 (timed tickets). Last admission to house 45 minutes before closing. West Wing rooms decorated for Christmas 21 November to 31 December. Everything except park closed 25 and 26 December. **Gallery open daily.

Shute Barton

Shute, near Axminster, Devon EX13 7PT

Map (1) H7 1959

Medieval manor house, with later Tudor gatehouse and battlemented turrets – now a holiday cottage. **Note**: only open the third weekend in May, June, September and October.

Finding out more: 01752 346585 or shute@nationaltrust.org.uk

Snowshill Manor and Garden

Snowshill, near Broadway, Gloucestershire WR12 7JU

Map (1) K1 1951

Charles Wade had a passion. From the age of seven, he collected and restored beautiful and interesting objects, living his whole life according to his motto 'Let nothing perish'. Seeing the true value of craftsmanship, colour and design, he housed his curious and unlikely finds in the Manor, and laid them out pictorially 'to inspire a thousand fancies'. Next to the manor house is the Priest's House, Charles Wade's humble home, set in a beautiful terraced garden with lovely views of the Cotswolds. Snowshill Manor and Garden is a quirky place, a world away from ordinary. **Note**: entry by timed ticket (including members), places limited. Opening hours may be extended.

Eating and shopping: restaurant serving cream teas, homemade cakes and lunches using homegrown produce where possible. Shop selling gifts, plants and local produce. Second-hand bookshop. Picnic tables.

Making the most of your day: **Indoors** Special tours and family trails. Handling collection. **Outdoors** Free children's trails. Introductory and garden talks. Special events, including Apple Festival. Downloadable circular walk.

Dogs: assistance dogs only.

Access:
Manor **Garden**
Sat Nav: follow signs from centre of village.
Parking: 500 yards.

Finding out more: 01386 852410 or
snowshillmanor@nationaltrust.org.uk

Snowshill Manor and Garden		M	T	W	T	F	S	S
Manor and Priest's House								
28 Mar–5 Jul	12–5*	·	·	**W**	**T**	**F**	**S**	**S**
6 Jul–31 Aug	11:30–4:30*	**M**	·	**W**	**T**	**F**	**S**	**S**
2 Sep–1 Nov	12–5*	·	·	**W**	**T**	**F**	**S**	**S**
Garden, shop and restaurant								
28 Mar–5 Jul	11–5:30	·	·	**W**	**T**	**F**	**S**	**S**
6 Jul–31 Aug	11–5	**M**	·	**W**	**T**	**F**	**S**	**S**
2 Sep–1 Nov	11–5:30	·	·	**W**	**T**	**F**	**S**	**S**
7 Nov–29 Nov	10:30–3:30	·	·	·	·	·	**S**	**S**
Manor by guided tour only (additional charge)								
7 Nov–29 Nov	11–3	·	·	·	·	·	**S**	**S**

Manor admission by limited timed tickets, places limited: tickets run out on peak days. Last admission to Manor one hour before closing. Open all Bank Holidays between April and October. *Priest's House opens at 11.

Snowshill Manor (below) and Garden (opposite) in Gloucestershire, with a detail of the Sancta Maria Byre (top right)

Stembridge Tower Mill

High Ham, Somerset TA10 9DJ

Map (1) 15 1969

Built in 1822, this is the last remaining thatched windmill in England – the only survivor of five in the area. **Note**: please respect the tenants' privacy in adjoining cottage. Sorry no toilet, limited parking.

Finding out more: 01935 823289 or
stembridgemill@nationaltrust.org.uk

Stoke-sub-Hamdon Priory

North Street, Stoke-sub-Hamdon, Somerset TA14 6QP

Map (1) 16 1946

Fascinating small complex of buildings, formerly the home of priests serving the Chapel of St Nicholas (now destroyed). **Note**: sorry no toilet or parking. Please respect the privacy of tenants in the main house.

Finding out more: 01935 823289 or
stokehamdonpriory@nationaltrust.org.uk

Why not share your pictures with us? #nationaltrust

Stourhead

near Mere, Wiltshire BA12 6QF

Map (1) J5 1946

'A living work of art' is how a magazine described Stourhead when it first opened over 250 years ago. The world-famous landscape garden surrounds a glistening lake. There are towering trees, exotic rhododendrons, classical temples and mystical grottoes to explore. Stourhead House was one of the first in the country to showcase Palladian architecture. With a unique Regency library, rare Chippendale furniture and inspirational paintings, this was a grand family home, shaped by generations of the Hoare family. Outside, views stretch across the Wiltshire countryside, and the lawns are perfect for picnics. Great for walking and wildlife spotting, with 1,072 hectares (2,650 acres) of chalk downs, ancient woods, Iron Age hill forts and farmland to explore.

Eating and shopping: large shop with local food, crafts, gifts and enticing garden and plant selection. Award-winning restaurant. 18th-century Spread Eagle Inn. Ice-cream parlour serving takeaway snacks and refreshments, Red Lion country pub, farm shop and art gallery (not National Trust). Picnics welcome.

Stourhead, Wiltshire (clockwise from top right): the landscape garden, Library and grand entrance

Making the most of your day: **Inside** The house is a great place to start your 'Harry's Story' journey. You can find out about the tragedies and joys of family life for Henry, Alda and their son Harry, the last owners of Stourhead. Alda wrote her letters in the Gothic Cottage, and you can share your memories there today. **Outside** The landscape garden changes in harmony with the seasons. From spring blooms and fresh greens of summer, to spectacular autumn colours and exposed winter views. There's lots to see in the productive walled garden. 'Harry's Story' trail reveals his family's garden paradise. **Dogs**: in garden on leads after 4 (March to October) and 3 (November), all day (December to February).

Access: **House** **Landscape Garden**
Parking: 400 yards. King Alfred's Tower 100 yards.

Finding out more: 01747 841152 or stourhead@nationaltrust.org.uk
Stourhead Estate Office, Stourton, Wiltshire BA12 6QD

Stourhead		M	T	W	T	F	S	S
Garden, shop and restaurant								
1 Jan–31 Mar	9–5*	M	T	W	T	F	S	S
1 Apr–30 Sep	9–6*	M	T	W	T	F	S	S
1 Oct–31 Dec	9–5*	M	T	W	T	F	S	S
House								
28 Feb–24 Oct	11–4:30	M	T	W	T	F	S	S
25 Oct–15 Nov	11–3:30	M	T	W	T	F	S	S
28 Nov–23 Dec**	11–3:30	M	T	W	T	F	S	S
Entrance Hall								
3 Jan–22 Feb	11–3	·	·	·	·	·	S	S
King Alfred's Tower								
1 Mar–31 Oct	12–4	·	·	·	·	·	S	S

*Shop opens at 10. **'The Christmas House' – selected rooms open and decorated. Everything closed 25 December. King Alfred's Tower also open on Bank Holidays.

Tintagel Old Post Office

Fore Street, Tintagel, Cornwall PL34 0DB

Map (1) D7 1903

One of the Trust's earliest acquisitions, this quaint house and garden was once in danger of being demolished. Dated *circa* 1380, it is a rare example of a medieval 'longhouse', modified over 600 years, yet retaining its charm. It has had many uses, most notably as a Victorian post office. **Note**: nearest toilet 54 yards in Trevena Square (not National Trust).

Eating and shopping: small souvenir shop in the Post Room selling stamps, crafts, gifts and books inspired by the Old Post Office's history. Picnics welcome in the cottage garden.

The Hall at Tintagel Old Post Office in Cornwall

Making the most of your day: **Indoors** Events held over the season, including traditional craft workshops, baking demonstrations and school holiday entertainment. **Outdoors** Family trail, games and dressing-up. **Dogs**: assistance dogs only.

Access: **Building** **Grounds**
Parking: in village car parks, not National Trust (charge including members). Nearest Trust parking at Glebe Cliff in Tintagel, ½ mile.

Finding out more: 01840 770024 or tintageloldpo@nationaltrust.org.uk

Tintagel Old Post Office		M	T	W	T	F	S	S
14 Feb–22 Feb	11–4	**M**	**T**	**W**	**T**	**F**	**S**	**S**
9 Mar–27 Mar	11–4	**M**	**T**	**W**	**T**	**F**	**S**	**S**
28 Mar–27 Sep	10:30–5:30	**M**	**T**	**W**	**T**	**F**	**S**	**S**
28 Sep–1 Nov	11–4	**M**	**T**	**W**	**T**	**F**	**S**	**S**

Tintinhull Garden

Farm Street, Tintinhull, Yeovil, Somerset BA22 8PZ

Map (1) I6 1953

The vision of Phyllis Reiss, amateur gardener, lives on in this small yet perfectly formed garden. You can stroll among clipped lawns, glinting pools and welcome shaded areas that punctuate 'living rooms' of colour and scent. It's just the place to sit, relax and get away from it all.

Eating and shopping: quaint tea-room serving cakes and cream teas. Small shop and plant sales.

Making the most of your day: village history exhibition (Tintinhull Archaeological Society). Why not combine with a visit to Montacute House or Lytes Cary Manor? Manor house available as holiday let. **Dogs**: welcome in courtyard only (reception has details of local walks).

Access: **Building** **Gardens**
Parking: 150 yards.

Entry is still possible at most places up to 30 minutes before closing

A quiet corner of delightful Tintinhull Garden, Somerset

Finding out more: 01935 823289 or tintinhull@nationaltrust.org.uk

Tintinhull Garden		M	T	W	T	F	S	S
15 Mar–31 May	11–5	·	·	W	T	F	S	S
2 Jun–28 Jul	11–5	·	T	W	T	F	S	S
29 Jul–1 Nov	11–5	·	·	W	T	F	S	S

Open Bank Holiday Mondays.

Treasurer's House, Martock

Martock, Somerset TA12 6JL

Map ① I6 1971

Completed in 1293, this medieval house includes a Great Hall, 15th-century kitchen and an unusual wall-painting. **Note**: private home, but open 15 March to 27 September, Sunday, Monday and Tuesday, 2 to 5. Sorry no toilets or parking.

Finding out more: 01935 825015 or treasurersmartock@nationaltrust.org.uk

Trelissick

Feock, near Truro, Cornwall TR3 6QL

Map ① C9 1955

On its own peninsula, commanding magnificent views over the Fal Estuary, Trelissick surely has one of the best natural settings of any estate in the country. There are 12 hectares (30 acres) of garden to explore, with twisting paths leading you through important collections of hydrangeas, rhododendrons and ginger lilies, together with woodland plants and herbaceous borders that provide year-round colour and interest. The wider parkland offers five miles of dog-friendly woodland and waterside walks, plus a beach for paddling and skimming stones. Trelissick House first opened its doors in 2014, and trial opening continues this year.

A magnificent view of the estuary from Trelissick, Cornwall

Eating and shopping: Crofters self-service licensed café open daily. The Barn Restaurant open for Sunday lunch. Gift and plant shop. Second-hand bookshop. Cornish art and craft gallery. Six holiday cottages.

Making the most of your day: **Indoors** Trelissick House offers amazing views. Christmas: house illuminated during evening openings. **Outdoors** Regular woodland activities and other countryside events for families. **Dogs**: welcome on woodland walks. Assistance dogs only in garden.

Access:
Reception **Stables**
Garden
Parking: 30 yards.

Finding out more: 01872 862090 or trelissick@nationaltrust.org.uk

Trelissick		M	T	W	T	F	S	S
Garden, café, shop, gallery and bookshop								
1 Jan–13 Feb	10:30–4:30	M	T	W	T	F	S	S
14 Feb–1 Nov	10:30–5:30	M	T	W	T	F	S	S
2 Nov–31 Dec	10:30–4:30	M	T	W	T	F	S	S
House trial opening								
1 Mar–1 Nov	10:30–5:30	·	·	W	T	F	S	S
Parkland and walks								
Open all year		M	T	W	T	F	S	S

Garden closes dusk if earlier. Closed 25 and 26 December.

The breathtaking setting of Trelissick, Cornwall

Trengwainton Garden

Madron, near Penzance, Cornwall TR20 8RZ

Map (1) B9 1961

When the craze for plant-hunting was at its height in the 1920s, some of those exotic new plants flowered in this country for the first time at Trengwainton. Award-winning magnolias and rhododendrons are still nurtured by those with a passion for plants, and subtropical species from around the world thrive in the shelter of the walled gardens, including a kitchen garden built to the dimensions of Noah's Ark. Winding wooded paths follow a half-mile incline to sea views across Mount's Bay, and the descent via the drive is bordered by a colourful stream garden and open meadows.

Lush and colourful corner of Trengwainton Garden, Cornwall

For other ways to get involved go to nationaltrust.org.uk/get-involved/volunteer

Eating and shopping: award-winning tea-room in its own walled garden (concession) with outdoor eating area. You can warm yourself by the woodburner in the shop, which sells souvenirs, gifts and plants you will find flowering in the garden, plus garden accessories.

Making the most of your day: numerous family fun events throughout the year, as well as a sensory trail. Nearby Godolphin can be visited on the same day. **Dogs**: welcome on leads.

Access: [access symbols] **Reception** [symbol] **Tea-room** [symbol] **Garden** [symbols]
Parking: 150 yards.

Finding out more: 01736 363148 or trengwainton@nationaltrust.org.uk

Trengwainton Garden		M	T	W	T	F	S	S
15 Feb–1 Nov	10:30–5	**M**	**T**	**W**	**T**	·	·	**S**
4 Dec–13 Dec	10:30–4	·	·	·	·	**F**	·	**S**

Open Good Friday. Tea-room opens at 10.

Trerice

Kestle Mill, near Newquay, Cornwall TR8 4PG

Map (1) C8 [symbols] 1953

This romantic Elizabethan manor house lies in a secluded wooded valley, with rare examples of Dutch gables, fine plaster ceilings and a magnificent Great Hall window. There is much to discover about the history of this unusual house and garden, the families who lived here, its architecture and the story of its restoration. The new formal garden is a re-created knot garden, inspired by the Great Chamber ceiling. The Great Chamber itself provides an ideal vantage point to view this garden from above and watch its progress. There is a wide range of events and family activities throughout the year.

Eating and shopping: self-service restaurant offering morning coffee, locally produced lunches, Sunday roasts, cakes and desserts, as well as our famous lemon meringue pie. Shop selling a range of local products, souvenirs and plants.

Romantic Elizabethan Trerice in Cornwall

Tudor-themed fun at Trerice in Cornwall

Making the most of your day: **Indoors** Tudor-themed craft activities, costume days, introductory talks, living history and conservation events. Replica armour to try on. **Outdoors** Family activities and trails, Cornish 'kayles' and other traditional games.
Dogs: welcome in car park only.

Access: **House**
Garden
Parking: 300 yards.

Finding out more: 01637 875404 or trerice@nationaltrust.org.uk

Trerice		M	T	W	T	F	S	S
House, garden, shop and tea-room								
14 Feb–1 Nov	10:30–5*	**M**	**T**	**W**	**T**	**F**	**S**	**S**
Great Hall, garden, shop and tea-room								
7 Nov–20 Dec	11–4	·	·	·	·	·	**S**	**S**

*House opens at 11.

Tyntesfield

Wraxall, Bristol, North Somerset BS48 1NX

Map (1) I4 2002

Just a stone's throw from Bristol, Tyntesfield was not built as a bold and extravagant statement of wealth, power or politics; instead its purpose was simple: to serve as a family home. Once hidden and inaccessible, the ordinary and extraordinary lives and possessions of four generations of the Gibbs family are ready for discovery. The garden and estate balance faded beauty and function with an abundance of nature – celebrated in the ornate Gothic carvings that decorate the house. Flower-filled terraces, an empty lake, woodland, champion trees and productive kitchen garden all give further opportunities for exploration. With each season you will experience a new side to Tyntesfield as we open doors and change perspectives on this much-loved family estate. **Note**: house tickets sell out very quickly during holiday periods. House now open daily.

Extraordinary Tyntesfield, North Somerset, seen from the air

Eating and shopping: converted cow barn serving dishes made from estate-grown ingredients. The Home Farm Visitor Centre offers a large shop with plant sales, local products and a second-hand bookshop. Light bites can be found in the Pavilion Café.

Making the most of your day: **Indoors** The house is now open every day all year, in some way, to showcase the collection and architecture. Activities and events, including behind-the-scenes discovery, workshops and lectures. Christmas at Tyntesfield features concerts, food and shopping, along with traditional festive fun and cheer. **Outdoors** Seasonal activities all year, including free garden tours (check times on arrival), open-air theatre and living history. Food and craft markets on the first Sunday of each month from April to November. Why not join us with your four-legged friend in the formal garden during the winter for Winter Walkies?
Dogs: welcome on two woodland walks (year-round); in formal gardens (November to February). Map available.

Access:
House **Grounds**
Parking: 550 yards from house.

Finding out more: 0344 800 4966 (Infoline). 01275 461900 or tyntesfield@nationaltrust.org.uk

Tyntesfield		M	T	W	T	F	S	S
House								
1 Jan–6 Mar	11–3	**M**	**T**	**W**	**T**	**F**	**S**	**S**
7 Mar–1 Nov	11–5	**M**	**T**	**W**	**T**	**F**	**S**	**S**
2 Nov–31 Dec	11–3	**M**	**T**	**W**	**T**	**F**	**S**	**S**
Garden, estate, restaurant, café and shop*								
1 Jan–6 Mar	10–5	**M**	**T**	**W**	**T**	**F**	**S**	**S**
7 Mar–1 Nov	10–6	**M**	**T**	**W**	**T**	**F**	**S**	**S**
2 Nov–31 Dec	10–5	**M**	**T**	**W**	**T**	**F**	**S**	**S**

Last admission to house 75 minutes before closing. Timed tickets to house (limited numbers): booking advisable. *Restaurant opens at 10:30; garden and estate close as above or dusk if earlier; restaurant, café and shop close 30 minutes before garden and estate. Tyntesfield is closed on 25 December. On 24 and 31 December house closes at 2, garden and estate close at 3.

The annunciator at Tyntesfield, North Somerset

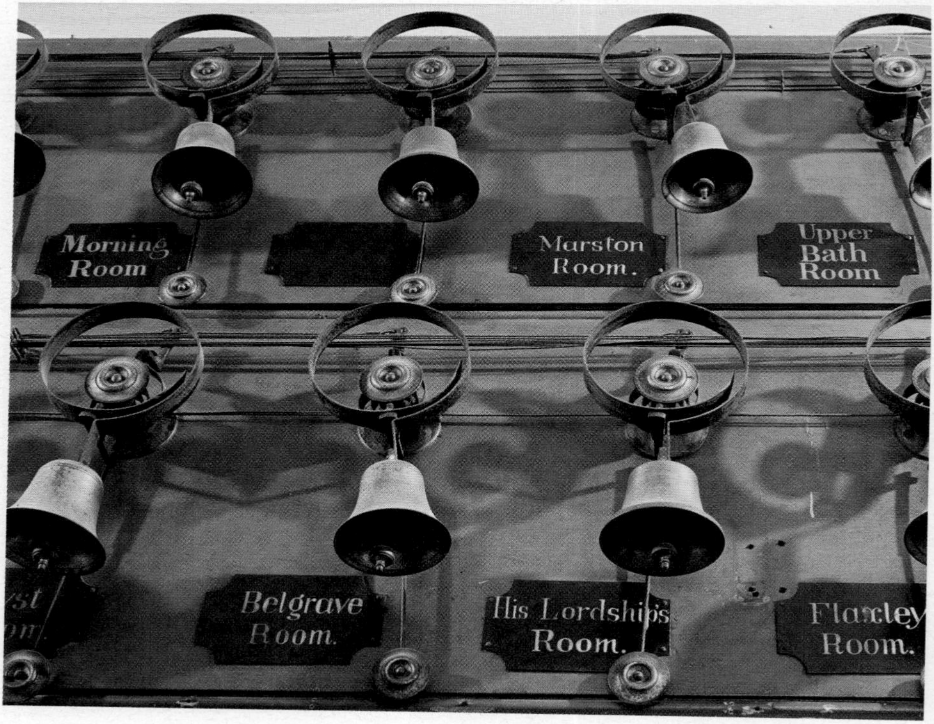

Westbury College Gatehouse

College Road, Westbury-on-Trym,
Bristol BS9 3EH

Map (1) I3 [house icon] 1907

15th-century gatehouse to 13th-century College of Priests – former home of theological reformer John Wyclif. **Note**: access by key, available from Holy Trinity Parish church office. Sorry no toilet.

Finding out more: 01275 461900 or westburycollege@nationaltrust.org.uk

Two views of Westbury Court Garden in Gloucestershire

Westbury Court Garden

Westbury-on-Severn, Gloucestershire GL14 1PD

Map (1) J2 [garden icon] 1967

Originally laid out between 1696 and 1705, this is the only restored Dutch water garden in the country. There are canals, clipped hedges, working 17th-century vegetable plots and many old varieties of fruit trees.

Making the most of your day: evening garden tours, Easter Egg trails, Apple Day.
Dogs: welcome on short leads at all times.

Access: [access icons] **Grounds** [access icons]
Parking: 300 yards.

Finding out more: 01452 760461 or westburycourt@nationaltrust.org.uk

Westbury Court Garden		M	T	W	T	F	S	S
11 Mar–28 Jun	10–5	·	·	W	T	F	S	S
1 Jul–31 Aug	10–5	M	T	W	T	F	S	S
2 Sep–25 Oct	10–5	·	·	W	T	F	S	S

Open Bank Holiday Mondays. Open other times by appointment.

 Please display your current sticker for free parking

Westwood Manor

Westwood, near Bradford-on-Avon, Wiltshire BA15 2AF

Map (1) J4 1960

Are you seeing double? Take a look at the topiary sculpture alongside this small Jacobean manor house, and see what you think. Inside the house, virtually untouched since 1650, there is decorative plasterwork, fine period furniture and tapestries. Particular highlights are two rare keyboard instruments: a spinet and a virginal. **Note**: Westwood Manor is a family home, administered by the tenants. Sorry no toilet.

Eating and shopping: new guidebook telling the fascinating history of Westwood, postcards and CD of Elizabethan music recorded on the virginal and spinet for sale.

Making the most of your day: children's quizzes (house suitable for over fives). Perfect for a short visit (one to two hours), so why not explore other Trust places nearby?

Access: Manor Garden
Parking: 90 yards.

Finding out more: 01225 863374 or westwoodmanor@nationaltrust.org.uk

Westwood Manor		M	T	W	T	F	S	S
1 Apr–30 Sep	2–5	·	**T**	**W**	·	·	·	**S**

Groups at other times by written application with the tenant.

White Mill

Sturminster Marshall, near Wimborne Minster, Dorset BH21 4BX

Map (1) K6 1982

An 18th-century corn mill built on a Domesday Book site with original wooden machinery in a peaceful riverside setting.

Finding out more: 01258 858051 or whitemill@nationaltrust.org.uk

Westwood Manor, Wiltshire: are you seeing double?

Map 2

South East

Runnymede, Surrey

Outdoors in the South East

With leafy woodlands, leisurely waterways, open chalk downland, sweeping coastline and rolling views, the South East region offers an eclectic mix of nature's jewels.

Ashridge Estate

near Berkhamsted, Hertfordshire

Map ② E3 1926

The vast countryside estate of Ashridge is one of the most beautiful parts of the Chilterns, a rich mosaic of woodland, rolling chalk hills and grassy meadows. Full of wildlife and criss-crossed with footpaths, Ashridge gives you the chance to get close to nature all year round, with carpets of bluebells in spring and herds of wild deer in autumn. From the top of the Bridgewater Monument there are panoramic views of the surrounding area, and the Wildwood Den near the visitor centre is the perfect place for children to play in a natural environment. **Note**: toilets only available when café open.

Eating and shopping: shop offers an ever-changing choice of gifts, local produce, books, local maps and self-guided walk leaflets. Al fresco dining at the Brownlow Café (concession).

Making the most of your day: events include guided wildlife walks and talks. Education programme and children's activities. Chilterns Countryside Festival in September. **Dogs**: allowed under close control (deer roam freely).

Access: Visitor centre
Grounds
Sat Nav: use HP4 1LT for visitor centre.
Parking: at visitor centre and Ivinghoe Beacon.

Glorious autumn colours on the Ashridge Estate, Hertfordshire

Finding out more: 01494 755557 (Infoline). 01442 851227 or ashridge@nationaltrust.org.uk

Ashridge Estate		M	T	W	T	F	S	S
Estate								
Open all year	Dawn–dusk	M	T	W	T	F	S	S
Visitor centre and shop*								
Open all year	10–5	M	T	W	T	F	S	S
Bridgewater Monument (weather dependent)								
4 Apr–1 Nov	11–4:30	·	·	·	·	·	S	S
Brownlow Café**								
Open all year	8–4	M	T	W	T	F	S	S

*Visitor centre, shop and café may close at dusk if earlier. Last entry to monument at 4. Monument open Bank Holiday Mondays. Visitor centre and shop closed 24 and 25 December. **Open until 6 from 21 March to 2 November. Café closed 25 December.

Badbury Hill

Coleshill, near Swindon, Wiltshire

Map (2) C4 2011

An Iron Age hill fort giving stunning views over the Upper Thames Valley. Varied circular walks and footpaths to explore. **Note**: for Sat Nav use SN6 7NJ.

Finding out more: 01793 762209 or badburyhill@nationaltrust.org.uk

Black Down

Haslemere, Surrey

Map (2) E7 1944

Highest point on the South Downs with breathtaking views. The heathland and woodland offer a true sense of the wild. **Note**: sorry no toilet. For Sat Nav use GU27 3AF.

Finding out more: 01428 652359 or blackdown@nationaltrust.org.uk

Panoramic view looking north-west from Coleshill, where Wiltshire meets Oxfordshire

The Buscot and Coleshill Estates

Coleshill, near Swindon, Wiltshire

Map (2) C4 1956

These countryside estates on the western border of Oxfordshire include the attractive, unspoilt villages of Buscot and Coleshill, each with a thriving tea-room. There are circular walks of differing lengths and a series of footpaths criss-crossing the estates, with breathtaking countryside and wildlife at Buscot Lock and Badbury Hill. **Note**: toilets in Coleshill Estate office yard and next to village shop and tea-room in Buscot.

Eating and shopping: Buscot tea-room offering lunches and afternoon tea. Locally sourced produce served at Coleshill shop and tea-room and The Radnor Arms (award-winning ales and microbrewery).

Making the most of your day: guided walks throughout the year, including tours of the Second World War bunker. **Dogs**: on leads only.

Access:
Sat Nav: use SN6 7PT. **Parking**: at Buscot village and Coleshill Estate office.

Finding out more: 01793 762209 or buscotandcoleshill@nationaltrust.org.uk

The Buscot and Coleshill Estates
Coleshill Watermill open second Sunday of the month: April to October, 2 to 5.

Cobham Wood and Mausoleum

near Cobham, Kent

Map (2) H5 2014

Once part of the Darnley family's estate, the woodland opens up to views of the mausoleum, designed by James Wyatt. **Note**: for Sat Nav use DA12 3BS.

Finding out more: 01732 810378 or cobham@nationaltrust.org.uk

Compton Bay and Downs

Compton, Isle of Wight

Map (2) C9 1961

Compton Bay has all the elements of a great day out, a sandy beach with plenty of space for families, as well as surfing and other non-motorised water sports. There is even a section of beach for dog walkers. The bay is also a prime site for fossil-hunting, and dinosaurs' fossilised foot casts can be seen in the rocks.

The multi-coloured cliffs provide a wonderful backdrop, while on the clifftop itself there are fine views to Tennyson Down and The Needles. A self-guided trail runs along part of this ridge, which is rich in wild flowers and butterflies.

Eating and shopping: licensed van selling hot and cold snacks, drinks and ice-cream.

Making the most of your day: one of the best spots on the Isle of Wight for swimming, surfing, fossil-hunting or just taking time out. **Dogs**: welcome on beach between Hanover Point and Brook Chine all year.

Access:
Sat Nav: use PO30 4HB. **Parking**: on site.

Finding out more: 01983 741020 or comptonbay@nationaltrust.org.uk

East Head

near Chichester, West Sussex

Map (2) E9 1966

One of the last surviving areas of natural coastline in West Sussex, with unspoilt sand dunes and fabulous views. **Note**: for Sat Nav use PO20 8AJ.

Finding out more: 01243 814730 or easthead@nationaltrust.org.uk

The wonderfully sandy beach at Compton Bay on the Isle of Wight, is perfect for a spot of serious digging

Ludshott Commons

near Headley Down, Hampshire

Map (2) E7 1908

One of the largest remaining heaths in Hampshire, dotted with footpaths through ancient heathland, wood-pasture and wetlands brimming with wildlife. **Note**: for Sat Nav GU26 6JE.

Finding out more: 01428 751338 or ludshott@nationaltrust.org.uk

Maidenhead and Cookham Commons

near Maidenhead, Berkshire

Map (2) E5 1934

Dotted around Maidenhead and Cookham, these attractive areas of common land are popular spots for walking, horse riding and picnicking. **Note**: for Sat Nav use SL6 6QD.

Finding out more: 01628 605069 or maidenheadandcookham@nationaltrust.org.uk

Runnymede

Egham, near Old Windsor, Surrey

Map (2) F5 1931

Seen by many as the birthplace of modern democracy, this picturesque open landscape beside the Thames was witness to King John's historic sealing of the Magna Carta 800 years ago. Today Runnymede offers the ideal space to enjoy ancient woodlands, waymarked countryside walks or tranquil picnics by the river, all within easy reach of the M25. Along with Lutyens' impressive Fairhaven Lodges, the peaceful landscape is also home to memorials for the Magna Carta, John F. Kennedy and Commonwealth Air Forces by Jellicoe and Maufe, making it the perfect place to remember and reflect upon important moments in world history. **Note**: toilets available during National Trust tea-room opening hours. Mooring and fishing (during fishing season) available for additional fee (including members).

Eating and shopping: newly opened and refurbished shop and tea-room serving freshly baked homemade produce, morning coffee, light lunches and afternoon teas.

A mown pathway through a meadow at Runnymede, Surrey (top), proves irresistible to young explorers

Making the most of your day: events throughout the year celebrating the 800th anniversary of the sealing of the Magna Carta. River boat trips available with French Brothers Boat Hire (01784 439626). **Dogs**: welcome on leads near livestock.

Access: Tea-room Grounds
Sat Nav: use TW20 0AE. **Parking**: either side of A308. Seasonal opening, check website for closing times.

Finding out more: 01784 432891 or runnymede@nationaltrust.org.uk

Runnymede		M	T	W	T	F	S	S
Tea-room								
Open all year	9–5*	M	T	W	T	F	S	S

*Closes dusk if earlier. Car parks are locked at 7, April to October and at dusk in the winter. Closed 25 December.

Selborne

near Alton, Hampshire

Map (2) E7 1933

These beech-wood hangers and flower-filled meadows inspired the pioneering naturalist Gilbert White, and are havens for wildlife and walkers alike. **Note**: traditional management with grazing animals in operation. For Sat Nav use GU34 3JR.

Finding out more: 01428 751338 or selborne@nationaltrust.org.uk

Toys Hill

near Brasted Chart, Kent

Map (2) G6 1898

Acres of mixed ancient woodland overlooking the Weald of Kent, with abundant wildlife and idyllic for peaceful walks. **Note**: for Sat Nav use TN16 1QG.

Finding out more: 01732 868381 or toyshill@nationaltrust.org.uk

The White Cliffs of Dover

Langdon Cliffs, Dover, Kent

Map (2) K7 1968

There can be no doubt that The White Cliffs of Dover are one of this country's most spectacular natural features. They are an official icon of Britain and have been a symbol of hope for generations. You can appreciate their beauty and enjoy their special appeal through the seasons by taking one of the country's most dramatic clifftop walks, which offers unrivalled views of the busy English Channel and the French coast.

While here, learn more about the fascinating military and penal history of The White Cliffs and savour the rare flora and fauna found only on this chalk grassland. **Note**: toilets available only when visitor centre is open.

Eating and shopping: shop selling gifts and outdoor goods. Coffee shop serving lunches and afternoon tea. Both with unrivalled views of the Port of Dover.

Making the most of your day: waymarked trail to the lighthouse. Spectacular viewpoints. Events and guided walks throughout the year. **Dogs**: under close control at all times (stock grazing).

Access: **Visitor centre**
Countryside
Sat Nav: use CT15 5NA. **Parking**: on site.

Finding out more: 01304 202756 or whitecliffs@nationaltrust.org.uk

The White Cliffs of Dover		M	T	W	T	F	S	S
Visitor centre								
1 Jan–1 Mar	11–4	**M**	**T**	**W**	**T**	**F**	**S**	**S**
2 Mar–1 Nov	10–5*	**M**	**T**	**W**	**T**	**F**	**S**	**S**
2 Nov–31 Dec	11–4	**M**	**T**	**W**	**T**	**F**	**S**	**S**

*Open until 5:30 from 13 July to 6 September.
Closed 24 and 25 December.

White Horse Hill

Uffington, Oxfordshire

Map (2) C4 1979

The oldest dated chalk figure in the country and an Iron Age hill fort. **Note**: archaeological monuments under English Heritage guardianship. Sorry no toilet.
Sat Nav: use SN7 7UK.

Finding out more: 01793 762209 or whitehorsehill@nationaltrust.org.uk

Woolbeding Countryside

Harting Down, near Midhurst, West Sussex

Map (2) E7/8 1958

With wide horizons and secluded places, you can wander and lose yourself among this rich blend of habitats and topography.
Note: sorry no toilet. For Woolbeding Parkland use GU29 9RR.

Finding out more: 01730 816638 or woolbedingcountryside@nationaltrust.org.uk

The vertiginous White Cliffs of Dover in Kent offer a thrilling experience to any walker with a head for heights and sense of adventure

New Forest

Mires, bogs, grassland, heathland and woodland, the New Forest contains an exciting mix of wild and beautiful terrains, perfect for both retreat and adventure.

A balancing act at Hale Purlieu in Hampshire

Hale Purlieu

Hale, near Fordingbridge, Hampshire

Map (2) B8 1947

This wild heathland is especially atmospheric on a misty morning, when the glorious bird song will send your spirits soaring.
Note: please stick to well-worn tracks, as some areas can be very boggy.

Finding out more: 01425 650035 or halepurlieu@nationaltrust.org.uk

Hightown Common

Ringwood, Hampshire

Map (2) B8 1929

Small but perfectly formed, this is the New Forest in miniature – a great place to explore with four-legged friends.

Finding out more: 01425 650035 or hightowncommon@nationaltrust.org.uk

Bramshaw Commons and Foxbury

near East Wellow, Hampshire

Map (2) C7 1928

Wide open spaces, gentle hillsides and hidden ponds can be discovered while exploring these recovering landscapes and their wildlife.
Note: we protect wildlife on this fragile conservation site by only opening for seasonal events. For Sat Nav use SO51 6AQ.

Finding out more: 01425 650035 or bramshaw@nationaltrust.org.uk

Ibsley and Rockford Commons

near Ringwood, Hampshire

Map (2) B8 1999

Wild expanses of purple heather and scented yellow gorse, littered with rambling paths in a centuries-old landscape shaped by man.
Note: steep hills and hidden tracks.

Finding out more: 01425 650035 or ibsleyandrockford@nationaltrust.org.uk

South Downs

Wild coast, varied wildlife, remarkable history – enjoy our top spots in Britain's newest National Park.

Birling Gap and the Seven Sisters

near Eastbourne, East Sussex

Map (2) H9 1931

Stretching between Birling Gap and Cuckmere Haven are the world-famous Seven Sisters chalk cliffs, one of the longest stretches of unspoilt coastline on the south coast. Here you can enjoy spectacular views along the coast, intricate wave-cut platforms, a stunning beach ideal for seaside picnics and networks of rock pools. Inland, there are lovely quiet walks across ancient chalk downland, rich in butterflies and flowers. Birling Gap is a delightful place to start your walk, with a National Trust café, shop and new visitor centre perched on the edge of the cliffs.

Eating and shopping: clifftop café serving breakfast, lunch, teas, snacks, homemade cakes and soups. Seaside shop selling local and seasonal items. Picnics welcome.

Making the most of your day: events and activities for all ages, information point at peak times. Chyngton Farm, Frog Firle Farm, Alfriston Clergy House and Monk's House nearby. **Dogs**: welcome, on leads in café, shop and visitor centre or near livestock.

Access: **Café** **Shop**
Sat Nav: use BN20 0AB. **Parking**: at Birling Gap.

Finding out more: 01323 423197 or birlinggap@nationaltrust.org.uk

Birling Gap and the Seven Sisters
Café, shop and visitor centre open 10 to 4 with extended hours in summer. Closed 24 and 25 December.

The world-famous Seven Sisters chalk cliffs in East Sussex provide a crisp white backdrop to seaside fun

Devil's Dyke

near Brighton, West Sussex

Map (2) G8 1995

At nearly a mile long, the Dyke Valley is the longest, deepest and widest 'dry valley' in the UK. Legend has it that the Devil dug this chasm to drown the parishioners of the Weald. On the other hand, scientists believe it was formed naturally just over 10,000 years ago in the last ice age. The walls of the Iron Age hill fort can be seen when you walk around the hill, and there is a carpet of flowers and a myriad of colourful insects to discover in the valley.

Eating and shopping: Devil's Dyke pub (not National Trust) beside car park.

Making the most of your day: self-guided walks leaflet, orienteering course map and family Discovery Packs available from information trailer (open April to September, weekends and some weekdays). Numerous bridleways offer great cycling.

Access:
Sat Nav: use BN1 8YJ. **Parking**: on site.

Finding out more: 01273 857712 or devilsdyke@nationaltrust.org.uk

Looking north from Devil's Dyke in West Sussex

Ditchling Beacon

near Ditchling, Westmeston, East Sussex

Map (2) G8 1953

Just 7 miles north of Brighton, at 248 metres above sea level, Ditchling Beacon is the highest point in East Sussex and offers panoramic views all around the summit. To the south visitors can see the sea, while to the north you look across the Weald or east–west across the Downs. The site also has the remains of an Iron Age hill fort. Situated on the South Downs Way, it makes an excellent place to start a walk heading west towards Devil's Dyke or east towards Black Cap and Lewes.

Dawn at Ditchling Beacon in East Sussex

Eating and shopping: refreshments available from ice-cream van. Picnics welcome.

Making the most of your day: great for bracing walks with amazing views on the South Downs. Traces of the rampart and ditch of the hill fort to discover. Why not visit nearby Ditchling Down? **Dogs**: welcome but must be kept on leads at all times.

Access: [P] [access]
Sat Nav: use BN6 8XG.
Parking: off Ditchling Road.

Finding out more: 01323 423197 or ditchlingbeacon@nationaltrust.org.uk

Saddlescombe Farm

near Brighton, West Sussex

Map (2) G8 1995

Saddlescombe Farm is a hidden gem on the South Downs Way, only 5 miles from Brighton. Documented in the Domesday Book, this unique example of a downland farm shows what life was really like throughout the past 1,000 years. Newtimber Hill is one of the finest examples of chalk grassland in the country and is home to many varieties of downland flowers and much wildlife, as well as ancient lime trees and 19th-century graffitied beech trees in the woodland.

Note: Saddlescombe is a working farm and is fully open only on special open days.

Eating and shopping: Hiker's Rest café (not National Trust) serving teas, cakes and light lunches (closed Wednesdays, and throughout January and February).

Making the most of your day: circular route to Devil's Dyke and walks up Newtimber Hill through ancient woodland. Cycling along the South Downs Way. Open days and events throughout the year. **Dogs**: welcome, on leads where livestock grazing.

Access: **Buildings**
Sat Nav: use BN45 7DE. **Parking**: very limited parking in lay-by opposite farm entrance (no parking in farm) or at Devil's Dyke.

Finding out more: 01273 857712 or saddlescombe@nationaltrust.org.uk

Saddlescombe Farm, West Sussex: a hidden gem on the South Downs Way

The folly on the ancient Slindon Estate in West Sussex

Slindon Estate

near Arundel, West Sussex

Map (2) E8 1950

The ancient Slindon Estate is an expansive patchwork of woodland, downland, farmland and parkland, with an unspoilt Sussex village at its centre. Countless historic features cover the landscape, such as Stane Street, the Roman road from Chichester to London soldiers once marched along. Slindon has a rich and wonderfully varied wildlife, and its sun-dappled woods are filled with wild flowers, with badgers and bats hunting there at dusk. The meadows are great places to spot butterflies and downland flowers, while expansive views take in the Weald and South Downs, continuing across the coastal plain to the sea.

Eating and shopping: The Forge in Slindon village (tenant-run) stocks everything from locally baked bread, deli items, fruit and vegetables, to sandwiches, biscuits and cakes. Fresh coffee and tea, beer, light breakfasts, lunches and afternoon tea are also available.

Making the most of your day: there are more than 25 miles of rights of way to explore on the estate, as well as the village to discover. **Dogs**: welcome under close control.

Access:
Sat Nav: use BN18 0QY for Park Lane; BN18 0SP Duke's Road; BN18 1PH Bignor Hill.
Parking: at Park Lane, Duke's Road and Bignor Hill.

Finding out more: 01243 814730 or slindonestate@nationaltrust.org.uk

Surrey Hills

This Area of Outstanding Natural Beauty offers some of South East England's most beautiful and accessible countryside, from rolling chalk downs and flower-rich grasslands, to heaths and woodlands.

Box Hill

Tadworth, Surrey

Map (2) F6 1914

A great place for family adventures: exploring the woods, braving the natural play trail, finding the tower or paddling in the River Mole at the stepping stones. On a clear day you can see for miles from the top of Box Hill, so if you're hiking up, the view is well worth it. You can pick up free walks guides from the shepherd's hut and café or find your own way along our many footpaths. Borrow a children's Tracker Pack or kite to explore the wild and make the most of the weather.

Eating and shopping: the Box Hill café, with its vintage crockery, has indoor and outdoor seating and serves light lunches, snacks and afternoon teas. Servery offers takeaway hot drinks, cakes, sandwiches and the famous revival flapjack!

Making the most of your day: school holiday activities and walks guides available; you are welcome to borrow a kite or Tracker Pack from the shepherd's hut. **Dogs**: under close control where livestock is grazing.

Access: Building Grounds
Sat Nav: use KT20 7LB. **Parking**: off the Box Hill Zig Zag road. Short walk to café and viewpoint.

Finding out more: 01306 888793 or boxhill@nationaltrust.org.uk

Box Hill		M	T	W	T	F	S	S
Shop, café, discovery zone and servery								
1 Jan–29 Mar	11–4	M	T	W	T	F	S	S
30 Mar–25 Oct	9–5	M	T	W	T	F	S	S
26 Oct–31 Dec	11–4	M	T	W	T	F	S	S

During bad weather the servery, shop, café and discovery zone may close early. Closed 25 December.

Denbies Hillside

near Dorking, Surrey

Map 2 F6 1963

Denbies Hillside is a dramatic chalk escarpment with panoramic views of the Surrey countryside. It's a great place for walking, picnics and wildlife-watching – you may even spot chalk downland species such as the Adonis blue and chalkhill blue butterflies.

Eating and shopping: picnic area with benches in Steers Field.

Making the most of your day: self-guided trail, spectacular views and several Second World War pillboxes to discover. Why not visit nearby Hackhurst Downs? **Dogs**: welcome on leads when livestock are grazing.

Access:
Sat Nav: use RH5 6SR. **Parking**: at Ranmore West car park and Denbies Hillside.

Finding out more: 01306 887485 or denbieshillside@nationaltrust.org.uk

The view from Box Hill (top) and Denbies Hillside (above) are two good reasons for visiting Surrey

Savouring the view at the Devil's Punch Bowl on Hindhead Commons, Surrey

Hindhead Commons and the Devil's Punch Bowl

near Hindhead, Surrey

Map (2) E7 1906

Spectacular views from Hindhead Commons and uninterrupted walks to the Devil's Punch Bowl make this an unforgettable place to relax and take in some of the best countryside in the South East. Since the opening of the A3 tunnel, paths, cycle routes and bridleways have been reconnected and natural contours restored. Peace and calm now reign and the glorious landscape, with its carpets of purple heather in the summer and grazing Highland cattle, is there to enjoy. There's plenty of space for family adventures and lovely spots for picnics.

Eating and shopping: café with indoor and outdoor seating, serving hot food, sandwiches and cakes.

Making the most of your day: walks leaflets available from the café and shepherd's hut. Children's Tracker Packs available to hire from the shepherd's hut at weekends. **Dogs**: under very close control during bird-nesting season (March to October).

Access: Café and shop **Grounds**
Sat Nav: use GU26 6AB.
Parking: off the London Road.

Finding out more: 01428 681050 (Rangers). 01428 608771 (café) or hindhead@nationaltrust.org.uk

Hindhead Commons		M	T	W	T	F	S	S
Café								
1 Jan–29 Mar	9-4*	M	T	W	T	F	S	S
30 Mar–25 Oct	9-5*	M	T	W	T	F	S	S
26 Oct–31 Dec	9-4*	M	T	W	T	F	S	S

*Open an hour later at weekends. Café closed on 25 December.

Leith Hill

near Coldharbour village, Dorking, Surrey

Map (2) F7 1923

There are unbeatable views from the top of the tower; at 1,000 feet above sea level, you can see all the way from London to the seaside. Every season is a riot of colour – don't miss spring at the Rhododendron Wood or autumn colour in the woodland. **Note**: sorry no toilet at tower.

Eating and shopping: tea, coffee, hot and cold snacks available at tower (not National Trust). Picnics welcome, but no barbecues please.

The Millennium Stones at Gatton Park in Surrey

Making the most of your day: **Indoors** Information room containing history of the tower. **Outdoors** Walks leaflets covering the whole estate. **Dogs**: on leads on heathland (April to July).

Access: **Tower** [access symbol]
Sat Nav: for Rhododendron Wood use RH5 6LU. For Leith Hill Lane use RH5 6LY.
Parking: for Starveall Corner use RH5 6LU, for Windy Gap RH5 6LX, for Landslip (Mosses Wood) RH5 6HG.

Finding out more: 01306 712711 or leithhill@nationaltrust.org.uk

Leith Hill		M	T	W	T	F	S	S
Tower and servery								
Open all year	10–3*	**M**	**T**	**W**	**T**	**F**	**S**	**S**

*Tower and servery open 9 to 5 on weekends and Bank Holidays. Closed on 25 December.

A frosty morning at Leith Hill Tower, Surrey

Reigate Hill and Gatton Park

near Reigate, Surrey

Map (2) G6 [symbol] 1912

Reigate Hill commands sweeping views across the Weald to the Sussex Downs. It's a great spot for walking, family picnics and wildlife-watching. A short walk away is Reigate Fort – a 19th-century defensive fort. The complex is open every day and the fort buildings open for special events. To the east of Reigate Hill is Gatton Park, designed by Lancelot 'Capability' Brown. **Note**: areas of Gatton Park open once a month by the Gatton Trust.

Eating and shopping: picnics welcome. Tea kiosk (not National Trust).

Making the most of your day: free walks leaflets (available from the noticeboards). Chalk downland species, such as the Adonis blue butterfly, to spot, as well as mysterious military structures on Reigate Hill.
Dogs: welcome, on leads when livestock grazing.

Access: [access symbols]
Sat Nav: use RH2 OHX. **Parking**: at Wray Lane car park.

Finding out more: 01342 843036 or reigate@nationaltrust.org.uk

Alfriston Clergy House

The Tye, Alfriston, Polegate,
East Sussex BN26 5TL

Map (2) H8 1896

This rare 14th-century Wealden 'hall-house' was the first building to be acquired by the National Trust, in 1896. The thatched, timber-framed house is in an idyllic setting, with views across the River Cuckmere, and is surrounded by a tranquil cottage garden full of wildlife. **Note**: nearest toilet in village car park.

Eating and shopping: shop selling souvenirs.

Making the most of your day: **Indoors** Children's quizzes and trails. Varied events all year. **Outdoors** Short circular walks and longer hikes over the South Downs.

Access: **Building** **Grounds**
Parking: in village car parks (not National Trust), 500 yards.

Finding out more: 01323 871961 or alfriston@nationaltrust.org.uk

Alfriston Clergy House		M	T	W	T	F	S	S
28 Feb–15 Mar	10:30–5	·	·	·	·	·	**S**	**S**
16 Mar–1 Nov	10:30–5	**M**	**T**	**W**	·	·	**S**	**S**
2 Nov–20 Dec	11–4	**M**	**T**	**W**	·	·	**S**	**S**

Open Good Friday.

Picturesque Alfriston Clergy House, East Sussex

The main avenue at Ascott, Buckinghamshire

Ascott

Wing, near Leighton Buzzard,
Buckinghamshire LU7 0PR

Map (2) E3 1949

This half-timbered Jacobean farmhouse, transformed by the de Rothschilds towards the end of the 19th century, now houses an exceptional collection of paintings, fine furniture and superb oriental porcelain. The extensive gardens are an attractive mix of formal and natural, with specimen trees, shrubs and beautiful herbaceous borders.

Making the most of your day: unusual features to spot in the gardens.
Dogs: assistance dogs only.

Access: **Building** **Grounds**
Parking: 220 yards.

Finding out more: 01296 688242 or ascott@nationaltrust.org.uk

Ascott		M	T	W	T	F	S	S
24 Mar–3 May	2–6	·	**T**	**W**	**T**	**F**	**S**	**S**
5 May–9 Jul	2–6	·	**T**	**W**	**T**	·	·	·
14 Jul–11 Sep	2–6	·	**T**	**W**	**T**	**F**	**S**	**S**

Open Bank Holiday Mondays and Good Friday. Last admission to gardens at 4:45; last admission to house at 5. Gardens open in aid of National Gardens Scheme on 4 May and 31 August (charges including members). Some garden areas may be roped off when ground conditions are bad.

Ashdown House, Berkshire: once a hunting lodge

Ashdown House

Lambourn, Newbury, Berkshire RG17 8RE

Map (2) C5 1956

Unique 17th-century chalk-block hunting lodge, with doll's-house appearance, built for the Queen of Bohemia by the Earl of Craven. The guided tour, which reveals an intriguing family history, leads up the staircase hung with fine 17th-century paintings. Outstanding rooftop views across three counties. **Note**: access to roof via 100-step staircase. Property is tenanted, so check opening times before visiting.

Making the most of your day: guided tour. **Dogs**: on leads in woodland only.

Access: Building Grounds
Sat Nav: follow local brown signs from B4000.
Parking: in main estate car park, 437 yards.

Finding out more: 01494 755569 (Infoline). 01793 762209 or ashdownhouse@nationaltrust.org.uk

Ashdown House		M	T	W	T	F	S	S
House*								
1 Apr–31 Oct	2–5	·	·	**W**	·	·	**S**	·
Woodland								
Open all year		**M**	**T**	**W**	**T**	·	**S**	**S**

*Admission by guided tour only at 2:15, 3:15 and 4:15.

Basildon Park

Lower Basildon, Reading, Berkshire RG8 9NR

Map (2) D5 1978

Lovingly restored and on a grand scale; Lord and Lady Iliffe made it their life's work to bring this fine Georgian mansion back to its full glory, dressing it with carefully chosen antique fine furnishings and important Old Master paintings. By contrast, 'below stairs' the 1950s kitchen and laundry are utterly of their period, and the everyday homeware and equipment provide nostalgic hands-on fun for visitors of all ages. Outside, the informal gardens and extensive parkland, inspired by 'Capability' Brown, offer family activities and seasonal trails that everyone will enjoy. Recently featured in *Downton Abbey*. **Note**: entrance to main show rooms of mansion on first floor – 21 steps from ground level.

The stately portico at Basildon Park in Berkshire

Eating and shopping: mansion tea-room serves light lunches between 12 and 2:30, with homemade cakes and cream teas available all day. The Parlour in the stableyard offers tasty treats and drinks. The shop sells books, plants, local food, ice-cream and much more.

Making the most of your day: **Indoors** Exhibition on Basildon's role as a film location for *Pride and Prejudice* and *Downton Abbey*. Guided house tours. **Outdoors** Woodland Walk and parkland walks. Play areas and family activities. **Dogs**: welcome on leads in grounds. Assistance dogs only in house.

Access:
Mansion **Grounds**
Sat Nav: not reliable, please follow brown tourist signs. **Parking**: 400 yards.

Finding out more: 01491 672382 or basildonpark@nationaltrust.org.uk

Basildon Park		M	T	W	T	F	S	S
House*								
Open all year	11-5**	**M**	**T**	**W**	**T**	**F**	**S**	**S**
Grounds, shop and tea-room								
Open all year	10-5**	**M**	**T**	**W**	**T**	**F**	**S**	**S**

*House tours only from 11 to 12. Access to house may also be by guided tours only at other times. **Closes dusk if earlier. Closed 24 and 25 December.

The Green Drawing Room at Basildon Park in Berkshire offered comfort in luxurious surroundings

Bateman's

Bateman's Lane, Burwash, East Sussex TN19 7DS

Map (2) H7 1940

Rudyard Kipling loved this place; it was his personal paradise, and somewhere he could enjoy family life. Surrounded by the wooded landscape of the Sussex Weald, this 17th-century house, with mullion windows, pretty secluded garden and acres of countryside, provided a tranquil sanctuary. The atmospheric oak-beamed rooms remain much as he left them. Outside, winding paths take in manicured lawns, a wildflower meadow and Kipling's 1928 Rolls-Royce Phantom 1, while beside the river sits a working 17th-century watermill.

Eating and shopping: shop selling Kipling souvenirs and a specialist second-hand Kipling bookstore, flour from our watermill and plants from the garden. Restaurant offering seasonal lunches using fresh produce from the kitchen garden, homemade cakes and light bites.

Making the most of your day: **Indoors** Children's house guide. **Outdoors** Re-enactment weekends, garden and countryside walks. Family fun days. Children's Tracker Packs, quizzes, trails and storytelling. Scotney Castle and Bodiam Castle nearby. **Dogs**: welcome in the gardens on a short lead.

Bateman's, East Sussex: Rudyard Kipling's paradise

Access:
Building **Grounds**
Parking: 30 yards.

Finding out more: 01435 882302 or
batemans@nationaltrust.org.uk

Bateman's		M	T	W	T	F	S	S
House								
Open all year	11–5*	**M**	**T**	**W**	**T**	**F**	**S**	**S**
Garden, shop and restaurant								
Open all year	10–5:30*	**M**	**T**	**W**	**T**	**F**	**S**	**S**

*Closes at dusk if earlier. Closed on 24 and 25 December. The restaurant closes at 5 from March to October.

Bembridge Fort

Bembridge Down, near Bembridge,
Isle of Wight PO36 8QY

Map (2) D9 1967

In a commanding position on top of Bembridge Down, this derelict Victorian fort is open for volunteer-run guided tours. **Note**: sorry no toilets. Access by guided tour, booking essential, £3.50 charge (including members), not suitable for children under ten.

Finding out more: 01983 741020 or
bembridgefort@nationaltrust.org.uk
c/o Longstone Farmhouse, Strawberry Lane,
Mottistone, Isle of Wight PO30 4EA

Bembridge Windmill

High Street, Bembridge,
Isle of Wight PO35 5SQ

Map (2) D9 1961

This little gem, the only surviving windmill on the Isle of Wight, is one of the island's most iconic images. Built *circa* 1700 and last operated in 1913, it still has most of its original machinery intact. Climb to the top and follow the milling process down its four floors.

Eating and shopping: ice-cream kiosk, hot and cold drinks, including tea, hot chocolate and various coffees. Postcards, sweets, gifts and souvenirs. Picnic tables in grounds.

Making the most of your day: walks, including the start of Culver Trail. Nature trails (school holidays). Bembridge Fort (booking essential) nearby. **Dogs**: welcome in grounds on leads. Assistance dogs only in windmill.

Access: **Building**
Sat Nav: do not use postcode, look for brown signs. **Parking**: free (not National Trust), 100 yards in lay-by.

Finding out more: 01983 873945 or
bembridgemill@nationaltrust.org.uk

Bembridge Windmill		M	T	W	T	F	S	S
14 Mar–1 Nov	10:30–5	**M**	**T**	**W**	**T**	**F**	**S**	**S**

Closes dusk if earlier. Conducted school groups and special visits March to end October (call or email to book).

Machinery at Bembridge Windmill on the Isle of Wight

Bodiam Castle in East Sussex looks just like a fairytale castle should – from a moat to high battlements

Boarstall Duck Decoy

Boarstall, near Bicester,
Buckinghamshire HP18 9UX

Map (2) D3 1980

One of the very few remaining decoys in the country, providing fascinating insights into a rare aspect of rural life.

Finding out more: 01280 817156 or boarstalldecoy@nationaltrust.org.uk

Boarstall Tower

Boarstall, near Bicester,
Buckinghamshire HP18 9UX

Map (2) D3 1943

Charming 14th-century moated gatehouse set in beautiful gardens, retaining original fortified appearance. Many rooms remain virtually unchanged. Grade I listed. **Note**: access to upper levels is via a spiral staircase.

Finding out more: 01280 817156 or boarstalltower@nationaltrust.org.uk

Bodiam Castle

Bodiam, near Robertsbridge,
East Sussex TN32 5UA

Map (2) I7 1926

A brooding symbol of power for over 700 years, the strong stone walls of Bodiam Castle rise up proudly from the peaceful river-valley setting. A wide moat encircles the seemingly untouched medieval exterior. Once inside, spiral stairways, tower rooms and battlements with dizzying viewpoints are ripe for exploration. The ruins of the inner rooms are brought to life through stories told by a range of medieval characters and a new audio adventure – 'A Knight's Peril'. **Note**: toilets in car park only. Popular with schools.

Eating and shopping: shop selling gifts, castle-themed products and local produce. Tea-room serving homemade lunches, teas, snacks and ice-cream. Seasonal snack kiosk.

Making the most of your day: medieval character talks, trails and activities. Choose your own interactive adventure, 'A Knight's Peril'. Events, including medieval-themed weekend, and family activities throughout the year. **Dogs**: welcome on leads in grounds only.

Access: [access symbols]
Castle [access symbols] **Grounds** [access symbols]
Parking: 400 yards.

Finding out more: 01580 830196 or bodiamcastle@nationaltrust.org.uk

Bodiam Castle		M	T	W	T	F	S	S
Open all year	10–5*	M	T	W	T	F	S	S

*Closes dusk if earlier. Castle opens at 10:30. Closed 24 and 25 December.

Buckingham Chantry Chapel

Market Hill, Buckingham, Buckinghamshire MK18 1JX

Map (2) D2 1912

Atmospheric 15th-century chapel, restored by Sir Gilbert Scott in 1875. Today it is a thriving coffee shop and second-hand bookshop.

Finding out more: 01280 817156 or buckinghamchantry@nationaltrust.org.uk

Buscot Old Parsonage

Buscot, Faringdon, Oxfordshire SN7 8DQ

Map (2) C4 1949

Beautiful early 18th-century house with small walled garden, on the banks of the Thames. **Note**: administered by a tenant (booking essential). Sorry no toilets.

Finding out more: 01793 762209 or buscot@nationaltrust.org.uk

Buscot Park

Faringdon, Oxfordshire SN7 8BU

Map (2) C4 1949

Lord Faringdon's family live in the house, maintain its interior, curate its contents on behalf of the Trustees of The Faringdon Collection and manage and develop the grounds and gardens. This unusual arrangement for a National Trust property gives it an idiosyncratic air and a different take on taste and presentation. As a result the whole entity becomes more fluid and more surprising. New works of art mingle with the old within the house, and new alleys and vistas stride out within the grounds. Paintings, statuary and objects by contemporary artists reinvigorate the whole – refreshing the spirit.
Note: administered on behalf of the National Trust by Lord Faringdon's family.

The Peto Water Garden at Buscot Park in Oxfordshire

Eating and shopping: tea-room (not National Trust), serving cream teas, sponge cakes, traybakes, ice-creams and selection of hot and cold drinks. Local honey and cider, peppermints, plants and kitchen garden produce (when available). Ice-cream and lollies available in ticket office. Picnic area.

Making the most of your day: occasional events in grounds and theatre (available for hire). **Dogs**: in Paddock (overflow car park) only.

Access: [icons] **House** [icons]
Grounds [icons]
Parking: on site.

Finding out more: 01367 240932 (Infoline). 01367 240786 or buscotpark@nationaltrust.org.uk buscotpark.com

Buscot Park		M	T	W	T	F	S	S
House, grounds and tea-room*								
1 Apr–30 Sep	2–6	·	·	**W**	**T**	**F**	·	·
Grounds only								
6 Apr–29 Sep	2–6	**M**	**T**	·	·	·	·	·

*Weekend opening: 4, 5, 18 and 19 April, 2, 3, 9, 10, 23 and 24 May, 13, 14, 27 and 28 June, 11, 12, 25 and 26 July, 8, 9, 22, 23, 29 and 30 August, 12, 13, 26 and 27 September, 2 to 6 (tea-room 2 to 5:30). Last admission to house one hour before closing. Open Bank Holiday Mondays.

Chartwell

Mapleton Road, Westerham, Kent TN16 1PS

Map (2) G6 [icons] 1946

Chartwell was a home and a place that truly inspired Sir Winston. The house is still much as it was when the family lived here, with pictures, books and personal mementoes. You may come across our resident cat, Jock, making his daily inspection of the grounds. The studio is home to the largest single collection of Churchill's paintings. The gardens reflect Churchill's love of the landscape and nature. They include the lakes he created, the kitchen garden and the Marycot, a playhouse designed for his youngest daughter Mary. The woodland estate offers family walks, trails, den-building, the Canadian camp and opportunities to blow away the cobwebs and stretch your legs. New temporary exhibition open in the winter.

Graceful Chartwell in Kent (above and right), provided refuge and inspiration for Sir Winston Churchill

Note: house entrance by timed ticket only, available from the visitor centre.

Eating and shopping: the Landemare Café serves seasonal dishes. We offer hot food, salads, light bites, cream teas and our usual delicious cakes. The shop stocks Churchill memorabilia, books, plants and much more. Regular tastings of local food are available.

Making the most of your day: **Indoors** Daily talks in the Studio about Sir Winston's painting. **Outdoors** Numerous events run throughout the season. Tours of Churchill's family garden on selected days. Families can get muddy in our woodland play area and make the most of our six tree swings. The woodland trail offers great views of the house and connects with the hilly five-mile circular Weardale Walk to Emmetts Garden. **Dogs**: are welcome on short leads in the gardens and estate.

Access: [icons]
Building [icons] **Grounds** [icons]
Parking: pay and display.

Finding out more: 01732 868381 or chartwell@nationaltrust.org.uk

Chartwell		M	T	W	T	F	S	S
House								
28 Feb–1 Nov	11–5*	**M**	**T**	**W**	**T**	**F**	**S**	**S**
Garden, exhibition, studio, shop and café								
Open all year	10–5*	**M**	**T**	**W**	**T**	**F**	**S**	**S**

The studio opens daily, times vary, closed in January, tours only in February. The exhibition closes for short periods to change the display. Entry to the house by timed ticket (places limited), available from the visitor centre. Last entry 45 minutes before closing. *Closes dusk if earlier. Closed 24 and 25 December.

Two views of the gardens at Chartwell (above and top)

Visitors learn about the garden on a tour at Chastleton House in Oxfordshire

Chastleton House

Chastleton, near Moreton-in-Marsh, Oxfordshire GL56 0SU

Map (2) C3 1991

A rare gem of a Jacobean country house and garden, Chastleton was created between 1607 and 1612 by Walter Jones, son of a prosperous wool merchant, as an impressive statement of wealth and power. Owned by the same, increasingly impoverished, family until 1991, it has remained essentially unchanged for more than 400 years, with the interiors and contents gradually succumbing to the ravages of time. With virtually no intrusion from the 21st century, this fascinating time capsule exudes an atmosphere of 'romantic neglect' in this glorious Cotswold valley. **Note**: entry by timed ticket only. You may have a wait at busy times.

Eating and shopping: plants and garden produce available (in season). Second-hand books, local publications and souvenirs. Refreshments available from local church (not National Trust), Wednesday to Saturday. Sunday teas at Chastleton. Picnics welcome in car park or stableyard.

Making the most of your day: **Indoors** Conservation in action and family explorer packs. **Outdoors** Croquet on the lawn, garden tours and family explorer packs. **Dogs**: welcome on leads in car park and Dovecote Field.

Access: **Building** **Garden**
Sat Nav: follow brown signs. **Parking**: 270-yard walk down steep gravel path.

Finding out more: 01494 755560 (Infoline). 01608 674981 or chastleton@nationaltrust.org.uk

Chastleton House		M	T	W	T	F	S	S
4 Mar–1 Nov	1–4*	·	·	**W**	**T**	**F**	**S**	**S**
28 Nov–13 Dec	11–3	·	·	·	·	·	**S**	**S**

*Open until 5 from 1 April to 30 September. Timed-ticket system on arrival, places limited.

Clandon Park

West Clandon, Guildford, Surrey GU4 7RQ

Map (2) F6 1956

Nearly 300 years ago, Clandon Park was the fashionable place to be seen. The family seat of the politically prominent Onslows, this Palladian mansion, with its glittering Marble Hall, was commissioned by the 2nd Lord Onslow to impress and entertain the names of the day. Today the mansion houses the Gubbay collection of 18th-century porcelain, tapestries and furniture. While the wider estate is owned by the Onslow family, you can enjoy the intimate gardens which are home to Hinemihi, the only Maori meeting house in the UK. Clandon is also home to the Surrey Infantry Museum. **Note**: booking essential for lift.

Eating and shopping: shop in 19th-century kitchen. Undercroft restaurant (concession). Picnic area.

Making the most of your day: Clandon's role as a First World War military hospital remembered. Children's trails, events, attic tours (selected Sundays). Surrey Infantry Museum. Combine with a visit to nearby Hatchlands Park. **Dogs**: assistance dogs only.

Access:
Building **Grounds**
Sat Nav: misleading, ensure you enter from A247 or use grid reference 186:TQ0446751369.
Parking: 250 yards.

Finding out more: 01483 222482 or clandonpark@nationaltrust.org.uk

Clandon Park		M	T	W	T	F	S	S
House, garden, museum, shop and restaurant								
17 Jan–15 Feb[1]	11-3	·	·	·	·	·	**S**	**S**
17 Feb–22 Feb[1]	11-4	·	**T**	**W**	**T**	·	·	**S**
1 Mar–1 Nov[2]	10:30-5*	·	**T**	**W**	**T**	·	·	**S**
Shop and restaurant†								
3 Nov–23 Dec	12-4	·	**T**	**W**	**T**	·	·	**S**
Surrey Infantry Museum††								
3 Nov–17 Dec	12-4	·	**T**	**W**	**T**	·	·	·

[1]Partial opening of house. *House opens at 11. [2]Also open Mondays in July and August. †Also open Mondays from 30 November. December restaurant booking essential. ††Museum open Mondays 7, 14 December and by appointment on Sundays in November and December. Whole property open Bank Holiday Mondays, Good Friday and Easter Saturday.

Clandon Park, Surrey: 'Three Graces' and the south front

Claremont Landscape Garden

Portsmouth Road, Esher, Surrey KT10 9JG

Map (2) F6 1949

Hidden in the heart of Surrey, this green oasis has always been a place to escape everyday life and enjoy simple pleasures with family and friends. For centuries the garden was a sanctuary for some of the wealthiest, most influential people in the country, however today everyone can enjoy it. The impressive turf amphitheatre offers wonderful views over the lake. Walks take in interesting features like the grotto and camellia terrace. As a child Queen Victoria loved relaxing here and the tradition of play continues today, with nine-pin bowling, two play areas and a cottage full of toys and games. **Note**: limited parking during busy times. Please park considerately to maximise spaces available.

Claremont Landscape Garden in Surrey (above and below): a place to go to escape the cares of everyday life

Eating and shopping: café (licensed) serving lunches and homemade cakes, biscuits and scones freshly baked every morning. Outside terraced seating area overlooking lake. Café is outside the pay barrier and situated close to the car park at the main entrance. Shop area within café. Free wi-fi.

Making the most of your day: events throughout the year, including children's trails, crafts and activities during school holidays. Guided walks. Belvedere Tower open on selected dates (May to October).
Dogs: welcome on leads between 1 November and 31 March only.

Access: **Grounds**
Sat Nav: unreliable, instead follow brown signs from Cobham and Esher. **Parking**: main car park at entrance. Space limited at busy times – use car park in West End Lane opposite.

Finding out more: 01372 467806 or claremont@nationaltrust.org.uk

Claremont Landscape Garden		M	T	W	T	F	S	S
1 Jan–31 Jan	10–5*	M	T	W	T	F	S	S
1 Feb–31 Mar	10–5	M	T	W	T	F	S	S
1 Apr–31 Oct	10–6	M	T	W	T	F	S	S
1 Nov–31 Dec	10–5*	M	T	W	T	F	S	S

Café and shop close 30 minutes earlier than garden.
*Closes at dusk if earlier, local closing times posted on website and at the property. Closed 25 December.

Some places are easy to get to on foot or by public transport. See page 3

Claydon

Middle Claydon, near Buckingham,
Buckinghamshire MK18 2EY

Map (2) D3 1956

Nestled in peaceful parkland with tranquil lakeside walks, this Georgian home hides a lavish interior that left the 18th-century Verney family facing financial ruin. Rococo carvings frame portraits of interesting characters, from Civil War heroes to Barbary buccaneers. An inspirational place, where Florence Nightingale, Lady Verney's sister, spent her summers.
Note: gardens (not National Trust) opened by permission of the Verney family. Garden entry charges apply (including members).

Eating and shopping: second-hand bookshop and small gift shop. Courtyard shops, seasonal kitchen garden produce, restaurant and tea-room (not National Trust). Picnics welcome.

Claydon, Buckinghamshire (above and below), sits in peaceful parkland and offers tranquil lakeside walks

Making the most of your day: **Indoors** Talking pictures and 17th-century Verney family costume exhibition. Children's activities, trails and replica costume to try on. **Outdoors** Family school holiday activities. Lakeside walks. Waddesdon Manor and Stowe nearby.
Dogs: welcome in park on leads.

Access:
House **Grounds**
Parking: on site.

Finding out more: 01296 730349 or claydon@nationaltrust.org.uk

Claydon		M	T	W	T	F	S	S
14 Mar–1 Nov	11–5	**M**	**T**	**W**	·	·	**S**	**S**

For garden opening times call 01296 730252. Restaurant open 12 to 3. Open Good Friday.

Cliveden

Cliveden Road, Taplow, Maidenhead, Buckinghamshire SL6 0JA

Map (2) E5 [1942]

Nestled high above the River Thames with panoramic views over the Berkshire countryside, these gardens capture the grandeur of a bygone age. Over the course of 300 years, each family that fell in love with this place added their own extravagant touch, creating a series of distinct gardens. From carpets of spring bulbs and vibrant floral displays on the elaborate Parterre, to the intimate Rose Garden and rich autumn colour in the oriental Water Garden, each area is designed purely for pleasure. Miles of walks meander through majestic beech woodlands and along riverbank paths, while a giant yew-tree maze, storybook-themed play area and acres of space to run around in, help make this a great place to play. **Note**: mooring charge on Cliveden Reach, £9 per 24 hours (including members), does not include entry.

Eating and shopping: Dovecote Coffee Shop serving morning coffee and afternoon tea. Lunch (12 to 2:30) and snacks available at the Orangery Café. Doll's House Café beside play area designed especially with families in mind. Shop, including plant sales. Picnic areas.

Making the most of your day: **Indoors** Short guided tour of part of the house (now a hotel) on certain days. Introductory film. **Outdoors** More than 30,000 plants create striking displays on the Parterre in spring and summer, with thousands more flowers filling the Long Garden each season. The Rose Garden blooms from late June. Walking and fitness trails. Highlights for families include a play area, maze, free seasonal trails, woodland play trail and den-building area. Events include open-air theatre, family fun days, guided garden walks and workshops. Boat trips on the Thames, April to October (additional charge including members). Greys Court and Hughenden nearby. **Dogs**: welcome under close control in woodlands only.

Access:
House (hotel) **Garden**
Sat Nav: for gardens use Cliveden Road and SL1 8NS. For woodlands use SL6 0HJ.
Parking: on site.

Finding out more: 01628 605069 or cliveden@nationaltrust.org.uk

Cliveden		M	T	W	T	F	S	S
Garden, shop, café and woodland*								
14 Feb–31 Dec	10–5:30**	**M**	**T**	**W**	**T**	**F**	**S**	**S**
Woodland only								
1 Jan–13 Feb	10–4	**M**	**T**	**W**	**T**	**F**	**S**	**S**
House (part), chapel								
2 Apr–25 Oct	3–5	·	·	·	**T**	·	·	**S**

*Café last orders 30 minutes before closing. **Closes dusk if earlier. Property closed 24 and 25 December. Admission to house by timed ticket only from Information Centre.

The Fountain of Love (below) and the elaborate Parterre (opposite) at Cliveden in Buckinghamshire

Dorneywood Garden

Dorneywood, Dorney Wood Road, Burnham, Buckinghamshire SL1 8PY

Map (2) E5 1942

Ministerial residence with country garden. Afternoon teas. Open selected afternoons (dates may change at short notice).
Note: no photography. Booking essential. Visitor details recorded for security reasons.

Finding out more: dorneywood@nationaltrust.org.uk

Emmetts Garden

Ide Hill, Sevenoaks, Kent TN14 6BA

Map (2) H6 1965

An Edwardian estate once owned by Frederic Lubbock, Emmetts is now a garden to enjoy with friends and family.

Delve a little deeper and there are exotic plants collected from around the world and a host of stories to be discovered. Best known for amazing spring colour, bluebell displays and vibrant autumn foliage, there is something to see all year round. Views reaching across the Weald of Kent can be enjoyed from our estate walks, or sit back and take it easy in the gardens with a picnic.

Eating and shopping: The Old Stables serving light refreshments. The shop sells a variety of plants and gifts including food and souvenirs.

Making the most of your day: events throughout the season. Garden tours (selected days). Children's activities. Walk guides available for the surrounding countryside.
Dogs: welcome on short leads in gardens and on estate.

Access: **Grounds**
Parking: 100 yards.

Finding out more: 01732 750367 or emmetts@nationaltrust.org.uk

Emmetts Garden		M	T	W	T	F	S	S
28 Feb–31 Dec	10–5*	M	T	W	T	F	S	S

Last entry 45 minutes before closing. *Closes dusk if earlier. All winter opening weather permitting. Closed 24 and 25 December.

A delightful figure adorns the fountain in the rose garden at Emmetts Garden in Kent

Great Coxwell Barn

Great Coxwell, Faringdon, Oxfordshire SN7 7LZ

Map ② C4 1956

Former 13th-century monastic barn, a favourite of William Morris, who would regularly bring his guests to wonder at its structure.
Note: sorry no toilet; narrow access lanes leading to property.

Finding out more: 01793 762209 or greatcoxwellbarn@nationaltrust.org.uk

Greys Court

Rotherfield Greys, Henley-on-Thames, Oxfordshire RG9 4PG

Map ② D5 1969

Greys Court takes modest centre stage at the head of a small Chiltern valley. From across an immaculate front lawn, the mellow Tudor manor house surveys its domain, taking in both the long views down the valley and the random patchwork of medieval buildings and characterful walls opposite the house. Hidden within the enclosed series of intimate spaces is an archetypal English country garden, full of detail to absorb and delight all year round. Equally, the house interior invites exploration and gently unfurls its memories of a comfortable and welcoming home life for the Brunner family throughout the mid-20th century.

Eating and shopping: tea-room serving morning coffee, afternoon tea, lunches and snacks. Family-inspired shop. Seasonal organic produce from gardens (when available).

Making the most of your day: children's explorer packs and open-air play area. Estate walks. Nuffield Place nearby. **Dogs**: welcome in the courtyard outside the tea-room and on the estate walk.

Interior and exterior views of Greys Court, Oxfordshire (above and right)

Access: **House** **Tea-room** **Grounds**
Parking: 220 yards.

Finding out more: 01491 628529 or greyscourt@nationaltrust.org.uk

Greys Court		M	T	W	T	F	S	S
Open all year†	10–5*	M	T	W	T	F	S	S

*House opens at 11. In January, February, November, December, entry to the house is by hourly tour between 11 and 3. For the rest of the year, there are house tours at 11 and 12, then free-flow from 1. On busy days timed tickets for the house may be in operation. All house tickets are available from visitor reception, first-come first-served. Closes at dusk if earlier. †Closed 6 September, 24 and 25 December.

Hartwell House Hotel, Restaurant and Spa

Oxford Road, near Aylesbury, Buckinghamshire HP17 8NR

Map (2) E3 2008

Elegant Grade I listed stately home, having both Jacobean and Georgian façades, contains magnificent main hall with rococo ceiling and elegant drawing-rooms serving morning coffee or afternoon tea. Set in beautifully landscaped grounds, including ruined Gothic church, lake, bridge and 36 hectares (90 acres) of parkland. Only one hour from central London.
Note: access is for paying guests of the hotel, including for luncheon, afternoon tea and dinner. Held on a long lease from the Ernest Cook Trust.

Finding out more: 01296 747444. 01296 747450 (fax) or info@hartwell-house.com hartwell-house.com

Hatchlands Park

East Clandon, Guildford, Surrey GU4 7RT

Map (2) F6 1945

Loved by families throughout the centuries, Hatchlands Park is an intimate Georgian country house and estate. The parkland is a tranquil space, perfect for relaxation or exploration. Waymarked walks lead through ancient woodland, wildflower meadows and open fields, and Little Wix Wood is known for its carpet of bluebells in the spring. The house is a family home, and contains Alec Cobbe's superb collection of paintings. The ground-floor rooms display the Cobbe Collection, Europe's largest array of keyboard instruments, including some which inspired such world-famous composers as J. C. Bach, Elgar and Chopin. **Note**: only six ground-floor rooms are open to the public.

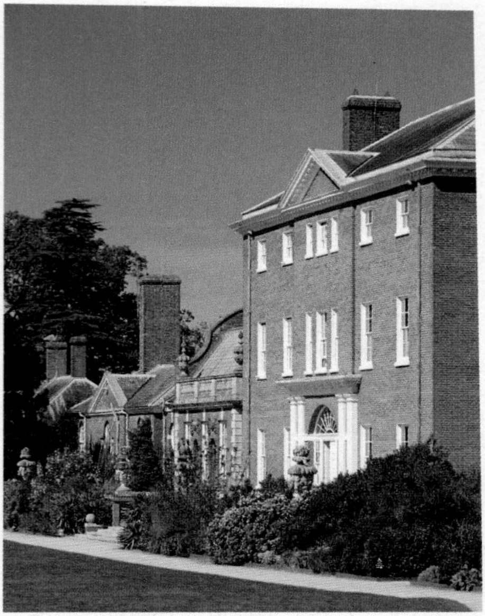

Hatchlands Park in Surrey: Georgian grace

Eating and shopping: tea-room in the original kitchen. Gift shop. Picnic areas.

Making the most of your day: **Indoors** Guided mansion tours most Thursdays. Cellar tours (selected days). Cobbe Collection concerts. **Outdoors** Children's trails, events and adventure area. Open-air theatre. NGS Quiet Garden. Clandon Park only 2 miles away. **Dogs**: welcome under close control in designated parkland areas.

Access:
Building **Grounds**
Sat Nav: misleading, instead follow brown signs to main entrance on A246 (grid reference TQ06349 51580). **Parking**: 300 yards.

Finding out more: 01483 222482 or hatchlands@nationaltrust.org.uk

Hatchlands Park		M	T	W	T	F	S	S
House and garden†								
1 Apr–1 Nov*	2–5:30	·	**T**	**W**	**T**	·	·	**S**
Shop, tea-room, park walks and NGS Quiet Garden††								
1 Apr–1 Nov	10:30–5:30	**M**	**T**	**W**	**T**	**F**	**S**	**S**

***Also open Fridays in August.** †Garden open 10:30 to 6 on house open days. Open Bank Holiday Mondays. Timed tickets may be used at busy periods. ††Park walks and NGS Quiet Garden open until 6.

 Places may occasionally close for events or bad weather

Hinton Ampner

Hinton Ampner, near Alresford,
Hampshire SO24 0LA

Map (2) D7 [icons] 1986

Hinton Ampner is the fulfilment of one man's vision. After a catastrophic fire in 1960, Ralph Dutton rebuilt his home in the light and airy Georgian style he loved. A passionate collector, he filled the sunny rooms with ceramics and art. Outside, Dutton designed a series of tranquil garden rooms, each with their own distinctive planting still apparent today. Geometric topiary, exotic coloured dahlias and borders of repeat-flowering roses lead onto terraces with panoramic views across the South Downs. Extensive lawns, a park with ancient oaks and beech woodland provide plenty of space to stroll, play, relax and picnic.

Eating and shopping: Stables tea-room serving seasonal dishes, homemade cakes and cream teas, made using produce grown in our walled garden. Shop selling many locally sourced products, including estate-grown plants. Picnics welcome.

Making the most of your day: **Indoors** Conservation demonstrations on Wednesday. **Outdoors** Estate walking trails and free seasonal garden walks. Children's trails and events. Uppark House and Garden and Winchester City Mill nearby. **Dogs**: welcome on leads in parkland, estate walks and tea-room courtyard.

Access: [icons] **Building** [icons]
Grounds [icons]
Sat Nav: use SO24 0NH – takes you to Hinton Arms pub, 21 yards west of main entrance.
Parking: on site.

Finding out more: 01962 771305 or
hintonampner@nationaltrust.org.uk

Hinton Ampner		M	T	W	T	F	S	S
Estate, garden, shop and tea-room								
Open all year	10–5*	M	T	W	T	F	S	S
House								
14 Feb–20 Dec**	11–4	M	T	W	T	F	S	S
Exhibition in main hall								
1 Jan–8 Feb	11–4	M	T	W	T	F	S	S
27 Dec–31 Dec	11–4	M	T	W	T	·	·	S

Closed 24 and 25 December. *Closes dusk if earlier.
**House closed 30 November to 4 December.

The south front of Hinton Ampner in Hampshire: the fulfilment of one man's vision

The Homewood

Portsmouth Road, Esher, Surrey KT10 9JL

Map (2) F6 [1999]

Extraordinary Modernist house and landscape garden, designed in 1938 by the architect Patrick Gwynne. **Note**: administered on behalf of the National Trust by a tenant. **Access is via minibus from Claremont Landscape Garden only**. Sorry no toilet. Additional charge for minibus and guided tour (including members).

Finding out more: 01372 476424 or thehomewood@nationaltrust.org.uk c/o Claremont Landscape Garden, Portsmouth Road, Esher, Surrey KT10 9JG

Hughenden

High Wycombe, Buckinghamshire HP14 4LA

Map (2) E4 [1947]

It's hardly surprising that the unconventional Victorian Prime Minister Benjamin Disraeli fell in love with Hughenden. His handsome home, set in an unspoilt Chiltern valley with its views of ancient woods and rolling hills, is full of the fascinating personal memorabilia of this charismatic and colourful statesman. Disraeli's hillside retreat became the headquarters for a top-secret, Second World War operation that put Hughenden high on Hitler's hit list. The re-created air-raid shelter, 1940s living room and ice-house bunker bring wartime Britain to life. The manor is surrounded by woodlands with winding footpaths and red kites soaring overhead.

Eating and shopping: Stableyard café selling hot meals, sandwiches, cakes and drinks. Shop stocks local produce, such as ales and honey, as well as Disraeli and 'Hillside' memorabilia. Second-hand bookshop and home-grown plants.

Hughenden, Buckinghamshire: Benjamin Disraeli's Chiltern retreat

Making the most of your day: **Indoors** Morning guided tour. Free introductory talks throughout day. Children's trails. **Outdoors** Woodland walks (map available) and children's trails in the walled garden. West Wycombe Park, Village and Hill nearby. **Dogs**: welcome in orchard, park and woodland. Assistance dogs only in formal gardens.

Access:
Manor **Grounds**
Parking: on site.

Finding out more: 01494 755565 (Infoline). 01494 755573 or hughenden@nationaltrust.org.uk

Hughenden		M	T	W	T	F	S	S
Open all year	10–5*	**M**	**T**	**W**	**T**	**F**	**S**	**S**

*Closes dusk, if earlier. **Manor and shop open 12 to 4 from 1 January to 13 February, thereafter open at 11.** Closed 24 and 25 December.

 Why not share your pictures with us? #nationaltrust

Ighthan Mote

Mote Road, Ivy Hatch, Sevenoaks, Kent TN15 0NT

Map (2) H6 1985

Hidden deep in the Kent countryside, a sense of magic surrounds this romantic, medieval moated manor house. Spanning centuries, if walls could talk, they would have a lot to say; the crypt of a medieval knight, the painted ceiling of a Tudor courtier, a Victorian gentleman's billiard-room and an American's take on an English country paradise. The tranquil garden features lakes, an orchard and flower borders, while the wider estate, with its secret glade, has wonderful views. **Note**: very steep slope from reception (lower drop-off point available).

Eating and shopping: Mote café serving hot lunches, sandwiches, cream teas, cakes and hot, cold, alcoholic and non-alcoholic beverages. Picnic facilities available. Shop selling gifts, local produce and plants.

Making the most of your day: **Indoors** Year-round events, including theatre productions, themed dining evenings, behind-the-scenes events, arts and crafts courses. **Outdoors** Countryside walks, activities and family fun days. Children's natural play area and discovery den.
Dogs: welcome on café patio and estate; assistance dogs only in gardens.

Access:
Building **Grounds**
Parking: 200 yards.

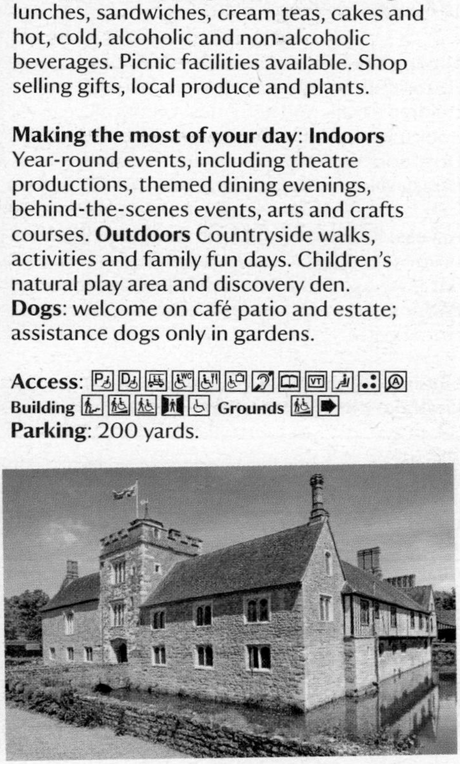

Romantic Ightham Mote in Kent (above and below): loved by all ages

Finding out more: 01732 810378 or ighthammote@nationaltrust.org.uk

Ightham Mote		M	T	W	T	F	S	S
House								
1 Jan–28 Feb	11–3	**M**	**T**	**W**	**T**	**F**	**S**	**S**
1 Mar–31 Oct	11–5*	**M**	**T**	**W**	**T**	**F**	**S**	**S**
1 Nov–31 Dec	11–3	**M**	**T**	**W**	**T**	**F**	**S**	**S**
Garden, café, exhibition and shop								
Open all year	10–5*	**M**	**T**	**W**	**T**	**F**	**S**	**S**

*Closes dusk if earlier. Partial access to house and grounds in winter months. Closed 24 and 25 December.

King's Head

King's Head Passage, Market Square, Aylesbury, Buckinghamshire HP20 2RW

Map (2) E3 1925

Historic public house dating back to 1455, with a pleasant family atmosphere. This is one of England's best-preserved coaching inns.
Note: Farmers' Bar leased by Chiltern Brewery.

Finding out more: 01296 718812 (Farmers' Bar). 01280 817156 (National Trust) or kingshead@nationaltrust.org.uk

Knole in Kent: this vast, complex palace is full of hidden treasures

Knole

Sevenoaks, Kent TN15 0RP

Map (2) H6 1946

Nestled in a medieval deer-park, Knole is vast, complex and full of hidden treasures. Originally an archbishop's palace, the house passed through royal hands to the Sackville family – Knole's inhabitants from 1603 to today. In 2012 a project to conserve Knole began with the support of the Heritage Lottery Fund. With external repairs complete, the next phase is to build a world-class conservation studio and painstakingly conserve the show rooms. In many ways, visitors this year will see more of Knole than ever before, as archaeologists search beneath floorboards and conservators unravel the secrets of Knole's collection. **Note**: opening times or visitor routes occasionally altered due to our conservation project.

Eating and shopping: hot drinks and cake available while you browse in our new Bookshop Café. Refreshments also served outdoors (open-air seating area available) while we refurbish our café space.

Making the most of your day: **Indoors** Historic show rooms to discover. Guided tours, children's trails and activities. Events all year. Bookshop Café and Orangery in Green Court. **Outdoors** Walks in the ancient parkland. **Dogs**: welcome in park on leads.

Access: **Show rooms** **Orangery** **Garden/park**
Sat Nav: use TN13 1HU and follow signs. **Parking**: 60 yards. Additional parking in town centre.

Finding out more: 01732 462100 or knole@nationaltrust.org.uk

Knole		M	T	W	T	F	S	S
Show rooms*								
7 Mar–1 Nov	11–4	·	**T**	**W**	**T**	**F**	**S**	**S**
Green Court: Visitor Welcome, bookshop café, Orangery								
7 Mar–31 Dec	10–5**	**M**	**T**	**W**	**T**	**F**	**S**	**S**
Outdoor café								
Open all year	10–5**	**M**	**T**	**W**	**T**	**F**	**S**	**S**
Parkland								
Open all year		**M**	**T**	**W**	**T**	**F**	**S**	**S**

*Last entry to show rooms 3:30; guided tours only 11 to 12. Show rooms open Bank Holiday Mondays, except 28 December. **November to February outdoor café and Green Court close dusk. Garden open Tuesdays only, 7 April until 29 September, 11 to 4. Whole property closed 24 and 25 December.

Lamb House

West Street, Rye, East Sussex TN31 7ES

Map (2) 18 1950

Georgian home of writers Henry James and E. F. Benson, who depicted the property in the Mapp and Lucia stories. **Note**: open Tuesday, Friday and Saturday, 11 to 5. Maintained on the National Trust's behalf by a tenant. Sorry no toilets.

Finding out more: 01580 762334 or lambhouse@nationaltrust.org.uk

Leith Hill Place

Leith Hill Lane, near Holmbury St Mary, Dorking, Surrey RH5 6LY

Map (2) F7 1945

Childhood home of English composer Ralph Vaughan Williams, once owned by the Wedgwood family and regularly visited by Charles Darwin. Opened to the public in 2013 for the first time in 40 years, it is a work in progress with an unusually informal atmosphere. Glorious views over the South Downs. **Note**: parking access across sloping field (can be muddy).

Eating and shopping: no café, but volunteer bakers provide freshly made cakes, scones and teas by donation. An original AGA is in use and visitors can sit in the stone-flagged dining-room or outside in the courtyard garden.

Making the most of your day: free soundscape audio tour (timed tickets). Everyone is welcome to play the piano, listen to music (often live), explore the cellar graffiti and children's trail. Summer concerts. **Dogs**: welcome on leads in grounds and house. Assistance dogs only in kitchen and Wedgwood Room.

Access: House Courtyard garden/ south terrace
Sat Nav: use RH5 6LU for car park.
Parking: Rhododendron Wood car park, 437 yards, in Tanhurst Lane.

Finding out more: 01306 711685 or leithhillplace@nationaltrust.org.uk

Leith Hill Place		M	T	W	T	F	S	S
27 Mar–1 Nov*	11–5	M	·	·	·	F	S	S
5 Dec–6 Dec	11–3:30	·	·	·	·	·	S	S

*Closed Sunday 2 August for Ride London cycle race. Closes at 4 from 25 October to 1 November.

Long Crendon Courthouse

Long Crendon, Aylesbury, Buckinghamshire HP18 9AN

Map (2) D4 1900

Superb example of a 14th-century courthouse with a wealth of local history – the second building acquired by the National Trust. **Note**: extremely steep stairs. Sorry no toilet.

Finding out more: 01280 817156 or longcrendon@nationaltrust.org.uk

Leith Hill Place, Surrey: opened to the public in 2013 for the first time in 40 years, the house has an unusually informal atmosphere

Monk's House

Rodmell, Lewes, East Sussex BN7 3HF

Map (2) G8 1980

This small 17th-century weatherboarded cottage in the village of Rodmell was the country retreat of novelist Virginia Woolf and her husband Leonard and a meeting place for the Bloomsbury Group. The garden features the room where she created her best-known works and includes cottage garden borders, orchard, allotments and ponds.
Note: no access to Rodmell from A26.

Making the most of your day: why not try your hand at a game of bowls? One of the favoured pastimes of the Woolfs.
Dogs: allowed in garden on leads.

Access: **Building** **Grounds**
Sat Nav: do not use. **Parking**: 100 yards. Please note height restriction barrier.

Finding out more: 01273 474760 or monkshouse@nationaltrust.org.uk

Monk's House		M	T	W	T	F	S	S
1 Apr–25 Oct*	1–5**	·	·	W	T	F	S	S

Last admission to house 15 minutes before closing. *Open Bank Holiday Mondays. **Admission to garden 12:30 to 5:30.

Pretty little Monk's House in East Sussex

Mottisfont

near Romsey, Hampshire SO51 0LP

Map (2) C7 1957

Once across the crystal-clear river, visitors enter a garden paradise. Ancient trees, babbling brooks and rolling lawns frame this lovely old house. An 18th-century home with a medieval priory at its heart, Mottisfont inspired a 1930s dream of creativity. Artists came here to relax and create works, some of which are still visible in our historic rooms. This tradition continues today, along with major exhibitions in our top-floor gallery. Outside, carpets of spring bulbs, a walled rose garden, rich autumn leaves and a colourful winter garden create a feast for the senses all year round. **Note**: National Collection of Old-fashioned Roses (usually flowering June).

Eating and shopping: Kitchen Café serving meals and cakes. Ice-cream parlour. Spacious shop. Second-hand books. Plant sales.

Making the most of your day: open-air theatre and events throughout the year. Free daily guided walks and talks. Family fun activities, including building dens, make-and-take days and a new wild play trail. Five major exhibitions in the art gallery every year, including a summer family show with a creative challenge quest trail. Seasonal variety in the Winter Garden, with 60,000 spring bulbs and late summer borders. Wider estate to explore on foot or by bike. **Dogs**: welcome on short leads at all times in most of grounds and garden.

Access:
House and gallery **Grounds**
Sat Nav: use SO51 0LN. **Parking**: on site.

Finding out more: 01794 340757 or mottisfont@nationaltrust.org.uk

Mottisfont		M	T	W	T	F	S	S
Garden, shop, café and art gallery*								
Open all year	10–5**	M	T	W	T	F	S	S
House								
1 Mar–1 Nov	11–5**	M	T	W	T	F	S	S

*Gallery opens at 11. Gallery closes for short periods to change exhibitions. **Closes dusk if earlier. Closed 24 and 25 December. Late opening during rose season in June and early July (except house and café) subject to weather, call for details.

For other ways to get involved go to nationaltrust.org.uk/get-involved/volunteer

Across a crystal-clear river lies the garden paradise of Mottisfont in Hampshire

Mottistone Gardens

Mottistone, near Brighstone,
Isle of Wight PO30 4ED

Map (2) C9 1965

Set in a sheltered south-facing valley, these gardens are full of surprises, with shrub-filled banks, hidden pathways and colourful herbaceous borders. Surrounding an attractive manor house (tenanted, not open), these 20th-century gardens have a Mediterranean-style planting scheme to take advantage of its southerly location, including drought-tolerant plants from subtropical regions. Other surprises include a monocot border, a small organic kitchen garden and a traditional tea-garden alongside The Shack, a unique cabin retreat designed as their summer drawing office by architects John Seely (2nd Lord Mottistone) and Paul Paget. There are also delightful walks across the adjoining Mottistone Estate. **Note**: manor house open two days a year.

Eating and shopping: shop selling gifts, books, cards and postcards. Plant stall. Second-hand books. Tea-garden serving ice-cream, hot and cold drinks, soup, sandwiches, cake and light refreshments (not National Trust). Picnic table.

Making the most of your day: family events and garden tours. Flowerpot trail and estate walks. Newtown Old Town Hall and The Needles Old Battery and New Battery nearby.
Dogs: welcome on leads.

Mottistone Gardens on the Isle of Wight (above and below) are full of surprises

Access:
The Shack **Garden**
Parking: 50 yards.

Finding out more: 01983 741302 or
mottistonegardens@nationaltrust.org.uk

Mottistone Gardens		M	T	W	T	F	S	S
Gardens and shop								
15 Mar–29 Oct	10:30–5	**M**	**T**	**W**	**T**	·	·	**S**
Shop								
5 Nov–12 Dec	11–3	·	·	·	**T**	**F**	**S**	·
13 Dec	11–3	·	·	·	·	·	·	**S**

Closes dusk if earlier. Manor house open two days only: Sunday 24 May (members only), guided tours 9:30 to 12 by timed ticket (available on day), free-flow 1 to 5; Monday 25 May open 10:30 to 5 (additional charges apply).

Some places are easy to get to on foot or by public transport. See page 3

The Needles Old Battery and New Battery

West High Down, Alum Bay,
Isle of Wight PO39 0JH

Map (2) C9 1975

Perched high above The Needles, amid acres of unspoilt countryside, is The Needles Old Battery, a Victorian fort built in 1862 and used throughout both World Wars. The Parade Ground has two original guns, and the fort's fascinating military history is brought to life with displays and models, plus a series of vivid cartoons by acclaimed comic book artist Geoff Campion. An underground tunnel leads to a searchlight emplacement with dramatic views over The Needles rocks. The New Battery, further up the headland, has an exhibition on the secret British rocket tests carried out there during the Cold War. **Note**: steep paths and uneven surfaces. Spiral staircase to tunnel. Toilet at Old Battery only.

Eating and shopping: clifftop 1940s-style tea-room serving soup, jacket potatoes, filled baguettes, cakes and light refreshments. Picnic tables (Parade Ground). Guardroom shop selling postcards, gifts and souvenirs. Refreshments, snacks and ice-cream available at New Battery kiosk.

Making the most of your day: **Indoors** Family events and activity packs. Inspector and soldier trails. **Outdoors** Clifftop walks to Tennyson Monument and beyond. **Dogs**: welcome on leads, although assistance dogs only in tea-room.

Access:
Old Battery **New Battery**
Parking: no parking on site (limited disabled parking by arrangement). Nearest at Alum Bay ¾ mile (not National Trust, minimum charge £4, including members). Freshwater Bay 3½ miles (not National Trust), or Highdown (SZ325856) 2 miles.

The Needles Old Battery on the Isle of Wight

Finding out more: 01983 754772 or needlesoldbattery@nationaltrust.org.uk

The Needles Batteries		M	T	W	T	F	S	S
Old Battery								
14 Mar–1 Nov	10:30–5*	M	T	W	T	F	S	S
New Battery								
14 Mar–1 Nov	11–4	M	T	W	T	F	S	S
Tea-room								
3 Jan–1 Mar**	11–3	·	·	·	·	·	S	S
14 Mar–1 Nov	10:30–5	M	T	W	T	F	S	S
7 Nov–13 Dec	11–3	·	·	·	·	·	S	S

*Closes dusk if earlier. Property closes in high winds.
**Open daily from 14 to 22 February. 10 May: no disabled vehicular access due to Walk the Wight. 27 June: Old Battery early opening (6:30) for Round the Island Yacht Race.

Newtown Old Town Hall

Newtown, near Shalfleet,
Isle of Wight PO30 4PA

Map (2) C9 1933

Tucked away in a tiny hamlet adjoining the National Nature Reserve, this small and quirky 17th-century building is the only remaining evidence of Newtown's former importance. It's hard to believe that this tranquil corner of the island once held, what were often turbulent, elections before sending two Members to Parliament. **Note**: nearest toilet in car park.

Newtown Old Town Hall, Isle of Wight: this 17th-century building witnessed a turbulent past

Eating and shopping: postcards and souvenirs available.

Making the most of your day: **Indoors** Children's quiz sheet. Exhibitions by local artists. **Outdoors** National Nature Reserve walks. Bird hide (April to September). Family activities run by Newtown Ranger from nearby Visitor Point (01983 531622).

Access: **Building**
Parking: 15 yards.

Finding out more: 01983 531785 or oldtownhall@nationaltrust.org.uk

Newtown Old Town Hall		M	T	W	T	F	S	S
15 Mar–28 Jun	2–5	·	**T**	**W**	**T**	·	·	**S**
29 Jun–6 Sep	2–5	**M**	**T**	**W**	**T**	·	·	**S**
8 Sep–22 Oct	2–5	·	**T**	**W**	**T**	·	·	**S**

Last admission 15 minutes before closing. Closes dusk if earlier. Open Bank Holiday Mondays.

 Please display your current sticker for free parking

Nuffield Place in Oxfordshire (above left), is the former home of the founder of Morris Motors Cars. The toy Morris Minor (above) is a reminder of this illustrious engineering history

Nuffield Place

Huntercombe, near Henley-on-Thames, Oxfordshire RG9 5RY

Map (2) D4 2011

William Morris, Lord Nuffield, at one time the richest man in the world, chose to live in the same comfortable house in the Oxfordshire countryside for 30 years. The founder of Morris Motor Cars was one of Britain's greatest philanthropists and influencers of the 20th century, and this intimate home exudes the tastes and interests of its remarkable owner. The house and garden are a perfect example of 1930s quiet good taste, and an evocative reflection of a man whose relatively modest home life was in complete contrast to his wealth and public persona.

Eating and shopping: tea-room serving light lunches and afternoon tea. Shop selling unique Nuffield Place products, gifts, books and postcards.

Making the most of your day: **Indoors** Lord Nuffield's bedroom with its secret workshop and Lady Nuffield's Wolseley Eight. **Outdoors** Pretty gardens that are being restored. Greys Court nearby. **Dogs**: on leads in woodland walks.

Access: **House** **Shop** **Grounds**
Parking: on site.

Finding out more: 01491 641224 or nuffieldplace@nationaltrust.org.uk

Nuffield Place		M	T	W	T	F	S	S
2 Mar–1 Nov	11–5	**M**	**T**	**W**	**T**	**F**	**S**	**S**

Closed Sunday 26 April, 28 June and Tuesday 9 July. Timed tickets for house entry may be used on busy days.

Nymans

Handcross, near Haywards Heath,
West Sussex RH17 6EB

Map (2) G7 1954

In the late 19th century, Ludwig Messel bought the Nymans Estate in the High Weald to make a dream family home. Inspired by the beautiful wooded surroundings, he created a stunning garden with plants collected from around the world. Here this creative family entertained friends and family and enjoyed relaxing, playing and picnicking in the garden and woods. Today Nymans is still a garden lovers' home – a place to relax all year round and enjoy a peaceful country garden. Partially destroyed by fire in 1947, the romantic ruins of a fairytale Gothic mansion remain alongside the surviving Messel Family Rooms. Nymans is one of the Trust's greenest properties and aims to inspire a more sustainable way of living.

The astonishing garden at Nymans, West Sussex (below and right), contains plants collected from all around the world

Any questions? Telephone 0344 800 1895 (seven days a week)

Eating and shopping: large shop, plant and garden centre offering Nymans' collection of plants. Café, with new indoor seating area, serving a choice of fresh, seasonal food. 'Grab and go' kiosk in the tea-garden. Woodland craft sales. Second-hand bookshop.

Making the most of your day: **Indoors** Small gallery in the house with changing exhibitions every season. Art and craft sessions run all year. **Outdoors** Daily guided walks and talks in the garden or woods. Mobility buggy tours of the garden or woods. Children will love our natural play trail, geocaching in the garden and woods, as well as the school holiday trails. Gardening workshops throughout the year. **Dogs**: in woodland only, on leads during bird nesting season (1 March to 31 July).

Access:
House **Gallery** **Garden**
Parking: on site.

Finding out more: 01444 405250 or nymans@nationaltrust.org.uk

Nymans		M	T	W	T	F	S	S
Open all year	10–5*	**M**	**T**	**W**	**T**	**F**	**S**	**S**

Gallery closes 30 minutes earlier and for short periods during the year to change exhibitions. *Closes dusk if earlier. Closed 25 and 26 December.

Oakhurst Cottage

Hambledon, near Godalming, Surrey GU8 4HF

Map (2) E7 1952

Quaint 16th-century cottage with contents spanning 400 years, and a delightful cottage garden. **Note**: sorry no toilet. Nearest visitor facilities at Winkworth Arboretum (4 miles approximately). Access by booked guided tour only and limited to a maximum of six visitors in the cottage at any one time.

Finding out more: 01483 208936 or oakhurstcottage@nationaltrust.org.uk

Old Soar Manor

Plaxtol, Borough Green, Kent TN15 0QX

Map (2) H6 [1947]

Dating from 1290, the remaining rooms of this knight's house offer a glimpse back to the time of Edward I. **Note**: sorry no toilet or tea-room. Narrow lanes, limited off-road parking.

Finding out more: 01732 810378 or oldsoarmanor@nationaltrust.org.uk

Owletts

The Street, Cobham, Gravesend, Kent DA12 3AP

Map (2) H5 [1938]

Dating back to the reign of Charles II, Owletts was the family home of the renowned architect Sir Herbert Baker.

Finding out more: 01732 810378 or owletts@nationaltrust.org.uk

Petworth House and Park

Petworth, West Sussex GU28 0AE

Map (2) E7 [1947]

Shaped by a family of collectors over the past 800 years, this 17th-century 'house of art' inspired countless artists, including England's greatest landscape painter J. M. W. Turner. The finest collection of art and sculpture in the National Trust, including world-famous paintings by Van Dyck, Reynolds, Blake and Turner, is displayed in the opulent state rooms and North Gallery. In contrast the atmospheric servants' quarters evoke the hustle and bustle of 'below stairs' life. Outdoors is a woodland Pleasure Ground and acres of 'Capability' Brown landscape deer-park with glorious views of the South Downs National Park.
Note: additional charge for Christmas Fair and Winter Art Exhibition (including members).

Eating and shopping: coffee shop and Audit Room Restaurant offering fresh seasonal food, barrista-style coffee and tempting homemade cakes. Gift shop, second-hand bookshop and plant sales.

Petworth House and Park, West Sussex: the fabulous house (opposite and this page) contains the finest collection of art and sculpture in the National Trust

Making the most of your day: **Indoors** Free daily introductory talks, specialist talks, costumed interpretation (monthly) and snapshot tours (Thursday and Friday). Children's activities. Selection of rooms available for private hire. **Outdoors** 4x4 tours of the park. Family events throughout the year. Trilingual multimedia guide (English, French and German) at small additional charge. Year-round events, culminating in Christmas Fair. **Dogs**: under close control in Petworth Park. Assistance dogs only in Pleasure Ground.

Access:
Building
Sat Nav: use GU28 9LR. **Parking**: on A283, 700 yards. Separate car park for Petworth Park.

Finding out more: 01798 342207 or petworth@nationaltrust.org.uk

Petworth House and Park		M	T	W	T	F	S	S
House								
14 Mar–4 Nov	11–5	**M**	**T**	**W**	·	·	**S**	**S**
19 Mar–30 Oct*	11–5	·	·	·	**T**	**F**	·	·
Pleasure Ground, shop and restaurant								
Open all year	10–5**	**M**	**T**	**W**	**T**	**F**	**S**	**S**

*On Thursdays and Fridays the house is partially open and specialist tours are available. **Closes dusk if earlier. Closed 24 and 25 December.

Pitstone Windmill

Ivinghoe, Buckinghamshire

Map (2) E3 1937

One of the oldest windmills in the UK, with stunning views of the Chilterns. **Note**: sorry no toilet. At the end of a rough track.

Finding out more: 01442 851227 or pitstonemill@nationaltrust.org.uk

'Delicious' Polesden Lacey, Surrey (above), contains such delights as the Pattisson children's portrait (below)

Polesden Lacey

Great Bookham, near Dorking, Surrey RH5 6BD

Map (2) F6 1942

'This is a delicious house…' remarked Queen Elizabeth, the Queen Mother, on her honeymoon at Polesden Lacey. This country retreat, with glorious views across the rolling Surrey Hills and acres of countryside, was home to formidable Edwardian hostess Mrs Greville. Visitors can soak up the atmosphere of the glittering Saloon, designed to impress kings and maharajahs; while the extensive collection of fine and decorative arts, ranging from world-famous Dutch Old Masters to sparkling Fabergé, is breathtaking. The gardens offer something for every season, including climbing roses (at their best in June), one of the longest double herbaceous borders in the country, and a winter garden bursting with yellow aconites. There are four waymarked walks around the wider estate. **Note**: for a quieter visit, come on a weekday morning (March to October) or winter weekend. Christmas events – additional charge (including members).

Eating and shopping: Granary Café and Cowshed Coffee Shop offering home cooking, drinks and snacks. Home and giftware, souvenirs and plants available to buy, all located outside the pay perimeter. Second-hand bookshop in the grounds.

Outside there is so much to discover, from fabulous displays of roses in June to glowing aconites in the winter

Making the most of your day: **Indoors** House tours covering the collections, conservation work and stories. If you want to get into the Edwardian party spirit, an ideal time to visit is at a weekend or Bank Holiday (March to October), or come for a Christmas event, when the house will be open all day and music is playing. **Outdoors** Free garden tours daily. Waymarked walks. Additional events for children in the holidays. Children will love our geocaching and other trails, which are always available. **Dogs**: on leads in designated areas, under close control on landscape walks, estate and farmland.

Access:
House **Grounds**
Parking: 200 yards.

Finding out more: 01372 452048 or polesdenlacey@nationaltrust.org.uk

Polesden Lacey		M	T	W	T	F	S	S
House*								
28 Feb–1 Nov	11–5**	**M**	**T**	**W**	**T**	**F**	**S**	**S**
Gardens, Granary Café, shop and coffee shop								
Open all year	10–5**	**M**	**T**	**W**	**T**	**F**	**S**	**S**

*House can only be visited by guided tours weekdays 11 to 12:30 and winter weekends, booking on arrival. Charges apply for Christmas (including members). **Closes dusk if earlier. Closed 10 February, 24 and 25 December.

Priory Cottages

1 Mill Street, Steventon, Abingdon, Oxfordshire OX13 6SP

Map (2) C5 1939

Now converted into two houses, these former monastic buildings were gifted to the National Trust by the famous Ferguson's Gang.
Note: Priory Cottage South only open. Administered by a tenant (booking essential). Sorry no toilet.

Finding out more: 01793 762209 or priorycottages@nationaltrust.org.uk

Quebec House

Quebec Square, Westerham, Kent TN16 1TD

Map (2) G6 [1918]

The childhood home of General James Wolfe, this 18th-century house retains much of its original charm and family feel, with a replica bed and examples of traditional pastimes the Wolfes would have enjoyed. An exhibition tells of the dramatic battle for North America, which tragically ended in General Wolfe's death.

Eating and shopping: second-hand bookshop. Souvenirs and guidebooks for sale in the Coach House, as well as hot and cold drinks and a selection of cakes.

Making the most of your day: house guided tours at 12 and 12:30 (book on arrival). Every Sunday we re-create Mrs Wolfe's recipes in the Georgian kitchen. Exhibition on the North American campaign. **Dogs**: welcome on short leads in the gardens.

Access: **Building** **Grounds**
Parking: 80 yards in main town car park on A25 (not National Trust).

Finding out more: 01732 868381 or quebechouse@nationaltrust.org.uk

Quebec House		M	T	W	T	F	S	S
28 Feb–1 Nov	11–5*	·	·	W	T	F	S	S
7 Nov–20 Dec	1–4	·	·	·	·	·	S	S

*House opens at 12. Open Bank Holiday Mondays. Closes dusk if earlier.

River Wey and Godalming Navigations and Dapdune Wharf

Navigations Office and Dapdune Wharf, Wharf Road, Guildford, Surrey GU1 4RR

Map (2) F6 [1964]

A hidden haven where you can take a boat trip, explore a restored barge, or enjoy scenic walks. Dapdune Wharf in Guildford brings to life stories of this historic waterway, along 20 miles of waterside towpath. A great place for children to have fun – and raid our dressing-up box. **Note**: boat trip charges, mooring and fishing fees apply to members.

Replica landing craft at Quebec House in Kent

Entry is still possible at most places up to 30 minutes before closing

Eating and shopping: small tea-room serving sandwiches, cakes, ice-cream and drinks. Small shop with plant sales. Picnic areas at Dapdune Wharf.

Making the most of your day: **Indoors** Dressing-up clothes for children. **Outdoors** Year-round events, including activities for children at Dapdune and guided walks along towpath and beyond. Guildford River Festival in September. Overnight moorings available. **Dogs**: on leads at Dapdune Wharf and lock areas; elsewhere under control.

Access: [access symbols] **Grounds** [access symbol]
Parking: at Dapdune Wharf.

Finding out more: 01483 561389 or riverwey@nationaltrust.org.uk

River Wey and Dapdune Wharf		M	T	W	T	F	S	S
Dapdune Wharf								
14 Mar–1 Nov*	11–5	**M**	·	·	**T**	**F**	**S**	**S**

*Open 7 days a week during local school half-term and summer holidays. River trips from Dapdune Wharf 11 to 4 (conditions permitting). Access to towpath during daylight hours all year.

St John's Jerusalem

Sutton-at-Hone, Dartford, Kent DA4 9HQ

Map (2) H5 [symbols] 1943

13th-century chapel surrounded by a tranquil moated garden, once part of the former Commandery of the Knights Hospitallers. **Note**: private residence, maintained and managed by a tenant on behalf of the National Trust.

Finding out more: 01732 810378 or stjohnsjerusalem@nationaltrust.org.uk

The tranquil River Wey in Surrey (above) on a frosty day

Sandham Memorial Chapel

Harts Lane, Burghclere, near Newbury, Hampshire RG20 9JT

Map (2) C6 1947

This tranquil yet powerful place contains an outstanding series of paintings by artist Stanley Spencer, inspired by his experiences as a First World War medical orderly and soldier. A new interactive exhibition tells the story of Sandham, while outside a new orchard garden provides space to picnic and reflect.
Note: timed-ticket system in operation.

Eating and shopping: small gift and tea shop. Gift shop selling books, postcards and Spencer-related products. Tea-room serving tea and cake.

Making the most of your day: new exhibition commemorating the First World War.
Dogs: in grounds on leads only.

Access: **Building** **Grounds**
Parking: opposite the entrance to the chapel.

Finding out more: 01635 278394 or sandham@nationaltrust.org.uk

Sandham Memorial Chapel		M	T	W	T	F	S	S
28 Mar–25 Oct	11–4	·	·	**W**	**T**	**F**	**S**	**S**

Entry by bookable timed ticket (online booking via website). Chapel closes at 3 in October. Open Bank Holiday Mondays.

Sandham Memorial Chapel, Hampshire: a place for reflection

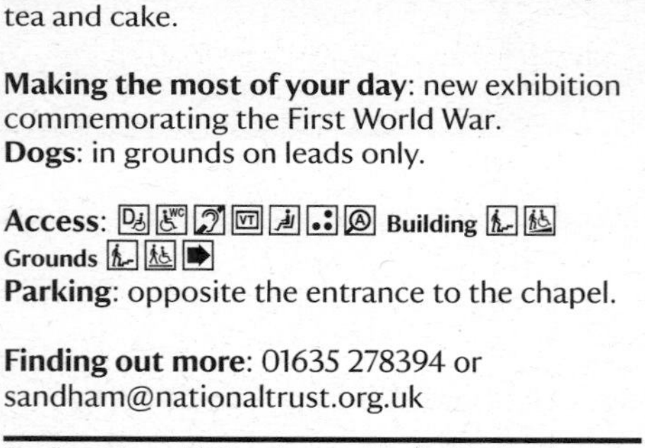

Scotney Castle

Lamberhurst, Tunbridge Wells, Kent TN3 8JN

Map (2) H7 1970

The medieval moated Old Scotney Castle lies in a peaceful wooded valley. In the 19th century its owner Edward Hussey III set about building a new house, partially demolishing the Old Castle to create a romantic folly, the centrepiece of his picturesque landscape. From the terraces of the new house, sweeps of rhododendrons and azaleas cascade down the slope in summer, followed by highlights of autumn leaf colour, mirrored in the moat. In the house three generations have made their mark, adding possessions and character to the homely Victorian mansion which enjoys far-reaching views out across the estate.

Eating and shopping: the coach house tea-room offers a selection of hot meals and sandwiches, as well as homemade cakes and scones. Take home your own part of Scotney with local honey, Scotney Ale and plant sales available in the shop.

The fairytale mix of moated castle, romantic garden and country house at Scotney Castle in Kent, combine to create a unique visit

Making the most of your day: **Indoors** Children's guided trails around house. **Outdoors** Garden tree trails in spring and autumn. Natural play. Estate trails. **Dogs**: welcome on leads on the estate.

Access: **House** **Grounds**
Parking: 130 yards (limited), overflow parking 440 yards.

Finding out more: 01892 893820 (Infoline). 01892 893868 or scotneycastle@nationaltrust.org.uk

Scotney Castle		M	T	W	T	F	S	S
Open all year	10-5**	**M**	**T**	**W**	**T**	**F**	**S**	**S**

House opens at 11. **Closes dusk if earlier. All visitors require timed ticket to visit house (places limited, early sell-outs possible). Estate walks available every day. Property may close during adverse weather. Closed 24 and 25 December.

Shalford Mill

Shalford, near Guildford, Surrey GU4 8BS

Map 2 F6 1932

You can feel the evocative stories of the past in the very structure of the mill, although the machinery no longer works. The wonderful story of the Ferguson's Gang is waiting for you – eccentric girls from the 1930s, determined to save the fabric of England for the future.
Note: sorry no toilet or parking on site.

Making the most of your day: **Indoors** Regular guided tours, evening talks and children's events. **Outdoors** Geocaching kits available on Sundays. **Dogs**: assistance dogs only.

Access: **Building**
Parking: none on site.

Finding out more: 01483 561389 or shalfordmill@nationaltrust.org.uk

Shalford Mill		M	T	W	T	F	S	S
1 Apr–1 Nov	11–5	·	·	**W**	·	·	·	**S**

Open Bank Holiday Mondays and Saturdays on Bank Holiday weekends.

Find out about the Ferguson's Gang at Shalford Mill, Surrey

Sheffield Park and Garden

Sheffield Park, Uckfield, East Sussex TN22 3QX

Map ② G7 1954

Sheffield Park and Garden is a horticultural work of art created through centuries of landscape design, with influences of 'Capability' Brown and Humphry Repton. Four lakes form the heart of the garden, with paths circulating through the glades and wooded areas surrounding them. The bordering parkland once played host to deer- and game-hunting for the guests at Sheffield Park House, thought to have included Henry VIII. Each owner has left their impression, which can still be seen today in the lakes, the construction of Pulham Falls, the planting of Palm Walk and the many different tree and shrub species from around the world.

Eating and shopping: Coach House tea-room serving homemade cakes, sandwiches, hot lunches and cream teas. A catering buggy is usually located in the garden. Shop selling local, garden-related, outdoor products and plants. Second-hand bookshop.

Making the most of your day: family activities all year, with extra activities in the school holidays. Garden tours on Tuesdays and Thursdays. Pulham Falls cascade, 12 to 1 (Tuesdays and Fridays). Natural play in the Ringwood Toll play trail, with tree-climbing, den-building, balance beams and much more. River, meadow and wildlife haven. Cricket matches most summer weekends. Carpets of bluebells in spring and outstanding autumn colour display. Bluebell Railway nearby and Sheffield Park station just a short walk across the parkland (weekend bus link operates spring and summer). **Dogs**: welcome in South or East Park. Assistance dogs only in garden.

Access:
Reception **Tea-room** **Garden**
Parking: on site. Overflow car park 600 yards.

Finding out more: 01825 790231 or sheffieldpark@nationaltrust.org.uk

Sheffield Park and Garden		M	T	W	T	F	S	S
Garden, shop and tea-room								
Open all year	10–5*	**M**	**T**	**W**	**T**	**F**	**S**	**S**
Parkland								
Open all year		**M**	**T**	**W**	**T**	**F**	**S**	**S**

Last admission to the garden is one hour before closing.
*Closes dusk if earlier. Garden, shop and tea-room closed 25 December.

Created over centuries, Sheffield Park and Garden in East Sussex (below and opposite), is a horticultural work of art

Some places are easy to get to on foot or by public transport. See page 3

Sissinghurst Castle Garden

Biddenden Road, near Cranbrook,
Kent TN17 2AB

Map (2) 17 1967

The garden of Sissinghurst Castle sits within the ruin of the great Elizabethan house – all surrounded by the rich Kentish landscape of woods, streams and farmland. The famous garden, with its fairytale tower, is the result of the creative tension between the formal design of Harold Nicolson and the lavish planting of Vita Sackville-West. The colour schemes, intimacy of the different garden 'rooms' and rich herbaceous borders are the epitome of an English garden. The wider estate, with its vegetable garden, lakes and rich variety of wildlife are waiting to be explored, while our year-round exhibitions tell Sissinghurst's stories and show how history and landscape have combined to shape this special place. **Note**: access to library, tower and gardens only.

Eating and shopping: restaurant serving lunch and afternoon tea made with produce from our vegetable garden and farm. The Old Dairy, offering sandwiches, cakes and drinks. Second-hand bookshop and plant shop selling produce grown in the Sissinghurst nursery.

Making the most of your day: **Indoors** Exhibitions and daily talks. The Library contains the National Trust's most significant collection of 20th-century literature, and visitors can learn how we conserve it. **Outdoors** Talks and activities, including dawn chorus walks and Ranger-led nature trails. Acres of ancient woodland to explore. Panoramic views across the Wealden countryside. Exploring equipment for children available to borrow. Smallhythe Place, Lamb House and Stoneacre nearby. **Dogs**: welcome on estate. Assistance dogs only in garden and vegetable garden.

Access:
Building **Grounds**
Parking: 315 yards.

Finding out more: 01580 710700 or sissinghurst@nationaltrust.org.uk

Sissinghurst Castle Garden		M	T	W	T	F	S	S
Garden								
3 Jan–8 Mar	Tour*	·	·	·	·	·	**S**	**S**
14 Mar–31 Oct	11–5:30**	**M**	**T**	**W**	**T**	**F**	**S**	**S**
1 Nov–31 Dec	Tour*	**M**	**T**	**W**	**T**	**F**	**S**	**S**
Shop and restaurant								
Open all year	10–5:30**	**M**	**T**	**W**	**T**	**F**	**S**	**S**
Estate								
Open all year	Dawn–dusk	**M**	**T**	**W**	**T**	**F**	**S**	**S**

*Garden access by guided tour only from 11, last tour at 3. **Closes dusk if earlier. Last garden entry 45 minutes before closing. Due to its fragile nature we regret we are unable to allow children's buggies in the garden, carriers are provided. Guide dogs only. Closed 24 and 25 December.

Sissinghurst Castle Garden, Kent (left and above): perfectly placed beside the ruin of the great Elizabethan house, this garden is the epitome of English horticultural design at its very finest

Smallhythe Place

Smallhythe, Tenterden, Kent TN30 7NG

Map (2) I7 1939

Nestled in the beautiful Weald of Kent, this early 16th-century cottage is full of the vibrant spirit of the adored Victorian actress Ellen Terry, and contains her fascinating theatrical collection. Voices of famous names who have graced the stage echo through our thatched Barn Theatre in the garden.

Eating and shopping: vintage-style tea-room (licensed) attached to Barn Theatre selling soup, sandwiches, cakes and drinks.

Making the most of your day: **Indoors** Wide range of plays and music in the Barn Theatre. **Outdoors** Open-air theatre in the garden. Sissinghurst Castle, Lamb House and Stoneacre nearby. **Dogs**: allowed on leads in grounds.

Access: **Building** **Grounds**
Parking: 50 yards (not National Trust).

Finding out more: 01580 762334 or smallhytheplace@nationaltrust.org.uk

Smallhythe Place		M	T	W	T	F	S	S
House								
4 Mar–1 Nov	11–5	·	·	W	T	F	S	S
Tea-room								
4 Mar–1 Nov	11:30–4:30	·	·	W	T	F	S	S

Open Bank Holiday Mondays 11 to 5. Closes dusk if earlier.

Roses adorn Smallhythe Place in Kent

Flying kites by South Foreland Lighthouse, Kent

South Foreland Lighthouse

The Front, St Margaret's Bay, Dover, Kent CT15 6HP

Map (2) K6 1989

This historic landmark, dramatically situated on the White Cliffs, guided ships past the infamous Goodwin Sands and has a fascinating tale to tell. It was the first lighthouse powered by electricity and the site of the first international radio transmission.
Note: no access for cars.

Eating and shopping: loose-leaf tea and homemade cakes served in Mrs Knott's tea-room. Shop selling ice-cream, cold drinks and gifts.

Making the most of your day: **Indoors** Tours run by knowledgeable guides. Interactive and hands-on displays. **Outdoors** Family fun with kite-flying and games. **Dogs**: in grounds only.

Access: **Lighthouse** **Tea-room** **Grounds**
Parking: none on site. Nearest at White Cliffs, 2 miles, or St Margaret's, 1 mile.

Finding out more: 01304 853281 or southforeland@nationaltrust.org.uk

South Foreland Lighthouse		M	T	W	T	F	S	S
Lighthouse*								
30 Mar–19 Apr	11–5:30	**M**	**T**	**W**	**T**	**F**	**S**	**S**
20 Apr–26 Jul	11–5:30	**M**	·	·	·	**F**	**S**	**S**
27 Jul–6 Sep	11–5:30	**M**	**T**	**W**	**T**	**F**	**S**	**S**
7 Sep–25 Oct	11–5:30	**M**	·	·	·	**F**	**S**	**S**
26 Oct–1 Nov	11–3	**M**	**T**	**W**	**T**	**F**	**S**	**S**
Tea-room								
7 Feb–29 Mar	11–3	·	·	·	·	·	**S**	**S**
30 Mar–6 Sep	11–5	**M**	**T**	**W**	**T**	**F**	**S**	**S**
7 Sep–25 Oct	11–5	**M**	·	·	·	**F**	**S**	**S**
26 Oct–1 Nov	11–3	**M**	**T**	**W**	**T**	**F**	**S**	**S**

*Open seven days a week during local school holidays.

Standen House and Garden

West Hoathly Road, East Grinstead, West Sussex RH19 4NE

Map (2) G7 1973

James and Margaret Beale chose an idyllic location with views across the Sussex countryside for their rural retreat. Designed by Philip Webb, the house is one of the finest examples of Arts and Crafts workmanship, with Morris & Co. interiors creating a warm and welcoming atmosphere. The house is dressed for a weekend stay in 1925, so you can imagine you are a guest of the family. A major restoration of the 5-hectare (12-acre) hillside garden showcases year-round seasonal highlights and an award-winning plant collection. On the wider estate, footpaths lead out into the woodlands and wider High Weald. **Note**: seasonal tours to top of water tower, £2 (including members).

Eating and shopping: William Morris-inspired gifts in the shop and online. Plant centre stocking the Standen Collection. Barn Café serving seasonal menus made from kitchen garden produce. Second-hand bookshop, woodland craft and kitchen garden barrow sales.

Making the most of your day: **Indoors** Daily introductory talks and tours. Changing exhibitions. **Outdoors** Seasonal guided walks and events. Play area. Themed family activities and trails. **Dogs**: welcome on short leads in the garden and woodlands.

Access:
House **Gardens**
Parking: 200 yards (steep hill).

Finding out more: 01342 323029 or standen@nationaltrust.org.uk

Standen House and Garden		M	T	W	T	F	S	S
House								
1 Jan–13 Feb	Tour	**M**	**T**	**W**	**T**	**F**	·	·
House, garden, café and shop*								
Open all year[1]	10–5**	**M**	**T**	**W**	**T**	**F**	**S**	**S**

*House opens at 11. Last entry to house one hour before closing. [1]Monday to Friday admission to house by guided tour only at certain times. **Closes dusk if earlier. Closed 24 and 25 December.

Standen House and Garden in West Sussex is one of the finest examples of Arts and Crafts workmanship in existence

Stoneacre

Otham, Maidstone, Kent ME15 8RS

Map (2) I6 [1928]

Medieval farmhouse surrounded by garden, orchard, rolling meadows and woodland. Home to famous designer and critic Aymer Vallance. **Note**: open Saturdays only, March to October, by tenants on behalf of the National Trust.

Finding out more: 01622 863247 or stoneacre@nationaltrust.org.uk

Stowe

Buckingham, Buckinghamshire MK18 5EQ

Map (2) D2 [1990]

The scale and beauty of Stowe is such that it has attracted visitors for over 300 years. Picture-perfect views, winding paths, lakeside walks and classical temples create a timeless landscape, reflecting the changing seasons. Full of hidden meaning and classical references, the gardens were created as an earthly paradise, and still cast their spell today.

Your visit starts at the New Inn visitor centre outside the gardens. This fusion of modern and restored 18th-century buildings was where visitors of the day were welcomed to Stowe. The sheer size and space is perfect for those who love the outdoors and enjoy walking. A short walk or a ride in a buggy takes you into the gardens, where another world awaits.

Eating and shopping: café inside New Inn, serving fresh homemade food – light lunches, cakes, soups and scones. Shop selling local products, gifts and plants, plus Restoration Ale and ceramics inspired by Stowe. Picnics welcome in gardens and wildflower paddock outside New Inn.

Making the most of your day: **Indoors** Restored 18th-century parlour rooms at New Inn. Stowe House state rooms (not National Trust) open. **Outdoors** Seasonal events, walks and trails and family activities throughout the year. Farmhouse kitchen garden. Family cycle trail. **Dogs**: welcome on leads.

Access: **Visitor centre**
Grounds
Parking: 545 yards.

Finding out more: 01280 817156 or stowe@nationaltrust.org.uk

Stowe		M	T	W	T	F	S	S
Gardens, shop, café and parlour rooms								
Open all year*	10–6**	**M**	**T**	**W**	**T**	**F**	**S**	**S**
Parkland								
Open all year	Dawn–dusk	**M**	**T**	**W**	**T**	**F**	**S**	**S**

*Landscape gardens closed 23 May but visitor centre, parkland, café and shop open. **Closes dusk if earlier. Last entry to the gardens is recommended 90 minutes before closing. Closed 25 December.

Just two of the many temples at Stowe in Buckinghamshire

Gracious Uppark House and Garden in West Sussex

Uppark House and Garden

South Harting, Petersfield,
West Sussex GU31 5QR

Map (2) E8 1954

Perched on its vantage point high on the South Downs ridge, Uppark commands views as far south as the English Channel. Outside, the intimate gardens are being gradually restored to their original 18th-century design, with plenty of space in the adjacent meadow to play and relax with a picnic. The nearby woodland is great for exploring and den-building. Uppark's Georgian interiors illustrate the comfort of life 'upstairs', in contrast to the 'downstairs' world of its servants. Highlights include one of the best examples of an 18th-century doll's-house in the country.

Eating and shopping: shop selling local products and peat-free plants. Café (licensed) serving homemade light lunches and cakes.

Making the most of your day: **Indoors** Family house trails. **Outdoors** Free garden tour every Thursday. Garden trails for families and outdoor toy chest on South Meadow. Hinton Ampner and Petworth House nearby. **Dogs**: on leads on woodland walk only. Please note: no shaded parking.

Access:
House **Gardens**
Parking: 300 yards.

Finding out more: 01730 825857 (Infoline). 01730 825415 or uppark@nationaltrust.org.uk

Uppark House and Garden		M	T	W	T	F	S	S
House*								
7 Mar–1 Nov	12:30–4:30	·	·	W	T	F	S	S
7 Nov–27 Dec	12–3	·	·	·	·	·	S	S
Garden, shop and café								
7 Mar–31 Dec	10–5**	M	T	W	T	F	S	S
Below stairs								
7 Mar–1 Nov	11–4:30	M	T	W	T	F	S	S
7 Nov–31 Dec	11–3	M	T	W	T	F	S	S

*House open daily in July and August 11 to 4:30 and on Bank Holidays. Print room open first Wednesday of each month March to October. **Property closes at dusk if earlier. Garden tours every Thursday from March to October. Closed 24 and 25 December.

The Vyne

Vyne Road, Sherborne St John, Basingstoke, Hampshire RG24 9HL

Map (2) D6 1956

Once an important Tudor palace, this atmospheric mansion has some illustrious connections, from Henry VIII to Jane Austen and J. R. R. Tolkien. Rare 16th-century interiors mix with elaborate 18th-century architecture, and there are rooms filled with treasures, including an ancient cursed ring and jewel-encrusted casket. Outside, acres of wildlife-rich gardens, meadows and woods create a wonderful space for relaxation and exploration, and a unique 'Hidden Realm' play space gives children freedom to let their imaginations take them on fantasy adventures. Sweeping lawns offer lakeside picnicking, and a short stroll reveals a cosy bird hide overlooking the water meadows. **Note**: occasional room closures for essential conservation work and filming.

Eating and shopping: tea-room serving soup and sandwiches, cakes and scones. Gift shop. Second-hand bookshop and plant sales. Picnics welcome.

Making the most of your day: **Indoors** Events and activities all year. Free guided tours, exhibitions and themed days. **Outdoors** Open-air theatre. Seasonal garden tours, trails and woodland walks. Geocaching, orienteering and inspirational 'Hidden Realm' playground. **Dogs**: welcome on short leads in woodlands and most of gardens.

Access:
Building **Grounds**
Sat Nav: not reliable, follow brown tourist signs. **Parking**: on site.

Finding out more: 01256 883858 or thevyne@nationaltrust.org.uk

The Vyne		M	T	W	T	F	S	S
Open all year	10–5*	**M**	**T**	**W**	**T**	**F**	**S**	**S**

*Closes dusk if earlier. House opens at 11 for either tour, free-flow or by timed ticket. Phone or check website for further details. Closed 24 and 25 December.

The Vyne, Hampshire: elegant both inside and out

Waddesdon Manor

Waddesdon, near Aylesbury, Buckinghamshire HP18 0JH

Map (2) D3 1957

Baron Ferdinand de Rothschild started building Waddesdon Manor in 1874 to display his outstanding collection of art treasures and entertain the fashionable world. The highest quality 18th-century French decorative arts are displayed alongside magnificent English portraits and Dutch Old Master paintings, while outside is one of the finest Victorian gardens in Britain, famous for its parterre and ornate working aviary. Today, the Manor continues its great tradition of entertainment and hospitality with a range of events celebrating food and wine. There are also opportunities to explore its history, collections and gardens through changing exhibitions and special interest days.

Note: managed by a Rothschild family charitable trust. House entrance by timed tickets only.

Eating and shopping: two licensed restaurants (not National Trust). Snacks and drinks available at the Summerhouse or Coffee Bar. Gift shop, wine shop and old-fashioned sweet shop with fudge made in our kitchens at the Stables.

Making the most of your day: **Indoors** Wide range of free activities on aspects of the house, collection and special exhibitions with experts. Rolling presentations on the Rothschilds and Waddesdon. Wine tastings. **Outdoors** Guided walks in the gardens. Woodland playground and Miss Alice's Drive Nature Trail. Special interest days and family events. Food markets and fairs. Advance booking advised.
Dogs: assistance dogs only.

Access: [access symbols]
Building [access symbols] **Grounds** [access symbols]
Parking: ¾ mile (bus transfer).

Finding out more: 01296 653226 or waddesdonmanor@nationaltrust.org.uk

Waddesdon Manor		M	T	W	T	F	S	S
Gardens, aviary, woodland playground, shops, restaurants								
10 Jan–22 Mar	10–5	·	·	·	·	·	**S**	**S**
16 Feb–20 Feb	10–5	**M**	**T**	**W**	**T**	**F**	·	·
25 Mar–31 Dec	10–5	·	·	**W**	**T**	**F**	**S**	**S**
House and wine cellars								
25 Mar–25 Oct	12–4*	·	·	**W**	**T**	**F**	**S**	**S**
11 Nov–31 Dec	11–4	·	·	**W**	**T**	**F**	**S**	**S**

*House opens one hour earlier at weekends. When house closes at 4, recommended last entry at 2:30, last tickets at 3:15. Open Bank Holiday Mondays. Open 7 April, 26 May, 26 and 27 October, 21, 22, 28 and 29 December and 1 to 3 January 2016. Closed 24 to 26 December. House operates by timed-ticket system (including members), available from booking office (01296 653226 £3 booking fee) or online at waddesdon.org.uk (tickets limited). To guarantee entry during busy periods, especially weekends, Christmas season and Bank Holidays, please book house entry tickets in advance. Admission to house must include gardens admission.

Waddesdon Manor in Buckinghamshire (above and top) boasts one of the finest Victorian gardens in Britain, as well as an outstanding collection of art treasures

The labyrinth at Wakehurst Place, West Sussex

Wakehurst Place

Ardingly, Haywards Heath,
West Sussex RH17 6TN

Map (2) G7 1964

This beautiful garden is the country estate of the Royal Botanic Gardens, Kew. It is internationally significant, not only for its collections but also for its scientific research and plant conservation. The glorious gardens, wetland and woodland contain plants from around the world. You may even spot kingfishers in their natural habitat at the Loder Valley Nature Reserve. A wide range of activities and events takes place throughout the year and a 'must see' is Kew's Millennium Seed Bank, a unique venue where science and horticulture work side-by-side to deliver Kew's mission: saving plants from around the world. **Note**: funded and managed by the Royal Botanic Gardens, Kew. International National Trust membership cards not accepted. **Parking charges apply (including members).**

Eating and shopping: Seed Café serving coffee, pastries, cakes, panini, soups and sandwiches. Stables Restaurant offering hot and cold food, as well as homemade cakes served all day. Wakehurst Bakery selling freshly baked bread and cakes. Gift shop. Plant centre (not National Trust).

Making the most of your day: free daily guided tours. Seasonal festival programme. Willow sculpture trail. Adventurous Journeys and natural play areas for families. Seasonal soup and stroll. Kingfisher, badger and bat-watching (charges apply). Various courses. **Dogs**: assistance dogs only.

Access: **Buildings**
Grounds
Parking: 50 yards.

Finding out more: 01444 894066 or wakehurst@kew.org. kew.org

Wakehurst Place		M	T	W	T	F	S	S
1 Jan–28 Feb	10–4:30*	M	T	W	T	F	S	S
1 Mar–31 Oct	10–6*	M	T	W	T	F	S	S
1 Nov–23 Dec	10–4:30*	M	T	W	T	F	S	S
26 Dec–31 Dec	10–4:30*	M	T	W	T	·	S	S

*Mansion and Millennium Seed Bank close one hour earlier. Shop closes 4:30 from 2 January to February, 5:30 March to October, 5 from November to 1 January 2016. Catering facilities available until 4 from 2 January to February, 5:30 March to October, 4:15 November to 1 January 2016. Property closed 24 and 25 December. Shop closed Easter Sunday. UK National Trust members free (reciprocal agreements made between the Trust and other parties do not apply).

West Green House Garden

West Green, Hartley Wintney, Hampshire RG27 8JB

Map (2) D6 1957

Nationally acclaimed gardens created by writer and designer Marylyn Abbott; celebrated walled garden and potager, exuberant planting and dazzling colour. **Note**: maintained on behalf of the National Trust by Marylyn Abbott. Facilities not National Trust.

Finding out more: 01252 844611 or westgreenhouse@nationaltrust.org.uk

West Wycombe Park, Village and Hill

West Wycombe, Buckinghamshire

Map (2) E4 1943

Alongside this historic village lies an exquisite country mansion. This lavish home and serene landscape garden reflect the wealth and personality of its creator, the infamous Sir Francis Dashwood, founder of the Hellfire Club. Still home to the Dashwood family and their fine collection, it remains a busy, private estate. **Note**: opened in partnership with the Dashwood family. Hellfire Caves and Café (not National Trust) are privately owned and members must pay admission fees.

Eating and shopping: refreshments available at the Hellfire Caves and Café and in the village (none National Trust). Variety of shops in National Trust village.

Making the most of your day: centuries-old village high street with historic cottages, coaching inns and courtyards. Nearby West Wycombe Hill: wildflower meadows, iconic Golden Ball and Mausoleum, far-reaching views and woodland walks. **Dogs**: welcome on West Wycombe Hill. Assistance dogs only in park.

Access: **Building**
Sat Nav: use HP14 3AJ. **Parking**: 250 yards.

Finding out more: 01494 755571 (Infoline). 01494 513569 or westwycombe@nationaltrust.org.uk

West Wycombe		M	T	W	T	F	S	S
House and grounds								
1 Jun–31 Aug	2–6	**M**	**T**	**W**	**T**	·	·	**S**
Grounds only								
1 Apr–31 Aug	2–6	**M**	**T**	**W**	**T**	·	·	**S**

Last admission 45 minutes before closing. Entry to house during June, July and August, Monday to Thursday, is by 40-minute guided tour with timed ticket. Free-flow system operates on Sundays and Bank Holidays.

Exploring West Wycombe Park in Buckinghamshire

Winchester City Mill

Bridge Street, Winchester,
Hampshire SO23 9BH

Map (2) D7 1929

For centuries, this ancient working watermill in the heart of historic Winchester has used the power of the River Itchen to mill stone-ground flour. A tranquil haven, it attracts plenty of wildlife, from trout and water voles to visiting otter families, which can be viewed on CCTV. **Note**: nearest toilet 220 yards (not National Trust).

Eating and shopping: shop selling local produce, gifts and books and our freshly milled wholemeal flour.

Making the most of your day: events and activities for families and children (school holidays). Milling and baking demonstrations and workshops. **Dogs**: assistance dogs only.

Access: Building
Sat Nav: do not use. **Parking**: at Chesil car park or park and ride.

Finding out more: 01962 870057 or winchestercitymill@nationaltrust.org.uk

Winchester City Mill		M	T	W	T	F	S	S
1 Jan–24 Dec	10–4*	**M**	**T**	**W**	**T**	**F**	**S**	**S**

*16 February to 1 November, open until 5.

Winkworth Arboretum

Hascombe Road, Godalming, Surrey GU8 4AD

Map (2) F7 1952

The National Trust's only arboretum is the result of one man's vision and passion. Dr Wilfrid Fox used the wooded valley and its lakes as a canvas to experiment with planting trees to 'paint a picture'. The fruits of his labour are now an award-winning collection of over 1,000 different plants, which offer stunning combinations of colour with every changing season. Famous for vibrant autumnal foliage and endless carpets of bluebells in spring; the azaleas, magnolias, witch hazel and snowdrops mean Winkworth is worth visiting all year for beautiful scenery, a picnic or the fun family events. **Note**: steep slopes; banks of lake and wetlands only partially fenced.

Some places are easy to get to on foot or by public transport. See page 3

Eating and shopping: small tea-room offers freshly baked scones, cakes and light lunches.

Making the most of your day: events and guided walks throughout the year. **Dogs**: welcome on leads.

Access: Grounds
Parking: on site, 100 yards.

Finding out more: 01483 208477 or winkwortharboretum@nationaltrust.org.uk

Winkworth Arboretum		M	T	W	T	F	S	S
1 Jan–31 Jan	10–5*	M	T	W	T	F	S	S
1 Feb–31 Mar	10–5	M	T	W	T	F	S	S
1 Apr–31 Oct	10–6	M	T	W	T	F	S	S
1 Nov–31 Dec	10–5*	M	T	W	T	F	S	S

Tea-room closes 30 minutes earlier than arboretum. *Closes at dusk if earlier; local closing times posted at the property. Car-park gates locked at closing time. Closed 25 December.

Three very different gems: Winchester City Mill, Hampshire (opposite), Winkworth Arboretum, Surrey (above) and Woolbeding Gardens in West Sussex (right)

Woolbeding Gardens

Midhurst, West Sussex GU29 9RR

Map (2) E7 1956

Described by Disraeli as 'the greenest valley with the prettiest river in the world', Woolbeding is a modern masterpiece, with colour-themed garden rooms and a landscape garden. Stunning views over the River Rother and beautiful floral displays are just a few of the surprises at this horticultural haven. **Note**: **booking essential**. Access by park-and-ride minibus from Midhurst only.

Eating and shopping: Coffee Bar serving sandwiches, cakes and hot and cold drinks. Shop selling gardening books, gifts and plants.

Making the most of your day: introductory talks, enchanted grotto and croquet lawn. Nearby properties include Petworth House and Park, Uppark House and Garden, and Hinton Ampner. **Dogs**: assistance dogs only.

Access: Reception Garden
Parking: no local parking or on site. Access by park and ride minibus from Midhurst only.

Finding out more: 0844 249 1895 or woolbedinggardens@nationaltrust.org.uk

Woolbeding Gardens		M	T	W	T	F	S	S
9 Apr–25 Sep	10:30–4:30	·	·	·	T	F	·	·

Advance booking essential: 0844 249 1895.
Access by park-and-ride only from Midhurst.

Map 2

London

Fenton House and Garden, Hampstead

Carlyle's House

24 Cheyne Row, Chelsea, London SW3 5HL

Map (2) G5 1936

A joy for anyone interested in the Victorian period and its leading characters, this Chelsea house was the home of a Victorian celebrity couple. Preserved since 1895, the house presents an entertaining view of the Carlyles' illustrious friends, including Charles Dickens, Charles Darwin, John Ruskin, the Brownings and Elizabeth Gaskell.

Access: **Building** **Grounds**
Parking: limited on street (metered).

Finding out more: 020 7352 7087 or carlyleshouse@nationaltrust.org.uk

Carlyle's House		M	T	W	T	F	S	S
7 Mar–1 Nov	11–4:30	·	·	**W**	**T**	**F**	**S**	**S**

Open Bank Holiday Mondays.

Carlyle's House, Chelsea: detail from 'A Chelsea Interior'

Eastbury Manor House

Eastbury Square, Barking, Essex IG11 9SN

Map (2) G5 1918

Remarkable brick-built Tudor gentry house in an unusual setting, completed around 1573 and little-altered since. **Note**: managed by London Borough of Barking and Dagenham. Some rooms closed for private functions. Special events and family days are charged at an additional cost.

Finding out more: 020 8227 2942 or eastburymanor@nationaltrust.org.uk

 For other ways to get involved go to nationaltrust.org.uk/get-involved/volunteer

Fenton House and Garden

Hampstead Grove, Hampstead, London NW3 6SP

Map (2) G5 [1952]

This 1686 town house is filled with world-class decorative and fine collections of musical instruments, ceramics, paintings, textiles and furniture. The ever-changing horticultural gem that is our garden, includes an orchard, kitchen garden, rose garden, formal terraces and lawns, and never fails to delight.

Fenton House and Garden, Hampstead (below and top right), contains world-class collections of fine art and musical instruments

Eating and shopping: small shop area selling local and National Trust items, garden plants and produce.

Making the most of your day: garden events, including annual Apple Weekend. Joint tickets with 2 Willow Road available. Combine with a visit to one of Hampstead's National Trust Partner attractions. **Dogs**: assistance dogs only.

Access: **Building** **Grounds**
Parking: none on site.

Finding out more: 020 7435 3471 or fentonhouse@nationaltrust.org.uk

Fenton House and Garden		M	T	W	T	F	S	S
28 Feb–1 Nov	11–5	·	·	**W**	**T**	**F**	**S**	**S**
28 Nov–20 Dec	11–4	·	·	·	·	·	**S**	**S**
Open Bank Holiday Mondays.								

George Inn

The George Inn Yard, 77 Borough High Street, Southwark, London SE1 1NH

Map (2) G5 [1937]

This public house, dating from the 17th century, is London's last remaining galleried inn. **Note**: leased to a private company. No table bookings (telephone for details).

Finding out more: 020 7407 2056 or georgeinn@nationaltrust.org.uk

Ham House and Garden

Ham Street, Ham, Richmond, Surrey TW10 7RS

Map (2) F5 1948

This rare and atmospheric Stuart house sits on the banks of the River Thames in Richmond. Internationally recognised for its superb collection of paintings, furniture and textiles – largely acquired 400 years ago – the house is reputed to be one of the most haunted in Britain. Outside, the restored 17th-century garden includes a productive kitchen garden containing many heritage crops, the formal 'Wilderness', complete with summerhouses, and many beautiful spots perfect for a picnic. **Note**: to protect our fragile textiles, some rooms have low light levels.

Whether exploring inside or out, there is so much to delight at the atmospheric Ham House and Garden in Richmond (above and below)

Eating and shopping: the recently refurbished Orangery Café serves light lunches and teas, using much of the produce from the walled kitchen garden. The Tea Shed sells refreshments (seasonal). Picnics welcome. Gift shop, including plant sales. Second-hand bookshop.

Making the most of your day: events throughout the year **Indoors** Ghost tours. Interactive rooms 'below stairs'. Family art activities and trails. **Outdoors** Free garden tours. Downloadable trails from local Underground and Overground stations to Ham. **Dogs**: assistance dogs only.

Access:
House **Café**
Grounds
Sat Nav: takes you to stables on Ham Street nearby. **Parking**: 380 yards (not National Trust) and on street.

Finding out more: 020 8940 1950 or hamhouse@nationaltrust.org.uk

Ham House and Garden		M	T	W	T	F	S	S
House								
23 Feb–12 Mar[1]	Tour	**M**	**T**	**W**	**T**	**F**	**S**	**S**
13 Mar–1 Nov[2]	12–4	**M**	**T**	**W**	**T**	**F**	**S**	**S**
Garden, below stairs, shop and café*								
Open all year	10–5**	**M**	**T**	**W**	**T**	**F**	**S**	**S**

[1]Guided tours of selected rooms, last tour 3:15, numbers limited, no free-flow. [2]**Fridays only by guided tour.**
*Below stairs open 10:30 to 4:30, or dusk if earlier – access to these rooms occasionally by tour. **Closes dusk if earlier. Whole property closed 24 and 25 December.

Morden Hall Park

Morden Hall Road, Morden, London SM4 5JD

Map (2) G5 1942

Hidden behind Grade II listed walls lies an Arcadian country estate, now enveloped by London but saved by a far-sighted philanthropist. This tranquil former deer-park – one of the few remaining estates which lined the River Wandle during its industrial heyday – now serves as London's gateway to the countryside. The park is yours to explore and enjoy whatever the season. There is so much to discover, from wildlife-rich meadows and atmospheric wetlands, to scented roses in the historic rose garden. At the heart of the park lies the handsome Victorian stableyard, now a sustainable visitor centre, powered using renewable energy. **Note**: admission charges apply (including members) to some events.

Eating and shopping: recently refurbished Potting Shed Café serving hot lunches, teas and cakes, and Potting Shed Shop selling gift range. Stableyard Café offering light refreshments and local ice-cream. Second-hand bookshop in the stables, artisan craft workshops and garden centre. Picnics welcome.

Making the most of your day: events throughout the year, including annual country show, open-air cinema and theatre. Family trails and tours. Natural play area. Unique recumbent bikes for hire. **Dogs**: welcome on leads around buildings and mown grass, including rose garden. Within sight elsewhere.

Access:
Snuff Mill
Visitor centre, café and shop
Parkland
Parking: next to garden centre.

Finding out more: 020 8545 6850 or mordenhallpark@nationaltrust.org.uk

Morden Hall Park	Open every day all year*

Rose Garden, stableyard and car park open 8 to 6. Garden centre open 9 to 6 Monday to Saturday, and 10:30 to 4:30 on Sundays. Potting Shed Café open 9 to 6 daily. *Closed 25 and 26 December. Stableyard Café opening dependent on weather and season.

Once a deer-park, tranquil Morden Hall Park in South London is now an oasis in the bustling city

As one of the last surviving country estates in London, Osterley Park and House in Isleworth offers a glimpse of a time before the city's boundaries spread so far

Osterley Park and House

Jersey Road, Isleworth, London TW7 4RB

Map (2) F5 1949

Osterley Park and House is one of the last surviving country estates in London. Only a short distance from the big city, you can explore the 18th-century house, designed by architect Robert Adam, and its beautiful gardens and hundreds of acres of parkland. A collection of rare family portraits and treasures has recently returned home to Osterley: come and celebrate this reunion. iTouch guides bring the stunning interiors to life. With our park, gardens and café now open all year, you can snooze in deckchairs on the Temple Lawn in summer and enjoy brisk walks in the vibrant Winter Garden.

Eating and shopping: Stables Café, serving light meals and homemade cakes with indoor and outdoor seating. Gift shop, second-hand bookshop and plant sales in the Stables courtyard. Free wi-fi. Picnics welcome in the park.

Making the most of your day: **Indoors** Year-round events and family activities, including free daily talks and tours and behind-the-scenes tours (Mondays and Tuesdays). **Outdoors** Adventure play trail and rope swings in the garden. **Dogs**: welcome in parkland areas, with designated on and off-lead areas.

Access: **House** **Garden**
Sat Nav: enter Jersey Road and TW7 4RD.
Parking: 400 yards.

Finding out more: 020 8232 5050 or osterley@nationaltrust.org.uk

Osterley Park and House		M	T	W	T	F	S	S
House and shop*								
28 Feb–1 Nov	11–5**	M	T	W	T	F	S	S
5 Dec–13 Dec	12–4	·	·	·	·	·	S	S
Garden and café								
Open all year	10–5†	M	T	W	T	F	S	S

*House: Monday and Tuesday 'behind-the-scenes' guided tours and only basement floor open. **House and shop open 12 to 4 from 28 February to 29 March and 28 September to 1 November. **Shop also open weekends in November.** †Closes dusk if earlier. Closed 25 and 26 December.

Places may occasionally close for events or bad weather

Rainham Hall

The Broadway, Rainham, London RM13 9YN

Map (2) H5 1949

A charming early 18th-century merchant's house, Rainham Hall has been home to a rich array of individuals over its 286-year history. One by one their stories will bring the house and garden to life, transforming Rainham Hall into a place to relax, inhabit, learn and participate. **Note**: property undergoing major restoration project, so opening date subject to change.

Eating and shopping: after major restoration, the stable block now houses a café serving seasonally inspired light lunches, home-baked cakes, barista coffee, teas and soft drinks. Gifts, guidebooks and postcards available.

Making the most of your day: **Indoors** Guided history tour and craft workshop. **Outdoors** One of London's largest orchards, beautiful garden and wide open skies. **Dogs**: assistance dogs only.

Access: **House** **Café** **Garden**

Parking: 300 yards, not National Trust.

Finding out more: 01708 525579 or rainhamhall@nationaltrust.org.uk

Rainham Hall		M	T	W	T	F	S	S
Stable block café and garden								
1 Aug–31 Dec	10–5*	M	T	W	T	F	S	S
House								
1 Aug–31 Oct	10–5	·	·	W	T	F	S	S
1 Nov–20 Dec	10–5	·	·	·	·	F	S	S

The property is undergoing major restoration so opening date subject to change. *Gardens close at dusk if earlier. Café and gardens closed 25 and 26 December.

The Red House in Kent (top right), is the only house that William Morris not only commissioned and created, but then lived in

Red House

Red House Lane, Bexleyheath, Kent DA6 8JF

Map (2) H5 2003

The only house commissioned, created and lived in by William Morris, founder of the Arts and Crafts Movement, Red House is a building of extraordinary architectural and social significance. When it was completed in 1860, it was described by Edward Burne-Jones as 'the beautifullest place on earth'.
Note: largely unfurnished, but contains original wall-paintings, features and furniture by Morris, Webb and Burne-Jones.

Eating and shopping: shop selling Red House specific and other Morris-related gifts and souvenirs. Café in original kitchen serving refreshments. Plants and second-hand books for sale. Picnics welcome in orchard.

Making the most of your day: **Indoors** Exhibition. Family fun in school holidays. Carols at Christmas. **Outdoors** Events, including Easter Fun, summer arts and crafts fair and autumn Apple Day. Garden games. **Dogs**: assistance dogs only.

Access: [icons] **Building** [icon]
Grounds [icons]
Sat Nav: use DA6 8HL – Danson Park car park.
Parking: Danson Park, 1 mile. Charge at weekends and Bank Holidays (including members).

Finding out more: 020 8304 9878 or redhouse@nationaltrust.org.uk

Red House		M	T	W	T	F	S	S
18 Feb–1 Nov	11–5	·	·	**W**	**T**	**F**	**S**	**S**
6 Nov–20 Dec	11–4:30	·	·	·	·	**F**	**S**	**S**

Free-flow 1:30 to 5 (booking not required). Admission by guided tour only at 11, 11:30, 12, 12:30 and 1 (booking essential). Last admission 45 minutes before closing. Last serving in tea-room 4:30 (4 in winter). Open Bank Holiday Mondays.

Sutton House

2 and 4 Homerton High Street, Hackney, London E9 6JQ

Map (2) G5 [icons] 1938

In the midst of modern-day Hackney, Sutton House – once the home of a Tudor courtier – is a window onto London's history

A Tudor courtier's house in thriving modern-day Hackney. With linenfold oak panelling, 17th-century wall-paintings and a tranquil courtyard, this is a haven in the heart of the city and a window onto London's history. Newly refurbished café and second-hand bookshop.

Eating and shopping: tea-room serving cream tea on vintage crockery. Second-hand books for sale in the dining-room.

Making the most of your day: Georgian panels can be opened to reveal Tudor arches. Family treasure chests to delve into. Tudor kitchen. Family days, craft fairs and cinema nights.
Dogs: assistance dogs only.

Access: [icons]
Building [icons]
Parking: no parking on site. Limited metered parking nearby.

Finding out more: 020 8986 2264 or suttonhouse@nationaltrust.org.uk

Sutton House		M	T	W	T	F	S	S
5 Feb–20 Dec*	12–5	·	·	**W**	**T**	**F**	**S**	**S**

*Open daily in August. Open Bank Holiday Mondays and Good Friday. Property regularly used by local community groups – rooms always open as advertised, but call if you would like to visit during a quiet time. Occasional 'Museum Lates' opening.

Why not share your pictures with us? #nationaltrust

575 Wandsworth Road, Lambeth, is a work of art

575 Wandsworth Road

575 Wandsworth Road, Lambeth,
London SW8 3JD

Map (2) G5 2010

Modest terraced house, transformed into a work of art, with a breathtaking hand-carved fretwork interior. **Note**: sorry no toilets. Access by guided tour only (booking fee for non-members).

Access: **House**
Parking: none on site.

Finding out more: 0844 249 1895 (bookings). 020 7720 9459 (enquiries) or 575wandsworthroad@nationaltrust.org.uk

575 Wandsworth Road		M	T	W	T	F	S	S
House tours								
1 Mar–1 Nov*	Tour	·	·	**W**	·	**F**	**S**	**S**

*House closed last Sunday of every month. Admission by booked guided tour only, booking essential (places limited). Tours on Wednesdays at 6:30, Fridays at 1:30 and 3:30, and Saturdays and Sundays at 11, 1:30 and 3:30.

2 Willow Road

Hampstead, London NW3 1TH

Map (2) G5 1994

This late 1930s house, an architect's vision of the future, paints a vivid picture of the creative and social circles in which Ernö and Ursula Goldfinger moved. Today you can explore the intimate and evocative interiors, innovative designs, intriguing personal possessions and impressive 20th-century art collection.
Note: nearest toilet at local pub.

Eating and shopping: a small table in the entrance hall has property-related items available for sale.

Making the most of your day: events, including late openings and tours. Fenton House nearby (joint tickets available). Combine your visit with one of Hampstead's National Trust Partners. **Dogs**: assistance dogs only.

Access: **Building**
Parking: very limited on-street parking nearby, pay and display (charge including members).

Finding out more: 020 7435 6166 or 2willowroad@nationaltrust.org.uk

2 Willow Road		M	T	W	T	F	S	S
28 Feb–1 Nov	11–5	·	·	**W**	**T**	**F**	**S**	**S**

Entry by guided tour only at 11, 12, 1 and 2 (places limited with tickets available on day at door only). Wednesday to Friday tours at 11 occasionally booked by groups. 3 to 5, self-guided viewing (timed entry when busy). Open Bank Holiday Mondays.

The entrance hall at 2 Willow Road in Hampstead

National Trust *Partner*

London partners

'National Trust Partner' is an exciting venture between the National Trust and a selection of small, independent heritage attractions and museums within London. The Partnership aims to bring enhanced benefits to National Trust members living in London or for those visiting the capital for a day out, helping to provide increased opportunities to explore our rich and diverse heritage.

Entry charges: 50 per cent discount for members on presentation of a valid membership card. For full visiting information (and access), please see individual National Trust Partner websites.

Benjamin Franklin House

The world's only remaining home of Benjamin Franklin, featuring a unique 'Historical Experience'.

Underground: Charing Cross or Embankment.
Train: Charing Cross.

Finding out more: 020 7925 1405 or benjaminfranklinhouse.org

Bevis Marks Synagogue

Dated 1701, Britain's oldest surviving synagogue contains Cromwellian and Queen Anne furniture.

Underground: Liverpool Street or Aldgate.
Train: Liverpool Street.

Finding out more: 020 7626 1274 or bevismarks.org.uk

Danson House

Beautiful Georgian villa with sumptuous interiors, built for pleasure and entertaining.

Train: Bexleyheath.

Finding out more: 020 8303 6699 or dansonhouse.org.uk

The Fan Museum

Unique collection of more than 4,000 fans, housed in elegant Georgian buildings.

Train: Cutty Sark (DLR) or Greenwich.

Finding out more: 020 8305 1441 or thefanmuseum.org.uk

Dr Johnson's House

Late 17th-century townhouse, once home to lexicographer and wit Samuel Johnson.

Underground: Chancery Lane or Blackfriars.
Train: Blackfriars.

Finding out more: 020 7353 3745 or drjohnsonshouse.org

Foundling Museum

Nationally important collection of 18th-century art, interiors, social history and music.

Underground: Russell Square, King's Cross St Pancras or Euston. **Train**: King's Cross, St Pancras or Euston.

Finding out more: 020 7841 3600 or foundlingmuseum.org.uk

Freud Museum London

The final home of pioneering psychoanalysts Sigmund Freud and his daughter Anna.

Underground: Finchley Road.
Train: Finchley Road and Frognal.

Finding out more: 020 7435 2002 or freud.org.uk

Leighton House Museum

Restored home of Victorian painter Lord Leighton, with priceless Islamic tile collection.

Underground: High Street Kensington or Holland Park.

Finding out more: 020 7602 3316 or leightonhouse.co.uk

Hall Place and Gardens

Stunning Tudor house with magnificent gardens.

Train: Bexley.

Finding out more: 01322 526574 or hallplace.org.uk

Museum of Brands

Intense experience of consumer culture: journey from Victorian times to your childhood.

Underground: Notting Hill Gate.

Finding out more: 020 7908 0880 or museumofbrands.com

The Old Operating Theatre Museum

Unique, atmospheric museum, hidden in the timbered Herb Garret of St Thomas's Church.

Underground: London Bridge.
Train: London Bridge.

Finding out more: 020 7188 2679 or thegarret.org.uk

Strawberry Hill House

Horace Walpole's beautifully restored Gothic-revival castle by the Thames in Twickenham.

Train: Strawberry Hill.

Finding out more: 020 8744 1241 or strawberryhillhouse.org.uk

National Trust
Partner

London partners

Entry charges: 50 per cent discount for members on presentation of a valid membership card. For full visiting information (and access), please see individual National Trust Partner websites.

Map 3

East of England

Blakeney National Nature Reserve, Norfolk

Outdoors in the East of England

Whether you love getting active, prefer a gentler pace, or simply want to be wowed by wildlife, you will be spoilt for choice in this spectacular region.

Blakeney National Nature Reserve

near Morston, Norfolk

Map (3) I3 1912

Wide open spaces and uninterrupted views of this unspoilt coastline make for an inspiring visit at any time of year. The reserve is an internationally important nature reserve hosting a range of flora and fauna; most notably the spectacular displays of the breeding seal and tern colony on Blakeney Point. **Note**: nearest toilet at Morston Quay and Blakeney Quay (not National Trust).

Eating and shopping: refreshments and seafood stall (not National Trust) at Morston Quay. Seafood, including seasonal mussels and crabs from local suppliers (not National Trust). Nearby pubs and hotels (not National Trust) offering locally themed menus.

Making the most of your day: visitor centres at Morston Quay and Lifeboat House on Blakeney Point. Extensive coastal walks on the Norfolk Coast Path. Guided walks available. Ferry trips (not National Trust) to Blakeney Point.

Dogs: some restrictions (particularly Blakeney Point), 1 April to mid-August.

Access: **Information centre** **Lifeboat House**
Sat Nav: use NR25 7BH for Morston Quay.
Parking: at Green Way Stiffkey Saltmarshes, Morston Quay and Blakeney Quay (not National Trust).

Finding out more: 01263 740241 or blakeneypoint@nationaltrust.org.uk

Blakeney		M	T	W	T	F	S	S
Lifeboat House (Blakeney Point)								
30 Mar–1 Nov	Dawn–dusk	**M**	**T**	**W**	**T**	**F**	**S**	**S**

Lifeboat House and toilets (Blakeney Point) open dawn to dusk. Refreshment kiosk (not National Trust) and Information Centre at Morston Quay open according to tides and weather.

Brancaster Estate

near Brancaster, Norfolk

Map (3) H3 1923

The estate encompasses Branodunum, an intriguing Scheduled Ancient Monument, and the golden sands at Brancaster Beach – ideal for sand castles. **Note**: for beach car park (not National Trust) use Sat Nav PE31 8AX. Nearest toilet Brancaster Beach. Natural England manages Scolt Head Island National Nature Reserve.

Finding out more: 01263 740241 or brancaster@nationaltrust.org.uk

Blakeney National Nature Reserve, Norfolk, is internationally important for its flora and fauna

Copt Hall Marshes

near Little Wigborough, Essex

Map (3) I9 1989

Working farm on the remote and beautiful Blackwater Estuary – a fantastic birdwatching spot, important for overwintering species. **Note**: for Sat Nav use CO5 7RD.

Finding out more: 01376 562226 or copthall@nationaltrust.org.uk

Danbury Commons and Blakes Wood

near Danbury, Essex

Map (3) H9 1953

Varied countryside, ranging from the lowland heath of Danbury Common to ancient woodland with stunning spring flowers at Blakes Wood. **Note**: sorry no toilets. Sat Nav: for Danbury Commons use CM3 4JH and for Blakes Wood use CM3 4AU. Danbury Commons main car park closes dusk.

Finding out more: 01245 227662 or danbury@nationaltrust.org.uk

Dunstable Downs and the Whipsnade Estate

near Dunstable, Bedfordshire

Map (3) E8 1928

Rich in wildlife, with acres of space to enjoy. Great for kite-flying and easy access to a variety of walks. Open all year round, so you can return to see the ever-changing scenery. **Note**: Chilterns Gateway Centre is owned by Central Bedfordshire Council and managed by the National Trust.

The windcatcher at Dunstable Downs in Bedfordshire

Eating and shopping: seasonal and regional products, kites and children's toys and activities for sale. Café serving locally produced food to eat in or take away – including the famous Bedfordshire Clanger.

Making the most of your day: events, including annual Kite Festival in July. Nature trail and playscape in Chute Wood. Waymarked routes. **Dogs**: under close control, on leads near livestock and ground-nesting birds.

Access:
Chilterns Gateway Centre **Dunstable Downs**
Sat Nav: use LU6 2GY (or LU6 2TA for older equipment). **Parking**: at Dunstable Downs, off B4541, and Whipsnade crossroads (Whipsnade Heath), junction of B4541 and B4540.

Finding out more: 01582 500920 or dunstabledowns@nationaltrust.org.uk

Dunstable Downs
Chilterns Gateway Centre: open 9:30 to 5 until November. November to February closes at 4. Closed 24 and 25 December. Please contact the centre for extended opening times in July and August.

Dunwich Heath and Beach in Suffolk: heather and gorse provide a blanket of vibrant colour above the gently curving sand of the shoreline

Dunwich Heath and Beach

Dunwich, Saxmundham, Suffolk

Map (3) K6 1968

A precious landscape on the Suffolk coast, Dunwich Heath offers peace and quiet and a true sense of being at one with nature. Within an Area of Outstanding Natural Beauty there is an abundance of wildlife to discover, as well as scarce species such as the Dartford warbler and nightjar. Quiet and serene, wild and dramatic, this is always an inspiring visit. Throughout the year we have a number of activities designed to deepen your understanding of this precious landscape, and our Dunwich Discovery app will help you plan and make the most of your visit.

Eating and shopping: clifftop tea-room serving breakfast, lunch, Sunday roasts, homemade cakes (gluten-free available) and ice-cream. Why not join the Scone Club to experience the amazing variety? Gift shop selling local products, National Trust best sellers, coastal-themed gifts and Dunwich-branded items. Picnic area.

Making the most of your day: self-guided trails, birdwatching and ranger walks. Family activities, including geocaching, pond dipping, bug hunting and nature trails. Heath Barn discovery area, children's play area and family beach. **Dogs**: welcome (*Woof* guide available).

Access: **Grounds**
Sat Nav: use IP17 3DJ. **Parking**: on site.

Finding out more: 01728 648501 or dunwichheath@nationaltrust.org.uk

Dunwich Heath and Beach		M	T	W	T	F	S	S
Tea-room								
1 Jan–2 Jan	10:30–3	·	·	·	T	F	·	·
28 Dec–30 Dec	10:30–3	M	T	W	·	·	·	·
Tea-room and shop								
3 Jan–15 Feb	10:30–3	·	·	·	·	·	S	S
18 Feb–1 Mar	10:30–3	·	·	W	T	F	S	S
4 Mar–29 Mar	10–4	·	·	W	T	F	S	S
1 Apr–30 Sep	10–5	M	T	W	T	F	S	S
1 Oct–31 Oct	10–4	·	·	W	T	F	S	S
1 Nov–27 Dec	10:30–3	·	·	·	·	·	S	S

Heath: open every day all year dawn to dusk. Tea-room may stay open later in summer.

Hatfield Forest

near Bishop's Stortford, Essex

Map (3) G8 1924

When Henry I established a royal hunting forest here in 1100, he could little have guessed that almost a millennium later it would be the best survivor of its kind in the world. The fine ancient trees are managed using ancient techniques and beneath them descendants of the original herd of fallow deer still roam. You can hire a boat or a bike in the summer or take a walk and enjoy the wide open plains, grazed by Red Poll cows. A great place for a family day out, with enough open space to ensure one can always find quiet.

Eating and shopping: shop selling local gifts, guidebook and maps, as well as Hatfield Forest venison and Red Poll beef. Café selling a wide range of hot and cold refreshments, with covered and outdoor dining area.

Making the most of your day: events programme. Trail bike and rowing boat hire available. Why not download our free mobile app with interactive map (iTunes/android) before you visit, or borrow a pre-loaded tablet? **Dogs**: welcome under control. On leads in lake area and near livestock.

Access: **Grounds**
Sat Nav: use CM22 6NE. **Parking**: on site.

Finding out more: 01279 874040 (Infoline). 01279 870678 or hatfieldforest@nationaltrust.org.uk

Hatfield Forest		M	T	W	T	F	S	S
Café								
1 Jan–22 Mar	10–3:30	·	·	W	T	F	S	S
23 Mar–1 Nov	9–5	M	T	W	T	F	S	S
4 Nov–31 Dec	10–3:30	·	·	W	T	F	S	S

Café and shop open daily 10 to 3:30 during February and December school holidays. Car parks open all year from 9, car parking limited in winter. Café closed 25 December. Shop closed 25 and 26 December.

Heigham Holmes

near Martham, Norfolk

Map (3) K5 1987

Remote island nature reserve, with grazing marshes and ditches, supporting the wildlife of this internationally important and vast broadland landscape. **Note**: admission by guided visits only (booking essential), due to restricted access via floating river crossing. Charge (including members).

Finding out more: 01493 393450 or heighamholmes@nationaltrust.org.uk

The wide open spaces within Hatfield Forest, Essex, are perfect for an active day out or just quiet reflection

Morven Park

Great North Road, near Potters Bar, Hertfordshire

Map (3) F9 1928

On the site of the original Potters Bar, these eight hectares (20 acres) of parkland are over 150 years old. **Note**: sorry no toilet. For Sat Nav use EN6 1HS.

Finding out more: 07795 126728 or morvenpark@nationaltrust.org.uk

Northey Island

near Maldon, Essex

Map (3) I9 1978

A peaceful retreat in the Blackwater Estuary, important for overwintering birds, Northey is also the oldest recorded battlefield in Britain. **Note**: access by causeway, so restricted by tides. Telephone in advance to arrange your visit. For Sat Nav use CM9 6PP.

Finding out more: 01621 853142 or northeyisland@nationaltrust.org.uk

Orford Ness National Nature Reserve

Orford, Woodbridge, Suffolk

Map (3) K7 1993

This is Suffolk's secret coast, only reached by National Trust ferry. Wild, remote and exposed, the 'Island' contains the ruined remnants of a disturbing past. Ranked among the most important shingle features in the world, rare and fragile wildlife thrives where weapons, including atomic bombs, were once tested and perfected.

One of the mysterious 'Pagodas' at Orford Ness National Nature Reserve in Suffolk

Note: limited tickets. Steep, slippery steps, long distances. Hazardous debris. Limited access: 'pagodas' only on tours. Charge for ferry crossing (including members).

Eating and shopping: cafés and pubs in village (none National Trust). Fresh fish available at quay. Local smokehouses.

Making the most of your day: guided tours and photography tours give safe access to Atomic Weapons Research Establishment site (booking essential for all tours).
Dogs: assistance dogs only.

Access: **Buildings** **Trails**
Sat Nav: use IP12 2NU. **Parking**: at Quay Street, not National Trust (charge including members), 150 yards to Trust Orford Quay office to buy ferry ticket.

Finding out more: 01728 648024 (Infoline). 01394 450900 (tour bookings) or orfordness@nationaltrust.org.uk

Orford Ness		M	T	W	T	F	S	S
4 Apr–27 Jun	10–2	·	·	·	·	·	**S**	·
30 Jun–26 Sep	10–2	·	**T**	**W**	**T**	**F**	**S**	·
3 Oct–31 Oct	10–2	·	·	·	·	·	**S**	·

The only access is by National Trust ferry from Orford Quay, with boats crossing regularly to the Ness between 10 and 2 only, the last ferry leaving the Ness at 5. Main visitor trail (Red Route) always available, other routes open seasonally.

Pin Mill

near Chelmondiston, Suffolk

Map (3) J8 1978

A woodland and heathland restoration site. A number of footpaths from the village with panoramic views over the River Orwell. **Note**: for Sat Nav use IP9 1JW.

Finding out more: 01206 298260 or pinmill@nationaltrust.org.uk

Rayleigh Mount

Rayleigh, Essex

Map (3) I10 1923

Medieval motte and bailey castle site, with adjacent windmill housing historical exhibition. **Note**: exhibition in windmill operated by Rochford District Council. For Sat Nav use SS6 7ED.

Finding out more: 01284 747500 or rayleighmount@nationaltrust.org.uk

Sharpenhoe

Sharpenhoe Road, Streatley, Bedfordshire

Map (3) F8 1939

Dominating the landscape, this steep chalk escarpment is crowned with beech woodland and traces of an Iron Age hill fort. **Note**: sorry no toilet.

Finding out more: 01582 873663 or sharpenhoe@nationaltrust.org.uk

Sheringham Park

Upper Sheringham, Norfolk NR26 8TL

Map (3) J4 1987

In 1812 landscape gardener Humphry Repton framed views of the North Norfolk coast that can still be enjoyed today, proclaiming Sheringham Park had more natural beauty and advantages than any place he had ever seen. Generations of the Upcher family implemented Repton's design and made their own mark with the planting of an extensive rhododendron collection together with a number of exotic tree species. For wildlife lovers there is lots to discover, with a wide range of woodland birds, skylarks performing on the clifftop and three species of deer. Look out for a steam train travelling through the park. **Note**: Sheringham Hall is privately occupied. April to September: limited access by written appointment with leaseholder.

Eating and shopping: gift shop selling souvenirs. Plant sales, including rhododendrons. Courtyard Café serving bacon rolls, chips, baps, cream teas and ice-cream. Picnics welcome in a number of areas.

Making the most of your day: self-guided trails and guided walks (suggested routes available to download from website). Why not climb the Gazebo to see coastal views enjoyed since Napoleonic times? Tracker Packs available for children. **Dogs**: on leads near livestock and visitor facilities.

Sheringham Park, Norfolk, offers numerous trails to enjoy

Glorious display of colour at Sheringham Park, Norfolk

Access: Building Grounds
Parking: 60 yards.

Finding out more: 01263 820550 or sheringhampark@nationaltrust.org.uk

Sheringham Park		M	T	W	T	F	S	S
Park								
Open all year	Dawn–dusk	M	T	W	T	F	S	S
Visitor centre and Courtyard Café								
3 Jan–8 Mar	11–4	·	·	·	·	·	S	S
14 Mar–27 Sep	10–5	M	T	W	T	F	S	S
28 Sep–1 Nov	10–5	M	·	·	T	F	S	S
7 Nov–27 Dec	11–4	·	·	·	·	·	S	S

Courtyard Café open from 8:45 every Saturday. Visitor centre and Courtyard Café: open daily 14 to 22 February and 24 October to 1 November, 10 to 5; 28 to 31 December, 11 to 4. Closed 26 December.

Sundon Hills Country Park

Harlington Road, Upper Sundon, Bedfordshire

Map (3) F8 2000

Extensive areas of chalk grassland and beech woodland, with views north towards the Greensand Ridge.

Finding out more: 01582 873663 or sundonhills@nationaltrust.org.uk

Totternhoe Knolls

Castle Hill Road, Totternhoe, Bedfordshire

Map (3) E8 2000

The dramatic earthworks of a Norman castle rise from important chalk grassland habitat, sitting high above the surrounding landscape.
Note: sorry no toilet.

Finding out more: 01582 873663 or totternhoeknolls@nationaltrust.org.uk

West Runton and Beeston Regis Heath

near West Runton, Norfolk

Map (3) J4 1925

A lovely place to walk among heath and woods, with fine views of the North Norfolk coast.
Note: sorry no toilets. For Sat Nav use NR27 9ND.

Finding out more: 01263 820550 or westrunton@nationaltrust.org.uk

Whipsnade Tree Cathedral

Whipsnade, Dunstable, Bedfordshire

Map (3) E8 1960

Peaceful place, with trees planted in the shape of a medieval cathedral. Created after First World War for fallen comrades.
Note: administered by Trustees of Whipsnade Tree Cathedral. Dogs allowed under close control. Small car park (open 9 to 5). For Sat Nav use LU6 2LQ. Donations welcome.

Finding out more: 01582 872406 or whipsnadetc@nationaltrust.org.uk

Wicken Fen National Nature Reserve in Cambridgeshire, is the epitome of a traditional fenland landscape

Wicken Fen National Nature Reserve

Lode Lane, Wicken, Ely, Cambridgeshire

Map (3) G6 1899

With vast skies above flowering meadows, sedge and reedbeds, Wicken Fen is a window onto a lost fenland landscape. A wealth of wildlife is at home in this important wetland, including rarities such as hen harriers and bitterns, numerous dragonflies, moths and wildfowl. The landscape feels wild, though people have managed it for years, as revealed by the fenman's yard, windpump and cottage. The Wicken Fen Vision, an ambitious landscape-scale conservation project, is opening up new areas for wildlife and you to explore. Grazing herds of Highland cattle and Konik ponies help create a diverse range of new habitats.

Eating and shopping: shop in the visitor centre selling wildlife and outdoor books, as well as local food and crafts. Café serving Newmarket sausage sandwiches, homemade soup, light lunches and afternoon teas. Picnics welcome.

Making the most of your day: you can explore by bike (why not cycle the Lodes Way?) or foot – the all-weather boardwalk/longer paths give access into the fen. Seasonal boat trips offer an alternative view. **Dogs**: welcome on leads on reserve and in visitor centre.

Access: **Building** **Grounds**
Sat Nav: use CB7 5XP. **Parking**: 120 yards.

Finding out more: 01353 720274 or wickenfen@nationaltrust.org.uk

Wicken Fen		M	T	W	T	F	S	S
Reserve, visitor centre and shop								
Open all year	10-5	M	T	W	T	F	S	S
Café								
1 Jan-15 Feb	10-4:30	·	·	W	T	F	S	S
16 Feb-1 Nov	10-5	M	T	W	T	F	S	S
4 Nov-31 Dec	10-4:30	·	·	W	T	F	S	S

Closed 25 December. Access to reserve dawn to dusk. Visitor centre closes dusk in winter.

Anglesey Abbey, Gardens and Lode Mill

Quy Road, Lode, Cambridge,
Cambridgeshire CB25 9EJ

Map (3) G7 1966

When you step into this elegant home, you journey back to a golden age of country-house living. The new Domestic Wing shows how the staff serving the meticulous Lord Fairhaven ran his household like clockwork. The celebrated garden, with its sweeping avenues, classical statuary and flower borders, offers captivating views, vibrant colours and delicious scents whatever the season. Children can play, explore and discover nature in the Wildlife Discovery Area. A visit to the historic working watermill and famous Winter Garden will complete your day.

Eating and shopping: Redwoods restaurant serving seasonal, local menu. Light refreshments and snacks in gardens during peak times. Shop selling local products and gifts. Freshly milled wholemeal flour available from the historic watermill. Plant centre selling plants and garden furniture. Second-hand bookshop.

Making the most of your day: **Indoors** Guided tours. Hands-on activities and demonstrations in Domestic Wing (Thursday and Friday). **Outdoors** Family activities. Weekday garden tours. Winter Lights: special event lighting the gardens at night (December weekends).

Elegant Anglesey Abbey, Gardens and Lode Mill in Cambridgeshire (above and below)

Dogs: assistance dogs only.

Access:
Abbey and mill **Grounds**
Parking: 50 yards.

Finding out more: 01223 810080 or angleseyabbey@nationaltrust.org.uk

Anglesey Abbey		M	T	W	T	F	S	S
Garden, restaurant, shop and plant centre								
1 Jan–29 Mar	10:30–4:30	M	T	W	T	F	S	S
30 Mar–25 Oct	10–5:30	M	T	W	T	F	S	S
26 Oct–31 Dec	10:30–4:30	M	T	W	T	F	S	S
House								
11 Mar–29 Mar	11–3	·	·	W	T	F	S	S
1 Apr–25 Oct	11–4	·	·	W	T	F	S	S
28 Oct–1 Nov	11–3	·	·	W	T	F	S	S
House (guided tours)								
31 Mar–20 Oct	11–4	·	T	·	·	·	·	·
Lode Mill								
1 Jan–29 Mar	11–3:30	·	·	W	T	F	S	S
1 Apr–25 Oct	11–4	·	·	W	T	F	S	S
28 Oct–31 Dec	11–3:30	·	·	W	T	F	S	S

Mill and house open on Bank Holiday Mondays. Tuesday house tours every 30 minutes, 11:30 to 3, not available during summer holidays (28 July to 1 September). Timed tickets to house on busy days. Last entry to house one hour before closing. Property closed 24 to 26 December. Snowdrop season: 26 January to 1 March.

Blickling Estate

Blickling, Aylsham, Norfolk NR11 6NF

Map (3) J4 1940

Nobody ever forgets their first sight of Blickling. The breathtaking mansion and ancient yew hedges sit within a magnificent garden and historic park, while inside the house is one of the most important book collections in the country. The landscape, ideal for walking and cycling, has changed little over the centuries. It is a hive of hidden activity, with farms, barns and cottages adding to its rural charm. You can meet the past residents, from ambassadors and airmen to kings' mistresses, who have used the estate as a place of quiet refuge while playing their part on the world's political stage. Blickling has always been a place of tranquility, and today it continues to extend the warmest of welcomes.

Blickling Estate, Norfolk (above and below): a magnificent mansion and unspoilt landscape to explore

Eating and shopping: two cafés and restaurant. Large second-hand bookshop. Stamp shop, gift shop, plant centre and pub (not National Trust).

Making the most of your day: **Indoors** Year-round events and activities for all ages. Changing local art, craft and photography exhibitions. Quizzes and trails, including 'Flo's basket'. Living history performances. A variety of house and garden tours for adults and family groups. RAF Oulton museum. **Outdoors** Events, including open-air theatre and summer music concerts. Fishing. Waymarked parkland walks (guides available from visitor reception). Pyramid mausoleum. Cycle hire along marked routes. Holiday cottages. Felbrigg Hall nearby. **Dogs**: welcome on leads in park and courtyard café. Assistance dogs only in formal garden.

Access: **House** **Gardens**
Parking: 400 yards.

Finding out more: 01263 738030 or blickling@nationaltrust.org.uk

Blickling Estate		M	T	W	T	F	S	S
House								
14 Feb–22 Feb	11-4	M	T	W	T	F	S	S
21 Mar–1 Nov	12-5	M	·	W	T	F	S	S
7 Nov–29 Nov*	11-3	·	·	·	·	·	S	S
5 Dec–20 Dec	11-5	·	·	·	·	·	S	S
Garden, shop, restaurant and bookshop								
1 Jan–4 Jan	11-4	·	·	·	T	F	S	S
5 Jan–11 Jan	11-4	M	·	·	T	F	S	S
15 Jan–15 Feb	11-4	·	·	·	T	F	S	S
16 Feb–1 Nov	10:15-5:30	M	T	W	T	F	S	S
5 Nov–20 Dec	10:15-4	·	·	·	T	F	S	S

Park and woodland: open every day all year dawn to dusk. Last ticket to house one hour before closing. House also open on Tuesday 31 March, 7 April, 26 May, 28 July, 4, 11, 18 and 25 August, 1 September and 27 October. *House offers shorter winter route in November.

Bourne Mill

Bourne Road, Colchester, Essex CO2 8RT

Map (3) I8 1936

Delightful piece of late Elizabethan playfulness built for banquets and converted into a mill, still with working waterwheel. **Note**: limited parking in mill grounds.

Finding out more: 01206 768145 or bournemill@nationaltrust.org.uk

Brancaster Activity Centre

Dial House, Harbour Way, Brancaster Staithe, Norfolk PE31 8BW

Map (3) H3 1984

Our newly refurbished residential activity centre offers comfortable accommodation and a variety of outdoor and coastal-themed activities, suitable for a wide range of groups, including schools and families. Located on the fringe of Brancaster Harbour, it is an ideal base for exploring the Norfolk coast and countryside. **Note**: please contact the centre for information on residential group bookings, activities and prices.

Blickling Estate garden (top left) and Brancaster Activity Centre (below): two good reasons to visit Norfolk

Eating and shopping: meals for residents prepared freshly on site, using locally sourced produce whenever possible (some grown in our garden). Small gift shop selling local and ethical products available for guests.

Making the most of your day: range of coastal discovery activities and adventurous pursuits. **Dogs**: please contact the centre.

Access: Activity Centre
Parking: limited within Harbour Way, Brancaster Staithe (not National Trust).

Finding out more: 01485 210719 or brancaster@nationaltrust.org.uk

Brancaster
Please contact the centre for more information on residential group bookings, courses and activities.

Elizabethan House Museum

4 South Quay, Great Yarmouth, Norfolk NR30 2QH

Map (3) K5 1943

An amazing hands-on museum that will enthral and fascinate all ages. The museum reflects the life and times of the families who lived in this 16th-century quayside building, from Tudor right through to Victorian times. **Note**: house managed by Norfolk Museums Service.

Elizabethan House Museum, Norfolk, will enthral all ages

Eating and shopping: small shop.

Making the most of your day: activity-packed toy room for children and hands-on activities, including Tudor dressing-up costumes.

Access: Building
Parking: at South Quay. Also in town centre, not National Trust (charge including members).

Finding out more: 01493 855746 or elizabethanhouse@nationaltrust.org.uk

Elizabethan House Museum		M	T	W	T	F	S	S
1 Apr–30 Oct	10–4	M	T	W	T	F	·	S

Felbrigg Hall, Gardens and Estate

Felbrigg, Norwich, Norfolk NR11 8PR

Map (3) J4 1969

Felbrigg Hall is full of delights, a surprising mixture of opulence and homeliness, where every room has something to feed the imagination. The decorative and productive walled garden traditionally provided fruit and vegetables for the kitchens of the Hall and now provides inspiration to visitors, flowers for the Hall and, occasionally, produce to the Squire's Pantry (licensed). The rolling landscape park, with a lake, 211 hectares (520 acres) of woods and miles of waymarked trails, is a great place to explore nature, spot wildlife, or just to get away from it all.

Eating and shopping: recently refurbished Squire's Pantry tea-room offering a relaxing atmosphere both indoors and out, with a choice of hot and cold food. Gift shop with a wide range of goods and plants. Well-stocked second-hand bookshop.

Making the most of your day: Indoors Occasional attics and cellars tours. Children's trails. Hall at Christmas event. **Outdoors** Children's trails. Events, including Chilli Fiesta and Honey Fair.
Dogs: on leads in parkland when stock grazing, under close control in woodland.

An opulent corner of Felbrigg Hall, Norfolk

Access: Hall
Gardens
Sat Nav: follow brown signs.
Parking: 100 yards.

Finding out more: 01263 837444 or felbrigg@nationaltrust.org.uk

Felbrigg Hall		M	T	W	T	F	S	S
House and bookshop								
28 Feb–24 Oct	11–5	M	T	W	·	·	S	S
20 Jul–28 Aug*	11–5	M	T	W	T	F	S	S
25 Oct–1 Nov	11–4	M	T	W	·	·	S	S
Gardens								
28 Feb–24 Oct	11–5:30	M	T	W	T	F	S	S
25 Oct–1 Nov	11–4	M	T	W	T	F	S	S
5 Nov–20 Dec	11–3	·	·	·	T	F	S	S
Refreshments and shop								
28 Feb–24 Oct	10:30–5	M	T	W	T	F	S	S
25 Oct–1 Nov	10:30–4	M	T	W	T	F	S	S
28 Dec–31 Dec	11–3	M	T	W	T	·	·	·
Refreshments, shop and bookshop								
3 Jan–22 Feb	11–3	·	·	·	·	·	S	S
5 Nov–20 Dec	11–3	·	·	·	T	F	S	S

House and bookshop open Good Friday. *20 July to 28 August: access to some areas of house may be limited on Thursdays and Fridays. Parkland: open every day all year dawn to dusk.

Flatford

Flatford, East Bergholt, Suffolk CO7 6UL

Map (3) 18 1943

The quiet hamlet of Flatford sits beside the River Stour, in the heart of the countryside of Dedham Vale. Surrounding Bridge Cottage are the locations which inspired many of Constable's iconic paintings. You can stand in the very same places that Constable stood so many years ago and enjoy views that he would recognise. Our small exhibition will give you an insight into Constable's paintings, then you could explore the countryside on foot or hire a boat and row along the river to immerse yourself in the history and beauty of Flatford. **Note**: no public access inside Flatford Mill, Valley Farm and Willy Lott's House.

Eating and shopping: riverside tea-room serving homemade cakes and light lunches. Shop selling plants, gifts and souvenirs.

Enjoying a quiet moment at Flatford in Suffolk

Some places are easy to get to on foot or by public transport. See page 3

Fun on the River Stour at Flatford, Suffolk (above), and the magnificent Grange Barn in Essex (below)

Making the most of your day: volunteer guides offer tours sharing their passion for Constable and show some of the locations he used. Waymarked countryside walks and family trails around Flatford. **Dogs**: welcome, but please be aware of livestock in fields.

Access:
Bridge Cottage **Grounds**
Parking: 100 yards.

Finding out more: 01206 298260 or flatford@nationaltrust.org.uk

Flatford		M	T	W	T	F	S	S
3 Jan–1 Mar	10:30–3:30	·	·	·	·	·	S	S
4 Mar–29 Mar	10:30–5	·	·	W	T	F	S	S
30 Mar–26 Apr	10:30–5	M	T	W	T	F	S	S
27 Apr–4 Oct	10:30–5:30	M	T	W	T	F	S	S
5 Oct–1 Nov	10:30–5	M	T	W	T	F	S	S
4 Nov–20 Dec	10:30–3:30	·	·	W	T	F	S	S

Grange Barn

Grange Hill, Coggeshall, Colchester, Essex CO6 1RE

Map (3) 18 1989

One of Europe's oldest timber-framed buildings, Grange Barn stands as a lasting reminder of the once powerful Coggeshall Abbey. With oak pillars soaring up to a cathedral-like roof, bearing the weight of centuries, this 13th-century building has truly stood the test of time.

Eating and shopping: takeaway refreshments, ice-cream, limited range of souvenirs and second-hand books available. Coffee shop at nearby Paycocke's House and Garden. Picnics welcome.

Making the most of your day: exhibition on the life and work of local wood carver, Bryan Saunders. Paycocke's House and Garden nearby. **Dogs**: welcome on leads in grounds.

Access: **Building** **Grounds**
Parking: on site.

Finding out more: 01376 562226 or grangebarncoggeshall@nationaltrust.org.uk

Grange Barn		M	T	W	T	F	S	S
25 Mar–27 Sep	11–4	·	·	W	T	F	S	S
30 Sep–1 Nov	11–3	·	·	W	T	F	S	S

Open Bank Holiday Mondays.

Horsey Windpump

Horsey, Great Yarmouth, Norfolk NR29 4EF

Map (3) K4 1948

See restoration in the making; the windpump's sails are off and we're busy restoring the building to get it into full working order. Here you'll find a great introduction to the Broads – and this is an excellent place to start a walk or just enjoy a cup of tea. **Note**: surrounded by Horsey Estate – managed by the Buxton family. Horsey Gap car park, not National Trust (charge including members).

Eating and shopping: Horsey Staithe Stores (next to Horsey Windpump) serving light refreshments and selling local gifts, souvenirs and books.

Horsey Windpump in Norfolk has its sails off while it is being restored to full working order

Making the most of your day: walking routes to Horsey Mere and to the beach, refreshments available at Horsey Staithe Stores. Boat trips (not National Trust) across Horsey Mere (holiday periods only). **Dogs**: welcome (on leads near wildlife and livestock).

Access: **Windpump** **Grounds**

Parking: on site. Alternatively, at Horsey Gap car park, 1 mile, not National Trust (charge including members).

Finding out more: 01493 393450 or horseywindpump@nationaltrust.org.uk Norfolk Coast Office, Friary Farm, Cley Road, Blakeney, Norfolk NR25 7NW

Horsey Windpump		M	T	W	T	F	S	S
Windpump								
28 Feb–29 Mar	10–4:30	·	·	·	·	·	**S**	**S**
30 Mar–1 Nov	10–4:30	**M**	**T**	**W**	**T**	**F**	**S**	**S**
Horsey Staithe Stores								
28 Feb–29 Mar	10–4:30	·	·	·	·	·	**S**	**S**
30 Mar–1 Nov	10–4:30	**M**	**T**	**W**	**T**	**F**	**S**	**S**

Car park open all year, dawn to dusk.

 Please display your current sticker for free parking

Young visitors get to grips with the wonderful machinery at Houghton Mill In Cambridgeshire

Houghton Mill and Waterclose Meadows

Houghton, near Huntingdon,
Cambridgeshire PE28 2AZ

Map (3) F6 [1939]

In a stunning riverside setting, surrounded by meadow walks, Houghton Mill is the oldest working watermill on the Great Ouse. There are hands-on activities for all the family, as well as milling demonstrations, and you can buy our flour, ground in the traditional way by our French burr millstones.

Eating and shopping: riverside tea-room serving snacks, cakes and scones made with our traditional stoneground flour. Small shop selling freshly ground Houghton Mill wholemeal flour, souvenirs and second-hand books.

Making the most of your day: **Indoors** Milling demonstrations and baking days. Family events. **Outdoors** Open-air theatre. Children's trails, activities and summer holiday events. Access to surrounding meadows via public footpaths. Riverside caravan and campsite. **Dogs**: welcome in grounds.

Access: **Building** **Grounds**
Parking: 20 yards.

Finding out more: 01480 301494 or houghtonmill@nationaltrust.org.uk

Houghton Mill		M	T	W	T	F	S	S
Mill								
21 Mar–1 Nov	11–5	·	·	·	·	·	**S**	**S**
25 Mar–23 Sep	1–5	**M**	**T**	**W**	·	·	·	·
Tea-room								
21 Mar–3 May	11–5	**M**	**T**	**W**	·	·	**S**	**S**
4 May–4 Sep	11–5	**M**	**T**	**W**	·	**F**	**S**	**S**
5 Sep–1 Nov	11–5	**M**	**T**	**W**	·	·	**S**	**S**

Open Bank Holiday Mondays and Good Friday 11 to 5. Caravan and campsite: now National Trust, open 20 March to 2 November, 1 to 8 (01480 466716). Car park: closes 8 or dusk if earlier. Toilets: as tea-room closed Thursday and Friday.

Ickworth

The Rotunda, Horringer, Bury St Edmunds, Suffolk IP29 5QE

Map (3) H7 1956

Classical Italy brought to Suffolk. Close to Bury St Edmunds, this estate reflects the Hervey family's passion for everything Italian, influenced by their European grand tours. The Rotunda is a Neo-classical showcase, intended by the 4th Earl of Bristol to house treasures; indeed an extensive collection of silver contains the finest examples by Huguenot silversmiths. Family history is documented in portraits by artists such as Gainsborough and Reynolds, while in the basement, 1930s domestic service is portrayed through memories of former staff. The Italianate garden mirrors the house architecture, with box hedges and Mediterranean planting, while an extensive Victorian stumpery, planted with shade-loving ferns, creates an air of mystery. Parkland walking and cycling routes have pastoral views with ancient oaks. **Note**: accommodation and dining – Ickworth Hotel (part of the Luxury Family Hotel Group), 01284 735350.

Eating and shopping: West Wing restaurant serving seasonal lunches, afternoon tea and snacks. Porter's Lodge outdoor café serving light snacks and refreshments. Roving catering buggy. Gift shop. Second-hand bookshop. New plant centre in main car park.

Making the most of your day: **Indoors** 'Ickworth Lives' exhibition and 1930s Living History days. Cooking workshops. Paintings by Titian, Velázquez, Reynolds and Gainsborough, as well as Georgian silver collection, Regency furniture, historic books and Italian porcelain. **Outdoors** Events and activities all year, including snowdrops, heritage daffodils, lambing and Easter Egg trails. Open-air theatre, archery and wildlife days. Wool Fair, Wood Fair and family Christmas weekends. Historic Walled Kitchen Garden and wildflower meadow to explore. Guided and waymarked walks through extensive parkland. Cycle routes, geocache sites and trim trail. Children's play area. **Dogs**: welcome on leads near livestock and close to house. Assistance dogs only in Italianate gardens.

Access: **House** **West Wing** **Grounds**
Parking: on site.

Finding out more: 01284 735270 or ickworth@nationaltrust.org.uk

Ickworth		M	T	W	T	F	S	S
House								
13 Mar–1 Nov*	11–4	**M**	**T**	·	**T**	**F**	**S**	**S**
20 Jul–30 Aug	11–4	**M**	**T**	**W**	**T**	**F**	**S**	**S**
7 Nov–20 Dec**	11–4	·	·	·	·	·	**S**	**S**
Shop and restaurant								
1 Jan–12 Mar	10:30–4	**M**	**T**	**W**	**T**	**F**	**S**	**S**
13 Mar–1 Nov	10:30–5	**M**	**T**	**W**	**T**	**F**	**S**	**S**
2 Nov–31 Dec	10:30–4	**M**	**T**	**W**	**T**	**F**	**S**	**S**
Plant and garden shop								
13 Mar–1 Nov	11–5	**M**	**T**	**W**	**T**	**F**	**S**	**S**
7 Nov–20 Dec	12–3	·	·	·	·	·	**S**	**S**
Outdoor café								
3 Jan–27 Dec	10–4	·	·	·	·	·	**S**	**S**
13 Mar–1 Nov	10–5	**M**	**T**	**W**	**T**	**F**	**S**	**S**

Italianate Gardens: open every day all year, 9 to 5:30. Parkland, woods and children's playground: open every day all year, 8 to 8 (parkland closes dusk if earlier). *Tours only in house until 12 every open day except Bank Holidays. **Entrance hall and basement only weekends in December. Last entry to the house 45 minutes before closing. Property closed 25 December. Italianate Garden and plant and garden shop may close earlier in winter. Porter's Lodge outdoor café may close in adverse weather.

Impressive Ickworth (clockwise from top left): the Rotunda brings a touch of classical Italy to rural Suffolk, the busy kitchen and enjoying the parachute game on the lawn

Lavenham Guildhall in Suffolk, tells the story of one of the wealthiest and best-preserved towns in Tudor England

Lavenham Guildhall

Market Place, Lavenham, Sudbury, Suffolk CO10 9QZ

Map (3) I7 1951

Set in the lovely village of Lavenham, the Guildhall of Corpus Christi tells the story of one of the best-preserved and wealthiest towns in Tudor England. When you step inside this fine timber-framed building, you'll feel the centuries melt away. You can discover the stories of the people who have used the Guildhall through almost 500 years at the heart of its community, and learn about the men and women who have shaped the fortunes of this unique village. Then you can explore the picturesque streets of Lavenham, lined with shops, galleries and more than 320 buildings of historic interest.

Eating and shopping: tea-room serving light lunches, cream teas and hot and cold drinks. Shop selling local gifts, souvenirs, books and plants.

Making the most of your day: Indoors Children's trails and dressing-up costumes. Changing exhibitions. **Outdoors** Guided walks and talks in summer.

Access: **Guildhall** **Garden**
Parking: in village.

Finding out more: 01787 247646 or lavenhamguildhall@nationaltrust.org.uk

Lavenham Guildhall		M	T	W	T	F	S	S
Guildhall and tea-room								
10 Jan–11 Jan	11–4	·	·	·	·	·	**S**	**S**
Guildhall, shop and tea-room								
17 Jan–1 Mar	11–4	·	·	·	·	·	**S**	**S**
2 Mar–1 Nov	11–5	**M**	**T**	**W**	**T**	**F**	**S**	**S**
5 Nov–20 Dec	11–4	·	·	·	**T**	**F**	**S**	**S**

Parts of property close occasionally for community use.
4 to 6 December: Lavenham Christmas Fair (free).

Teddy bear's picnic on the lawn at Melford Hall, Suffolk

Melford Hall

Long Melford, Sudbury, Suffolk CO10 9AA

Map (3) 17 1960

There are so many stories to discover in this eclectic home. Melford Hall has had its share of trials and tribulations, but it's thanks to many generations, from medieval monks to the Hyde Parker family, that this home still stands. Devastated by fire in 1942, Melford Hall was nurtured back to life by the Hyde Parker family and it remains their much-loved family home to this day. It is their stories of family life – from visits by their cousin Beatrix Potter to our visitors today – that make this house more than bricks and mortar.

Eating and shopping: small tea-room or Park Room serving sandwiches and cream teas. Gatehouse shop selling souvenirs, gifts, second-hand books, souvenir story books and plants.

Making the most of your day: walks, talks and family events. Children's spot-it quiz and trail.
Dogs: on leads in car park and park walk only.

Access: **Building** **Grounds**
Parking: on site.

Finding out more: 01787 376395 (Infoline). 01787 379228 or melford@nationaltrust.org.uk

Melford Hall		M	T	W	T	F	S	S
1 Apr–30 Oct	1–5	·	·	**W**	**T**	**F**	·	·
4 Apr–1 Nov	12–5*	·	·	·	·	·	**S**	**S**

*Saturday and Sunday house open 12 to 1 for guided tours only. Open Good Friday and Bank Holiday Mondays.

Melford Hall is still a much-loved family home

Oxburgh Hall

Oxborough, near Swaffham, Norfolk PE33 9PS

Map (3) H5 1952

No one forgets their first sight of Oxburgh. Built in 1482 by the Catholic Bedingfeld family, it is the enduring legacy of their survival through turbulent times. There are 500 years of history to explore and you can learn how each generation of the family left its mark while discovering hidden doors, climbing inside the secret priest's hole and enjoying panoramic rooftop views. Exhibitions include needlework made by Mary, Queen of Scots, and colourful wallpapers from the mid-19th century. The moated Hall is surrounded by nearly 28 hectares (70 acres), containing gardens with seasonal interest, streams and woodland walks.

Eating and shopping: tea-room in old Kitchen and Servants' Hall. The Pantry is a seasonal kiosk serving light refreshments. Picnic in the grounds or the area by the car park. Gift shop selling gifts, games and local products. Plant sales. Second-hand bookshop.

Making the most of your day: **Indoors** Introductory talks most days, March to October. Variety of family trails. **Outdoors** Daily guided garden tours and winter weekend snowdrop walks. Children's activities and new den-building area. Year-round events.
Dogs: assistance dogs only.

Access: **Hall** **Chapel** **Garden**
Parking: on site.

Finding out more: 01366 328258 or oxburghhall@nationaltrust.org.uk

Oxburgh Hall		M	T	W	T	F	S	S
Garden, shop and tea-room								
3 Jan–8 Feb	11–4	·	·	·	·	·	**S**	**S**
14 Feb–13 Mar	10:30–4	**M**	**T**	**W**	·	**F**	**S**	**S**
3 Oct–1 Nov	10:30–5	**M**	**T**	**W**	·	**F**	**S**	**S**
7 Nov–20 Dec	11–4	·	·	·	·	·	**S**	**S**
House, garden, shop and tea-room								
14 Mar–2 Oct*	11–5	**M**	**T**	**W**	·	**F**	**S**	**S**
House								
14 Feb–13 Mar	12–3	**M**	**T**	**W**	·	**F**	**S**	**S**
3 Oct–1 Nov	11–4	**M**	**T**	**W**	·	**F**	**S**	**S**

*Admission to garden, shop and tea-room from 10:30.

Owned by one family since 1482, moated Oxburgh Hall in Norfolk contains many secrets, from hidden doors to a priest's hole

Paycocke's House and Garden in Essex: dappled sunlight plays on the lawn

Paycocke's House and Garden

25 West Street, Coggeshall, Colchester, Essex CO6 1NS

Map (3) 18 1924

Exquisitely carved half-timbered Tudor cloth merchant's house, with a beautiful and tranquil cottage garden. Visitors can follow the changing fortunes of the house over its 500 years of history, as it went from riches to rags, and see how it was saved from demolition and restored to its former glory.
Note: toilet on first floor.

Eating and shopping: coffee shop serving cream teas, coffee, cakes and soft drinks (courtyard and garden). Picnics welcome. Ice-cream available. Shop selling gifts, local and gardening products. Plants for sale at our garden stall. Second-hand bookshop.

Making the most of your day: **Indoors** Events all year, including changing annual exhibition. Children's activities and costumes. **Outdoors** Relax or play garden games. Why not combine with a visit to nearby Coggeshall Grange Barn? **Dogs**: welcome in garden only.

Access: **Building** **Grounds**
Parking: at Coggeshall Grange Barn, ½ mile, or at Stoneham Street car park, ¼ mile (not National Trust). Limited roadside parking.

Finding out more: 01376 561305 or paycockes@nationaltrust.org.uk

Paycocke's		M	T	W	T	F	S	S
25 Mar–1 Nov	11–5	·	·	**W**	**T**	**F**	**S**	**S**

*Garden opens at 10:30. Open Bank Holiday Mondays.

Vivid crimson, scented blooms create a fiery feast for the senses at Peckover House and Garden, Cambridgeshire

Peckover House and Garden

North Brink, Wisbech, Cambridgeshire PE13 1JR

Map (3) G5 1943

Peckover House is a secret gem, an oasis hidden away in an urban environment. A classic Georgian merchant's town house, it was lived in by the Peckover family for 150 years. The Peckovers were staunch Quakers, which meant they had a very simple lifestyle, yet at the same time they ran a successful private bank, the story of which can be seen in our banking exhibition. The 1-hectare (2½-acre) garden is an outstanding sensory delight, with an Orangery, summerhouses, croquet lawn, herbaceous borders and more than 60 varieties of rose.

Eating and shopping: lunch or afternoon tea available in the Reed Barn. Gift shop. Second-hand bookshop. Plant sales.

Making the most of your day: **Indoors** Grand piano to play. Behind-the-scenes tours. Handling collection and children's trails. First World War exhibition. Lord Peckover's Library. Octavia Hill's Birthplace House opposite. **Outdoors** Free garden tours. Croquet (summer). **Dogs**: assistance dogs only.

Access: **House** **Garden**

Sat Nav: use PE13 1RG or PE13 2RA for nearest car parks. **Parking**: nearest is Chapel Road or Somers Road, 500 yards (not National Trust).

Finding out more: 01945 583463 or peckover@nationaltrust.org.uk

Peckover House and Garden		M	T	W	T	F	S	S
House, garden, shop and tea-room								
10 Jan–22 Feb	12–4*	·	·	·	·	·	S	S
Garden and tea-room								
28 Feb–23 Mar	11–5	M	·	·	·	·	S	S
28 Mar–12 Apr	11–5	M	T	W	T	F	S	S
13 Apr–28 Jun	11–5	M	T	W	·	·	S	S
29 Jun–5 Jul	11–5	M	T	W	T	F	S	S
6 Jul–1 Nov	11–5	M	T	W	·	·	S	S
House								
28 Feb–23 Mar	12–4:30	M	·	·	·	·	S	S
28 Mar–12 Apr	12–4:30	M	T	W	T	F	S	S
13 Apr–28 Jun	12–4:30	M	T	W	·	·	S	S
29 Jun–5 Jul	12–4:30	M	T	W	T	F	S	S
6 Jul–1 Nov	12–4:30	M	T	W	·	·	S	S
House, garden, shop and tea-room								
5 Dec–6 Dec	11–5	·	·	·	·	·	S	S
7 Dec–13 Dec	11–5	M	T	·	·	·	S	S

*10 January to 22 February, admission to house by timed conservation talk only, 1:30 and 3. Gift shop open 12 to 5 on open days from 28 February.

Ramsey Abbey Gatehouse

Abbey School, Ramsey, Huntingdon, Cambridgeshire PE26 1DH

Map (3) F6 [1952]

This fascinating medieval gatehouse, along with the Lady Chapel, are all that remain of the great Benedictine abbey at Ramsey. **Note**: exterior open all year. Gatehouse and Lady Chapel in Abbey open first Sunday of month, April to September (1 to 5). Sorry no toilet.

Finding out more: 01284 747500 or ramseyabbey@nationaltrust.org.uk

St George's Guildhall

29 King Street, King's Lynn, Norfolk PE30 1HA

Map (3) H5 [1951]

The largest surviving medieval guildhall in England, with many original features – now a theatre. **Note**: managed by King's Lynn and West Norfolk Borough Council and King's Lynn Arts Centre Trust.

Finding out more: 01553 779095. 01553 764864 (box office) or stgeorgesguildhall@nationaltrust.org.uk

Shaw's Corner

Ayot St Lawrence, near Welwyn, Hertfordshire AL6 9BX

Map (3) F9 [1944]

You can follow in the footsteps of one of the world's greatest playwrights, George Bernard Shaw, as you explore his fascinating home and enjoy the beauty and tranquility of his inspiring garden. **Note**: access roads very narrow.

Eating and shopping: souvenir and gift shop. Second-hand bookshop. Ice-cream and soft drinks available in garden. Pre-1950s varieties of plants for sale.

Making the most of your day: events, including open-air performances of George Bernard Shaw's plays (summer). **Dogs**: assistance dogs only.

Access: **House** **Grounds**
Sat Nav: use AL6 9BX (some routes might take you through a ford and a route not signposted to Shaw's Corner). **Parking**: very limited (not suitable for large vehicles).

Finding out more: 01438 829221 (Infoline). 01438 820307 or shawscorner@nationaltrust.org.uk

Shaw's Corner		M	T	W	T	F	S	S
House								
21 Mar–1 Nov	1–5	·	·	**W**	**T**	**F**	**S**	**S**
Garden								
21 Mar–1 Nov	12–5:30	·	·	**W**	**T**	**F**	**S**	**S**

Last entry 4:30. Open Bank Holiday Mondays.

The great man's writing shed at Shaw's Corner, Hertfordshire

This striking replica warrior's helmet gives a flavour of the numerous breathtaking treasures unearthed at Sutton Hoo in Suffolk

Sutton Hoo

Tranmer House, Sutton Hoo, Woodbridge, Suffolk IP12 3DJ

Map (3) J7 1998

Days before the outbreak of the Second World War, an Anglo-Saxon king and his treasured possessions were unearthed by archaeologist Basil Brown. These ancient graves kept their secrets for 1,300 years, but what was found here changed our perceptions of the past for ever. The atmospheric ancient burial mounds, breathtaking replica treasure, original finds and reconstruction of the king's burial chamber bring this fascinating story to life. Edith Pretty's country house takes you back to that remarkable discovery, while sitting and relaxing in true 1930s style. Stunning views overlook the River Deben on walks across this Anglo-Saxon landscape.

Eating and shopping: café serving hot meals, snacks, children's menu and cream teas (outdoor seating and views to the River Deben). You'll be inspired by the range of gifts in our shop, including exclusive locally made pottery. Second-hand bookshop in stables.

Making the most of your day: events and family activities throughout the year. Burial mound tours, Anglo-Saxon encampments, living history, children's play area (dress up as a Saxon), as well as wildlife and nature walks. **Dogs**: welcome on leads in park and café terrace area only.

Access: **Buildings** **Grounds**
Parking: on site.

Finding out more: 01394 389700 or suttonhoo@nationaltrust.org.uk

Sutton Hoo		M	T	W	T	F	S	S
1 Jan–4 Jan	11–4	·	·	·	**T**	**F**	**S**	**S**
10 Jan–8 Feb	11–4	·	·	·	·	·	**S**	**S**
14 Feb–22 Feb	11–4	**M**	**T**	**W**	**T**	**F**	**S**	**S**
28 Feb–8 Mar	11–4	·	·	·	·	·	**S**	**S**
14 Mar–1 Nov	10:30–5	**M**	**T**	**W**	**T**	**F**	**S**	**S**
7 Nov–20 Dec	11–4	·	·	·	·	·	**S**	**S**
28 Dec–31 Dec	11–4	**M**	**T**	**W**	**T**	·	·	·

Estate walks open daily all year, 9 to 6
(except for some Thursdays, November to end January).

Theatre Royal Bury St Edmunds

Westgate Street, Bury St Edmunds, Suffolk IP33 1QR

Map (3) I7 1974

This Grade I listed theatre, one of the country's most significant theatre buildings and the only surviving Regency playhouse in Britain, will give you an intimate and unique theatrical experience. We offer year-round tours and self-explore sessions alongside a varied programme of performances. **Note**: managed by Bury St Edmunds Theatre Management Ltd. Admission charges apply to live shows and selected guided tours (including members). Please call before visiting, as opening times may vary due to performances.

Grade I listed, the Theatre Royal Bury St Edmunds in Suffolk is England's only surviving Regency playhouse

Eating and shopping: gifts and souvenirs on sale. Light snacks available in Greene Room.

Making the most of your day: why not combine your guided tour or self-explore with a performance from our varied programme?

Access: **Building**
Parking: on Westgate Street; alternatively at Swan Lane, 546 yards, not National Trust (charge including members).

Finding out more: 01284 769505 or theatreroyal@nationaltrust.org.uk

Theatre Royal Bury St Edmunds		M	T	W	T	F	S	S
5 Feb–19 Feb	10:30–12:30**	·	·	W	T	·	·	·
4 Mar–1 Apr	10:30–12:30**	·	·	W	T	·	S	·
9 Apr–25 Apr	10:30–12:30**	·	·	W	T	·	S	·
2 May–27 Jun	10:30–12:30**	·	·	W	T	·	S	·
16 Jul–30 Jul	10:30–12:30**	·	·	W	T	·	S	·
16 Sep–14 Nov	10:30–12:30**	·	·	W	T	·	S	·

Guided tours: February to July and September to November; Wednesdays, Thursdays and Saturdays at 11 (75 minutes).
**Please call before visiting, these are our standard opening times. We do at times have to make unscheduled closures due to being a working theatre. For details of special tours, events and performance details contact Box Office, 01284 769505.

Willington Dovecote and Stables

Willington, Church End, near Bedford, Bedfordshire MK44 3PX

Map (3) F7 1914

A hidden gem in a tranquil setting; were these magnificent Tudor stone buildings built for Henry VIII's 1541 visit? **Note**: exterior open daily. Open Days last Sunday of month (April to September). Groups by appointment with Mrs J Endersby, 01234 838278.

Finding out more: 01480 301494 or willingtondovecote@nationaltrust.org.uk

Wimpole Estate

Arrington, Royston, Cambridgeshire SG8 0BW

Map (3) G7 1976

With its changing owners driven by passions and purposeful agendas, Wimpole is both a place to escape to and a place to get involved. We continue with the 3rd Earl of Hardwicke's passion for trail-blazing food production and design, sharing the latest ideas, celebrating the estate's past magnificence and echoing Elsie Bambridge's 20th-century revival. As owners changed, a roll-call of ingenious architects, artists, thinkers and landscape designers cultivated magnificence. Money was spent to combine practicality with extravagant fashions. Even the most humble farm building was designed to be beautiful. Wimpole was shaped and designed by the best minds of its day. Today we seek out the best minds to inform our future and influence and inspire others in our turn.

 Some places are easy to get to on foot or by public transport. See page 3

Three views of the Wimpole Estate, Cambridgeshire: the impressive mansion sits at the heart of a unique working estate, which contains a traditional farm, productive walled garden and pleasure grounds

Note: half-price entry to Home Farm for members.

Eating and shopping: Old Rectory Restaurant and Farm Café serving dishes made with walled garden and Home Farm produce. Shop selling gifts, Wimpole rare-breed meat, flour, bread and eggs. Garden shop and plant sales. Toy and fudge shop, second-hand bookshop.

Making the most of your day: **Indoors** Basement tours. Top Hat and Mob Cap trail for families. **Outdoors** Guided walks, tractor rides, gardens tours, free family trails, Tracker Packs and geocaching. Daily farm activities such as grooming the donkey, meeting the Shire horse and rabbits, feeding the pigs and milking the cow (seasonal). Cycle and running trails. Events, including lambing time, open-air theatre, *50 things to do before you're 11¾*, craft fair and Christmas events. **Dogs**: welcome on leads in park.

Access:
Hall **Farm** **Gardens**
Sat Nav: entrance via A603, not A1198.

Parking: 275 yards.

Finding out more: 01223 206000 or wimpole@nationaltrust.org.uk

Wimpole Estate		M	T	W	T	F	S	S
Garden, Old Rectory Restaurant and stable block								
1 Jan–13 Feb	11–4	**M**	**T**	**W**	**T**	**F**	**S**	**S**
14 Feb–1 Nov	10–5	**M**	**T**	**W**	**T**	**F**	**S**	**S**
2 Nov–31 Dec	11–4	**M**	**T**	**W**	**T**	**F**	**S**	**S**
Home Farm and Farm Café								
3 Jan–8 Feb	11–4	·	·	·	·	·	**S**	**S**
14 Feb–1 Nov	10:30–5	**M**	**T**	**W**	**T**	**F**	**S**	**S**
7 Nov–27 Dec	11–4	·	·	·	·	·	**S**	**S**
Hall								
14 Feb–1 Nov	11–5	**M**	**T**	**W**	**T**	·	**S**	**S**
Hall (guided basement tour)								
7 Nov–29 Nov	11–3	·	·	·	·	·	**S**	**S**

Park: open every day all year dawn to dusk. Home Farm: open 1 to 5 January and 27 to 31 December, daily, 11 to 4. Estate: closed 25 and 26 December, except park and stable block (servery and gift shops) open 26 December, 11 to 4. Bookshop as shop, but closed Monday mornings. Car park: open 7:30 to 6:30.

Midlands

Calke Abbey, Derbyshire

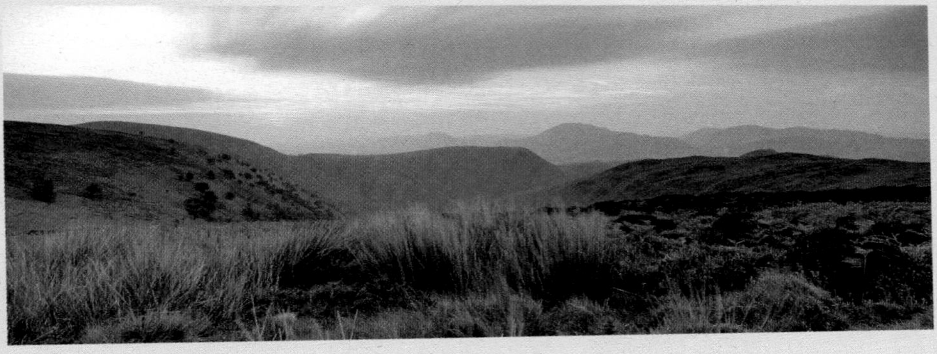

The view from the head of Carding Mill Valley in Shropshire shows why this is an Area of Outstanding Natural Beauty

Outdoors in the Midlands

With a huge variety of landscapes and places to enjoy, the Midlands offers countryside on your doorstep that is waiting to be explored.

Carding Mill Valley and the Shropshire Hills

Church Stretton, Shropshire

Map (4) H5 1965

Covering 2,000 hectares (4,942 acres) of heather-covered hills featuring iconic views of the Shropshire Hills Area of Outstanding Natural Beauty, this is an important place for wildlife, geology, landscape and archaeology. There are numerous paths for walking, cycling and horse riding.

Eating and shopping: Chalet Pavilion tea-room serving local food, including hot lunches, drinks and ice-cream. Shop selling gifts, souvenirs, maps and pond nets.

Making the most of your day: events all year. Free walks cards available in Carding Mill Valley. **Dogs**: under close control (grazing livestock).

Access: **Building** **Grounds**
Sat Nav: use SY6 6JG. **Parking**: 50 yards.

Finding out more: 01694 725000 or cardingmill@nationaltrust.org.uk

Carding Mill Valley		M	T	W	T	F	S	S
Tea-room								
1 Jan–13 Feb	10–4	**M**	**T**	**W**	**T**	**F**	**S**	**S**
14 Feb–1 Nov	10–5	**M**	**T**	**W**	**T**	**F**	**S**	**S**
2 Nov–31 Dec	10–4	**M**	**T**	**W**	**T**	**F**	**S**	**S**
Shop*								
1 Jan–2 Jan	11–4	·	·	·	**T**	**F**	·	·
3 Jan–8 Feb	11–4	·	·	·	·	·	**S**	**S**
14 Feb–1 Nov	11–5	**M**	**T**	**W**	**T**	**F**	**S**	**S**
2 Nov–31 Dec	11–4	**M**	**T**	**W**	**T**	**F**	**S**	**S**

*Shop opens at 10 on Saturday and Sunday. Tea-room and shop closed on 25 December. Toilets and information hut open 9 to 7, February half-term to October; 9 to 4:30 November to early February.

Clent Hills

near Romsley, Worcestershire

Map (4) J6 1959

Set on the edge of Birmingham and the Black Country, this green oasis with panoramic views is the perfect place for a refreshing walk or a picnic on a sunny day. Families can create their own adventures – building dens, hunting for geocaches or simply getting closer to nature. **Note**: nearest facilities at Nimmings Wood entrance.

This 19th-century 'mock' stone circle on the Clent Hills, Worcestershire, is just one of the attractions of this green oasis

Eating and shopping: café (not National Trust) at Nimmings Wood car park serving light meals and refreshments.

Making the most of your day: guided rambles (bookable). Families can drop in to our Outdoor Challenge Trails (Wednesdays during summer holidays). Natural play area. **Dogs**: welcome, but please be considerate to other visitors.

Access:
Sat Nav: use B62 0NL for Nimmings Wood entrance. **Parking**: at Nimmings Wood; additional parking at Adam's Hill and Walton Hill.

Finding out more: 01562 712822 or clenthills@nationaltrust.org.uk

Clent Hills
Nimmings Wood car-park gates open 8 and close 5 winter, 9 in summer. Closed 25 December.

Downs Banks

near Stone, Staffordshire

Map (4) J3 1950

A little wilderness of woodlands and heath, with easy access walks, in the heart of the Midlands. **Note**: sorry no toilets. Some steep paths. For Sat Nav use ST15 8UU.

Finding out more: 01889 882825 or downsbanks@nationaltrust.org.uk

Duffield Castle

Duffield, Derbyshire

Map (3) C4 1899

Remains of one of England's largest 13th-century castles, a place to relax and soak up the history. **Note**: sorry no toilets. Steep steps. For Sat Nav use DE56 4DW.

Finding out more: 01332 842191 or duffieldcastle@nationaltrust.org.uk

Ulverscroft Nature Reserve

near Copt Oak, Loughborough, Leicestershire

Map (3) D5 1945

Part of the ancient forest of Charnwood, Ulverscroft is especially beautiful during the spring – with heathland and woodland habitats. **Note**: assistance dogs only. Sorry no toilet. Access by permit from Leicestershire and Rutland Wildlife Trust (0116 262 9968) – apply several days before visit.

Finding out more: 01332 863822 or ulverscroftnaturereserve@nationaltrust.org.uk

Peak District

The Peak District has stunning scenery and breathtaking landscapes for you to enjoy throughout the year.

Ilam Park, Dovedale and the White Peak

Ilam, Ashbourne, Derbyshire

Map (3) B3 1906

The White Peak offers year-round walking in the wildlife-rich limestone countryside. Ilam Park features a formal Italian Garden with the rugged backdrop of Thorpe Cloud and Bunster Hill. Paths through woodlands and the River Manifold make it a popular choice for families and dog walkers. Just a mile from Ilam Park, the stepping stones in Dovedale are one of many reasons to explore the famous limestone valley. Huge hills and rock formations, wild flowers, fossils and caves all attract visitors to this special spot in the Peak District. The thickly wooded Manifold Valley offers a traffic-free cycling route. **Note**: Ilam Hall is let to the Youth Hostel Association.

Eating and shopping: Manifold Tea-Room at Ilam Park, with uninterrupted views towards Dovedale, serving homemade lunches and cake. Shops at Ilam Park and Dovedale Barn offering postcard-sized walk maps, gifts and information. Café at Wetton Mill (not National Trust) overlooking the River Manifold.

Making the most of your day: self-led family trails (school holidays). Free weekly guided walks (March to November). Postcard-sized walk cards (from shop). Holiday cottage, caravan site, bunkhouse. Ilam Hall Youth Hostel (not National Trust). **Dogs**: under close control, on leads near livestock and ground-nesting birds.

Access:
Ilam Park stableyard **Winster Market House**
Ilam Park grounds

Parking: at Ilam Park. Also at Dovedale and Wetton Mill, not National Trust (charge including members).

Finding out more: 01335 350503 or peakdistrict@nationaltrust.org.uk

Ilam Park, Dovedale, White Peak		M	T	W	T	F	S	S
Ilam Park tea-room								
1 Jan–15 Feb	11–4	M	T	W	T	F	S	S
16 Feb–1 Nov	10:30–5	M	T	W	T	F	S	S
2 Nov–31 Dec	11–4	M	T	W	T	F	S	S
Ilam Park shop								
1 Jan–15 Feb	11–4	M	T	W	T	F	S	S
16 Feb–1 Nov	11–5	M	T	W	T	F	S	S
2 Nov–31 Dec	11–4	M	T	W	T	F	S	S
Dovedale mobile barn								
28 Mar–27 Sep	11–5	M	T	W	T	F	S	S

Tea-room and shop: closed 24 and 25 December. Ilam bunkhouse: open all year (01335 350301). Ilam Park Caravan Site: open 27 February to 1 November, Darfar and Redhurst holiday cottages: available to let throughout the year (0344 800 2070). Ilam Hall: available for overnight accommodation via the Youth Hostel Association (01335 350212).

Dovedale, Derbyshire: tackling the giant stepping stones across the River Dove (left) and discovering one of the many footpaths (above)

Kinder, Edale and the Dark Peak

near Hope Valley, Derbyshire

Map (3) B2 1936

The Dark Peak from Kinder to the Derwent edges and the Vale of Edale provide exhilarating walks, dramatic landscapes, stories and wild nature. You can explore heather moors, high gritstone edges and windswept tors, ancient peat bogs, quiet wooded cloughs, rugged upland farms and even towering limestone crags. Why not escape for a day on the Kinder Scout National Nature Reserve, site of the 1932 Mass Trespass, following in the footsteps of the early champions of access to wild places? Discover the Shivering Mountain, make the short climb up Mam Tor to savour unrivalled views around the ancient hilltop fortress. **Note**: nearest toilets in adjacent villages and at visitor centres at Ladybower Reservoir, Edale and Castleton.

Eating and shopping: Penny Pot in Edale, serving cooked breakfasts, soup, sandwiches and cakes, teas and coffees. Seating and bike racks outside, sofas and log burner inside.

Making the most of your day: downloadable leaflet with walks and geocache details. Information barns. Stay longer at our Dalehead bunkhouse in Edale. **Dogs**: under close control, on leads near livestock and ground-nesting birds.

Walkers on Mam Tor footpath (above) and the rock formations at Kinder Scout (below), both part of Kinder, Edale and the Dark Peak, Derbyshire

Access:

Parking: at Mam Nick, by Mam Tor. Also at Edale, Castleton, Bowden Bridge, Hayfield, Sett Valley, Hayfield and Upper Derwent Valley, none National Trust (charge including members).

Finding out more: 01433 670368 or peakdistrict@nationaltrust.org.uk

Kinder, Edale and the Dark Peak		M	T	W	T	F	S	S
Penny Pot Café								
2 Jan–15 Mar	10–4	·	·	·	·	F	S	S
16 Mar–1 Nov	10–4:30	M	T	W	T	F	S	S
2 May–27 Sep	8:30–4:30	·	·	·	·	·	S	S
6 Nov–20 Dec	10–4	·	·	·	·	F	S	S
27 Dec–31 Dec	10–4	M	T	W	T	·	·	S

Closed 24, 25 and 26 December, open 27 to 31 December. Information shelters open all year: Edale End (SK161864), Lee Barn (SK096855) and Dalehead (SK101843) in Edale; South Head (SK060854) at Kinder; Grindle Barns above Ladybower Reservoir (SK189895). Dalehead bunkhouse open all year (01433 670368); camping and bed and breakfast available at some farms. Mam Nick car park open all year (SK123832).

Families enjoying Longshaw, Derbyshire (above and below). Known as the 'Pocket Peak District', access for all is excellent

Longshaw, Burbage and the Eastern Moors

Longshaw, near Sheffield, Derbyshire

Map (3) C2 1931

The 'Pocket Peak District' of Longshaw, Burbage and the Eastern Moors offers easy access through an excellent network of paths, bridleways and open access to much of what makes Britain's first National Park so special. Gritstone edges and tors, ancient woods and grasslands, meadows, tumbling streams and heather moorland support diverse wildlife and reveal traces and layers of our past. Ancient settlements and mysterious remains, abandoned millstone quarries and packhorse routes surround the designed landscape of Longshaw, a former grouse-shooting estate. Walking, climbing, cycling, riding, nature-watching, playing, exploring, relaxing and discovering the past, there is something for everyone. **Note**: National Trust/RSPB manage Eastern Moors for Peak District National Park Authority. National Trust helps manage Burbage for Sheffield City Council.

Eating and shopping: Longshaw tea-room (with outdoor seating for a panoramic view) serving soup, scones and dishes using fresh seasonal produce from the kitchen garden. Shop selling outdoor and wildlife-themed products, maps and guides.

Making the most of your day: Boggarts magical world with 'Play Longshaw!' for children. Events, including Cycle to the Cinema and muck-in days. Free walks (Wednesday/Sunday). Walk routes map available (shop). Kitchen garden. Geocaching. **Dogs**: under close control, on leads near livestock and ground-nesting birds.

Access: **Building**
Grounds
Parking: at Woodcroft, Wooden Pole and Haywood for Longshaw and at Curbar Gap, Birchen Edge and Shillito Wood for the Eastern Moors. Additional car parks at Surprise View and Burbage, not National Trust (charge including members).

Finding out more: 01433 637904 (Longshaw). 01433 630316 (Eastern Moors) or peakdistrict@nationaltrust.org.uk

Longshaw, Burbage, Eastern Moors		M	T	W	T	F	S	S
Tea-room and shop								
1 Jan–15 Feb	10:30–4	M	T	W	T	F	S	S
16 Feb–1 Nov	10:30–5	M	T	W	T	F	S	S
2 Nov–31 Dec	10:30–4	M	T	W	T	F	S	S

Last orders in tea-room 30 minutes before closing. Closed 24 and 25 December. Lodge is not open to the public. White Edge Lodge available as holiday cottage throughout year (0344 800 2070).

Attingham Park

Atcham, Shrewsbury, Shropshire SY4 4TP

Map (4) H4 1947

Attingham was designed for 1st Lord Berwick by George Steuart in the 1780s and sits at the heart of a grand Repton landscape. You can learn how the Berwick fortunes rose and fell and how their legacy lives on today as the family's stories are brought to life. Discovering Attingham's acres of parkland and miles of walks, walled kitchen garden, large playfield and welcoming mansion will easily take a day. Whether you are a family looking for activities, both inside and out, or are simply in search of a traditional inspirational visit to an historic house and parkland, you'll find it here. Attingham, Shropshire's leading year-round place to visit, has something to inspire and intrigue all our visitors. **Note**: 'Attingham Re-discovered Goes Through the Roof': conservation in action – John Nash's picture gallery and staircase.

Eating and shopping: the four catering units and two shops offer a variety of experiences and styles, including the Carriage House Café (open daily), Lady Berwick's waitress-service afternoon tea (bookings accepted), Mansion tea-room, Greedy Pig Catering, Stables shop and Grooms second-hand bookshop.

Making the most of your day: **Indoors** Themed tours, Attingham Christmas in mansion. Conservation in action, with mansion's 'Attingham Re-discovered' project. **Outdoors** Early opening (at 8) from spring and late park opening (to 7) in summer. Seasonal spectaculars, including winter snowdrops, spring bluebells, summer blossom and autumn tree colour. Events, including Easter, Hallowe'en, Christmas, food and harvest markets. Daily family activities during local school holidays. Sporting activities to help you get active, including regular running and walking groups. Holiday activity days, drop-in activities and competitions. Visitors can witness the Walled Garden and Pleasure Grounds projects, which continue to transform, conserve and restore Attingham.

Attingham Park, Shropshire (above and opposite): there is so much to see and do, that a day is barely enough

Dogs: welcome in grounds (identified on and off-lead areas). Dog walkers' guide available.

Access: **Mansion** **Carriage House Café** **Grounds**
Parking: 25 to 100 yards.

Finding out more: 01743 708123 (Infoline). 01743 708162 or attingham@nationaltrust.org.uk

Attingham Park		M	T	W	T	F	S	S
Park and playfield								
1 Jan–31 Mar	9–6*	M	T	W	T	F	S	S
1 Apr–30 Jun	8–6	M	T	W	T	F	S	S
1 Jul–31 Aug	8–7	M	T	W	T	F	S	S
1 Sep–30 Sep	8–6	M	T	W	T	F	S	S
1 Oct–31 Dec	9–6*	M	T	W	T	F	S	S
Walled Garden and Carriage House Café[1]								
1 Jan–28 Feb	9–5*	M	T	W	T	F	S	S
1 Mar–31 Oct	9–6	M	T	W	T	F	S	S
1 Nov–31 Dec	9–5*	M	T	W	T	F	S	S
Mansion								
7 Mar–1 Nov	10:30–5:30**	M	T	W	T	F	S	S
28 Nov–23 Dec	10:30–4	M	T	W	T	F	S	S
Mansion winter tours[2]								
2 Jan–1 Mar	11–3	·	·	·	·	F	S	S
Lady Berwick's Luncheons and Afternoon Tea[3]								
7 Mar–1 Nov	1–5	·	·	W	T	F	S	S
28 Nov–13 Dec	12:30–4	·	·	·	·	·	S	S
19 Dec–23 Dec	12:30–4	M	T	W	·	·	S	S

*Park, garden, playfield: January, February, November, December, closes 5 or dusk if earlier. [1]Carriage House Café: July and August closes one hour before park. **Mansion: March to November; 10:30 tour then free-flow from 11. Last admission one hour before closing. [2]Winter tours: 12 tour bookable. [3]Lady Berwick's: last seating one hour before closing. Mansion tea-room: 1 January to 13 February and 2 to 27 November open weekends only, 14 February to 1 November and 28 November to 3 January 2016 open daily from 11. Greedy Pig playfield catering: from 11 weekends and daily during school holidays. Stables shops: daily from 10. Property closed 25 December.

 Please display your current sticker for free parking

Attingham Park Estate: Cronkhill

near Atcham, Shrewsbury, Shropshire SY5 6JP

Map (4) H5 1947

Significant and delightful Italianate hillside villa designed by Regency architect John Nash, with beautiful views across the Attingham Estate. **Note**: open six days a year. 'Cronkhill Restored' project ongoing. House ground floor, garden and stables open as part of visit. Property contents belong to tenants.

Finding out more: 01743 708162 or cronkhill@nationaltrust.org.uk

Attingham Park Estate: Town Walls Tower

Shrewsbury, Shropshire SY1 1TN

Map (4) H4 1930

This last remaining 14th-century watchtower sits on what were once the medieval fortified, defensive walls of Shrewsbury. **Note**: open six days a year. Sorry no toilet or car parking and 40 extremely steep, narrow steps to top floor. Visit by guided tours.

Finding out more: 01743 708162 or townwallstower@nationaltrust.org.uk

A sanctuary since the 15th century, magical Baddesley Clinton in Warwickshire (above and opposite) continues to offer refuge. Although today's visitors are fleeing the noise and bustle of 21st-century life, rather than religious persecution

Baddesley Clinton

Rising Lane, Baddesley Clinton, Warwickshire B93 0DQ

Map (4) K6 1980

The magic of Baddesley Clinton comes from its secluded, timeless setting deep within its own parkland. From refuge to haven, this atmospheric moated manor house has been a sanctuary since the 15th century. This year discover Baddesley's fascinating late-medieval and Tudor history, from hiding persecuted Catholics in its three priest's holes to discovering the history of the Ferrers family who lived at Baddesley for more than 500 years. The peaceful gardens include fish pools, romantic lake and walled garden filled with colours for every season.

Eating and shopping: the Barn Restaurant serving hot meals, drinks and snacks;
The Stables offering light refreshments.
Shop selling seasonal gifts, local foods and plants. Second-hand bookshop.

Making the most of your day: **Indoors** Events, including supper lectures and Murder Mystery evening. **Outdoors** Open-air theatre. Family Fun every holiday, as well as Playful Journeys around the estate all year. Welcome talks and garden tours, plus walking trails around the estate and surrounding countryside. Packwood House and Coughton Court are nearby.
Dogs: welcome on leads in car park and public footpaths across estate. Assistance dogs only in gardens.

Access: **Building** **Grounds**
Parking: 100 yards.

Finding out more: 01564 783294 or baddesleyclinton@nationaltrust.org.uk

Baddesley Clinton		M	T	W	T	F	S	S
1 Jan–13 Feb	9–4*	**M**	**T**	**W**	**T**	**F**	**S**	**S**
14 Feb–1 Nov	9–5*	**M**	**T**	**W**	**T**	**F**	**S**	**S**
2 Nov–31 Dec	9–4*	**M**	**T**	**W**	**T**	**F**	**S**	**S**

*House open at 11. Admission to house by timed ticket, tickets available from reception (not bookable). Closed 24 and 25 December.

Belton House

Grantham, Lincolnshire NG32 2LS

Map (3) E4 1984

Belton's architectural significance and quality of collections, formal gardens and historic deer-park mean that it's often cited as being the perfect example of an English country-house estate. Begun for Sir John Brownlow in 1685, Belton House boasts one of the most important silver collections in the country and the second largest library held by the National Trust. One of Belton's most noteworthy connections is with the Machine Gun Corps, which had its first base and training centre in the park in 1915.

Throughout the year and to mark the 100th anniversary of its formation, there will be interpretation, events and installations focusing on the story of the Machine Gun Corps at Belton House. **Note**: all visitors (including members) need to obtain an admission sticker from visitor reception on arrival.

Eating and shopping: Stables Restaurant serving hot meals at lunchtime, including Belton's award-winning venison (when in season). Snacks and light meals served in the Ride Play Café. Two large shops selling gifts, plants and local produce. Extensive second-hand bookshop in the stableyard.

Making the most of your day: **Indoors** You can explore the house at your own pace, with no set visitor route, then discover more about Belton House with themed interpretation,

The perfect example of an English country-house estate, Belton House, Lincolnshire (left and top), also played an important part in the First World War (above)

guided tours and resource rooms. Pick up a timed ticket for one of the 'below stairs' tours (from 11 daily). Events and activities all year, including specialist talks. Indoor adventure play café plus Discovery Centre for free family activities. **Outdoors** Guided walks, markets, open-air theatre and cinema, plus family trails and archaeology activities. Christmas themed events. New adventure playground opening in March. Downloadable parkland and garden walks. Woolsthorpe Manor, home of Sir Isaac Newton, is nearby. **Dogs**: welcome on leads in parkland and stableyard.

Access:
House
Grounds
Sat Nav: use NG32 2LW.
Parking: on site.

Finding out more: 01476 566116 or belton@nationaltrust.org.uk

Belton House		M	T	W	T	F	S	S
House								
14 Mar–1 Nov	12:30–5	·	·	**W**	**T**	**F**	**S**	**S**
Park, gardens, shops, restaurant and Ride Play Café								
1 Jan–28 Feb	9:30–4	**M**	**T**	**W**	**T**	**F**	**S**	**S**
1 Mar–1 Nov	9:30–5:30	**M**	**T**	**W**	**T**	**F**	**S**	**S**
2 Nov–31 Dec	9:30–4	**M**	**T**	**W**	**T**	**F**	**S**	**S**
Adventure playground								
14 Mar–1 Nov	9:30–5:30	**M**	**T**	**W**	**T**	**F**	**S**	**S**
2 Nov–31 Dec	9:30–4	**M**	**T**	**W**	**T**	**F**	**S**	**S**

House: open Bank Holiday Mondays (March to October); no set visitor route in the house. Specialist tours most days and timed tickets for 'below-stairs' tours daily from the Marble Hall. Bellmount Woods: open daily, access from separate car park. Bellmount Tower and Boathouse open occasionally. House closes in poor light. Closed 25 December.

Benthall Hall

Broseley, Shropshire TF12 5RX

Map (4) I5 1958

Within this fine stone house, you can discover the history of the Benthall family from the Saxon period to the present day. Outside, the garden includes a beautiful Restoration church, a restored plantsman's garden with pretty crocus displays in spring and autumn, and an old kitchen garden.

Eating and shopping: tea-room serving drinks, cakes and ice-creams.

Making the most of your day: Elizabethan skittle alley. Circular walks through the park and woodland. **Dogs**: in park and woodland only.

Access: **Building**
Parking: 100 yards.

Finding out more: 01952 882159 or benthall@nationaltrust.org.uk

Benthall Hall		M	T	W	T	F	S	S
Garden								
7 Feb–1 Mar	1–4:30	·	·	·	·	·	S	S
3 Mar–28 Oct	12:30–5:30	·	T	W	·	·	S	S
House and tea-room								
7 Feb–1 Mar*	1–4	·	·	·	·	·	S	S
3 Mar–28 Oct**	1–5	·	T	W	·	·	S	S

*Last entry to the house at 3. **House and tea-room open at 1 and last entry at 4:30. Open Good Friday and Bank Holiday Mondays. Closes dusk if earlier.

The elegant drawing-room at Benthall Hall in Shropshire

Berrington Hall, Herefordshire, from across the lake – which was created as part of 'Capability' Brown's 1780s landscaping

Berrington Hall

near Leominster, Herefordshire HR6 0DW

Map (4) H6 1957

This fine Georgian mansion, designed by Henry Holland, sits within one of 'Capability' Brown's final landscapes. Home to the Harley, Rodney and Cawley families with jewel-like interiors and interesting stories. This year, you can uncover the world of 18th-century glamour and find out about the fashion inspirations of the time. You can experience for yourself some of the extremes of this period in the wig and bum shop, play Georgian-inspired games or enjoy walks on the level around the parkland, while taking in Berrington's beautiful and airy landscape.

Eating and shopping: shop selling gifts, local products and preserves made from our fruit. Tea-room serving light lunches, afternoon tea and cakes, often using produce from the garden. Second-hand bookshop.

Making the most of your day: **Indoors** Costume collection on view. House quizzes, family activities and dressing-up. Servants' quarters to explore. **Outdoors** Stables and walled garden to discover. Natural play area. Waymarked estate walks. **Dogs**: welcome on leads in parkland and in parts of garden.

Access: [access symbols] **Building** [access symbols] **Grounds** [access symbols]
Parking: 30 yards.

Finding out more: 01568 615721 or berrington@nationaltrust.org.uk

Berrington Hall		M	T	W	T	F	S	S
1 Jan–4 Jan	10–4	·	·	·	**T**	**F**	**S**	**S**
10 Jan–8 Feb	10–4	·	·	·	·	·	**S**	**S**
14 Feb–1 Nov	10–5	**M**	**T**	**W**	**T**	**F**	**S**	**S**
7 Nov–20 Dec	10–4	·	·	·	·	·	**S**	**S**
28 Dec–31 Dec	10–4	**M**	**T**	**W**	**T**	·	·	·

Mansion opens 11. Last admission one hour before closing.

Biddulph Grange Garden

Grange Road, Biddulph, Staffordshire ST8 7SD

Map (4) J2 1988

Biddulph Grange Garden is a remarkable survival – a high Victorian horticultural masterpiece and a quirky, playful paradise full of intrigue and surprise. Created by its visionary owner, James Bateman, its design expresses and attempts to reconcile both his deeply held religious convictions and his passion for geology, botany and plant collecting. His plant collection comes from all over the world – a visit takes you on a journey from an Italian terrace to an Egyptian pyramid, via a Himalayan glen and Chinese-inspired garden.

The collection includes rhododendrons, dahlias, Wellingtonias and the oldest surviving golden larch in Britain. **Note**: there are 400 steps throughout the garden. The Geological Gallery is open but unrestored.

Eating and shopping: self-service tea-room. Gift shop. Plant centre.

Making the most of your day: talks, guided tours, events and children's trails all year. Summer activities. **Dogs**: assistance dogs only in garden.

Access: [access symbols] **Garden** [access symbol]
Parking: 50 yards.

Finding out more: 01782 517999 or biddulphgrange@nationaltrust.org.uk

Biddulph Grange Garden		M	T	W	T	F	S	S
1 Jan–13 Feb	11–3:30	**M**	**T**	**W**	**T**	**F**	**S**	**S**
14 Feb–13 Mar	11–4	**M**	**T**	**W**	**T**	**F**	**S**	**S**
14 Mar–25 Oct	11–5:30	**M**	**T**	**W**	**T**	**F**	**S**	**S**
26 Oct–1 Nov	11–4	**M**	**T**	**W**	**T**	**F**	**S**	**S**
2 Nov–31 Dec	11–3:30	**M**	**T**	**W**	**T**	**F**	**S**	**S**

Open Bank Holiday Mondays. Closes dusk if earlier. Closed 25 December.

The Chinese Temple at Biddulph Grange Garden in Staffordshire

Birmingham Back to Backs

55-63 Hurst Street/50-54 Inge Street, Birmingham, West Midlands B5 4TE

Map (4) J5 [icons] 2004

An atmospheric glimpse into the extraordinary lives of the ordinary people who crammed into Birmingham's last surviving court of back to backs: 11 houses built, literally, back to back around a communal courtyard. Knowledgeable and engaging guides will take you on a journey in time, from the 1840s through to the 1970s. With fires alight in the grates, and sounds and smells from the past, you will experience an evocative and intimate insight into life and work at the Back to Backs. **Note**: visits by guided tour only (advance booking essential). Eight flights of steep and winding stairs.

Eating and shopping: shop offering a range of Birmingham-based memorabilia and traditional toys and games. 1930s-style sweet shop (not National Trust).

Making the most of your day: year-round events. Ground-floor tour also available if you are unable to manage our steep, winding stairs (booking essential).

Access: [icons] **Building** [icons]
Parking: nearest at Arcadian Centre, Bromsgrove Street (not National Trust).

Finding out more: 0121 666 7671 (booking line). 0121 622 2442 or backtobacks@nationaltrust.org.uk

Birmingham Back to Backs		M	T	W	T	F	S	S
3 Feb–6 Sep	Tour	·	**T**	**W**	**T**	**F**	**S**	**S**
12 Sep–23 Dec	Tour	·	**T**	**W**	**T**	**F**	**S**	**S**

Admission by timed ticket and guided tour only, booking essential. Open Bank Holiday Mondays (but closed next day). During term-time property closed 10 to 1 on Tuesdays, Wednesdays and Thursdays for schools. Last tour times vary in winter. Closed 7 to 11 September.

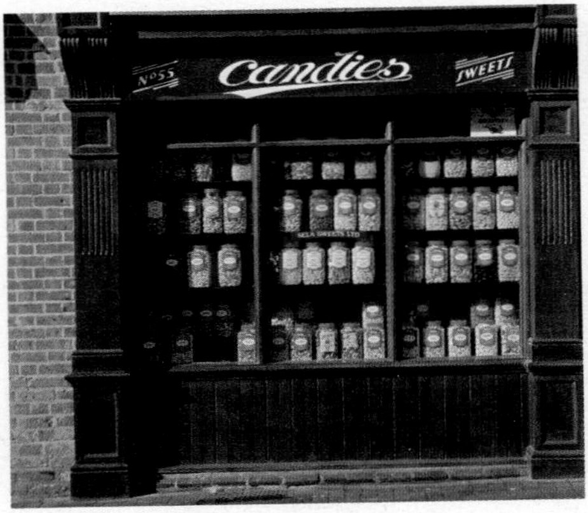

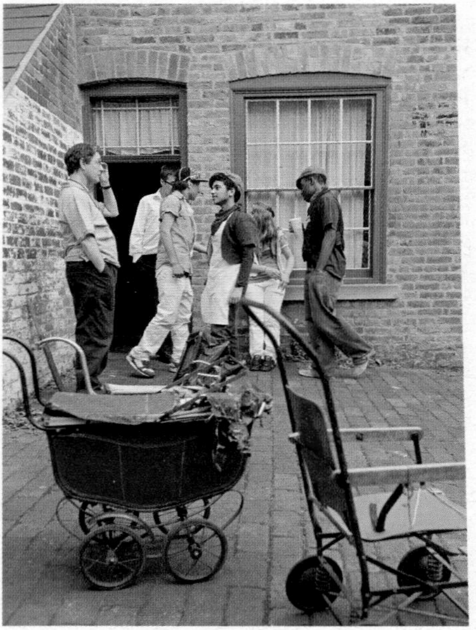

These three views of the Birmingham Back to Backs, West Midlands (right), hint at the evocative and immersive experience awaiting visitors

Brockhampton Estate

Bringsty, near Bromyard,
Herefordshire WR6 5TB

Map (4) I7 1946

This medieval moated manor house sits at the heart of a 688-hectare (1,700-acre) Anglo-Saxon settlement site, in an unspoilt romantic parkland redesigned in the 19th century. There are many walks through the estate, with its traditional orchards and hedgerows, working farmland, woodland, streams and countryside views. You can even spot wildlife on the nature trail. The manor house (now fully open) is entered via a charming timber-framed gatehouse. Through the stories of its residents, from 1425 to the present day, visitors discover how farming remains continually important, whereas life and practices have changed dramatically.

Eating and shopping: Old Apple Store tea-room serving seasonal food. Granary farm shop at Lower Brockhampton offering sandwiches and refreshments. Gifts, award-winning estate jams, local farm products, honey and beer. Second-hand bookshop. Brockhampton Craft and Produce Market, first Saturday of month, 12 to 3. Picnics welcome.

Making the most of your day: **Indoors** Year-round activities, plus demonstrations, exhibitions and historical re-enactments. Weekend tours. **Outdoors** Countryside event days, family trails and games. Natural play trail and geocache. Waymarked walks and orienteering routes. **Dogs**: welcome on leads in grounds, woods and parkland.

Access:
Building
Grounds
Parking: 100 yards and 1 mile.

Finding out more: 01885 482077 (Infoline). 01885 488099 or brockhampton@nationaltrust.org.uk

Brockhampton Estate		M	T	W	T	F	S	S
Estate								
Open all year	10–5	M	T	W	T	F	S	S
Tea-room								
1 Jan–2 Jan	10–4	·	·	·	T	F	·	·
3 Jan–15 Feb	10–4	·	·	·	·	·	S	S
16 Feb–1 Nov	10–5	M	T	W	T	F	S	S
7 Nov–27 Dec	10–4	·	·	·	·	·	S	S
House, grounds and shop								
3 Jan–15 Feb	11–4	·	·	·	·	·	S	S
16 Feb–1 Nov	11–5	M	T	W	T	F	S	S
7 Nov–27 Dec	11–4	·	·	·	·	·	S	S

Brockhampton Estate in Herefordshire: timber-framed gatehouse (top) and inside the medieval Great Hall (right)

Calke Abbey

Ticknall, Derby, Derbyshire DE73 7LE

Map (3) C4 [1985]

With peeling paintwork and overgrown courtyards Calke Abbey tells the story of the dramatic decline of a grand country-house estate. The house and stables are little restored, with many abandoned areas vividly portraying a period in the 20th century when numerous country estates did not survive to tell their story. Outdoors there are beautiful, yet faded, walled gardens and the orangery, auricula theatre and kitchen gardens to explore. The more adventurous can discover the ancient and fragile habitats of Calke Park and its National Nature Reserve, a haven for wildlife. Enjoy a variety of walks in 243 hectares (600 acres), from limeyards and wetlands, to woodland and ponds. **Note**: everyone requires admission tickets for house and garden, including members. House admission by timed ticket.

Eating and shopping: restaurant serving meals, including estate-reared meat. Café, coffee van and BBQ available at peak times. Large gift shop selling seasonal gifts, plants and local food.

Making the most of your day: **Indoors** Family activities in Squirt's Stable at weekends and during school holidays, from February to October. House tours on Thursday and Friday. Children's activity sheets. **Outdoors** Events all year, whatever the weather, and activities including guided park and garden walks. Children's play areas – play map available. Tramway cycling and walking circuit suitable for all the family. We also offer Tracker Packs, discovery trails and geocaching.
Dogs: welcome under control in park and on leads in stables.

Access:
House **Stables** **Grounds**
Sat Nav: use DE73 7JF. **Parking**: on site.

The grand exterior of Calke Abbey, Derbyshire, gives little hint that this is a house in dramatic decline. The interiors and beautiful, yet faded, garden (top right and bottom) tell the true story

 For other ways to get involved go to nationaltrust.org.uk/get-involved/volunteer

Finding out more: 01332 863822 or calkeabbey@nationaltrust.org.uk

Calke Abbey		M	T	W	T	F	S	S
Calke Park National Nature Reserve								
Open all year*	7:30–7:30	**M**	**T**	**W**	**T**	**F**	**S**	**S**
House								
21 Feb–1 Nov**	12:30–5	**M**	**T**	**W**	·	·	**S**	**S**
House tours								
21 Feb–1 Nov†	Tour	**M**	**T**	**W**	·	·	**S**	**S**
26 Feb–30 Oct†	Tour	·	·	·	**T**	**F**	·	·
Garden and stables								
7 Feb–1 Nov	10–5	**M**	**T**	**W**	**T**	**F**	**S**	**S**
Restaurant and shop								
1 Jan–20 Feb	10–4	**M**	**T**	**W**	**T**	**F**	**S**	**S**
21 Feb–1 Nov	10–5	**M**	**T**	**W**	**T**	**F**	**S**	**S**
2 Nov–31 Dec††	10–4	**M**	**T**	**W**	**T**	**F**	**S**	**S**

*Closes dusk if earlier. **House: admission by timed ticket. Last admission to house and garden 4:15. Guided tours may replace free-flow during adverse weather conditions. †Part-house tours Saturday to Wednesday, last tour 11:45; Thursday and Friday, last tour 3:30. ††Closed 25 December.

Canons Ashby

near Daventry, Northamptonshire NN11 3SD

Map (3) D7 1981

Tranquil Elizabethan manor house set in beautiful 18th-century gardens. Built by the Drydens using the remains of a medieval priory, the house and gardens have survived largely unaltered since 1710, and are presented as they were during the time of Sir Henry Dryden, a Victorian antiquary, passionate about the past. The warm and welcoming house features grand rooms, stunning tapestries and Jacobean plasterwork, contrasting with the domestic detail of the servants' quarters. Strolling through the historic parkland, you will glimpse early medieval landscapes, while a wander through the priory church reveals the story of the canons of Canons Ashby. **Note**: admission by timed tickets on busy days.

Eating and shopping: Stables tea-room and tea-gardens. Coach House shop selling home and garden gifts. Second-hand bookshop (donations welcome).

Canons Ashby, Northamptonshire: the stone-flagged kitchen, with its enormous range and servants' bells, is the same shape as the original Tudor house

Making the most of your day: **Indoors** Events all year, including costumed weekends. **Outdoors** Live music in the gardens and priory. Guided walks. Family fun activities on Mothering Sunday, Easter, Hallowe'en Christmas and school holidays. **Dogs**: welcome on leads in car park, paddock, tea-garden and parkland only.

Access: **Building** **Church** **Grounds**
Parking: 218 yards.

Finding out more: 01327 861900 or canonsashby@nationaltrust.org.uk

Canons Ashby		M	T	W	T	F	S	S
House								
13 Feb–22 Feb*	11:30–3:30	M	T	W	T	F	S	S
27 Feb–8 Mar*	11:30–3:30	·	·	·	·	F	S	S
13 Mar–1 Nov†	11–5	M	T	W	·	F	S	S
6 Nov–29 Nov*	11:30–3:30	·	·	·	·	F	S	S
4 Dec–13 Dec**	11:30–3:30	M	T	W	·	F	S	S
Tea-room, gardens, shop, church and parkland								
13 Feb–22 Feb	10:30–3:30	M	T	W	T	F	S	S
27 Feb–8 Mar	10:30–3:30	·	·	·	·	F	S	S
13 Mar–1 Nov	10:30–5	M	T	W	T	F	S	S
6 Nov–29 Nov	10:30–3:30	·	·	·	·	F	S	S
4 Dec–13 Dec**	10:30–3:30	M	T	W	·	F	S	S

House: closed on Thursdays, except 19 February.
†Free-flow admission to house from 1; entry by taster tours between 11 and 1 (30 minutes showing three rooms).
*Some rooms may be closed due to conservation needs.
**Whole property closed on Thursday 10 December.

Some places are easy to get to on foot or by public transport. See page 3

Charlecote Park

Wellesbourne, Warwick,
Warwickshire CV35 9ER

Map (4) K7 1946

The scene of Shakespeare's reputed poaching exploits, Charlecote Park was already in its middle age by the time Queen Elizabeth I arrived, along the carriage drive through the Tudor Gatehouse and on to the welcoming red-brick mansion. Generations of the Lucy family have left their mark on the buildings, gardens and parkland where visitors are intrigued to this day by the family's continuing presence. Protected by the unnavigable rivers Dene and Avon and by its distinctive cleft-oak paling fences, Charlecote presents a picture of peace and repose. It is a park where people picnic, play, walk and wander amongst the Jacob sheep and fallow deer that still roam across the 'Capability' Brown landscape.

Eating and shopping: The Orangery serves a range of hot meals and light snacks. The Servants' Hall gift shop and Pantry shop sell a range of Charlecote specific and locally sourced produce. Picnics welcome.

The riverside setting (above) of turreted Charlecote Park, Warwickshire (below), ensured protection in the past and offers peace and repose today

Making the most of your day: **Indoors** Hands-on activities bring the Victorian kitchen and outbuildings to life. The house is festively decorated during weekends in December. **Outdoors** Activities throughout the year, including guided park walks, talks, trails and a range of sporting activities. **Dogs**: assistance dogs only.

Access:
Building **Grounds**
Parking: 300 yards.

Finding out more: 01789 470277 or charlecotepark@nationaltrust.org.uk

Charlecote Park		M	T	W	T	F	S	S
Park, gardens, restaurant and shop								
1 Jan–26 Jan*	10:30–4	**M**	**T**	**W**	**T**	**F**	**S**	**S**
30 Jan–27 Feb*	10:30–4	**M**	**T**	**W**	**T**	**F**	**S**	**S**
28 Feb–1 Nov*	10:30–5:30	**M**	**T**	**W**	**T**	**F**	**S**	**S**
2 Nov–31 Dec*	10:30–4	**M**	**T**	**W**	**T**	**F**	**S**	**S**
House								
14 Feb–27 Mar	12–3:30	**M**	**T**	·	**T**	**F**	**S**	**S**
28 Mar–1 Nov	11–4:30	**M**	**T**	·	**T**	**F**	**S**	**S**
7 Nov–20 Dec	12–3:30	·	·	·	·	·	**S**	**S**

Outbuildings open as park. *Restaurant and shop close 30 minutes earlier. Closed: 27, 28 and 29 January, 23, 24 and 25 December. May close at dusk if earlier. House: parts of ground floor open only in November and December. Some rooms closed in February. Admission to the house by timed tickets on busy days.

A corner of the drawing-room at Charlecote Park, Warwickshire

Clumber Park

Worksop, Nottinghamshire S80 3BE

Map (3) D2 1946

With 1,537 hectares (3,800 acres) of parkland, including gardens, woodland, the longest double lime-tree avenue in Europe and a lake at its heart, Clumber Park retains the grandeur of its past as the country estate of the Dukes of Newcastle. A cedar avenue leads to the Walled Kitchen Garden with its impressive glasshouse, herbaceous borders and vegetable beds containing hundreds of varieties. There's plenty to experience, from the Gothic-style chapel to the peace and tranquility of the Pleasure Ground and heathlands.

With a lake at its heart (above) and avenues of gracious trees (top right), Clumber Park in Nottinghamshire provides everything visitors could possibly need for an active day in the great outdoors

Eating and shopping: café serving home-cooked food, using produce grown on site. Snacks, hot meals, cream teas and children's menu. BBQ at peak times. Gift shop, plant sales and seasonal produce. Second-hand bookshop. Bicycle hire and sales. Designated BBQ site and picnic area.

Making the most of your day: **Indoors** Year-round activities for all ages and interests to enjoy, including rotating exhibitions and workshops and the Burrow play area for pre-school children. The Discovery Centre is perfect for trying out some of the *50 things to do before you're 11¾* activities. **Outdoors** 20 miles of walking and cycle routes. Tours. Play areas and bicycles for hire. Why not stay longer at our campsite? Choice of self-led or organised activities. **Dogs**: welcome, some restrictions apply.

Access: **Buildings** **Grounds**
Parking: 250 yards.

Finding out more: 01909 544917 or clumberpark@nationaltrust.org.uk

Clumber Park		M	T	W	T	F	S	S
Visitor facilities								
1 Jan–28 Mar	10–4	**M**	**T**	**W**	**T**	**F**	**S**	**S**
29 Mar–24 Oct	10–5*	**M**	**T**	**W**	**T**	**F**	**S**	**S**
25 Oct–31 Dec	10–4	**M**	**T**	**W**	**T**	**F**	**S**	**S**
Walled Kitchen Garden								
3 Jan–8 Feb	11–3	·	·	·	·	·	**S**	**S**
14 Feb–28 Mar	11–3	**M**	**T**	**W**	**T**	**F**	**S**	**S**
29 Mar–24 Oct	10–5	**M**	**T**	**W**	**T**	**F**	**S**	**S**
25 Oct–1 Nov	10–4	**M**	**T**	**W**	**T**	**F**	**S**	**S**
7 Nov–27 Dec	11–3	·	·	·	·	·	**S**	**S**

Visitor facilities include tea-room, café, shop, plant sales, cycle hire, chapel, Discovery Centre and children's play areas. Open daily except 25 December. *Visitor facilities close at 6 on Saturday and Sunday. Café: open daily at 9.

Coughton Court

Alcester, Warwickshire B49 5JA

Map (4) K6 1946

Coughton has been home to the Throckmorton family for 600 years. Facing persecution for their Catholic faith, they were willing to risk everything. You can explore their fascinating story this year through 'Consequences of Conflict' – illustrating a family's ingenuity, resilience and resolve to overcome conflict in all its guises, from political and religious to conflicts of the heart. Coughton is very much a family home with an intimate feel; the Throckmorton family still live here. They created and manage the stunning gardens, including a riverside walk, bog garden and beautiful display of roses in the walled garden.

Coughton Court, Warwickshire (above and below): the fabulous gardens and opulent, yet comfortable, interiors offer a warm welcome

Eating and shopping: the Coughton Kitchen serving lunch and teas. Drinks and ice-cream available from the Stables Coffee Bar. Coach House shop selling local food and seasonal gifts. Throckmorton family plant sales.

Making the most of your day: **Indoors** Welcome talks. **Outdoors** Events, including Cheese and Pickle and Winter festivals. Open-air theatre and concerts. Holiday family fun, playground and games. Walking trails. Baddesley Clinton and Packwood House nearby. **Dogs**: welcome on leads in car park and public footpaths. Assistance dogs only in gardens.

Access:
House **Grounds**
Parking: 150 yards.

Finding out more: 01789 400777 or coughtoncourt@nationaltrust.org.uk

Coughton Court		M	T	W	T	F	S	S
House, shop and restaurant[1]								
1 Mar–29 Mar	11–5	·	·	·	**T**	**F**	**S**	**S**
House, shop, restaurant and garden[2]								
1 Apr–27 Sep	11–5	·	·	**W**	**T**	**F**	**S**	**S**
1 Oct–1 Nov	11–5	·	·	·	**T**	**F**	**S**	**S**
Taster tours[3]								
1 Apr–25 Sep	10:45–11:15	·	·	**W**	**T**	**F**	·	·
House, shop and restaurant†								
28 Nov–6 Dec	11–5	**M**	**T**	**W**	**T**	**F**	**S**	**S**

Open Bank Holiday Mondays. Closed Good Friday, 11 and 12 July. Admission by timed ticket on weekends and busy days. [1]Parts of the house may be closed due to building work. [2]The walled garden opens at 12. [3]One tour per day focusing on parts of the collection, subject to availability. †Coughton Winter Festival.

Still a family home after 1,000 years, Croft Castle and Parkland in Herefordshire has many compelling stories to tell

Croft Castle and Parkland

Yarpole, near Leominster, Herefordshire HR6 9PW

Map (4) H6 1957

This intimate house has been the Croft family home for 1,000 years. Indeed they still live here today. There are many compelling 20th-century stories to discover and this year you can find out how the First World War affected Croft, the parish and the family. Children can experience life on the home front as a wartime child, and you can learn how the landscape changed during this period and see the restoration of the wood pasture. There is a walled garden and Iron Age hill fort to explore, with Croft's glorious giants – veteran trees – to spot along the way.

Eating and shopping: tea-room serving hot meals, homemade cakes, local beers, ciders, ice-cream and Sunday roasts. Fresh produce used straight from the garden. Children's and half portions available. Shop selling local gifts, plant sales, home accessories and gardening gifts. Second-hand bookshop. Picnic area.

Making the most of your day: **Indoors** Tours and family room. **Outdoors** Iron Age hill fort, medieval church, walled garden and glasshouse. Natural, as well as castle-inspired, play areas. Waymarked walks, dog-walking and orienteering courses. **Dogs**: welcome, on leads in parkland only.

Access: **Castle** **Grounds**
Sat Nav: use HR6 0BL. **Parking**: 100 yards.

Finding out more: 01568 780246 or croftcastle@nationaltrust.org.uk

Croft Castle and Parkland		M	T	W	T	F	S	S
Tea-room, garden and parkland								
1 Jan–4 Jan	10–4	·	·	·	T	F	S	S
10 Jan–8 Feb	10–4	·	·	·	·	·	S	S
28 Dec–31 Dec	10–4	M	T	W	T	·	·	·
Tea-room, garden, shop and parkland								
14 Feb–22 Feb	10–4:30	M	T	W	T	F	S	S
1 Mar–1 Nov	10–5	M	T	W	T	F	S	S
7 Nov–20 Dec	10–4	·	·	·	·	·	S	S
Castle								
14 Feb–22 Feb	11–4:30	M	T	W	T	F	S	S
1 Mar–1 Nov	11–5	M	T	W	T	F	S	S
7 Nov–20 Dec	11–4:30	·	·	·	·	·	S	S
Countryside								
Open all year	Dawn–dusk	M	T	W	T	F	S	S

Play area: open as parkland. Shop: opens 11. Tea-room open winter weekends 10 to 4.

Croome

near High Green, Worcester,
Worcestershire WR8 9DW

Map ④ J7 1996

Expect the unexpected. After stepping into what remains of a secret wartime air base, now our visitor centre, where thousands of people lived and worked in the 1940s, you walk through a masterpiece in landscape design, 'Capability' Brown's first commission. Over the past 17 years we have restored what was once lost and overgrown parkland and we're continuing this work today. At the heart of the park lies Croome Court, with its stories of loss and survival, which is being transformed from a house of faded beauty into one of wonder. You can see the repairs for yourself and get up close to the action every day – a new way of visiting a country house. **Note**: major repair work continues this year.

Eating and shopping: 1940s-style restaurant and shop at the visitor centre. 1940s tea-car serving snacks on busy days. Second-hand bookshop in the visitor centre run by the Friends of Croome. Limited catering in the house this year due to the repair works.

Making the most of your day: **Indoors** You can experience something different with 'Croome Court Uncovered', where you can see the house repair and conservation work up close, join a tour of the work and take part in many hands-on activities (themes change monthly). Events and activities all year, including regular guided tours of the house and imaginative family house trail.
Outdoors Regular guided tours of the park. Outer eye-catcher open days. Family trail around the park, with an explorer pack to take with you. Special fun trails throughout the school holidays. RAF-themed playground and natural play area close to visitor centre.
Dogs: welcome on leads. Assistance dogs only in house, restaurant and shop.

Access: **House**
Park
Parking: on site.

Croome, Worcestershire: the grotto (opposite) and the north front as seen from the original driveway (above)

Finding out more: 01905 371006 or croome@nationaltrust.org.uk
Estate Office, The Builders' Yard, High Green, Severn Stoke, Worcestershire WR8 9JS

Croome		M	T	W	T	F	S	S
Park, restaurant and shop								
1 Jan–13 Feb	10–4:30	M	T	W	T	F	S	S
14 Feb–1 Nov	10–5:30	M	T	W	T	F	S	S
2 Nov–23 Dec	10–4:30	M	T	W	T	F	S	S
26 Dec–31 Dec	10–4:30	M	T	W	T	·	S	S
House								
1 Jan–13 Feb*	11–4	M	·	W	T	F	S	S
14 Feb–1 Nov	11–4:30	M	·	W	T	F	S	S
2 Nov–23 Dec*	11–4	M	·	W	T	F	S	S
House**								
26 Dec–31 Dec	Tour	M	T	W	T	·	S	S

*Winter weekdays house open for guided tours only before 1:30. **House open for timed tours only.

Cwmmau Farmhouse

Brilley, Whitney-on-Wye,
Herefordshire HR3 6JP

Map ④ G7 1965

Sitting deep in the heart of Herefordshire countryside, this early 17th-century black-and-white timbered farmhouse has many original features to explore. **Note**: open four days, in June and October – available at other times as holiday cottage (0344 800 2070).

Finding out more: 01568 780246 or cwmmaufarmhouse@nationaltrust.org.uk

Dudmaston Estate

Quatt, near Bridgnorth, Shropshire WV15 6QN

Map (4) 15 1978

Enchanting wooded parkland, sweeping gardens and a house with a surprise collection; Dudmaston is nestled in the Shropshire countryside. A much-loved home for over 875 years, the family rooms are scattered with photos with perhaps an odd pair of shoes peeping out from under a table. Unexpected galleries, designed by the last owner Rachel, Lady Labouchere, for her and her husband's modern and traditional art collections, create a total contrast. The tranquil gardens offer amazing vistas, and families will love the orchard playground, Big Pool and Dingle woods. The wider estate provides extensive walking and cycling routes all year.
Note: the family home of Mr and Mrs Mark Hamilton-Russell.

Eating and shopping: shop selling gifts. Orchard tea-room offering lunch and afternoon tea. Ice-cream parlour and Apple Store snacks. Second-hand bookshop.

Making the most of your day: traditional outdoor games and children's woodland playground. Garden tours. Varied events and family activities. **Dogs**: welcome on leads in parkland and orchard only.

Access:
Building **Grounds**
Parking: on site or at The Holt and Hampton Loade.

Finding out more: 01746 780866 or dudmaston@nationaltrust.org.uk

Dudmaston Estate		M	T	W	T	F	S	S
Park, tea-room and shop								
14 Feb-22 Feb**	12-4	·	·	·	·	·	S	S
15 Mar-31 Mar	11:30-5	M	T	W	T	·	·	S
1 Apr-30 Sep	11-5:30	M	T	W	T	·	·	S
1 Oct-29 Oct	11:30-5	M	T	W	T	·	·	S
1 Nov-13 Dec**	11:30-4	·	·	·	·	·	S	S
Galleries								
15 Mar-31 Mar	1-5	M	T	W	T	·	·	S
1 Oct-29 Oct	1-5	M	T	W	T	·	·	S
House and galleries								
1 Apr-30 Sep	1-5*	M	T	W	T	·	·	S
Garden and second-hand bookshop								
15 Mar-31 Mar	12-5	M	T	W	T	·	·	S
1 Apr-30 Sep	12-5:30	M	T	W	T	·	·	S
1 Oct-29 Oct	12-5	M	T	W	T	·	·	S

No entry to the car park before opening time. *House and galleries open at 2 on Sundays. **Restricted park access – Dingle walks only.

The enchanting Dudmaston Estate in Shropshire

Why not share your pictures with us? #nationaltrust

The Library at Eyam Hall in Derbyshire

Eyam Hall and Craft Centre

Main Street, Eyam, Derbyshire S32 5QW

Map (3) B2 [2013]

Eyam Hall is an unspoilt example of a gritstone Jacobean manor house, set within a walled garden. Completed in 1672, it was home to the Wright family for 11 generations. Explore the legendary plague history of the village and the surrounding Peak District countryside.

Eating and shopping: gift and craft shops. Buttery café (not National Trust) serving lunch and refreshments.

Making the most of your day: Indoors Seasonal events. Family activities during school holidays and themed workshops. **Outdoors** 'Thought walks' exploring some of the village stories and plague history. Hardwick Hall nearby. **Dogs**: welcome on 'thought walks'. Assistance dogs only in walled gardens.

Access: **Building**
Parking: 43 yards.

Finding out more: 01433 639565 or eyam@nationaltrust.org.uk

Eyam Hall and Craft Centre		M	T	W	T	F	S	S
Craft Centre								
Open all year*	10:30–4:30	·	**T**	**W**	**T**	**F**	**S**	**S**
Hall and garden								
7 Feb–1 Nov	10:30–4:30	·	·	**W**	**T**	**F**	**S**	**S**
28 Nov–31 Dec**	10:30–3	·	·	**W**	**T**	**F**	**S**	**S**

*National Trust shop and information centre closed Mondays. Independent craft shops and café opening hours may vary from National Trust. Also open Bank Holidays April to August.
**Christmas decorations: reduced number of rooms are available to view in December. Closed 23 to 26 December. Open 27 to 31 December.

Farnborough Hall

Farnborough, near Banbury,
Warwickshire OX17 1DU

Map (4) L7 [1960]

Honey-coloured stone house with stunning library and treasures collected during the Grand Tour, surrounded by landscape garden with country views. **Note**: occupied and administered by the Holbech family.

Finding out more:
01295 690002 (Farnborough Hall).
01295 670266 (Upton House) or
farnboroughhall@nationaltrust.org.uk

The Fleece Inn

Bretforton, near Evesham,
Worcestershire WR11 7JE

Map (4) K7 [1978]

Originally a half-timbered medieval longhouse and barn, now a traditional village inn known for folk music, Morris dancing and asparagus.

Finding out more: 01386 831173 or fleeceinn@nationaltrust.org.uk

Grantham House

Castlegate, Grantham, Lincolnshire NG31 6SS

Map (3) E4 1944

Handsome town house, one of the oldest buildings in Grantham, with riverside walled garden. **Note**: leased by the National Trust and the lessee is responsible for arrangements and facilities. Appointments may be needed.

Finding out more: 01476 564705 or granthamhouse@nationaltrust.org.uk

Greyfriars' House and Garden

Friar Street, Worcester, Worcestershire WR1 2LZ

Map (4) J7 1966

Set in the heart of historic Worcester, Greyfriars is a charming timber-framed merchant's house – perfect for getting away from the hustle and bustle. This unique house and garden were rescued by two extraordinary people with a vision to revive this medieval gem and create a peaceful oasis.

Charming Greyfriars' House and Garden, Worcestershire

Eating and shopping: light refreshments served in walled garden (in house during winter). Plants grown at nearby Hanbury Hall for sale, plus a selection of second-hand books.

Making the most of your day: **Indoors** Themed events throughout the year. Children's activity room, trails and tours. **Outdoors** Garden games and geocaching. **Dogs**: welcome in garden.

Access: **House**
Parking: no parking on site. Nearest parking at Corn Market, Kings Street and Cathedral Plaza (pay and display). Park and ride service from city outskirts.

Finding out more: 01905 23571 or greyfriars@nationaltrust.org.uk

Greyfriars		M	T	W	T	F	S	S
17 Feb–28 Mar	1–5	·	**T**	**W**	**T**	**F**	**S**	·
31 Mar–3 Oct*	11–5	·	**T**	**W**	**T**	**F**	**S**	·
6 Oct–19 Dec**	1–5	·	**T**	**W**	**T**	**F**	**S**	·

Open Bank Holiday Mondays. *Taster tours available from 11 to 1 (last tour at 12:30), tour tickets allocated on arrival. Free-flow access 1 to 5. **Worcester Christmas Fayre, open 11 to 5 and 6 to 9 on 26 and 27 November. Open 11 to 5 on 28 November.

Gunby Hall and Gardens

Gunby, Spilsby, Lincolnshire PE23 5SS

Map (3) G3 1944

Gunby Hall was the Massingberd family home from 1700 until 1967. The Hall feels homely and cherished, and many visitors remark 'I could live here'. It has a magnificent music room, dining-room and 3 hectares (8 acres) of gardens, which include immaculate lawns and a wonderful rose garden.

Eating and shopping: courtyard tea-room offering cakes, sweet treats and hot and cold drinks. Well-stocked second-hand bookshop in the basement. Seasonal plants and produce for sale when available.

Making the most of your day: events throughout year, from open-air theatre to

It is hard not to feel at home at Gunby Hall and Gardens, Lincolnshire, as the house feels so comfortable and cherished

Regency re-enactments and Apple Days. Public footpaths run across the wider historic park and estate. **Dogs**: welcome on leads in the gardens, courtyard tea-room terrace and grounds.

Access: [icons] **Building** [icons] **Grounds** [icons]
Sat Nav: may misdirect – entrance is off roundabout and not beyond or before.
Parking: on site.

Finding out more: 01754 890102 or gunbyhall@nationaltrust.org.uk

Gunby Hall and Gardens		M	T	W	T	F	S	S
House*								
14 Feb–1 Nov	11–5	**M**	**T**	**W**	·	·	**S**	**S**
28 Nov–13 Dec	11–3	·	·	·	·	·	**S**	**S**
Gardens and tea-room**								
14 Feb–1 Nov	11–5	**M**	**T**	**W**	**T**	**F**	**S**	**S**
28 Nov–13 Dec	11–3	·	·	·	·	·	**S**	**S**
Parkland and car park								
Open all year	11–5	**M**	**T**	**W**	**T**	**F**	**S**	**S**

*Last admission to house one hour before closing.
On busy days admission to the house may be by timed ticket.
**Tea-room service ceases at 4:30. May close dusk or earlier.

Gunby Hall Estate: Monksthorpe Chapel

Monksthorpe, near Spilsby,
Lincolnshire PE23 5PP

Map (3) G3 [+] [2000]

Remote late 17th-century Baptist chapel in tranquil grounds with rare open-air baptistry. **Note**: grounds accessible at all times. Chapel key available from tea-room at nearby Gunby Hall and Gardens (£20 refundable deposit required).

Finding out more: 01754 890102 or monksthorpe@nationaltrust.org.uk

Hanbury Hall and Gardens

School Road, Hanbury, Droitwich Spa, Worcestershire WR9 7EA

Map (4) J6 1953

An early 18th-century house built by Thomas Vernon, lawyer and Whig MP for Worcester. Discover the story behind the magnificent Sir James Thornhill wall and ceiling-paintings and the Hercules rooms, which feature views of the formal gardens and Malvern Hills.

Outside, the restored George London garden, originally commissioned by Thomas Vernon, includes a parterre, grove, bowling green and fruit garden. Why not see if you can find the mushroom house and ice house? For a longer walk, the 162-hectare (400-acre) park has paths up to the church and on to the Droitwich canal system.

Eating and shopping: extended gardening range and walled-garden plants for sale. Servants' hall tea-room serving meals made using home-grown produce (where possible) and home-baked cakes and sweet treats. Chambers tea-room serving sandwich lunches and afternoon teas. Stableyard outdoor café (open busy days only).

The parterre at Hanbury Hall and Gardens, Worcestershire

Making the most of your day: **Indoors** Art exhibitions and themed weekends. **Outdoors** Regular garden tours and introductory talks. Varied events, including family activity days, concerts and open-air theatre. Free park walks leaflet. **Dogs**: on leads in park and short leads in stableyard. Assistance dogs only in gardens.

Access: **Building** **Grounds**
Parking: 150 yards.

Finding out more: 01527 821214 or hanburyhall@nationaltrust.org.uk

Hanbury Hall and Gardens		M	T	W	T	F	S	S
1 Jan–28 Jan	11-4	**M**	**T**	**W**	**T**	**F**	**S**	**S**
30 Jan–28 Mar	11-4	**M**	**T**	**W**	**T**	**F**	**S**	**S**
29 Mar–24 Oct	10:30-5	**M**	**T**	**W**	**T**	**F**	**S**	**S**
25 Oct–23 Dec	11-4	**M**	**T**	**W**	**T**	**F**	**S**	**S**
26 Dec–31 Dec	11-4	**M**	**T**	**W**	**T**	·	**S**	**S**

January to 13 February, 2 November to 31 December, house admission by guided tour only. All tour tickets allocated on arrival (non-bookable). 5 to 20 December: limited free-flow access. 14 February to 1 November: house admission by guided tour until 1 (last tour at 12:20), 1 to 4 or 1 to 5 free-flow (depending on time of year as listed above). Whole property closed 29 January and 24 and 25 December. Admission to house by timed ticket on busy days. Bank Holiday Mondays: free-flow access, 11 to 5.

Hardwick Estate: Stainsby Mill

Doe Lea, Chesterfield, Derbyshire S44 5RW

Map (3) D3 1976

A fully operational Victorian flour mill giving an insight into the workplace of a 19th-century miller. There has been a mill on this site for hundreds of years, providing flour for the local villages and the Hardwick Estate. Flour is ground regularly showing the cogs and machinery in action. **Note**: nearest toilets and refreshments at Hardwick Hall.

Eating and shopping: Stainsby freshly milled flour for sale. You can learn more about the mill with a full colour souvenir guide. Restaurant and Stables gift shop at nearby Hardwick Hall.

Making the most of your day: why not start your day at Stainsby Mill, with its children's trail and activity sheets? Visitors are welcome to have a go grinding flour on the hand quern. **Dogs**: welcome on leads in Hardwick Park.

Access: **Building** **Grounds**
Parking: limited on-road parking (not National Trust).

Finding out more: 01246 850430 or stainsbymill@nationaltrust.org.uk

Hardwick Estate: Stainsby Mill		M	T	W	T	F	S	S
7 Feb–1 Nov	10-4	·	·	**W**	**T**	**F**	**S**	**S**

Open Bank Holiday Mondays. 23 May to 6 September open until 5.

Inspecting the freshly ground flour at Stainsby Mill on the Hardwick Estate in Derbyshire

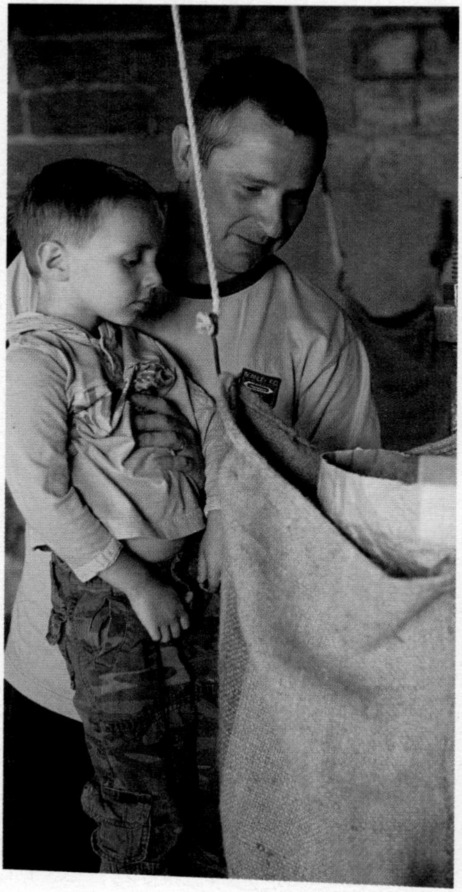

Hardwick Hall

Doe Lea, Chesterfield, Derbyshire S44 5QJ

Map (3) D3 1959

The Hardwick Estate is made up of stunning houses and beautiful landscapes that have been created by a cast of thousands. It was the formidable Bess of Hardwick who first built Hardwick Hall in the late 16th century, and in the centuries since then, gardeners, builders, decorators, embroiderers and craftsmen of all kinds have contributed and made Hardwick their creation. This year we are celebrating the 400th anniversary of Lady Arbella Stuart. You can discover how Hardwick was at the heart of England's social, political and religious turmoil, through the eyes of Lady Arbella – a royal granddaughter and prisoner to her destiny. There's so much to see and do, for all ages, throughout the year. **Note**: Old Hall owned by the National Trust and administered by English Heritage (01246 850431).

Eating and shopping: Great Barn Restaurant serving hot meals, seasonal specials and homemade cakes. Stables shop selling gifts, souvenirs and local produce. Outdoors shop and plant sales and (many propagated in the nursery at Hardwick). Picnic areas in the stableyard and parkland.

Making the most of your day: **Indoors** Seasonal events, including Easter, Hallowe'en and Christmas. **Outdoors** Open-air films during the summer and themed tours and talks. You can see the garden change throughout the seasons, from spring bulbs to autumn colours. There are also walking trails around the estate and surrounding countryside. Family woodland trail and Tracker Packs available daily and family fun activities during all school holidays. Stainsby Mill and Eyam Hall are nearby.
Dogs: welcome on leads in park and car park. Assistance dogs only in gardens.

Access:
Hall **Restaurant** **Garden**
Sat Nav: use S44 5RW.
Parking: 600-space car park.

Finding out more: 01246 850430 or hardwickhall@nationaltrust.org.uk

Hardwick Hall		M	T	W	T	F	S	S
Park, garden and restaurant								
Open all year	9-6*	**M**	**T**	**W**	**T**	**F**	**S**	**S**
Shop								
Open all year	10-6*	**M**	**T**	**W**	**T**	**F**	**S**	**S**
Hall								
7 Feb-1 Nov	12-4:30**	·	·	**W**	**T**	**F**	**S**	**S**
28 Nov-20 Dec	10:30-3:30†	·	·	**W**	**T**	**F**	**S**	**S**

*Park, garden, restaurant and shop close at 5 during winter months (November to February) and close 25 December.
**Hall also opens Bank Holiday Mondays (April to August).
Property may close early if weather is bad during winter.
†Reduced number of rooms visible during Christmas opening.

Hardwick Hall, Derbyshire: a full-length portrait of Lady Arbella Stuart at 13 years old (right), and visitors take a detailed look at a piece of furniture (opposite)

Some places are easy to get to on foot or by public transport. See page 3

Hawford Dovecote

Hawford, Worcestershire WR3 7SG

Map (4) J6 1973

Picturesque dovecote, which has survived virtually unaltered since the late 16th century, retaining many nesting boxes.

Note: sorry no toilet or tea-room. Please park carefully to one side of lane.

Finding out more: 01527 821214 or hawforddovecote@nationaltrust.org.uk

A bed fit for a king at Kedleston Hall, Derbyshire. The posts of this State Bed are carved as palm trees, with gilt roots forming feet and sprays supporting the canopy

Kedleston Hall

near Quarndon, Derby, Derbyshire DE22 5JH

Map (3) C4 1987

Kedleston is one of the grandest and most perfectly finished houses designed by architect Robert Adam as 'a temple of the arts' and the location for lavish entertainment. The main house was never meant to be a family home; instead it was merely a canvas on which to showcase the finest collection of paintings, sculpture and furniture belonging to the Curzon family. Set in beautiful naturalistic parkland, which blends seamlessly into the surrounding countryside, the 332 hectares (820 acres) are perfect for walks, picnics and spotting wildlife, as well as being home to more than 100 ancient trees.

 Please display your current sticker for free parking

Note: medieval All Saints church, containing many family monuments, run by the Churches Conservation Trust.

Eating and shopping: gift shop, plant sales and second-hand bookshop. The Great Kitchen Restaurant serving hot and cold lunches, cakes and teas. Refreshments available from coffee shop kiosk (peak times only).

Making the most of your day: **Indoors** Meet Mrs Garnett, our 18th-century housekeeper. Tours and children's trail. **Outdoors** Five waymarked walks. Talks and tours. Events all year, whatever the weather. **Dogs**: welcome on leads in park and pleasure grounds.

Access:
Ground floor **State floor**
Grounds
Sat Nav: follow brown signs.
Parking: 200 yards.

Finding out more: 01332 842191 or kedlestonhall@nationaltrust.org.uk

Kedleston Hall		M	T	W	T	F	S	S
Hall								
7 Feb–22 Feb	11–3	M	T	W	T	·	S	S
Whole property Conservation in Action*								
7 Mar–1 Nov	12–5	M	T	W	T	·	S	S
Hall introductory tour								
7 Mar–1 Nov	11–11:30	M	T	W	T	·	S	S
Park and Pleasure Grounds**								
1 Jan–6 Mar	10–4	M	T	W	T	F	S	S
7 Mar–1 Nov	10–6	M	T	W	T	F	S	S
2 Nov–31 Dec	10–4	M	T	W	T	F	S	S
Restaurant and shop								
7 Feb–22 Feb	10:30–3	M	T	W	T	F	S	S
7 Mar–1 Nov	10:30–5	M	T	W	T	·	S	S
7 Nov–20 Dec	10:30–4	·	·	·	·	·	S	S
26 Dec–31 Dec	10:30–3	M	T	W	T	·	S	S

Hall, restaurant and shop open Good Friday. Restaurant and shop open Fridays in school holidays. Hall: last admission 45 minutes before closing (will close early if light level is poor). Not all rooms may be open as part of introductory tour. **Occasional park and pleasure grounds closure in adverse weather and in winter. Property closed 25 December. *7 to 22 February Conservation in Action event with family activities and trail.

Kinver Edge and the Rock Houses

Holy Austin Rock Houses, Compton Road, Kinver, near Stourbridge, Staffordshire DY7 6DL

Map (4) I5 1917

The Holy Austin Rock Houses, inhabited until the 1950s, have no equivalent in the whole of England. Visitors can discover how a few extraordinary people carved themselves homes in this famous sandstone ridge. There is an extra treat if you walk on to Kinver Edge – dramatic views across three counties.

Eating and shopping: tea-room inside restored Rock House serving drinks, cakes and snacks, including our famous rock cakes.

Making the most of your day: **Indoors** Traditional games and range. **Outdoors** Adder Adventure Play Trail. Monthly guided rambles (booking required). **Dogs**: welcome on leads within grounds of Rock Houses.

Access: **Building** **Grounds**
Parking: by Warden's Lodge, Comber Road, for the Edge and Compton Road or Kingsford Lane overflow car park for the Rock Houses.

Finding out more: 01384 872553 or kinveredge@nationaltrust.org.uk

Kinver Edge and the Rock Houses		M	T	W	T	F	S	S
Rock Houses and tea-room								
19 Feb–29 Nov	11–4	·	·	·	T	F	S	S

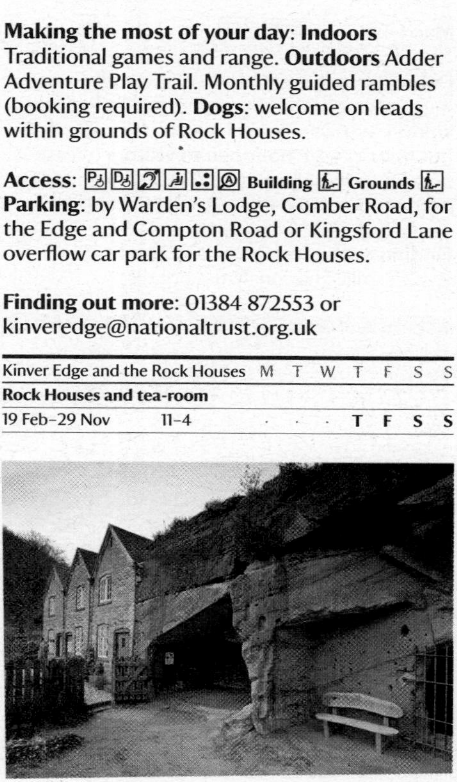

The extraordinary Holy Austin Rock Houses, Staffordshire, have no equivalent in the whole of England

Kinwarton Dovecote

Kinwarton, near Alcester,
Warwickshire B49 6HB

Map (4) K7 1958

Rare 14th-century circular dovecote with metre-thick walls, hundreds of nesting holes and original rotating ladder. **Note**: stock may be grazing. Sorry no toilet.

Finding out more: 01789 400777 or kinwartondovecote@nationaltrust.org.uk

Knowles Mill

Dowles Brook, Bewdley, Worcestershire DY12 2LX

Map (4) I6 1938

Dating from the 18th century, the mill retains much of its machinery, including the frames of an overshot waterwheel. **Note**: mill open daily, but Mill Cottage not open to visitors (please respect the resident's privacy). Sorry no toilets or tea-room. No parking at Mill Cottage.

Finding out more: 01527 821214 or knowlesmill@nationaltrust.org.uk

Letocetum Roman Baths and Museum

Watling Street, Wall, near Lichfield,
Staffordshire WS14 0AW

Map (4) K5 1934

Remains of a once-important Roman staging post and settlement, including *mansio* (Roman inn) and bathhouse. **Note**: in the guardianship of English Heritage.

Finding out more: 0870 333 1181 (English Heritage) or letocetum@nationaltrust.org.uk

Lyveden New Bield

Harley Way, near Oundle,
Northamptonshire PE8 5AT

Map (3) E6 1922

Tucked away in the heart of the Northamptonshire countryside lies a mysterious garden, a remarkable example of Renaissance design and craftsmanship. Started by Sir Thomas Tresham in 1595 but never completed, the garden contains many features desired by wealthy Elizabethan landowners, such as a water garden, bizarrely placed on top of a hill, and an eerie garden lodge covered in religious symbols – some features of which remain unexplained to this day. Our audio guide describes Sir Thomas's dream and how it all ended in a nightmare for the Tresham family with their involvement in the Gunpowder Plot.

Eating and shopping: small traditional Northamptonshire cottage tea-room, serving homemade cakes and cream teas. Ice-cream available from visitor reception. Picnics welcome.

Making the most of your day: free audio guide. Children's trail and volunteer-led tours. Numerous countryside walks. **Dogs**: welcome on leads only.

Access:
Building **Grounds**
Parking: 100 yards.

Finding out more: 01832 205158 or lyveden@nationaltrust.org.uk

Lyveden New Bield		M	T	W	T	F	S	S
3 Jan–28 Feb	11–4	·	·	·	·	·	S	S
1 Mar–31 Oct	10:30–5	M	T	W	T	F	S	S
1 Nov–27 Dec	11–4	·	·	·	·	·	S	S

Lyveden New Bield, Northamptonshire: this remarkable example of Renaissance design and craftsmanship was started in 1595 but never completed

The knot garden at Moseley Old Hall in Staffordshire: this atmospheric farmhouse holds many secrets

Middle Littleton Tithe Barn

Middle Littleton, Evesham, Worcestershire WR11 8LN

Map (4) K7 1975

The largest and finest restored 13th-century tithe barn in the country. **Note**: sorry no toilets.

Finding out more: 01905 371006 or middlelittleton@nationaltrust.org.uk

Morville Hall

Morville, near Bridgnorth, Shropshire WV16 5NB

Map (4) I5 1965

Stone-built house set in attractive gardens. Elizabethan in origin, extended around 1750, giving it the appearance of a Georgian home.

Finding out more: 01746 780838 or morvillehall@nationaltrust.org.uk

Moseley Old Hall

Moseley Old Hall Lane, Fordhouses, Wolverhampton, Staffordshire WV10 7HY

Map (4) J5 1962

This atmospheric farmhouse holds many secrets. Charles II hid here while fleeing for his life after the Battle of Worcester in 1651 and you can see where he hid, the bed he slept on and find out how he escaped Cromwell's army. Meanwhile daily life continues, and while a log fire crackles in the grate, the domestic world of the 17th century carries on around you. Outside, protected within the walled garden, are herbs, vegetables, an orchard and a knot garden. Beyond is King's Walk Wood, part of the Monarch's Way Trail.

Eating and shopping: tea-room serving light lunches, homemade cakes and scones – freshly baked throughout the day. Shop selling gifts and plants. Second-hand bookshop.

Making the most of your day: **Indoors** Guided tours, have-a-go sessions and re-creations of 17th-century life all year. **Outdoors** Children's activities, including Tracker Packs, tree-house and den-building. Wightwick Manor nearby. **Dogs**: welcome on leads in garden and grounds.

A peacock displays in the garden of Moseley Old Hall

Access: [access symbols] House [access symbols]
Grounds [access symbols]
Parking: on site.

Finding out more: 01902 782808 or
moseleyoldhall@nationaltrust.org.uk

Moseley Old Hall		M	T	W	T	F	S	S
House, tea-room and shop								
14 Feb–11 Mar	11–4	M	T	W	·	·	S	S
14 Mar–1 Nov	11–5	M	T	W	·	·	S	S
7 Nov–20 Dec	11–4	·	·	·	·	·	S	S
21 Dec–23 Dec	11–3	M	T	W	·	·	·	·
Tea-room and shop								
7 Aug–25 Sep	11–5	·	·	·	·	F	·	·

Grounds: open as tea-room and shop. House: opens 30 minutes after property, except Bank Holidays. In February, March, November, December, last entry is at 3 and, for safety, access to top floor may be limited; rest of year at 4. Guided tours available from 11:30 onwards, free-flow from 11:45.

The Old Manor

Norbury, Ashbourne, Derbyshire DE6 2ED

Map (3) B4 1987

Medieval hall featuring a rare king post, Tudor door and 17th-century Flemish glass.
Note: parking limited (cars only).

Finding out more: 01283 585337 or
oldmanor@nationaltrust.org.uk

Packwood House

Packwood Lane, Lapworth,
Warwickshire B94 6AT

Map (4) K6 1941

Surrounded by beautiful gardens and countryside, Packwood was described by a guest in the 1930s as 'a house to dream of, a garden to dream in'. Lovingly restored at the beginning of the 20th century by Graham Baron Ash, the house has a fascinating architectural history. This year you can discover the detail behind the man, his passion for collecting and his collection. The gardens include brightly coloured, 'mingled style' herbaceous borders, famous sculpted yews, an 18th-century gentleman's kitchen garden and playful sculpture in the park.

Eating and shopping: new Garden Kitchen café serving hot food, soup, salads, sandwiches, cakes and snacks. Shop selling seasonal gifts, local foods and plants, many grown in our own nursery. Picnics welcome.

The famous sculpted yews at Packwood House in Warwickshire

Making the most of your day: events, including Family Fun, open-air theatre and evening garden tours. Countryside walking trails, playful sculpture in the park and woodland Welly Walk. Baddesley Clinton and Coughton Court nearby. **Dogs**: welcome on leads in car park and park footpaths. Assistance dogs only in gardens.

Access: House Grounds
Parking: 150 yards.

Finding out more: 01564 782024 or packwood@nationaltrust.org.uk

Packwood House		M	T	W	T	F	S	S
House, garden and gift shop								
14 Feb–19 Jul	11–5	·	**T**	**W**	**T**	**F**	**S**	**S**
20 Jul–31 Aug	11–5	**M**	**T**	**W**	**T**	**F**	**S**	**S**
1 Sep–1 Nov	11–5	·	**T**	**W**	**T**	**F**	**S**	**S**
Café, shop and park								
1 Jan–13 Feb	9–4	·	**T**	**W**	**T**	**F**	**S**	**S**
14 Feb–19 Jul	9–5	·	**T**	**W**	**T**	**F**	**S**	**S**
20 Jul–31 Aug	9–5	**M**	**T**	**W**	**T**	**F**	**S**	**S**
1 Sep–1 Nov	9–5	·	**T**	**W**	**T**	**F**	**S**	**S**
3 Nov–31 Dec	9–4	·	**T**	**W**	**T**	**F**	**S**	**S**
House and garden tours*								
1 Jan–13 Feb	11–3	·	**T**	**W**	**T**	**F**	**S**	**S**
3 Nov–31 Dec	11–3	·	**T**	**W**	**T**	**F**	**S**	**S**

Open Mondays during school holidays (16 February, 30 March, 6 April and 26 October) and on Bank Holiday Mondays. Admission to the house by timed ticket (not bookable). *Tours run at intervals throughout the day, subject to availability. Closed 24 and 25 December.

Mysterious path at Packwood House, Warwickshire

Priest's House, Easton on the Hill

38 West Street, Easton on the Hill, near Stamford, Northamptonshire PE9 3LS

Map (3) E5 1966

Delightful small late 15th-century building, with interesting local architecture and museum exploring Easton on the Hill's industrial past. **Note**: open all year, 10 to 5. Access from neighbouring keyholders (details on property noticeboard).

Finding out more: 01832 205158 or priestshouse2@nationaltrust.org.uk

Rosedene

Victoria Road, Dodford, near Bromsgrove, Worcestershire B61 9BU

Map (4) J6 1997

Restored 1840s cottage, organic garden and orchard illustrating the mid-19th-century Chartist Movement. **Note**: available to hire as a 'back to basics' holiday cottage. Visit by booked tours only (first Sunday of the month, March to December).

Finding out more: 01527 821214 or rosedene@nationaltrust.org.uk

The fine Georgian mansion at Shugborough Estate, Staffordshire

Shugborough Estate

Milford, near Stafford, Staffordshire ST17 0XB

Map (4) J4 1966

Shugborough is a working, historic estate, featuring a fine Georgian mansion, working servants' quarters, farm with costumed servants and redeveloped walled garden. Home to the Earls of Lichfield, Shugborough is set in 364 hectares (900 acres) of Grade I listed parkland, peppered with unusual monuments. **Note**: entirely operated by Staffordshire County Council. Charge for members for all areas, apart from the house and gardens. Parking charge (including members), refunded on purchase of all-sites ticket.

Eating and shopping: licensed tea-room serving homemade cream teas and meals, including Shugborough's own-recipe sausage and mash and game casserole. Gift shop, ice-cream parlour, old-fashioned sweetshop and craft outlets making and selling handmade goods.

Making the most of your day: **Indoors** Mansion guided tours, 11 to 1. Regular demonstrations of milling, baking and cheese-making. **Outdoors** Events all year, including craft fairs, theatre and family activities. **Dogs**: on leads in formal gardens and main visitor routes.

Access:
Building **Grounds**

Parking: £3 (pay and display, including members). Refunded on purchase of all-sites ticket.

Finding out more: 0845 459 8900 or shugborough@nationaltrust.org.uk

Shugborough Estate		M	T	W	T	F	S	S
House and walled garden								
13 Mar–23 Oct	11–5	**M**	·	**W**	**T**	**F**	**S**	**S**
Parkland, gardens, tea-room and shop								
13 Mar–23 Oct	11–6*	**M**	**T**	**W**	**T**	**F**	**S**	**S**
Shop								
24 Oct–23 Dec	11–4	**M**	**T**	**W**	**T**	**F**	**S**	**S**

Servants' quarters and farm open as house. Access to house by guided tour only 11 to 1. *Tea-room and shop close at 5.

Staunton Harold Church

Staunton Harold Estate, Ashby-de-la-Zouch, Leicestershire LE65 1RW

Map (3) C4 1954

One of the few churches built between the outbreak of the English Civil War and the Restoration period. **Note**: nearest toilets 500 yards (not National Trust). Parking not National Trust; Staunton Harold Estate, charges apply (including members).

Finding out more: 01332 863822 or stauntonharold@nationaltrust.org.uk

Stoneywell

Whitcroft's Lane, Ulverscroft,
Leicestershire LE67 9QE

Map (3) D5 [icons] 2012

Built as a summer home by Arts and Crafts architect-designer Ernest Gimson for his brother Sydney, Stoneywell zigzags from its rocky outcrop, amid rhododendrons and heather. Every turn conjures childhood memories of holiday excitement, dashing down the winding steps – one way to the fort, the other to the woods beyond. **Note**: booking essential (due to the size of Stoneywell everyone, including members, must book in advance).

Eating and shopping: Stables tea-room (for use by booked visitors only) serving light lunches, cakes and cream teas. Small range of Arts and Crafts-inspired gifts and books available. Picnics welcome in grounds.

Making the most of your day: **Indoors** Beautifully crafted furniture, original to Stoneywell. **Outdoors** Games and swing in the garden. Woodland walks. **Dogs**: assistance dogs only.

Access: [icons] **Stables** [icons] **Cottage** [icons] **Gardens** [icons]
Sat Nav: use LE67 9QE. **Parking**: for booked visitors only.

Finding out more: 01530 248040 (Infoline). 01530 248048 (bookings) or stoneywell@nationaltrust.org.uk

Stoneywell		M	T	W	T	F	S	S
2 Feb–30 Nov	10–5	M	T	W	T	F	S	S

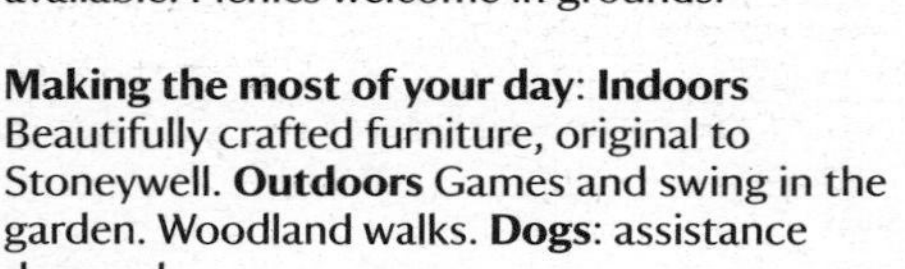

Stoneywell in Leicestershire (below) and the hallway of Mr Straw's House, Nottinghamshire (above)

Mr Straw's House

5–7 Blyth Grove, Worksop,
Nottinghamshire S81 0JG

Map (3) D2 [icons] 1990

You can discover how a grocer's family lived in a Midlands market town in this extraordinary home, virtually unchanged since 1923 and full of their treasured possessions and household objects. **Note**: to enable you to enjoy your visit we operate timed tickets, please book in advance.

Eating and shopping: shop selling jam, biscuits, plants, souvenirs and gifts. Coffee area. Picnic benches.

Making the most of your day: changing exhibitions. Tours and other events throughout the year.

Access: [icons] **Buildings** [icons] **Garden** [icons]
Parking: on site, in orchard.

Finding out more: 01909 482380 (bookings) or mrstrawshouse@nationaltrust.org.uk

Mr Straw's House		M	T	W	T	F	S	S
3 Mar–2 Apr	11-5*	·	T	W	T	F	S	·
4 Apr–31 Oct	11-5*	·	T	W	T	F	S	·

*Admission by tour only with timed ticket, booked in advance. Last tours start at 4. Closed Sundays, Mondays and Good Friday.

Some places are easy to get to on foot or by public transport. See page 3

Sudbury Hall and the National Trust Museum of Childhood

Sudbury, Ashbourne, Derbyshire DE6 5HT

Map (3) B4 1967

There's so much to see and do at Sudbury Hall and the Museum of Childhood. The Hall has one of the most surprising, light and beautiful long galleries in England and is the result of George Vernon's aspirations to create a perfect new home. You can get a glimpse of life 'below stairs' in the kitchen and basement, and picture yourself at home in some of the smaller family rooms. The Museum is a place of fun and fascination for all ages. View childhood from the Victorian period to the present day; send your little one up a chimney, play with our hands-on toys and games and join a lesson in the Victorian Schoolroom.

Eating and shopping: gift shop, plant sales, sweets and toys. Tea-room serving light lunches and homemade cakes. Additional refreshments available at peak times.

The re-created Victorian classroom at the National Trust Museum of Childhood (above) and Sudbury Hall (below) in Derbyshire

Making the most of your day: **Indoors** Hands-on toys in the museum. You can see behind the scenes and go to places not normally open to visitors on our themed Hall tours. **Outdoors** Events throughout the year, whatever the weather. Why not take part in a range of family activities during school holidays? Or you could pick up a trail sheet and test your skills in our woodland play area, then discover the wildlife in the Boat House.

Access:
Hall **Museum** **Grounds**
Parking: 500 yards.

Finding out more: 01283 585337 or sudburyhall@nationaltrust.org.uk

Sudbury Hall		M	T	W	T	F	S	S
Whole property Conservation in Action*								
7 Feb–22 Feb	11-3	**M**	**T**	**W**	**T**	**F**	**S**	**S**
Hall								
7 Mar–1 Nov	1-5	·	·	**W**	**T**	**F**	**S**	**S**
Hall tours								
7 Mar–1 Nov	11:30-12	·	·	**W**	**T**	**F**	**S**	**S**
7 Apr–27 Oct	11:30-2:30	·	**T**	·	·	·	·	·
Museum								
7 Mar–5 Apr	11-5	·	·	**W**	**T**	**F**	**S**	**S**
6 Apr–1 Nov	11-5	**M**	**T**	**W**	**T**	**F**	**S**	**S**
5 Nov–20 Dec	11-4	·	·	·	**T**	**F**	**S**	**S**
Tea-room and shop								
7 Feb–22 Feb	10:30-3	**M**	**T**	**W**	**T**	**F**	**S**	**S**
7 Mar–5 Apr	10:30-5	·	·	**W**	**T**	**F**	**S**	**S**
6 Apr–1 Nov	10:30-5	**M**	**T**	**W**	**T**	**F**	**S**	**S**
5 Nov–20 Dec	10:30-4	·	·	·	**T**	**F**	**S**	**S**

*7 to 22 February Conservation in Action event with family activities and trail. Open Bank Holidays. Last admission 45 minutes before closing (Hall will close early if light level is poor). Not all rooms may be open as part of tour.

Lessons at the National Trust Museum of Childhood

A game of skittles on the lawn at Sunnycroft, Shropshire

Sunnycroft

200 Holyhead Road, Wellington, Telford, Shropshire TF1 2DR

Map (4) I4 1999

This rare suburban villa and mini estate, tucked away in Wellington, is an Edwardian time capsule. Its original contents and features will transport you back to the pre-First World War 'country-house' lifestyle. Sunnycroft tells the story of a brewer, a widow and three generations of a local industrialist family.

Eating and shopping: small Edwardian tea-room serving light lunches, cakes, ice-creams and drinks. Picnics welcome on the lawn. Sunnycroft souvenirs, second-hand bookshop and plant sales available.

Making the most of your day: **Indoors** Guided tours and children's trails. Edwardian Christmas. **Outdoors** Garden tours and use of garden games, including croquet, badminton and skittles. Collection-themed events, including summer fête.

Dogs: welcome on leads in grounds only.

Access: [access symbols] **Building** [symbol] **Grounds** [symbols]
Sat Nav: use TF1 2DP. **Parking**: 150 yards. Additional parking in Wrekin Road car park (not National Trust).

Finding out more: 01952 242884 or sunnycroft@nationaltrust.org.uk

Sunnycroft		M	T	W	T	F	S	S
17 Jan–8 Mar	10:30–2	·	·	·	·	·	S	S
13 Mar–23 Mar	10:30–4	M	·	·	·	F	S	S
27 Mar–7 Apr	10:30–4	M	T	·	·	F	S	S
10 Apr–27 Jul	10:30–4	M	·	·	·	F	S	S
31 Jul–25 Aug	10:30–4	M	T	·	·	F	S	S
28 Aug–1 Nov	10:30–4	M	·	·	·	F	S	S
7 Nov–6 Dec	10:30–2	·	·	·	·	·	S	S
11 Dec–22 Dec	10:30–3	M	T	·	·	F	S	S

Entry by timed tickets with ten-minute introductory talk, then free-flow. Daily guided tours available in main season (not bookable). Free-flow throughout house on Bank Holiday weekends, 11 to 22 December and event days.

Tattershall Castle

Sleaford Road, Tattershall, Lincolnshire LN4 4LR

Map (3) F3 [symbols] 1925

Standing proudly on the edge of the Lincolnshire Fens, Tattershall Castle is a bold statement of late medieval style, architecture and achievement. Ralph Cromwell, Lord Treasurer to Henry VI, used his position and wealth to build the finest red-brick castle in the 15th century. The castle has been a home to lords, ladies, soldiers and cows and was saved from demolition in 1911 by Lord Curzon of Kedleston. Now the site is home to ducks, bats and moorhens, the birds living on the two moats. You might even spot the historic planes from the Battle of Britain Memorial Flight overhead. **Note**: access to the tower is via a spiral staircase only (149 steps).

Eating and shopping: Guardhouse shop selling sandwiches, wrapped cakes, hot and cold drinks, ice-cream, gifts and souvenirs. Picnics welcome.

Making the most of your day: **Indoors** Free audio guides for children and adults. **Outdoors** Events throughout the year, including Easter Egg trails, medieval re-enactments, open-air theatre and Christmas market. **Dogs**: welcome on leads in grounds only.

Access: [access symbols] **Castle** [symbol]
Parking: 150 yards.

Finding out more: 01526 342543 or tattershallcastle@nationaltrust.org.uk

Tattershall Castle		M	T	W	T	F	S	S
Castle, grounds and shop								
14 Feb–1 Nov	11–5	M	T	W	T	F	S	S
7 Nov–20 Dec	11–3	·	·	·	·	·	S	S
Countryside								
Open all year	Dawn–dusk	M	T	W	T	F	S	S

Last admission one hour before closing. Last audio guides issued one hour before closing. Some areas of the property may be temporarily closed for a wedding ceremony.

Tattershall Castle, Lincolnshire, stands proudly on the edge of the fens

Upton House and Gardens

near Banbury, Warwickshire OX15 6HT

Map (4) L7 1948

In 1939, Lord and Lady Bearsted vacated Upton, allowing the family-owned merchant bank to move in and escape the London air-raids. The evacuated staff set up a typing pool and canteen in the Long Gallery surrounded by Upton's great art collection, including works by Canaletto, Jan Steen and fine Chelsea porcelain. Those days are being re-created, with rooms dressed as though staff had slipped away for a coffee break. Outside, the sweeping lawn gives way to tumbling terraces, colourful borders and the sparkling mirror pool. There are also spring bulbs, a tranquil bog garden and kitchen garden to enjoy.

Eating and shopping: licensed restaurant serving hot lunches and freshly baked cakes and teas, including gluten-free and vegetarian options. Shop selling gifts, accessories, art books, plants and souvenirs.

Making the most of your day: **Indoors** Contemporary art exhibition, evocative house tours, treasure boxes and family dressing-up. **Outdoors** Woodland adventure and games. Home of National Collection of Asters (flowering in September). Two holiday cottages. **Dogs**: assistance dogs only in grounds.

Access:
House and gallery **Grounds**
Sat Nav: follow brown signs to car park once you arrive at postcode location.
Parking: 300 yards.

Finding out more: 01295 670266 or uptonhouse@nationaltrust.org.uk

Upton House and Gardens		M	T	W	T	F	S	S
Gardens, restaurant and shop*								
3 Jan–8 Feb	12–4	·	·	·	·	·	**S**	**S**
14 Feb–1 Nov	11–5	**M**	**T**	**W**	·	**F**	**S**	**S**
2 Nov–21 Dec	12–4	**M**	·	·	·	**F**	**S**	**S**
26 Dec–31 Dec	12–4	**M**	**T**	**W**	**T**	·	**S**	**S**
House and exhibition								
3 Jan–8 Feb	12–4	·	·	·	·	·	**S**	**S**
14 Feb–1 Nov	1–5	**M**	**T**	**W**	·	**F**	**S**	**S**
2 Nov–21 Dec	12–4	**M**	·	·	·	**F**	**S**	**S**

House admission each day is by timed ticket. Open every day in July and August. *November to March: gardens open by winter walk only. 14 February to 1 November: themed tours 11 to 1 (timed tickets available on arrival). 26 to 31 December: exhibition open. Open 1 January 2016.

The wood-panelled inglenook in the Picture Room at Upton House and Gardens, Warwickshire

Some places are easy to get to on foot or by public transport. See page 3

Springtime at The Weir in Herefordshire. This riverside garden is completely captivating, whatever the season

The Weir

Swainshill, Hereford, Herefordshire HR4 7QF

Map (4) H7 1959

Whatever the season, the natural beauty of this riverside garden is completely captivating. In spring, the ground beneath the ancient trees is carpeted with bulbs; then, in summer, a picnic by the river while watching the wildlife is irresistible. In autumn the walled garden is bursting with seasonal produce. **Note**: sturdy footwear recommended.

Eating and shopping: self-service tea and coffee available. Picnics welcome.

Making the most of your day: events, including walks and talks. Historical secrets to discover, from giant fish to Roman remains. Family trails during school holidays. Brockhampton Estate, Croft Castle and Parkland and Berrington Hall nearby.
Dogs: assistance dogs only (other dogs allowed in the car park).

Access: Grounds
Parking: on site.

Finding out more: 01981 590509 or theweir@nationaltrust.org.uk

The Weir		M	T	W	T	F	S	S
17 Jan–25 Jan	10:30–4	·	·	·	·	·	S	S
31 Jan–1 Nov	10:30–4:30	M	T	W	T	F	S	S
7 Nov–15 Nov	10:30–4	·	·	·	·	·	S	S

Wichenford Dovecote

Wichenford, Worcestershire WR6 6XY

Map (4) I7 1965

Small but striking 17th-century half-timbered dovecote at Wichenford Court. **Note**: no access to Wichenford Court (privately owned). Sorry no toilet or tea-room. Please consider local residents when parking.

Finding out more: 01527 821214 or wichenforddovecote@nationaltrust.org.uk

The Great Parlour (above) and formal garden (below) at Wightwick Manor and Gardens in the West Midlands

Wightwick Manor and Gardens

Wightwick Bank, Wolverhampton,
West Midlands WV6 8EE

Map (4) J5 1937

The haven of a romantic industrialist, Wightwick's timber beams and barley-twist chimneys, rich William Morris furnishings and Pre-Raphaelite paintings, gardens of wide lawns, yew hedges and roses, make it an idyllic time capsule of Victorian nostalgia for medieval England. If you delve deeper, you will find stories of the remarkable politician, Geoffrey Mander, who fought social injustice and European fascism and felt the need to share this unique property with the nation. More than 75 years since that gift, the magic and warmth of the home is as enthralling and enchanting as ever.

Eating and shopping: specialist shop selling William Morris and Arts and Crafts-inspired range and plant centre (also available online). Tea-room serving range of light lunches, sandwiches and sweet treats.

Please display your current sticker for free parking

Making the most of your day: **Indoors** Events, including specialist talks and tours, throughout the year. **Outdoors** Year-round garden orienteering map, family activities in school holidays. Moseley Old Hall nearby.
Dogs: welcome on leads in garden.

Access:
Manor **Gardens**
Sat Nav: use WV6 8BN.
Parking: entrance off A454.

Finding out more: 01902 761400 or wightwickmanor@nationaltrust.org.uk

Wightwick Manor and Gardens		M	T	W	T	F	S	S
Garden, tea-room and shop								
1 Jan–13 Feb	11–4	M	T	W	T	F	S	S
14 Feb–1 Nov	11–5	M	T	W	T	F	S	S
2 Nov–31 Dec	11–4	M	T	W	T	F	S	S
House								
1 Jan–13 Feb	12–4	M	·	W	T	F	S	S
14 Feb–5 Jul	12–5	M	·	W	T	F	S	S
6 Jul–30 Aug	12–5	M	T	W	T	F	S	S
31 Aug–1 Nov	12–5	M	·	W	T	F	S	S
2 Nov–31 Dec	12–4	M	·	W	T	F	S	S

Last entry to house one hour before closing.
Closed 25 December. A reduced number of rooms will be open January to mid-February and after 26 December.

Wilderhope Manor

Longville, Much Wenlock, Shropshire TF13 6EG

Map (4) H5 1936

Beautiful Elizabethan manor house, restored by John Cadbury in 1936, surrounded by farmland managed for landscape and wildlife.
Note: youth hostel, access may be restricted. Open Sundays throughout the year, and Wednesdays, April to September.

Finding out more: 01694 771363 (Hostel Warden YHA) or wilderhope@nationaltrust.org.uk

Winster Market House

Main Street, Winster, Matlock, Derbyshire DE4 2DJ

Map (3) C3 1906

An excellent example of its type and the first Peak District place to be acquired by the Trust. It cost £50 and became a listed building in 1951. Its origins are in the 16th century, when cheese and cattle fairs featured prominently in the daily life of the area. **Note**: Winster Market House is unstaffed.

Making the most of your day: information room with interpretation panels and a scale model of Winster village. Ilam Park and Dovedale nearby.

Access:
Parking: on street or at small village car parks (not National Trust).

Finding out more: 01335 350503 or winstermarkethouse@nationaltrust.org.uk

Winster Market House		M	T	W	T	F	S	S
28 Mar–1 Nov	11–5	M	T	W	T	F	S	S

Winster Market House, Derbyshire, dates from the 16th century

Woolsthorpe Manor

Water Lane, Woolsthorpe by Colsterworth, near Grantham, Lincolnshire NG33 5PD

Map (3) E4 1943

A small manor house but the birthplace of a great mind – Sir Isaac Newton, world-famous scientist, mathematician, alchemist and Master of the Royal Mint. During the plague years of 1665–6, he returned to the family farm and produced some of his most important work on physics and mathematics here, including his crucial experiment to split white light into a spectrum of colours. Today you can still see the famous apple tree and explore some of Newton's ideas for yourself in the hands-on Science Centre.

Eating and shopping: coffee shop and small shop in ticket office. Second-hand bookshop.

Woolsthorpe Manor, Lincolnshire: the birthplace of Sir Isaac Newton

Making the most of your day: **Indoors** Demonstrations of 17th-century food and crafts. Hands-on science and children's activity room. Volunteer-led 'Tales from Woolsthorpe' and science talks. Film. Family events all year. **Outdoors** Don't miss Isaac's apple tree! **Dogs**: welcome in car park only.

Access: **House** **Science Centre** **Grounds**
Parking: 50 yards.

Finding out more: 01476 860338 or woolsthorpemanor@nationaltrust.org.uk
23 Newton Way, Woolsthorpe by Colsterworth, near Grantham, Lincolnshire NG33 5NR

Woolsthorpe Manor		M	T	W	T	F	S	S
Manor house								
2 Jan–20 Mar	11–3	**M**	·	·	·	**F**	**S**	**S**
21 Mar–25 Oct	11–5	**M**	·	**W**	**T**	**F**	**S**	**S**
26 Oct–28 Dec*	11–3	**M**	·	·	·	**F**	**S**	**S**
Science Discovery Centre and coffee shop								
1 Jan–20 Mar	11–3	**M**	**T**	**W**	**T**	**F**	**S**	**S**
21 Mar–25 Oct	11–5	**M**	**T**	**W**	**T**	**F**	**S**	**S**
26 Oct–31 Dec*	11–3	**M**	**T**	**W**	**T**	**F**	**S**	**S**

Film and grounds open as Science Discovery Centre.
Guided tours to manor house during winter opening.
*Closed 24 and 25 December.

The Workhouse, Southwell in Nottinghamshire (above and below): this austere building implemented a harsh regime

The Workhouse, Southwell

Upton Road, Southwell,
Nottinghamshire NG25 0PT

Map (3) D3 2002

Walking up the pauper's path towards The Workhouse it is easy to imagine how the Victorian poor might have felt as they sought refuge here. This austere building, the most complete workhouse in existence, was built in 1824 as a place of last resort for the destitute. Its architecture was influenced by prison design and its harsh regime became a blueprint for workhouses throughout the country. The stories of those who lived and worked here in the 1840s help bring the building to life and prompt reflection on how society has tackled poverty through the centuries.

Eating and shopping: refreshment room offering drinks and snacks. Shop selling gifts, seasonal produce from the vegetable garden. Picnic benches in the garden.

Making the most of your day: **Indoors** Wide range of events for all, including living history days, storytelling and special tours. Children's trails and hands-on activities. **Outdoors** Re-created Victorian vegetable garden planted with heritage varieties.

Access:
Building **Grounds**
Sat Nav: use NG25 0QB. **Parking**: 200 yards.

Finding out more: 01636 817260 or theworkhouse@nationaltrust.org.uk

The Workhouse, Southwell		M	T	W	T	F	S	S
14 Feb–31 Jul	12–5	·	·	W	T	F	S	S
1 Aug–31 Aug	12–5	M	T	W	T	F	S	S
2 Sep–1 Nov	12–5	·	·	W	T	F	S	S

Guided tour of the outside and other buildings at 11 (places limited). Open Bank Holidays. Last admission one hour before closing.

North West

Sizergh, Cumbria

Outdoors in the North West

From Cheshire's diverse countryside to the stunning Lancashire coast or the Lake District's inspiring landscape, the North West is one of the best places to enjoy the outdoors.

Alderley Edge and Cheshire Countryside

Nether Alderley, Macclesfield, Cheshire

Map (5) D8 1946

The dramatic red sandstone escarpment of Alderley Edge has far-reaching views over the Cheshire Plain and towards the Peak District. Numerous paths meander through open pasture, mature pine and beech woodland. The site, designated a Site of Special Scientific Interest for its geology and history of copper mining dating back to the Bronze Age, is also noted for its legend and *The Weirdstone of Brisingamen* novel. For similar countryside experiences, why not visit Bickerton, Bulkeley and Helsby Hills on the Sandstone Ridge, Thurstaston Common on the Wirral, and The Cloud and Mow Cop on the Staffordshire border? **Note**: toilets at Alderley Edge car park only.

Eating and shopping: Alderley Edge: Wizard Tea-room (weekends and some Bank Holidays only) and Wizard Inn (neither National Trust). Ice-cream vendor (when weather is fine). Picnic area close to car park.

Walkers in the fields below Alderley Edge in Cheshire

Making the most of your day: 'Baffled by Humps and Hollows' guided walk at Alderley Edge. Circular walk through woodland and pasture to Hare Hill. Orienteering. Mine tours: Derbyshire Caving Club, twice yearly. **Dogs**: under close control. On leads where livestock present.

Access: **Grounds**
Sat Nav: for Alderley Edge use SK10 4UB.
Parking: at Alderley Edge, Mow Cop and Bickerton (plus roadside elsewhere).

Finding out more: 01625 584412 or alderleyedge@nationaltrust.org.uk

Alderley Edge		M	T	W	T	F	S	S
Countryside								
Open all year	Dawn–dusk	M	T	W	T	F	S	S
Alderley Edge car park								
1 Jan–31 Mar	8–5	M	T	W	T	F	S	S
1 Apr–31 May	8–5:30	M	T	W	T	F	S	S
1 Jun–30 Sep	8–6	M	T	W	T	F	S	S
1 Oct–31 Dec	8–5	M	T	W	T	F	S	S

Formby

near Formby, Liverpool

Map (5) B7 1967

Formby's sand dunes and wide beaches command sea views over Liverpool Bay to the hills of North Wales. Pinewood walks with red squirrels lead to open fields and the Formby asparagus trail. Footprint trails, 5,000 years old, sometimes re-appear as the sea erodes ancient mudflats. **Note**: toilets close at 5.30 in summer, 4 in winter.

Eating and shopping: ice-cream, soft drinks, coffee and confectionery available from mobile vans. Picnics welcome (safe barbecue area).

Making the most of your day: guided walks. Trail guides. Circular and longer walks linked to the Sefton Coastal Path. Orienteering and geocaching. **Dogs**: under close control (vulnerable wildlife).

Access: **Grounds**
Sat Nav: use L37 1LJ. **Parking**: on site.

Finding out more: 01704 878591 or formby@nationaltrust.org.uk

Formby		M	T	W	T	F	S	S
Car park								
1 Jan–1 Feb	9–4	M	T	W	T	F	S	S
2 Feb–29 Mar	9–4:30	M	T	W	T	F	S	S
30 Mar–25 Oct	9–5:30	M	T	W	T	F	S	S
26 Oct–29 Nov	9–4:30	M	T	W	T	F	S	S
30 Nov–31 Dec	9–4	M	T	W	T	F	S	S

Closed 25 December.

Formby near Liverpool: sand dunes and wide beaches

Lake District

Whether you want a great day out, a gentle stroll and splash in the lake, challenging hike to the mountaintops, or a picnic spot with a view, we've got it all.

Aira Force and Ullswater

near Watermillock, Penrith, Cumbria

Map (6) D7 1906

Aira Force is a showcase for the power and beauty of nature, it's a place to escape the ordinary. For 300 years visitors have been drawn here, where rainwater runs from the fells into Aira Beck (right) and thunders in one 65-foot leap over the falls. Yet, Aira Force is much more than an impressive waterfall. A network of trails weave their way from Ullswater lakeshore to Gowbarrow summit, passing towering Himalayan firs, rare red squirrels, woodland glades, picnic spots, and views out across Ullswater. This year, for the first time, you can leave the car behind in Glenridding and arrive on an Ullswater Steamer, taking in the sights of Ullswater valley along the way.

Eating and shopping: tea-room serving light lunches, cakes, ice-cream and hot and cold drinks. Shop selling gifts and souvenirs. Light refreshments for sale in picnic area.

Making the most of your day: new *Aira Force Guide* available at the shop for walking trails, points of interest and Rangers' tips. Red squirrel trail and natural play area. Canoe launching at Glencoyne car park. Picnic and pebble skimming at Aira Green. Boat rides with Ullswater Steamers. Wordsworth's daffodils on Ullswater lakeshore in spring. New off-road footpath from Aira Force to Glencoyne Bay. Walks to Gowbarrow summit, the best spot for panoramic views across the Lakeland fells. **Dogs**: under close control (stock grazing).

Aira Force in Cumbria: exploring on the woodland trail

Access: Grounds
Parking: at Aira Force, Aira Force High Cascades, Aira Force Park Brow and Glencoyne Bay.

Finding out more: 017684 82067 or ullswater@nationaltrust.org.uk

Aira Force and Ullswater		M	T	W	T	F	S	S
Tea-room								
14 Feb–24 Dec	10:30–4	**M**	**T**	**W**	**T**	**F**	**S**	**S**
Shop								
1 Jan–24 Dec	10:30–4	**M**	**T**	**W**	**T**	**F**	**S**	**S**

Opening times may vary.

Ambleside

near Windermere, Cumbria

Map (6) D8 1927

Sitting on the northern tip of Lake Windermere, the town of Ambleside is surrounded by countryside. Skelghyll Wood is home to Cumbria's tallest trees. In spring, Stagshaw Gardens bursts into life with displays of azaleas and rhododendrons, and Jenkyn's Field is great for a lakeshore picnic and paddle.

Making the most of your day: Bridge House, Ambleside's smallest building, built on a bridge over a beck. Tall Tree Trail at Skelghyll Woods. New information panels at Ambleside Roman Fort. Townend nearby. **Dogs**: welcome under close control (stock grazing).

Access: **Bridge House**

Sat Nav: use LA22 9AN.
Parking: at Stagshaw Gardens.

Finding out more: 015394 46402 or ambleside@nationaltrust.org.uk

Ambleside		M	T	W	T	F	S	S
Bridge House								
24 Mar–1 Nov	11–4	**M**	**T**	**W**	**T**	**F**	**S**	**S**
Stagshaw Gardens								
Open all year	Dawn–dusk	**M**	**T**	**W**	**T**	**F**	**S**	**S**

Stagshaw Gardens at their best April to July.

Borrowdale and Derwentwater

near Keswick, Cumbria

Map (6) D7 1902

Derwentwater is often called the 'Queen of the Lakes', and as you canoe between the islands with your picnic at the ready it's easy to see why. The boardwalk across the wetlands makes the 9-mile circular lake walk a delight, and the jewel in the crown is Derwent Island House, open to visitors for five special days each year. As Borrowdale winds the 7 miles from Keswick to Seathwaite, there are eight car parks from which you can start your adventure into the fells. Directions for iconic routes like Castle Crag (below) and Cat Bells are in our *Rangers' Guide*. **Note**: charges apply to members on Force Crag Mine and Derwent Island House open days.

Eating and shopping: Derwentwater lakeside shop and visitor centre selling souvenirs, refreshments and ice-cream. Selection of tenant-run cafés serving local treats.

Discovering Force Crag Mine, Borrowdale, Cumbria

Making the most of your day: five days a year, you can don a hard-hat for a guided tour of Force Crag Mine processing mill. Windswept and atmospheric, it's a fascinating glimpse into Lakeland's industrial heritage. **Dogs**: under close control at lambing time.

Access: Island House Mine Foreshore
Sat Nav: use CA12 5DJ for lakeside shop and CA12 5XN for Seatoller (at foot of Honister Pass). **Parking**: at Great Wood, Ashness Bridge, Surprise View, Watendlath, Kettlewell, Bowder Stone, Rosthwaite, Seatoller and Honister Pass.

Finding out more: 017687 74649 or borrowdale@nationaltrust.org.uk

Borrowdale and Derwentwater

Visit our website for Force Crag Mine and Derwent Island House open days.

Buttermere Valley

near Cockermouth, Cumbria

Map (6) C7 1935

Looking down from Grey Knotts summit you'll see Buttermere, Crummock Water and Loweswater offering lakeshore walks and fell-top reflections. **Note**: sorry no toilets at Crummock Water or Loweswater. For Sat Nav use CA13 9UZ for Buttermere, CA13 0RT for Crummock Water, CA13 0RU for Loweswater. For Loweswater bothy bookings please see nationaltrust.org.uk/camping.

Finding out more: 017687 74649 or buttermere@nationaltrust.org.uk

Claife Viewing Station and Windermere West Shore

near Far Sawrey, Cumbria

Map (6) D8 1962

The western shore of Windermere is perfect for a car-free adventure. Why not come on the ferry and check out Claife Viewing Station? The 4-mile track from here leads to Wray Castle, so this part of the Lakes is great for exploring on your bike or on foot. **Note**: toilets at Ferry House (near Claife Viewing Station).

Eating and shopping: pop-up café at Wray Castle serving freshly made cakes, sandwiches, snacks and drinks. Picnics welcome along the West Shore. The Wray Castle shop stocks gifts, treats and essential castle kit, such as swords and archery sets.

Making the most of your day: why not let the passenger ferry bring you across the lake so you can enjoy the view from Claife and a walk along the lakeshore without bringing the car?
Dogs: allowed in countryside, under close control.

Access: Viewing Station
Parking: at Ash Landing and Harrowslack, near Windermere lakeshore, for Claife Viewing Station.

Finding out more: 015394 41456 or claife@nationaltrust.org.uk

Claife Viewing Station
Works taking place this year may restrict access to the Viewing Station at certain times.

Ennerdale

Cleator, Cumbria

Map (6) C7 1927

Home of the Wild Ennerdale project with 30 miles of traffic-free tracks and paths – the quiet side of Lakeland. **Note**: sorry no toilet. For Sat Nav use CA23 3AU for Bowness Knott and CA23 3AS for Bleach Green.

Finding out more: 017687 74649 or ennerdale@nationaltrust.org.uk

Eskdale and Duddon Valley

Eskdale, near Ravenglass; Duddon Valley, near Broughton in Furness

Map (6) D8 1926

Eskdale is a valley of contrasts, with upper Eskdale leading to the high mountains, including Scafell, Esk Pike and Bowfell. On the valley floor are meandering riverside and woodland paths. Across high mountain passes lies the Duddon Valley. A diverse landscape with wildflower meadows, woodlands, mountains, hill farms and rivers.

Eating and shopping: pubs at Eskdale Green, Boot and Seathwaite; shops at Eskdale Green, Boot and Ulpha Post Office; café and shop at Dalegarth station (none National Trust).

Making the most of your day: walks from the La'al Ratty Railway, running through Eskdale (Ravenglass to Dalegarth). Hardknott Roman Fort to explore. Woodland paths in Duddon Valley. Upland walks to Harter Fell and Seathwaite Tarn.
Dogs: please follow local and seasonal guidance.

Access:
Parking: in lay-bys, along roadsides and at some small village car parks (not National Trust).

Finding out more: 019467 23466 or eskdaleandduddon@nationaltrust.org.uk

Fell Foot

Newby Bridge, Windermere, Cumbria

Map (6) D9 1948

Sitting on the southern tip of Lake Windermere with views across the water to the mountains above, this family-friendly park has green lawns sloping down to the lakeshore that are a great place for playing, a picnic or barbecue. It offers the perfect opportunity to get outdoors, stroll along the lakeshore or explore, and is one of the best spots to soak up Lake Windermere in all its beauty. With easy lake access, the park is ideal

Fun on Windermere (below) at Fell Foot (top), Cumbria

for paddling, swimming and boating. If you want to take to the water, then boats can be hired from the Boathouse Café. **Note**: building works possible later in the year. Launch/slipway facilities available for a wide variety of craft, charges apply (including members).

Eating and shopping: Boathouse Café serving hot and cold drinks, soup and snacks, homemade cakes and pastries. A small selection of children's toys, gifts, maps, picnic rugs and seasonal goods available in the shop. Picnics welcome.

Making the most of your day: seasonal rowing boat hire, April to October (weather permitting). Events. Adventure playground, volleyball pitch and easy lake access with 'beach' for paddling. Quiet spots and easy meadow walk. **Dogs**: welcome on leads.

Access: **Grounds**
Sat Nav: use LA12 8NN.
Parking: two large car parks.

Finding out more: 015395 31273 or fellfoot@nationaltrust.org.uk

Fell Foot		M	T	W	T	F	S	S
Park								
1 Jan–27 Mar	Dawn–dusk	M	T	W	T	F	S	S
28 Mar–6 Sep	8–8	M	T	W	T	F	S	S
7 Sep–31 Dec	Dawn–dusk	M	T	W	T	F	S	S
Catering facilities								
14 Feb–27 Mar	11–4	M	T	W	T	F	S	S
28 Mar–6 Sep	10–5	M	T	W	T	F	S	S
7 Sep–1 Nov	11–4	M	T	W	T	F	S	S
Retail facilities								
28 Mar–17 Jul	11–4	M	T	W	T	F	S	S
18 Jul–6 Sep	10–5	M	T	W	T	F	S	S
7 Sep–1 Nov	11–4	M	T	W	T	F	S	S

Boat hire available daily from April to October, weather permitting. Catering facilities: opening times may vary.

Sticklebarn and The Langdales

near Ambleside, Cumbria

Map (6) D8 1925

Sticklebarn is a traditional pub with panoramic views of the iconic Langdale Pikes. It's the only pub run by the National Trust – we want to ensure that every penny we make goes back into looking after Langdale. Sticklebarn sits at the heart of miles of walking routes and, with crackling fires, real ales and Lakeland food, there's no better place to unwind after a day on the fells. The ambitious can tackle the major peaks, but it's not all about high-level scrambling. The circular route around Blea Tarn is easily accessible, with views of Little and Great Langdale.

Eating and shopping: pub (below) serving food and drink all day. Outdoor eating on the terrace. Wood-fired pizza oven. Good helpings of hearty Lakeland food, including the irresistible Stickle Toffee Pudding. A range of Cumbrian real ales and our own Sticklebarn Bedrock Gin.

Making the most of your day: ghyll scrambling and rock climbing. Our *Rangers' Guide to the Langdales* available at the pub. Live music, adventure film nights and family film matinées at Sticklebarn. Autumn Pumpkinfest.
Dogs: welcome under control.

Access: **Pub** **Grounds**
Sat Nav: use LA22 9JU for Sticklebarn.
Parking: at Stickle Ghyll, Old Dungeon Ghyll, Blea Tarn and Elterwater village.

Finding out more: 015394 37356 (Sticklebarn). 015394 35665 (Grasmere Information Centre) or sticklebarn@nationaltrust.org.uk

Sticklebarn and The Langdales		M	T	W	T	F	S	S
Sticklebarn								
1 Jan–4 Jan	12–11*	·	·	·	T	F	S	S
26 Jan–27 Mar	12–6**	M	T	W	T	F	S	S
28 Mar–1 Nov	12–11*	M	T	W	T	F	S	S
2 Nov–20 Dec	12–6**	M	T	W	T	F	S	S
26 Dec–31 Dec	12–11*	M	T	W	T	·	S	S

*Closes 10:30 in the evening on Sundays. **Friday, Saturday and Sunday: open until 9 in the evening.

Tarn Hows and Coniston

near Coniston, Cumbria

Map (6) D8 1943

Stunning Tarn Hows offers an accessible circular walk (1¾ miles) through beautiful countryside with majestic mountain views. We have off-road mobility scooters available to hire for less-able visitors. The area around the tarn and Coniston village is a great place to begin your wider Lake District adventure.

Eating and shopping: ice-cream van on site, also selling hot and cold drinks. Numerous catering options nearby, particularly in Coniston and Hawkshead. Picnics welcome.

Making the most of your day: theme your day around water and come to Tarn Hows via a Steam Yacht Gondola cruise on Coniston. Nearby Wray Castle on Windermere's west shore is great for families. **Dogs**: on leads (stock grazing).

Access: **Grounds**
Parking: on site at Tarn Hows; also at Glen Mary in Coniston (not National Trust).

Finding out more: 015394 41456 or tarnhows@nationaltrust.org.uk

Wasdale

near Gosforth, Cumbria

Map (6) D8 1920

The birthplace of British mountaineering and it's easy to see why. Wasdale Head lies beneath towering mountains, including England's highest – Scafell Pike. People have lived in the valley since earliest times and the intricate network of walled fields is testimony to the long history of farming in this area. Here too lies England's deepest lake, Wastwater, with the Screes sweeping down from the top of Illgill Head to the lake below, creating ever-changing images on the surface of the water. Towards the southern end of the lake and Nether Wasdale, there are natural woodlands with winding paths. **Note**: limited toilet facilities (we are planning improvements and raising money towards this project).

Eating and shopping: shop at National Trust campsite in Wasdale. Pub and shop at Wasdale Head and pubs in Nether Wasdale and Santon Bridge (none National Trust).

Wasdale, Cumbria: pausing to admire 'Britain's favourite view' with England's deepest lake, Wastwater, glimmering in the distance

Making the most of your day: walking and climbing in England's highest mountains. Lakeside, riverbank and woodland rambles. Wild-swimming and paddling in Wastwater and rivers. Herdwick sheep graze in fields and on fells. **Dogs**: well-behaved dogs welcome. Please follow local and seasonal guidance.

Access: [icon]
Sat Nav: use CA20 1EX. **Parking**: at Lake Head.

Finding out more: 019467 26064 or wasdale@nationaltrust.org.uk

Whitehaven Coast

Whitehaven, Cumbria

Map ⑥ C7

This post-industrial coastline holds hidden gems with clifftop walks from the Georgian harbour and views to the Isle of Man. **Note**: sorry no toilet. For Sat Nav use CA28 9BG for Haig and CA28 7LY for Whitehaven harbour.

Finding out more: 017687 74649 or whitehavencoast@nationaltrust.org.uk

Morecambe Bay Coast

Sand dunes, cliffs, fascinating wildlife and amazing views make this coast a perfect backdrop for a day at the beach.

Arnside and Silverdale

near Arnside, Cumbria

Map ⑤ C4 1929

With a wildlife-rich mosaic of limestone grassland, pavement, woodland and meadows this coastal countryside offers fine views over Morecambe Bay and miles of footpaths.

Arnside Knott, Cumbria: a lone Scots pine stands sentinel

Arnside Knott and Eaves Wood are home to butterflies and flowers; Jack Scout's cliffs are perfect for watching the setting sun or migrant birds passing through.

Eating and shopping: variety of small shops, galleries and cafés in and around Arnside and Silverdale villages (not National Trust). Nearest National Trust café at Sizergh.

Making the most of your day: toposcope viewpoint (short uphill from Arnside Knott car park). Silverdale Lots footpath to the cove perfect for strolls. Silverdale village heritage walk. **Dogs**: welcome under control (on leads where stock grazing).

Access: [icon]
Parking: at Arnside Knott (signposted from Arnside Promenade) and Eaves Wood, Silverdale. Also in Silverdale village (not National Trust).

Finding out more: 01524 702815 or arnsidesilverdale@nationaltrust.org.uk

Heysham Coast

Heysham, near Morecambe, Lancashire

Map (6) D10 1996

A beautiful sandstone walk in coastal grassland and peaceful woodland, leading to a unique ruined Saxon chapel and rock-cut graves. **Note**: nearest facilities in village (not National Trust); park in the main village car park. For Sat Nav use LA3 2RN.

Finding out more: 01524 701178 or heysham@nationaltrust.org.uk

Sandscale Haws National Nature Reserve

near Barrow in Furness, Cumbria

Map (6) D9 1984

Home to natterjack toads, these wild, grass-covered sand dunes and beach are the perfect habitat for rare wildlife. **Note**: toilets (not National Trust). Car park open all year. For Sat Nav use LA14 4QJ.

Finding out more: 01229 462855 or sandscalehaws@nationaltrust.org.uk

Near Old Dungeon Ghyll car park, Great Langdale, Cumbria

Additional coastal and countryside car parks in the North West

Borrowdale and Derwentwater	
Great Wood	NY 272 213
Kettlewell	NY 269 196
Ashness Bridge	NY 270 195
Surprise View	NY 268 190
Watendlath	NY 276 164
Bowderstone	NY 254 167
Rosthwaite	NY 257 148
Seatoller	NY 246 137
Buttermere Valley	
Honister Pass	NY 225 135
Buttermere	NY 172 173
Lanthwaite Wood	NY 149 215
Ullswater	
Aira Force	NY 401 201
Glencoyne Bay	NY 387 188
High Cascades	NY 397 211
Wasdale	
Lake Head	NY 182 074
Overbeck	NY 168 068
Nether Wasdale	NY 128 038
The Langdales	
Blea Tarn	NY 295 043
Old Dungeon Ghyll	NY 285 062
Stickle Ghyll	NY 295 064
Elterwater	NY 329 047
Coniston	
Glen Mary	SD 321 998
Tarn Hows	SD 326 995
Windermere West Shore	
Red Nab	SD 385 995
Harrowslack	SD 388 960
Ash Landing	SD 388 955
Coast	
Sandscale Haws	SD 200 756
Arnside Knott	SD 458 776
Eaves Wood (Silverdale)	SD 457 749
Formby	SD 275 082
Cheshire Countryside	
Alderley Edge	SJ 860 776
Mow Cop	SJ 857 573
Bickerton	SJ 498 529

Acorn Bank

Temple Sowerby, near Penrith, Cumbria CA10 1SP

Map (6) E7 1950

At the heart of the Eden Valley, with spectacular views to the Lake District, Acorn Bank is a tranquil haven with an almost forgotten industrial past. Its wide estate has hidden gypsum-mining remains and an abundance of wildlife. The walled gardens shelter a medicinal herb collection and traditional orchards. Woodland paths along Crowdundle Beck lead to the watermill, now working again after more than 70 years. The unfurnished, 17th-century, sandstone house is partially open to the public while restoration work progresses. In spring the woods are awash with daffodils, a legacy of donor D. U. Ratcliffe, lady of a million daffodils. **Note**: access to fragile grass paths may be restricted after wet weather. Members pay on Apple Day, 11 October (opening arrangements differ on that day, see note in table for details).

Spectacular border at Acorn Bank in Cumbria

Eating and shopping: tea-room serving light lunches, cakes and scones made using herbs and fruit from the garden and flour from the mill. Shop selling gifts and plants.

Making the most of your day: watermill machinery operates most weekend afternoons. Apple Day is a great family day out.
Dogs: welcome on leads on woodland walks and garden courtyard. Apple Day: assistance dogs only.

Access: **Watermill** **House** **Grounds**
Parking: on site, limited.

Finding out more: 017683 61893 or acornbank@nationaltrust.org.uk

Acorn Bank		M	T	W	T	F	S	S
House, garden, watermill, woodland walks and shop								
14 Feb–8 Mar	11–4	·	·	·	·	·	S	S
14 Mar–1 Nov*	10–5	M	·	W	T	F	S	S
7 Nov–20 Dec	11–4	·	·	·	·	·	S	S
Tea-room								
14 Feb–8 Mar	11–4	·	·	·	·	·	S	S
14 Mar–1 Nov	10:30–4:30	M	·	W	T	F	S	S
7 Nov–20 Dec	11–4	·	·	·	·	·	S	S

*Apple Day: Sunday 11 October, 11 to 4:30 (access for event only).

Allan Bank and Grasmere

near Ambleside, Cumbria LA22 9QB

Map (6) D8 1920

A visit to this former home of William Wordsworth isn't a typical National Trust experience. Only partially restored and decorated, muddy boots (and paws) are welcome. Grasmere's valley unfolds from the picture windows and woodland grounds. Secret hideaways like the Victorian viewing tunnel create an air of mystery. You could have something to eat, watch red squirrels as you read by the fire or picnic on the lawn, write on the walls, dig the garden, paint and draw. Canon Rawnsley, National Trust founder, was inspired here – and there's even more to discover today. **Note**: no parking on site. Follow directions from Miller Howe Café in centre of village, 450 yards.

Eating and shopping: at Allan Bank light lunches, snacks and tasty cakes are available from the homely kitchen. Picnics welcome in the gardens. Church Stile shop in Grasmere selling unusual gifts, ice-cream, local books and maps.

Making the most of your day: **Indoors** Drawing and painting, board games and children's activities. Mountaineering and climbing books in the Mountain Heritage Library. **Outdoors** Deckchairs on the lawn. Kitchen garden, woodland trail and walks. **Dogs**: welcome under control.

Access: **Allan Bank** **Countryside**
Sat Nav: use LA22 9SW for nearest car park.
Parking: nearest in village, pay and display, not National Trust (charge including members).

Finding out more: 015394 35143 or allanbank@nationaltrust.org.uk

Allan Bank and Grasmere		M	T	W	T	F	S	S
Allan Bank								
14 Feb–22 Feb	10:30–4	M	T	W	T	F	S	S
27 Feb–22 Mar	10:30–4	·	·	·	·	F	S	S
23 Mar–1 Nov	10–5	M	T	W	T	F	S	S
6 Nov–20 Dec	10:30–4	·	·	·	·	F	S	S
29 Dec–31 Dec	10:30–4	·	T	W	T	·	·	·
Grasmere gift shop								
1 Jan–1 Feb	10–4	M	·	·	T	F	S	S
2 Feb–22 Mar	10–4	M	T	W	T	F	S	S
23 Mar–1 Nov	9:30–5:30	M	T	W	T	F	S	S
2 Nov–31 Dec	10–4	M	T	W	T	F	S	S

Grasmere gift shop: closed 25 and 26 December.
Grasmere Gallop: Saturday 6 June.

Allan Bank, Cumbria, in its woodland setting

20 Forthlin Road, Liverpool: McCartney's childhood home

The Beatles' Childhood Homes

Woolton and Allerton, Liverpool

Map (5) C8 2002

A combined tour to Mendips and 20 Forthlin Road, the childhood homes of John Lennon and Paul McCartney, is your only opportunity to see inside the houses where The Beatles met, composed and rehearsed many of their earliest songs. You can walk through the back door into the kitchen and imagine John's Aunt Mimi cooking him his tea, or stand in the spot where Lennon and McCartney composed 'I Saw Her Standing There'. The custodians take you on a fascinating trip down memory lane in these two atmospheric period houses, so typical of Liverpool life in the 1950s. **Note**: access to these houses is by National Trust minibus tour only from Liverpool city centre or Speke Hall (charge including members).

Eating and shopping: guidebooks and postcards available at both houses and Speke Hall shop. Speke Hall's Home Farm restaurant serving regional specialities, such as Scouse and Wet Nelly.

Making the most of your day: departures from convenient pick-up points (city centre and Speke Hall). Our comfortable minibus and easy online booking service allow you to relax, as we take the strain out of visiting.

Access: **Building**
Parking: numerous car parks near collection point (not National Trust) for tours from city centre, or at Speke Hall for tours departing from there.

Finding out more: 0844 800 4791 (Infoline). 0151 427 7231 (booking line) or thebeatleshomes@nationaltrust.org.uk

The Beatles' Childhood Homes		M	T	W	T	F	S	S
25 Feb–29 Nov	Tour*	·	·	W	T	F	S	S

*Admission by guided tour only. Times and pick-up locations vary. Please visit website or call for details and to book tickets.

Beatrix Potter Gallery and Hawkshead

Main Street, Hawkshead, Cumbria LA22 0NS

Map (6) D8 1944

This quirky 17th-century building, once the office of Beatrix Potter's husband, is now home to the National Trust's collection of original Potter artwork. By popular demand, our 'On Holiday with Beatrix Potter' exhibition has been extended for 2015. With new exhibits and classic illustrations alongside rarely seen gems, it makes a great visit for Beatrix Potter fans of any age. Hawkshead village is the perfect base for exploring the countryside that has inspired countless artists, authors and poets. All profits from the National Trust's Hawkshead Corner Shop go into funding our conservation work in this area of the Lakes. **Note**: nearest toilet 300 yards in main village car park (not National Trust).

Eating and shopping: the National Trust Corner Shop in Hawkshead stocks local products and gifts (online shop: shop.nationaltrust.org.uk/beatrixpotter). Meals and refreshments available at various pubs and cafés in Hawkshead village (none National Trust).

Making the most of your day: **Indoors** Children's gallery quiz and books to read in the cosy reading corner. **Outdoors** Walking routes around Hawkshead. Hill Top, Tarn Hows or Wray Castle are all nearby.
Dogs: assistance dogs only.

Access: **Gallery**
Parking: 300 yards, pay and display, not National Trust (charge including members).

Finding out more: 015394 36355 (gallery). 015394 36471 (shop) or beatrixpottergallery@nationaltrust.org.uk

Beatrix Potter Gallery/Hawkshead		M	T	W	T	F	S	S
Gallery								
14 Feb–19 Mar	10:30–3:30	M	T	W	T	·	S	S
21 Mar–21 May	10:30–5	M	T	W	T	·	S	S
23 May–3 Sep	10:30–5	M	T	W	T	F	S	S
5 Sep–1 Nov	10:30–5	M	T	W	T	·	S	S
Shop								
3 Jan–8 Feb	10–4	·	·	·	·	·	S	S
14 Feb–1 Nov	10–5	M	T	W	T	F	S	S
2 Nov–23 Dec*	10–4	M	T	W	·	·	S	S

Gallery open various Fridays throughout the year. At busy periods, timed entry system in operation. Hawkshead Courthouse: 21 March to 1 November by key from the National Trust shop in Hawkshead, no parking facilities. *Hawkshead shop also open 24 December.

Beatrix Potter Gallery, Cumbria, has original artworks on display

Dalton Castle

Market Place, Dalton-in-Furness,
Cumbria LA15 8AX

Map (6) D9 1965

Formerly the manorial courthouse of Furness Abbey, this eye-catching 14th-century tower was built to assert the Abbot's authority. **Note**: opened on behalf of the National Trust by the Friends of Dalton Castle.

Finding out more: 015395 60951 or daltoncastle@nationaltrust.org.uk

Dunham Massey is the Stamford Military Hospital

Altrincham, Cheshire WA14 4SJ

Map (5) D8 1976

A group of the up patients, nursin
sons on their ponies.

'This evening at 5.30 a telephone message came through: "Expect 16 patients tomorrow at 11.30".' During the First World War this Georgian house, set in a magnificent deer-park, opened its doors as the Stamford Hospital, offering a sanctuary from the trenches for 282 wounded soldiers. To mark the centenary of the First World War, Dunham Massey has been transformed into the hospital once again as we tell the stories of the soldiers, nurses and family who lived here. Why not spend time in the ward, recreation room and operating theatre? You will encounter staff and patients as you experience the hospital as it once was. Treasures: a special exhibition showcases some of the most fascinating objects in this significant collection. **Note**: everyone requires entry and timed ticket (including members), available from reception on the day.

Eating and shopping: café in visitor centre with indoor and outdoor seating serving a range of food and drinks. Ice-cream parlour and kiosk. Stables Restaurant near clock tower serving hot lunches. Shop selling gifts, local products and a range of plants.

Making the most of your day: wounded soldiers experienced the 'fresh air cure' – Dunham Massey has a garden for all seasons. Spring bulbs brighten borders, the recently established rose garden, with its very own *Rosa* 'Dunham Massey', blooms in summer, autumn brings shades of red and gold and Britain's largest winter garden awaits your discovery. The Mill is the oldest building on the estate. Free guided walks in the garden and deer-park. Children's trails in garden. Events all year, including open-air theatre and garden parties. Family activities during school holidays. Cycling for under-fives. **Dogs**: welcome under close control and on leads in deer-park.

Access:
House **Garden and grounds**
Parking: 200 yards.

Dunham Massey is the Stamford Military Hospital, Cheshire: a group of soldiers injured in the First World War and their nurses (left) and a re-created ward (below)

Finding out more: 0161 942 3989 (Infoline). 0161 941 1025 or dunhammassey@nationaltrust.org.uk

Dunham Massey		M	T	W	T	F	S	S
House/hospital*								
14 Feb–11 Nov	11–5	**M**	**T**	**W**	·	·	**S**	**S**
Garden**								
1 Jan–13 Feb	11–4	**M**	**T**	**W**	**T**	**F**	**S**	**S**
14 Feb–11 Nov	11–5:30	**M**	**T**	**W**	**T**	**F**	**S**	**S**
12 Nov–31 Dec	11–4	**M**	**T**	**W**	**T**	**F**	**S**	**S**
Café and shop								
1 Jan–13 Feb	10–4	**M**	**T**	**W**	**T**	**F**	**S**	**S**
14 Feb–11 Nov	10–5	**M**	**T**	**W**	**T**	**F**	**S**	**S**
12 Nov–31 Dec	10–4	**M**	**T**	**W**	**T**	**F**	**S**	**S**
Park†								
Open all year	9–5	**M**	**T**	**W**	**T**	**F**	**S**	**S**
Mill								
14 Feb–11 Nov	12–4	**M**	**T**	**W**	·	·	**S**	**S**

*Last entry to house at 4, closes at 5 or dusk if earlier. House open Good Friday. **Closes at specified time or dusk if earlier. Wednesdays and Fridays in June: garden open from 11 to 8. †March to October: gates and car park open until 7:30. White Cottage open on last Sunday of each month from 29 March to 25 October, 2 to 5 (booking essential on 0161 928 0075). Dunham Massey closed 25 November and 25 December (including car park).

The ornate kitchen range at Gawthorpe Hall, Lancashire

Gawthorpe Hall

Burnley Road, Padiham, near Burnley, Lancashire BB12 8UA

Map (5) D6 1972

This imposing house, set in the heart of urban Lancashire, contains fabulously opulent interiors, created by Sir Charles Barry in the 19th century. The Hall displays textiles from the Gawthorpe Textile Collection, including needlework, lace and embroidery, while outside the grounds are popular with dog walkers. **Note**: financed and run in partnership with Lancashire County Council.

Eating and shopping: tea-room serving light snacks.

Making the most of your day: **Indoors** Guided tours, talks and exhibitions. Events all year, including Victorian Christmas. **Outdoors** Open-air theatre in July and other events, including some for children. **Dogs**: under close control in grounds.

Access: **Building**
Grounds
Parking: 150 yards, narrow access road (passing places).

Finding out more: 01282 771004 or gawthorpehall@nationaltrust.org.uk

Gawthorpe Hall		M	T	W	T	F	S	S
House								
1 Apr–1 Nov	12–5	·	·	**W**	**T**	**F**	**S**	**S**
Tea-room								
1 Apr–1 Nov	11–5	·	·	**W**	**T**	**F**	**S**	**S**
Grounds								
Open all year	8–7	**M**	**T**	**W**	**T**	**F**	**S**	**S**

Hall and tea-room open Bank Holidays.
Opening times may change.

The Hardmans' House

59 Rodney Street, Liverpool, Merseyside L1 9ER

Map (5) B8 2003

59 Rodney Street – at this Liverpool address renowned photographer E. Chambré Hardman and his talented wife Margaret lived and worked together for 40 years, keeping everything, changing nothing. This remarkable Georgian house is a time capsule of post-war years and the life of an extraordinary couple. **Note**: admission by guided tour only – booking advised. Visitor entrance on Pilgrim Street.

The Hardmans' House, Merseyside: tools of the trade

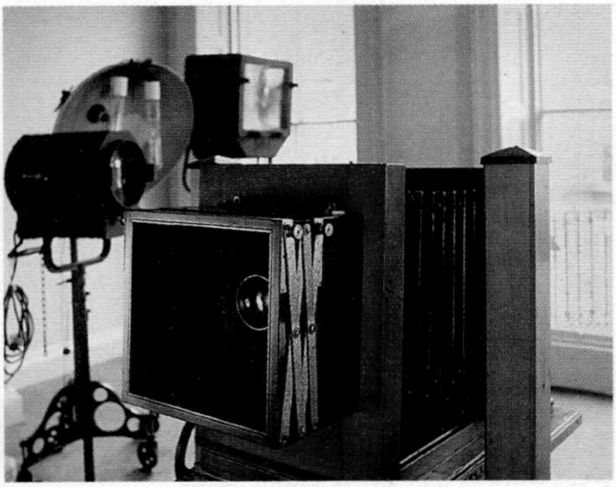

Eating and shopping: shop selling unique photographic prints, postcards and guidebooks.

Making the most of your day: tours (book your place to avoid disappointment). Virtual tour of house. Children's quiz trail. New exhibition for 2015.

Access: **Building**
Parking: none on site. Car parks at Anglican Cathedral and Slater Street, not National Trust (charge including members).

Finding out more: 0151 709 6261 or thehardmanshouse@nationaltrust.org.uk

The Hardmans' House		M	T	W	T	F	S	S
18 Mar–31 Oct	11–3:30	·	·	**W**	**T**	**F**	**S**	·

Admission by timed ticket only, booking advisable (places limited). Open Bank Holiday Mondays.

Hare Hill

Over Alderley, Macclesfield, Cheshire SK10 4PY

Map (5) D8 1978

Set within an idyllic landscaped park, this glorious informal woodland garden comes alive in spring with established plantings of rhododendrons, magnolias, azaleas and other unusual shrubs and bulbs. At its heart is the delightful walled White Garden, inspired by Colonel Brocklehurst, a tranquil place to relax in the summer.

Eating and shopping: hot drinks vending machine. Picnics welcome in Walled Garden. Plants for sale at the kiosk. Small second-hand book stall located in the Form.

Making the most of your day: carved wooden hares to spot and follow through grounds. Bird hide. Croquet lawn. Waymarked circular walk through mature woodland and parkland to Alderley Edge. **Dogs**: assistance dogs only in Walled Garden (dog park provided). On leads/under close control elsewhere.

Access: **Grounds**
Sat Nav: use SK10 4PY to take you 109 yards west of car park. **Parking**: on site.

Enjoying idyllic Hare Hill in Cheshire

Finding out more: 01625 584412 or harehill@nationaltrust.org.uk

Hare Hill		M	T	W	T	F	S	S
1 Mar–1 Nov	10–5	·	**T**	**W**	**T**	**F**	**S**	**S**

Open Bank Holiday Mondays. Last admission one hour before closing. Car park closes at 5.

Hill Top

Near Sawrey, Hawkshead, Ambleside, Cumbria LA22 0LF

Map (6) D8 1944

A time capsule of Beatrix Potter's life, this small house, with its fragile interiors, is full of her favourite things, while the garden is a haphazard mix of flowers, herbs, fruit and vegetables – just as it would have been in her day. Let the sights and sounds of Beatrix Potter's house inspire the senses, as you warm yourself by the fire and hear the clock strike the hours, following her footsteps through this place, which was so loved by Beatrix. Hill Top can be very busy and visitors may sometimes have to wait to enter the house.
Note: timed-ticket entry system operating, early sell-outs possible when particularly busy.

Eating and shopping: Sawrey House Hotel and Tower Bank Arms (neither National Trust) serving meals, afternoon tea and refreshments. The Hill Top shop sells a great range of Beatrix Potter books and collectables. Shop online at shop.nationaltrust.org.uk/beatrixpotter or mail-order: hilltop.shop@nationaltrust.org.uk.

Making the most of your day: children's garden trail and you could combine Hill Top with a visit to nearby Hawkshead and the Beatrix Potter Gallery. Why not visit by boat, bus, boot or bike? **Dogs**: assistance dogs only.

Access: **House** **Shop** **Garden**
Parking: limited.

Iconic Hill Top house, Cumbria (top right), where children can try the garden trail

Finding out more: 015394 36269. 015394 36801 (shop) or hilltop@nationaltrust.org.uk

Hill Top		M	T	W	T	F	S	S
House								
14 Feb–19 Mar	10:30–3:30	M	T	W	T	·	S	S
21 Mar–21 May	10–4:30	M	T	W	T	·	S	S
25 May–3 Sep	10–5:30	M	T	W	T	·	·	·
23 May–30 Aug	10–4:30	·	·	·	·	·	S	S
5 Sep–1 Nov	10–4:30	M	T	W	T	·	S	S
Shop and garden								
14 Feb–20 Mar	10:30–4	M	T	W	T	F	S	S
21 Mar–24 May	10–5	M	T	W	T	F	S	S
25 May–3 Sep	10–5:45	M	T	W	T	·	·	·
29 May–30 Aug	10–5	·	·	·	·	F	S	S
4 Sep–1 Nov	10–5	M	T	W	T	F	S	S
2 Nov–23 Dec	10–4	M	T	W	T	F	S	S

Entry by timed ticket (places limited). Small car park. Access to garden and shop free during opening hours. House open various Fridays throughout the year.

Keld Chapel

Keld Lane, Shap, Cumbria CA10 3NW

Map (6) E7 1918

With its rustic stone floor and walls, this 16th-century chapel is thought to have been the chantry for Shap Abbey. **Note**: sorry no facilities. Access daily (for key, see the notice on chapel door). For Sat Nav use CA10 3NW.

Finding out more: 017683 61893 or keldchapel@nationaltrust.org.uk

Little Moreton Hall

Congleton, Cheshire CW12 4SD

Map (5) D9 1938

The Cheshire-based Moreton family certainly experienced the highs and lows of life in the 16th century. Throughout the last 500 years this timber-framed hall, surrounded by a moat and set within a small pretty garden, survived the Civil War, spent 250 years tenanted, was in serious danger of falling over and is as intriguing as it is wonky! Colourful Tudor times are brought to life through fantastic guided tours, traditional festivals and celebrations. A rare pre-Reformation chapel, topsy-turvy long gallery and early wallpaper ensure the genuine 'wow' factor is experienced more than once at this iconic Tudor treasure.

Eating and shopping: The Little Tea Room with outdoor orchard seating and Mrs Dale's Pantry serve scrummy homemade food produced in the on-site bakery. Ice-cream kiosk (open on sunny days). Large shop in the car park selling gifts, refreshments and local products.

Making the most of your day: **Indoors** Free guided tours. Tudor-themed daily craft activities. Costumes to try on. Exhibitions and family trails. **Outdoors** Theatre in the summer and Yuletide celebrations in December.
Dogs: on leads in car park and front lawn only.

Access:
Hall **Reception**
Grounds
Parking: 100 yards.

Finding out more: 01260 272018 or littlemoretonhall@nationaltrust.org.uk

Little Moreton Hall		M	T	W	T	F	S	S
14 Feb–22 Feb	11–5	M	T	W	T	F	S	S
25 Feb–5 Apr	11–5	·	·	W	T	F	S	S
6 Apr–19 Apr	11–5	M	T	W	T	F	S	S
22 Apr–24 May	11–5	·	·	W	T	F	S	S
25 May–31 May	11–5	M	T	W	T	F	S	S
3 Jun–19 Jul	11–5	·	·	W	T	F	S	S
20 Jul–6 Sep	11–5	M	T	W	T	F	S	S
9 Sep–25 Oct	11–5	·	·	W	T	F	S	S
26 Oct–1 Nov	11–5	M	T	W	T	F	S	S
7 Nov–20 Dec	11–4	·	·	·	·	·	S	S

Open Bank Holiday Mondays. Upper floors may close early if light levels are poor.

No one can fail to be won over by the wonderfully wonky Little Moreton Hall in Cheshire (above and left)

Some places are easy to get to on foot or by public transport. See page 3

Lyme Park, House and Garden

Disley, Stockport, Cheshire SK12 2NR

Map (5) E8 [icons] 1947

Home of the Legh family for more than 600 years, Lyme Park sits in 570 hectares (1,400 acres) of parkland, with glorious views across Manchester and the Cheshire Plain. Its lavish interiors reflect the life of a great estate, from its earliest beginnings to its Edwardian 'Golden Era' – the heyday of aristocratic life, with its social whirl of parties and engagements, all of which ended with the start of the First World War. In more recent times, Lyme has featured as 'Pemberley' in the BBC adaptation of *Pride and Prejudice* starring Colin Firth. Lyme's gardens with the Reflection Lake, orangery and Rose Garden are an ideal place to relax and stroll.
Note: owned and managed by the National Trust, but partly financed by Stockport Metropolitan Borough Council.

Eating and shopping: restaurant serving light snacks, lunches and desserts. Servants' Hall tea-room offering drinks and sweet treats; Timber Yard Café snacks, cakes and drinks. Salting Room Tea Parlour and Garden – full afternoon tea – booking essential. Gifts, book and plant shop. Pre-loved bookshop.

Lyme Park, House and Garden, Cheshire: the imposing façade (opposite), Palladian courtyard (below) and stags in front of The Cage, an Elizabethan hunting tower

Making the most of your day: **Indoors** Activities such as reading in the Library, home to the 15th-century *Lyme Missal* – a rare Caxton prayer book – taking part in Edwardian theatricals in the Long Gallery, dressing-up in Edwardian costumes in the wardrobe department, writing a letter in the Morning Room or visiting Mr Truelove the Butler's rooms 'below stairs'. **Outdoors** Regular Saturday Park runs and Xplorer family orienteering course (changes every month), self-led woodland and moorland walks, and adventurous play in Crow Wood Playscape for five- to 12-year-olds. Events, including Easter trails, summer holiday activities, Hallowe'en, winter exhibition and Christmas celebrations.
Dogs: under close control in park; leads near livestock and vehicles; selected days in garden.

Access: [icons]
House [icons] **Garden** [icons]
Parking: 200 yards.

Finding out more: 01663 762023 or lymepark@nationaltrust.org.uk

Lyme Park		M	T	W	T	F	S	S
House and restaurant*								
16 Feb–1 Nov	11–5	**M**	**T**	·	·	**F**	**S**	**S**
Garden and hall shop								
16 Feb–1 Nov	11–5	**M**	**T**	**W**	**T**	**F**	**S**	**S**
Park								
Open all year	8:30–6	**M**	**T**	**W**	**T**	**F**	**S**	**S**
30 Mar–4 Oct	8–8	**M**	**T**	**W**	**T**	**F**	**S**	**S**
Timber Yard Café and shop**								
Open all year	11–4	**M**	**T**	**W**	**T**	**F**	**S**	**S**
Servants' Hall tea-room								
4 May–27 Sep	11–5	**M**	**T**	**W**	**T**	**F**	**S**	**S**
Winter exhibition, garden, shop and restaurant								
3 Jan–15 Feb	11–3	·	·	·	·	·	**S**	**S**
7 Nov–27 Dec	11–3	·	·	·	·	·	**S**	**S**

*Last entry to house at 4. **Timber Yard Café and shop: 16 February to 1 November, open 10 to 5.

Nether Alderley Mill

Congleton Road, Nether Alderley, Macclesfield, Cheshire SK10 4TW

Map (5) D8 1950

Restored double-overshot waterwheels turn as modern millers demonstrate how corn was ground at this evocative 16th-century Cheshire mill. **Note**: view by guided tour only. Sorry no toilet or visitor facilities. Uneven floor, steep stairs and low ceilings throughout. Limited parking.

Finding out more: 01625 527468 or netheralderleymill@nationaltrust.org.uk

Austere Quarry Bank Mill, Cheshire (bottom) and the Apprentice House School Room (below)

Quarry Bank

Styal, Wilmslow, Cheshire SK9 4LA

Map (5) D8 1939

Deep in a Cheshire valley by the River Bollin, Samuel Greg built Quarry Bank. While exploring, you will discover the compelling and contrasting stories of mill workers and entrepreneurs, with the Apprentice House offering a window into the lives of pauper children. Inside the mill, the clatter of machinery, hiss of steam engines and churn of Europe's most powerful working waterwheel demonstrate technological developments. The Greg family loved the outdoors, creating formal gardens and planting exotic and native trees, as well as an extensive collection of rhododendrons, which bloom alongside the river path. Northern and Southern Woods are perfect for long walks, and fields lead to the cottages of Styal village, built as a community to house the mill workers. **Note**: steep hill with 61 steps from car park.

Please display your current sticker for free parking

Eating and shopping: shop selling gifts, including fabric and glass cloths produced in the mill. Second-hand bookshop. Small range of plants on sale. Café serving lunch and afternoon tea. Coffee and ice-cream available from the Pantry (open during busy periods only). Picnic facilities.

Making the most of your day: **Indoors** Changing exhibitions throughout the year. Special events on Easter, autumn and Christmas weekends. Activities and trails for all the family in the school holidays. **Outdoors** Tracker Packs available for the garden. Guided walks. **Dogs**: under close control on estate. On leads in garden, Mill Yard and Mill Meadow.

Access:
Building **Grounds**
Parking: 200 yards (steep hill).

Finding out more: 01625 527468 or quarrybankmill@nationaltrust.org.uk

Quarry Bank		M	T	W	T	F	S	S
Mill and Apprentice House								
1 Jan–13 Feb	11–3:30	·	·	W	T	F	S	S
14 Feb–1 Nov	11–5	M	T	W	T	F	S	S
4 Nov–31 Dec	11–3:30	·	·	W	T	F	S	S
Garden								
14 Feb–1 Nov	10:30–5*	M	T	W	T	F	S	S
Shop, café and ticket/information office								
1 Jan–13 Feb	10:30–4	·	·	W	T	F	S	S
14 Feb–1 Nov	10:30–5	M	T	W	T	F	S	S
4 Nov–31 Dec	10:30–4	·	·	W	T	F	S	S

Completely closed 5 to 9 January for essential maintenance. Closed 21 to 25 December, open daily 26 December to 1 January 2016. Apprentice House: limited timed tickets only, available from ticket office (early arrival advised). Popular destination for schools. *Garden closes dusk if earlier.

Rufford Old Hall

200 Liverpool Road, Rufford, near Ormskirk, Lancashire L40 1SG

Map (5) C6 1936

Home to the Hesketh family for 500 years, Rufford Old Hall has plenty of stories to tell. Its Tudor Great Hall hosted theatrical productions in Shakespeare's time. Did Shakespeare himself spend a short time at Rufford in his youth? And what was the 'moveable' screen used for in the Great Hall? Why not find the answer to these intriguing questions yourself and discover Rufford's fascinating past. Outside, the Victorian-style garden and grounds are accessible to all, offering seasonal displays of colours and views across the Leeds & Liverpool Canal.

Rufford Old Hall, Lancashire: plenty of stories to tell

Eating and shopping: you can experience local tastes with Lancashire Tea in the Victorian tea-room. The shop offers special treats or gifts to keep memories of Rufford Old Hall fresh.

Making the most of your day: **Indoors** Daily house talks and seasonal children's trail. Christmas experience with Santa's Grotto. **Outdoors** Guided garden tours. Events, including open-air theatre. Seasonal children's trails and Tudor and Victorian games. **Dogs**: on leads in courtyard and woodland only.

Access:
Building
Grounds
Parking: on site.

Finding out more: 01704 821254 or
ruffordoldhall@nationaltrust.org.uk

Rufford Old Hall		M	T	W	T	F	S	S
14 Feb–22 Feb	11–4	M	T	W	T	·	S	S
23 Feb–25 Mar	11–4	M	T	W	·	·	S	S
28 Mar–12 Apr	11–5	M	T	W	T	·	S	S
13 Apr–24 May	11–5	M	T	W	·	·	S	S
25 May–31 May	11–5	M	T	W	T	·	S	S
1 Jun–26 Jul	11–5	M	T	W	·	·	S	S
27 Jul–6 Sep	11–5	M	T	W	T	·	S	S
7 Sep–25 Oct	11–5	M	T	W	·	·	S	S
26 Oct–1 Nov	11–5	M	T	W	T	F	S	S
7 Nov–20 Dec	11–4	·	·	·	·	·	S	S

Open Good Friday. Car park closes 30 minutes after times above. Tudor Great Hall occasionally closed until 1 on Saturdays for weddings.

Sizergh

Sizergh, near Kendal, Cumbria LA8 8AE

Map (6) E8 1950

With more than 700 years of history and centuries-old portraits sitting alongside modern family photographs, this medieval house certainly feels lived in; indeed it is still home to the Strickland family. It is surrounded by rich gardens and a 647-hectare (1,600-acre) estate with limestone pastures, orchards and semi-natural woodland, inhabited by a rich and diverse wildlife. There is a limestone rock garden, where colours change with the passing of the seasons, and its timeless atmosphere makes this the perfect place to relax. Sizergh has many tales to tell and it is an unexpected treasure on the edge of the Lake District. **Note**: Sizergh is a family home; consequently there are some opening restrictions.

Eating and shopping: contemporary licensed café serving a selection of hot and cold drinks, meals and snacks. Shop selling local products, home accessories, gifts, toys and plants. Nearby Strickland Arms pub (tenant-run). Picnics available.

Making the most of your day: **Indoors** Exhibitions, virtual and guided tours, as well as Elizabethan carving of international significance. **Outdoors** The garden includes the National Trust's largest limestone rock garden, four National Collections of Hardy Ferns and a kitchen garden with bees and hens. A bird hide and feeding area, as well as a network of footpaths, guided walks and orienteering, are available in the wider estate. Children can enjoy a natural play trail, pond dipping and quizzes. **Dogs**: welcome on estate footpaths. Assistance dogs only in house and garden.

Access: **Building**
Grounds
Sat Nav: use LA8 8DZ. **Parking**: 250 yards.

Finding out more: 015395 60951 or
sizergh@nationaltrust.org.uk

Sizergh		M	T	W	T	F	S	S
House*								
8 Mar–1 Nov	12–4	M	T	W	T	·	·	S
Garden, café and shop**								
10 Jan–8 Feb	10–4	·	·	·	·	·	S	S
14 Feb–7 Mar	10–4	M	T	W	T	F	S	S
8 Mar–1 Nov	10–5	M	T	W	T	F	S	S
2 Nov–31 Dec	10–4	M	T	W	T	F	S	S
Estate†								
Open all year	9–7	M	T	W	T	F	S	S

*Three guided house tours at 11, 11:20 and 4 (places limited, charges apply). **Parts of the garden closed every Friday and Saturday and during January, February, November and December. †Car park opens 10 to 4, 1 January to 7 March and 2 November to 31 December. Closed 25 December.

Sizergh, Cumbria: wild flowers growing in the garden (opposite) and a moment's peace by the pond (below)

Magnificent Tudor Speke Hall, Liverpool (main picture and top right), is surrounded by glorious gardens and woodland (opposite)

Speke Hall

Speke, Liverpool L24 1XD

Map (5) C8 1944

This magnificent Tudor manor house with beautiful Victorian interiors has witnessed more than 400 years of turbulent history. Built by the Catholic Norris family during the unsettled and dangerous religious Tudor period, Speke has several 16th-century hidden security features, including priest's and spy holes. Some of Speke's interior rooms have been brought back to life in the Victorian Arts and Crafts style. The Hall is surrounded by glorious gardens and woodland, with seasonal displays of rhododendrons, daffodils and bluebells – a tranquil oasis from modern life. Bordering the Speke Estate, the coastal reserve along the shores of the River Mersey is perfect for a bracing walk or wildlife watch, set against stunning views of the Welsh hills.

Note: administered and financed by the National Trust, assisted by a grant from National Museums Liverpool.

Eating and shopping: local gifts, products and plants available. Home Farm restaurant serving regional specialities, such as Scouse and Wet Nelly. Stable Tea-room, near the house, offering hot drinks and homemade cakes.

Making the most of your day: **Indoors** Activities such as costumed guided tours, dressing-up, Victorian billiard-table for visitors to play. Hallowe'en, Tudor and Victorian Christmas events. **Outdoors** Easter trails, May Day celebrations and open-air theatre in the summer. Gardens, coastal and woodland walks, Victorian maze, restored kitchen garden and children's playground. The new woodland trail is a great space to build a den, climb tree stumps or ride the zipwire. **Dogs**: welcome on leads in the woodland and on signed estate walks.

Access:
Hall **Grounds**
Parking: on site.

Finding out more: 0151 427 7231 or spekehall@nationaltrust.org.uk

Speke Hall		M	T	W	T	F	S	S
14 Feb–22 Feb	11–4	·	·	**W**	**T**	**F**	**S**	**S**
28 Feb–15 Mar	11–4	·	·	·	·	·	**S**	**S**
18 Mar–19 Jul	11–5	·	·	**W**	**T**	**F**	**S**	**S**
21 Jul–30 Aug	10:30–5	·	**T**	**W**	**T**	**F**	**S**	**S**
2 Sep–1 Nov	11–5	·	·	**W**	**T**	**F**	**S**	**S**
7 Nov–13 Dec	11–4	·	·	·	·	·	**S**	**S**

House: entry before 12:30 by guided tour only (places limited); free-flow access from 12:30. Hall open Bank Holiday Mondays. Some rooms under cover 14 February to 15 March for conservation reasons. Car park closes 30 minutes after times stated.

Steam Yacht Gondola on Coniston, Cumbria

Steam Yacht Gondola

Coniston Pier, Lake Road, Coniston, Cumbria LA21 8AN

Map (6) D8 1980

Rebuilt from the original Victorian Gondola, today's passengers can experience the nostalgia of a cruise once enjoyed by the Victorians. Based on the design of a Venetian *burchiello*, Gondola allows you to watch the steam engine in action and experience a gentle gliding motion in near silence. In the saloons, you can go first class and pretend to be a member of the 'hoi polloi' or be an 'oik' in third. Either way, we don't segregate you as the Victorians did: the whole boat is worth exploring and the crew love to tell tales about her chequered past. **Note**: sailings depart from Coniston Pier (subject to weather conditions). Sorry no toilet on scheduled sailings. Gondola is an historic ship and extremely costly to run. Members are required to pay with a small discount in recognition of their support.

Eating and shopping: small shop on board selling souvenirs. Bluebird Café at Coniston Pier serving local, freshly prepared food. Disembark at Brantwood jetty for Jumping Jenny's café (licensed). Catering provided for private hire (not National Trust). Picnic cruises and gift vouchers available online.

Making the most of your day: themed events, downloadable trails from Gondola's jetties and joint tickets with partner attractions. **Dogs**: in outside areas only.

Access: **Gangway**
Sat Nav: use LA21 8AN.
Parking: at Coniston Pier, 50 yards, not National Trust (charge including members).

Finding out more: 01539 432733 or sygondola@nationaltrust.org.uk
Booking Office, Low Wray Campsite, Low Wray, Ambleside, Cumbria LA22 0JA

Steam Yacht Gondola
Daily sailing 27 March to 1 November. See website or call for timetable. Piers at Coniston, Monk Coniston, Parkamoor and Brantwood (not National Trust).

Tatton Park

Knutsford, Cheshire WA16 6QN

Map (5) D8 1960

One of the most complete historic estates open to visitors. The early 19th-century Wyatt house sits amid a 400-hectare (1,000-acre) deer-park and is opulently decorated, providing a fine setting for the Egerton family's collections of pictures, books, china, glass and specially commissioned Gillows furniture. The theme of Victorian grandeur extends into the garden, with its Fernery, Orangery, Rose Garden, Tower Garden, Pinetum, Walled Garden with glasshouses, plus Italian and Japanese gardens (viewed from the perimeter). Other features include a 1930s working rare-breeds farm, Tudor Old Hall, adventure playground, speciality shops and restaurants. **Note**: managed/financed by Cheshire East Council. For tours, RHS show, Christmas and other events supplementary charges may apply (including members). Park car entry charge, £6 (including members).

Eating and shopping: Stableyard shopping and dining, including Stables self-service restaurant and Gardener's Cottage table service tea-room. Speciality shops, including the Housekeepers' Store for the best in local speciality food and drink, gift shop, garden shop and tuck shop.

Making the most of your day: tattonpark.org.uk for over 100 events and learning courses for adults and children. Members – free to mansion and gardens only; half-price to farm. Old Hall special openings. Large deer-park to explore. **Dogs**: on leads at farm and under close control in park only.

Access:
Building **Grounds**
Sat Nav: use WA16 6SG. **Parking**: park car entry charge, £6 (including members).

Finding out more: 01625 374435 (Infoline). 01625 374400 or tatton@cheshireeast.gov.uk tattonpark.org.uk

Tatton Park, Cheshire (top), sits within a deer-park (above)

Tatton Park		M	T	W	T	F	S	S
Parkland, gardens, restaurant and tea-room								
1 Jan–27 Mar*	10–5	·	T	W	T	F	S	S
28 Mar–25 Oct*	10–7	M	T	W	T	F	S	S
27 Oct–31 Dec*	10–5	·	T	W	T	F	S	S
Mansion								
28 Mar–27 Sep	1–5	·	T	W	T	F	S	S
29 Sep–1 Nov	12–4	·	T	W	T	F	S	S
Farm								
3 Jan–22 Mar	11–4	·	·	·	·	·	S	S
28 Mar–25 Oct	12–5	·	T	W	T	F	S	S
31 Oct–27 Dec	11–4	·	·	·	·	·	S	S
Shops								
1 Jan–27 Mar	12–4	·	T	W	T	F	S	S
28 Mar–25 Oct	11–5	M	T	W	T	F	S	S
27 Oct–31 Dec	12–4	·	T	W	T	F	S	S

*Gardens, restaurant and tea-room close one hour earlier. Open Bank Holiday Mondays. Parkland, mansion, farm and garden last admission one hour before closing. Guided mansion tours Tuesday to Sunday 28 March to 27 September at 12 by timed ticket (places limited), small charge including members. Old Hall special opening arrangements. Closed 25 December.

Townend

Troutbeck, Windermere, Cumbria LA23 1LB

Map (6) D8 1948

The Brownes of Townend were a simple farming family, but their home and belongings bring to life more than 400 years of extraordinary stories. The farmhouse kitchen has a real fire burning most afternoons and a quirky collection of domestic tools. Throughout the house, intricately carved furniture provides a window into the personality of George Browne. The library contains the family's well-used collection of books, including 45 that are the only remaining copies in the world. Outside, the colourful cottage-style garden is a lovely place to while away some time among the flowers.

Eating and shopping: small selection of souvenirs available. Second-hand books. Picnics welcome.

Making the most of your day: **Indoors** 'A Taste of Townend'; food displays every day. Living history demonstrations on Thursdays. Children's trail. **Outdoors** Garden trail for children. Traditional games. Guided tours at 11 and 12.

Access: **Building** **Grounds**
Parking: 300 yards.

Finding out more: 015394 32628 or townend@nationaltrust.org.uk

Townend		M	T	W	T	F	S	S
House tours								
14 Mar–1 Nov	11–1*	·	·	**W**	**T**	**F**	**S**	**S**
House								
14 Mar–1 Nov	1–5	·	·	**W**	**T**	**F**	**S**	**S**

*11 to 1 entry by guided tour only at 11 and 12 (places limited). Open Bank Holiday Mondays. May close early due to poor light.

A 17th-century meal is prepared in the homely kitchen at Townend, Cumbria

Some places are easy to get to on foot or by public transport. See page 3

Wordsworth House and Garden, Cumbria: inside and out

Wordsworth House and Garden

Main Street, Cockermouth, Cumbria CA13 9RX

Map (6) C7 1938

William and Dorothy's award-winning birthplace is a home from home. This lovely Georgian town house offers an unforgettable chance to learn the horrible truth about 18th-century life, meet ghostly family members and share their stories. The servants and our 21st-century guides offer a taste of history in the working kitchen. The garden is packed with vegetables, fruit, herbs and flowers, just as it would have been in William's day. His early life here inspired some of his most moving poems. Whatever the weather, you're guaranteed a warm welcome – and great baking in our café! Featured on ITV.

Eating and shopping: shop selling Wordsworth and local souvenirs. Café serving light lunches and cakes.

Making the most of your day: **Indoors** Audio and guided house tours. Talks, harpsichord music, cooking demonstrations and Georgian recipe tastings. Dressing up, traditional toys and family activities during school holidays. **Outdoors** Garden tours. **Dogs**: on leads in front garden only.

Access:
Building **Grounds**
Parking: in town centre car parks, none National Trust (charge including members). Please note long-stay car park signposted as coach park, 300 yards, Wakefield Road.

Finding out more: 01900 820884 (Infoline). 01900 824805 or wordsworthhouse@nationaltrust.org.uk

Wordsworth House and Garden		M	T	W	T	F	S	S
House, garden and café								
7 Mar–1 Nov*	11–5	M	T	W	T	·	S	S
Shop								
7 Mar–1 Nov	10–5	M	T	W	T	·	S	S
3 Nov–24 Dec	10–4	·	T	W	T	F	S	·

*Café: open 10:30 to 4:30. House: last entry 4. Timed tickets may operate on busy days. Property open on selected Fridays in holidays, please ring for information.

Wray Castle

Low Wray, Ambleside, Cumbria LA22 0JA

Map (6) D8 1929

Wray Castle makes for a new and exciting National Trust visit; it's a place for all the family to enjoy, so don't worry about running around and making as much noise as you like! You could try a guided tour, castle building or dressing-up. As a developing property things change quickly, so check our Facebook page for more information and feel free to share your ideas with us. Our jetty allows you to arrive in style by boarding one of the regular cruises from Ambleside, or why not hop on the shuttle bus at Ferry Nab and call in at Hill Top and the Beatrix Potter Gallery on the way? **Note**: car park fills up quickly at peak times. We suggest using alternative transport where possible.

Arrive in style (opposite) at Wray Castle, Cumbria (above), then explore the castle. Maybe on a guided tour?

Eating and shopping: 'pop-up' café (run by National Trust tenants from the Tower Bank Arms in Near Sawrey) serving hot and cold drinks, cakes, snacks and sandwiches freshly prepared every day. Picnics welcome.

Making the most of your day: **Indoors** Guided tours and family activities, including dressing-up, crafts and castle building. **Outdoors** Walks and tree trails, as well as an exciting play area and the lakeshore to explore. Events throughout the year. Why not stay on the doorstep at Low Wray campsite – just a short walk away from the castle beside the lake and through woodland? You can arrive by boat at the castle's own boathouse or cycle here along the lakeshore path from Ferry Nab on Windermere's western shore. **Dogs**: welcome in grounds on leads, assistance dogs only in castle.

Access: **Castle**
Parking: limited – fills up quickly at peak times.

Finding out more: 015394 33250 or wraycastle@nationaltrust.org.uk

Wray Castle		M	T	W	T	F	S	S
Castle								
21 Mar–1 Nov	10–5	**M**	**T**	**W**	**T**	**F**	**S**	**S**
6 Nov–20 Dec	10:30–4	·	·	·	·	**F**	**S**	**S**
Grounds								
Open all year	Dawn–dusk	**M**	**T**	**W**	**T**	**F**	**S**	**S**

Extra openings possible.

Yorkshire and North East

Rievaulx Terrace, North Yorkshire

Outdoors in Yorkshire and the North East

Between them, these two contrasting areas offer unspoilt coastline and beautiful beaches, as well as rugged countryside, moorland and green valleys.

Allen Banks and Staward Gorge

near Ridley Hall, Bardon Mill, Hexham, Northumberland

Map (6) F5 1942

With its deep gorge, created by the River Allen and the largest area of ancient semi-natural woodland in Northumberland, this 250-hectare (617-acre) site provides the perfect excuse for an adventure. There are many miles of waymarked walks and the ornamental woods are home to a fantastic array of wildlife.

Eating and shopping: picnics welcome at the numerous beauty spots – in the woodland and garden or by the river.

Making the most of your day: events and downloadable trails. Victorian suspension bridge, medieval pele-tower and reconstructed Victorian summerhouse. **Dogs**: welcome under close control.

Allen Banks and Staward Gorge, Northumberland

Access: **Grounds**
Parking: at Allen Banks.

Finding out more: 01434 321888 or allenbanks@nationaltrust.org.uk

Bridestones, Crosscliff and Blakey Topping

near Pickering, North Yorkshire

Map (5) I3 1944

Spectacular all year, the Bridestones are a geological wonder – with rock formations, moorland vistas, woodland walks and grassy valleys. **Note**: nearest toilets at Staindale Lake car park. For Sat Nav use YO18 7LR. Dalby Forest drive starting 2½ miles north of Thornton le Dale – toll charges (including members).

Finding out more: 01723 870423 or bridestones@nationaltrust.org.uk

Brimham Rocks

near Summerbridge, Harrogate, North Yorkshire

Map (5) F4 1970

These rock formations tower over heather moorland, offering panoramic views across Nidderdale. Dating back 320 million years, it is now a haven for climbers and walkers and a natural playground for families to enjoy picnics and nature-spotting. For magical photographs, visit all year and see this landscape through all seasons. **Note**: beware of cliff edges. Nearest toilets 600 yards from car park.

Eating and shopping: shop selling books, gifts and the popular locally made bilberry jam. Hot and cold refreshments and ice-cream available from kiosk. Picnic tables with views of the rocks and seating inside the visitor centre.

The fabulously shaped Brimham Rocks in North Yorkshire

Making the most of your day: regular guided walks, events, family activities and climbing days. Visitor centre exhibition space reveals the story of the rocks, conservation work and views to the Vale of York. **Dogs**: welcome, on moors under control and on leads April to June (ground-nesting birds).

Access: **Building** **Grounds**
Sat Nav: HG3 4DW. **Parking**: on site.

Finding out more: 01423 780688 or brimhamrocks@nationaltrust.org.uk

Brimham Rocks		M	T	W	T	F	S	S
Countryside								
Open all year	8-dusk	**M**	**T**	**W**	**T**	**F**	**S**	**S**
Visitor centre, shop and kiosk								
14 Feb-22 Feb	11-5	**M**	**T**	**W**	**T**	**F**	**S**	**S**
28 Feb-22 Mar	11-5	·	·	·	·	·	**S**	**S**
28 Mar-12 Apr	11-5	**M**	**T**	**W**	**T**	**F**	**S**	**S**
18 Apr-17 May*	11-5	·	·	·	·	·	**S**	**S**
23 May-27 Sep	11-5	**M**	**T**	**W**	**T**	**F**	**S**	**S**
3 Oct-18 Oct	11-5	·	·	·	·	·	**S**	**S**
24 Oct-1 Nov	10:30-4	**M**	**T**	**W**	**T**	**F**	**S**	**S**
7 Nov-27 Dec*	10:30-4	·	·	·	·	·	**S**	**S**

*Also open Bank Holiday 4 May, 26 December and 1 January 2016.

Farne Islands

Northumberland

Map (6) H2 1925

Probably the most exciting seabird colony in England. The boat trip from Seahouses rewards you with a close-up peek into the world of 23 nesting species of seabird, including thousands of puffins, Arctic terns and guillemots. In autumn, you can see the grey seal colony, with over 1,000 pups. **Note**: basic toilet facilities on Inner Farne only. Access by boat from Seahouses (charge including members).

Eating and shopping: shop in Seahouses selling a range of gifts and local produce. Some souvenirs also available on the islands.

Making the most of your day: St Cuthbert's Chapel, with vibrant stained glass, and Victorian lighthouse. Visitor centre. Easy-access boardwalk. Seasonal tours and events. Lindisfarne Castle and Northumberland Coast nearby. **Dogs**: not allowed (including assistance dogs) due to very sensitive nature of the colony.

Access: **Grounds**
Sat Nav: NE68 7RQ. **Parking**: in Seahouses, not National Trust (charge including members).

Birdwatching on the Farne Islands, Northumberland

Finding out more: 01665 721099. 01289 389244 (Lindisfarne Castle) or farneislands@nationaltrust.org.uk

Farne Islands		M	T	W	T	F	S	S
Inner Farne Island								
28 Mar–30 Apr	10:30–6	M	T	W	T	F	S	S
1 May–31 Jul	1:30–5:30	M	T	W	T	F	S	S
1 Aug–1 Nov	10:30–6	M	T	W	T	F	S	S
Staple Island								
1 May–31 Jul	10:30–1:30	M	T	W	T	F	S	S

Landings only on Inner Farne and Staple Islands. Seahouses information centre and shop open all year, 10 to 5.

Hardcastle Crags

near Hebden Bridge, West Yorkshire

Map (5) E6 1950

This beautiful wooded valley, with its deep ravines, tumbling streams and glorious waterfalls, has miles of footpaths through woodlands rich in wildlife – don't forget to listen out for the ever-changing birdsong. The seasonal colours are simply stunning, with carpets of bluebells in spring and golden leaves in autumn. Nestling alongside the river is Gibson Mill, a former cotton mill and entertainment emporium, now a visitor centre powered by sustainable energy. You can discover more about the valley's 200-year history here with exhibitions, tours and family fun. **Note**: steep paths and rough terrain.

Eating and shopping: Weaving Shed Café serving sandwiches, soup, cakes and ice-cream. Shop selling books, gifts, cards and sweets.

Gibson Mill at Hardcastle Crags, West Yorkshire

Making the most of your day: **Indoors** Tours and dressing-up in period costume at Gibson Mill. **Outdoors** Variety of trails with downloadable options, plus guided walks and seasonal events. **Dogs**: under close control at all times.

Access: **Building** **Grounds**

Sat Nav: for Midgehole car park use HX7 7AA; Clough Hole car park HX7 7AZ.
Parking: at Clough Hole, 1 mile, and Widdop Road (steep walk).

Finding out more: 01422 844518 (weekdays). 01422 846236 (weekends) or hardcastlecrags@nationaltrust.org.uk

Hardcastle Crags		M	T	W	T	F	S	S
Gibson Mill and Weaving Shed Café								
3 Jan–29 Mar	11–3	·	·	·	·	·	S	S
31 Mar–1 Nov*	11–4	·	T	W	T	·	S	S
7 Nov–27 Dec	11–3	·	·	·	·	·	S	S

*Café open 10 to 5 weekends 2 May to 27 September. Weaving Shed Café open seven days and Gibson Mill open Saturday to Thursday during Calderdale school holidays. Café and Mill open Bank Holidays.

Marsden Moor Estate

Marsden, Huddersfield, West Yorkshire

Map (5) E7 1955

The landscape and history of Marsden Moor, within the South Pennines and Peak District National Park, will bring out the explorer in you. Pule Hill and Buckstones offer breathtaking views, and there are miles of footpaths and bridleways to enjoy, while spotting the wildlife which inhabits this internationally important habitat.
Note: sorry no toilet.

Eating and shopping: tea-rooms, restaurants and shops in Marsden village (none National Trust).

Making the most of your day: events, family activities and guided walks all year. Walking routes available (OS map required) from Estate Office exhibition room. Why not visit the 'Framing the Landscape' artwork and Stanza Stone? **Dogs**: welcome on leads.

Exploring Marsden Moor Estate, West Yorkshire

Access: **Exhibition Room** [icon] **Grounds** [icon]
Sat Nav: use HD7 6DH for Marsden village.
Parking: at Marsden village (not National Trust), Buckstones and Wessenden Head.

Finding out more: 01484 847016 or marsdenmoor@nationaltrust.org.uk

Marsden Moor Estate		M	T	W	T	F	S	S
Exhibition Centre								
Open all year	9-5	**M**	**T**	**W**	**T**	**F**	**S**	**S**
Closed 25 December.								

Northumberland Coast

Northumberland

Map (6) H2   1935

From Lindisfarne to Druridge Bay, you'll find wide open skies above white sands and blue seas. This unspoilt coastline boasts pretty fishing villages and deserted beaches, with excellent rock pools. It's also a haven for spotting wonderful wildlife, including seals, wading shorebirds and nesting terns at the Long Nanny.

Eating and shopping: shops on Holy Island and Seahouses. Cafés, pubs and shops in coastal towns and villages (none National Trust).

Making the most of your day: little tern nesting colony at Long Nanny (June to August), access from High Newton. Events, including guided walks and wildlife spotting. Farne Islands, Dunstanburgh Castle and Lindisfarne Castle nearby. **Dogs**: welcome, some local restrictions may apply.

Access: [icon]
Parking: limited at Druridge Bay. Also at Holy Island, Seahouses, Beadnell, Newton by the Sea and Craster, not National Trust (charge including members).

Finding out more: 01289 389244 or northumberlandcoast@nationaltrust.org.uk

Dunes on the glorious Northumberland Coast

Penshaw Monument

near Penshaw, Tyne & Wear

Map (6) H5   1939

Enjoy walks and magnificent views from this 70-foot high tribute to the 1st Earl of Durham. An iconic Wearside landmark. **Note**: sorry no toilets. Access staircase to the top of monument by guided tour only (advance booking via website advised). For Sat Nav use DH4 7NJ.

Finding out more: 01723 870423 or penshaw.monument@nationaltrust.org.uk

Roseberry Topping

near Newton-under-Roseberry, North Yorkshire

Map (5) G2 1985

Affectionately known as 'Yorkshire's Matterhorn', layers of geological history have shaped this iconic hill. Stunning views, woodland walks and wildlife. **Note**: sorry no toilet. For Sat Nav use TS9 6QR.

Finding out more: 01723 870423 or roseberrytopping@nationaltrust.org.uk

Yorkshire Coast

near Ravenscar, North Yorkshire

Map (5) I2 1976

The coastline from Saltburn to Filey is breathtakingly dramatic, with sea views, clifftop walks, cycling routes and sandy bays with excellent rock-pooling and fossil-hunting. Ravenscar Visitor Centre will give you lots of ideas and there's also a coastal exhibition at the Old Coastguard Station, Robin Hood's Bay.

Eating and shopping: Old Coastguard Station and Ravenscar Visitor Centre shops sell gifts, books, maps and children's toys. Ice-cream and light refreshments available at Ravenscar. Indoor seating and outdoor picnic area.

Making the most of your day: **Indoors** Regular art exhibitions at the Old Coastguard Station. **Outdoors** Family events, geocaching, wildlife activities and guided walks from Ravenscar Visitor Centre and the Old Coastguard Station. **Dogs**: welcome on lead at most events. Assistance dogs only in visitor centre and Old Coastguard Station.

Access: **Visitor centre** **Grounds**
Parking: on roadside at Ravenscar. Pay and display at Saltburn, Runswick Bay and Robin Hood's Bay, not National Trust (charge including members).

Finding out more: 01723 870423 or yorkshirecoast@nationaltrust.org.uk

Yorkshire Coast		M	T	W	T	F	S	S
Old Coastguard Station								
1 Jan–4 Jan	10–4	·	·	·	T	F	S	S
10 Jan–8 Feb	10–4	·	·	·	·	·	S	S
14 Feb–22 Feb	10–4	M	T	W	T	F	S	S
28 Feb–22 Mar	10–4	·	·	·	·	·	S	S
28 Mar–1 Nov	10–5	M	T	W	T	F	S	S
7 Nov–20 Dec	10–4	·	·	·	·	·	S	S
27 Dec–31 Dec	10–4	M	T	W	T	·	·	S
Ravenscar Visitor Centre								
28 Mar–1 Nov	10–4:30	M	T	W	T	F	S	S

Enjoying the sea view on the Yorkshire Coast

Yorkshire Dales

Whatever your ability, you will find a walk that suits you here. There are riverside beauty spots, picturesque villages, limestone uplands and flower-rich meadows to discover.

Malham Tarn Estate

Waterhouses, Settle, North Yorkshire

Map (5) D4 1946

With stunning views across limestone pavements and the Tarn's rippling water, the peacefulness of the National Nature Reserve is the perfect place to enjoy the great outdoors. Popular with walkers and cyclists, it is wonderful for a stroll, picnic or family adventure.

Note: nearest toilet at Malham National Park car park or Orchid House exhibition.

Eating and shopping: tea-rooms, pubs and facilities in Malham village (none National Trust).

Making the most of your day: guided walks, events, outdoor activities. Accessible boardwalk through reserve. Cycle trails around the tarn. Family events during holidays. Orchid House exhibition. Walking routes for all abilities, tramper available to hire.
Dogs: welcome on leads (livestock roaming).

Access: **Town Head Barn** [icon] **Grounds** [icons]
Sat Nav: use BD24 9PT. **Parking**: off-road at Waterhouses and at Watersinks car park, south side of Malham Tarn.

Finding out more: 01729 830416 or malhamtarn@nationaltrust.org.uk

Malham Tarn Estate		M	T	W	T	F	S	S
Town Head Barn								
14 Feb–31 Oct	10–4	**M**	**T**	**W**	**T**	**F**	**S**	**S**

Hiking on the Malham Tarn Estate, North Yorkshire

Exploring Upper Wharfedale, North Yorkshire

Upper Wharfedale

near Buckden, North Yorkshire

Map (5) E4 [icons] 1989

The spectacular landscapes in this part of the Dales are great for walking and cycling. The characteristic drystone walls and barns look striking in the summer, surrounded by beautiful flowering hay meadows. Combined with river and woodland valleys, this is a wonderful place to relax and explore the great outdoors.

Eating and shopping: village tea-rooms, shops, pubs and farm shops (not National Trust).

Making the most of your day: guided walks, events, workshops and activities. Family events during school holidays. Exhibition at Town Head Barn in Buckden. **Dogs**: welcome on leads due to livestock.

Access: [icons] **Town Head Barn** [icon] **Grounds** [icon]
Sat Nav: use BD23 5JA. **Parking**: in Kettlewell and Buckden, pay and display, not National Trust (charge including members).

Finding out more: 01729 830416 or upperwharfedale@nationaltrust.org.uk

Upper Wharfedale		M	T	W	T	F	S	S
Town Head Barn								
14 Feb–31 Oct	10–4	**M**	**T**	**W**	**T**	**F**	**S**	**S**

Beningbrough Hall, Gallery and Gardens

Beningbrough, York,
North Yorkshire YO30 1DD

Map (5) G4 1958

Inspired by his Grand Tour, John Bourchier created Beningbrough, an Italian Palace nestled between York, Harrogate and Leeds.
The impressive rooms are a perfect backdrop for the rich collection of portraits on loan from the National Portrait Gallery, Beningbrough's long-term partner. The paintings feature people who have made, and are making, British history and culture, and in 2015 include contemporary portraits in a display of 'Royals: then and now'. A working walled garden, grand herbaceous borders, sweeping lawns and a play area for children to let off steam, creates a year-round garden. Picture-postcard views can be seen from the garden, and the parkland offers opportunities to explore riverside walks, ancient trees and discover hidden wildlife.

Eating and shopping: the Walled Garden restaurant serves morning coffee, afternoon tea and hot lunches, which include freshly picked produce. The shop has an extensive home and garden range. Second-hand books can be found in the library in the hall.

Making the most of your day: **Indoors** The hands-on interactive galleries at this award-winning property; Making Faces – 18th-century Style, are perfect for discovering history and portraiture. Sitting for your own virtual digital portrait is a great way to send a lasting memory home, or Clarence the Corgi can be your guide on the free family royal trail. A taste of servant life is found in the Victorian laundry, and the friendly team bring the stories to life in the house. **Outdoors** The hidden gem of a garden continues to evolve and offers quiet corners to relax in and luxurious borders to inspire.
Dogs: welcome on leads in parkland. Assistance dogs only in gardens and grounds.

Access: **Mansion** **Stable block** **Grounds**
Parking: on site.

The entrance hall (opposite) at Beningbrough Hall, Gallery and Gardens, North Yorkshire, and enjoying the grounds (above)

Finding out more: 01904 472027 or beningbrough@nationaltrust.org.uk

Beningbrough Hall		M	T	W	T	F	S	S
Gardens, shop, restaurant, house and interactive galleries*								
28 Feb–5 Jul	11-5	·	T	W	T	F	S	S
6 Jul–31 Aug	11-5	M	T	W	T	F	S	S
1 Sep–1 Nov	11-5	·	T	W	T	F	S	S
Gardens, shop, restaurant and interactive galleries**								
3 Jan–15 Feb	11-3:30	·	·	·	·	·	S	S
17 Feb–22 Feb	11-3:30	·	T	W	T	F	S	S
7 Nov–27 Dec	11-3:30	·	·	·	·	·	S	S

*House and interactive galleries open at 12.
**Interactive galleries open at 11:30. Open Bank Holiday Mondays and 1 January 2016.

Braithwaite Hall

East Witton, Leyburn, North Yorkshire DL8 4SY

Map (5) E3 1941

This beautiful 17th-century tenanted farmhouse lies in the heart of Coverdale.
Note: sorry no toilet. Parts of the Hall are open to visit in June, July and August (by arrangement in advance with the tenant).

Finding out more: 01969 640287 or braithwaitehall@nationaltrust.org.uk

Cherryburn

Station Bank, Mickley, Stocksfield,
Northumberland NE43 7DD

Map (6) G5 1991

Set in a tranquil garden with views across the picturesque Tyne Valley, this unassuming Northumbrian farmstead is the birthplace of famous artist and naturalist Thomas Bewick. You can enjoy the natural world that inspired his work, explore the museum with Bewick's pioneering wood engravings and meet the quirky farm animals.

Eating and shopping: gift shop offering an array of handmade Bewick prints, souvenirs and books. Farmhouse café serving homemade scones and ice-creams with farmyard picnic area.

Making the most of your day: **Indoors** Printing demonstrations every weekend. **Outdoors** Family trail, mini-adventure play area and school holiday activities following in young Tom's footsteps. Paddock walk. Monthly folk music in the farmyard. **Dogs**: welcome on short leads in garden and grounds (animals in farmyard).

Access:
Birthplace **Café and museum**
Grounds
Sat Nav: use NE43 7DD. **Parking**: 100 yards.

Cherryburn, Northumberland: Thomas Bewick illustration

Finding out more: 01661 843276 or cherryburn@nationaltrust.org.uk

Cherryburn		M	T	W	T	F	S	S
14 Feb–28 Jun	11–5	M	T	·	T	F	S	S
29 Jun–30 Aug	10–5	M	T	W	T	F	S	S
31 Aug–1 Nov	11–5	M	T	·	T	F	S	S

Cragside

Rothbury, Morpeth, Northumberland NE65 7PX

Map (6) G3 1977

Trip the light fantastic to the home where modern living began. Lord and Lady Armstrong used their wealth, art and science in a most ingenious way – Cragside was the first house in the world to be lit by hydroelectricity, making it a wonder of the Victorian age, while outside, their shared passion for landscaping and gardening was daring and demonstrated engineering on a spectacular scale. There are towering North American conifers and great drifts of rhododendrons, as well as rocky crags and tumbling water. The house is one of the finest examples of Arts and Crafts workmanship in the country.
Note: challenging terrain and distances (stout footwear essential).

Eating and shopping: tea-rooms serving hot meals and snacks, hand-crafted sweet treats and afternoon tea. Outlets at visitor centre, near the house, and play area offering takeaway snacks and sandwiches. Shop selling Northumbrian gifts, books and cards. Picnics welcome.

Making the most of your day: **Indoors** We have installed the Archimedes Screw, so now the house is illuminated by water power once more. Family activities, special exhibitions and seasonal events throughout the year. Lord Armstrong's hydroelectric engineering collection. **Outdoors** Fantasy landscape, including a rhododendron labyrinth. Six-mile estate drive through woodland. Lakeside trails and walks for all abilities, from family strolls to challenging hikes. Free shuttle bus between key features. Wallington and Lindisfarne Castle nearby. **Dogs**: welcome on leads outdoors.

The grounds at Cragside, Northumberland (above and below), offer so much for adventurers – whatever their age

Access:
House **Visitor Centre** **Estate**
Parking: nine car parks on estate.

Finding out more: 01669 620333 or
cragside@nationaltrust.org.uk

Cragside		M	T	W	T	F	S	S
House								
24 Feb–30 Oct*	1–5	·	**T**	**W**	**T**	**F**	**S**	**S**
28 Mar–19 Apr	11–5	**M**	**T**	**W**	**T**	**F**	**S**	**S**
23 May–31 May	11–5	**M**	**T**	**W**	**T**	**F**	**S**	**S**
18 Jul–31 Aug	11–5	**M**	**T**	**W**	**T**	**F**	**S**	**S**
24 Oct–1 Nov	11–5	**M**	**T**	**W**	**T**	**F**	**S**	**S**
Gardens and woodland								
14 Feb–22 Feb	11–4	**M**	**T**	**W**	**T**	**F**	**S**	**S**
24 Feb–1 Nov**	10–7	·	**T**	**W**	**T**	**F**	**S**	**S**
6 Nov–20 Dec	11–4	·	·	·	·	**F**	**S**	**S**

*House open from 11 weekends February to October. House (ground floor only) also open from 14 to 22 February 12 to 4. House open Bank Holiday Mondays 11 to 5. Entry is controlled (queueing at busy times). **Gardens and woodland open Mondays 10 to 7 when house is open. Last access to estate drive 5:30.

Dunstanburgh Castle

Craster, Alnwick, Northumberland NE66 3TT

Map (6) H3 1961

Iconic castle ruin occupying a dramatic position with spectacular views of the Northumberland coastline – only a mile walk from Craster. **Note**: managed by English Heritage. National Trust members free. Sorry no toilets, see English Heritage website for further information. Parking at Craster, pay and display, not National Trust (charge including members).

Finding out more: 01665 576231 or dunstanburghcastle@nationaltrust.org.uk

East Riddlesden Hall

Bradford Road, Riddlesden, Keighley, West Yorkshire BD20 5EL

Map (5) E5 1934

Imagine stepping 400 years back in time and entering into the home of James Murgatroyd, a 17th-century cloth merchant. James used his wealth to make some major changes to his Tudor home, although sadly these were never completed – come and discover why. Today, James's tale is brought to life through fascinating stories shared by our room guides. Outside, the intimate garden offers an oasis to relax and unwind in, while families can enjoy hiding in the hobbit house, balancing on logs or letting off some steam in the natural play areas.

Eating and shopping: traditional tea-room on first floor of 17th-century building serving a selection of cakes and drinks. Downstairs table available. Ground-floor shop selling gifts, books, plants and ice-cream.

Making the most of your day: **Indoors** Family trails and dressing-up. Historic barn with original timber beams. **Outdoors** Bird hide. Discovery garden featuring hobbit house and mud-pie kitchen. Riverside walk. Playground and natural play areas. **Dogs**: assistance dogs only.

Access:
Building **Grounds**
Parking: 100 yards.

Finding out more: 01535 607075 or eastriddlesden@nationaltrust.org.uk

East Riddlesden Hall		M	T	W	T	F	S	S
House, shop and tea-room								
14 Feb–22 Feb	10:30–4:30	M	T	W	·	·	S	S
28 Feb–15 Mar	10:30–4:30	·	·	·	·	·	S	S
21 Mar–1 Nov	10:30–4:30	M	T	W	·	·	S	S
Shop and tea-room								
7 Nov–20 Dec	11–4	·	·	·	·	·	S	S

Also open Good Friday. Entry to house may be by guided tour. Last admission to tea-room 15 minutes before closing.

East Riddlesden Hall, West Yorkshire: this 17th-century home has so many tales to tell

Fountains Abbey and Studley Royal Water Garden

near Ripon, North Yorkshire HG4 3DY

Map (5) F4 1983

For centuries people have been drawn to this inspiring place. From humble beginnings, the magnificent Abbey was established by devout monks seeking a simpler existence. The atmospheric ruins that remain are a window into a way of life which shaped the medieval world. When the socially ambitious John Aislabie inherited Studley Royal, he set about creating an elegant water garden of mirror-like ponds, statues and follies, incorporating the romantic ruins into his design. Green lawns stretch down to the riverside, a perfect spot for a picnic. Riverside paths lead to the deer-park, home to red, fallow and sika deer and ancient trees – limes, oaks and sweet chestnuts. One-of-a-kind, this special place is now recognised as a World Heritage Site. **Note**: cared for in partnership with English Heritage.

Fountains Abbey (below) and Studley Royal Water Garden (above), a World Heritage Site in North Yorkshire

Eating and shopping: large restaurant serving breakfast, lunch, daily specials and Sunday dinner. Studley and Abbey tea-rooms in spectacular settings. Large visitor centre shop selling homeware, gardenware, plants, books and artisan products. Smaller shop at Studley entrance. Picnics welcome.

Red deer at Fountains Abbey and Studley Royal Water Garden in North Yorkshire

Making the most of your day: **Indoors** In Porter's Lodge you can uncover the story of the monks who founded the Abbey, or see the mill created by these skilful masters of machinery. You can explore the opulent interior of St Mary's Church. Fountains Hall has changing art exhibitions. Why not stay longer in one of the holiday apartments? **Outdoors** The hidden herb garden beside the River Skell is waiting to be found. Nature walks and tours guide you through the estate and its history. You can clamber, swing and slide in the playground or find a geocache. **Dogs**: welcome on leads.

Access: **Abbey** **Fountains Hall** **Grounds**
Parking: main car park at visitor centre.

Finding out more: 01765 608888 or fountainsabbey@nationaltrust.org.uk

Fountains Abbey		M	T	W	T	F	S	S
Abbey and Water Garden*								
1 Jan–31 Jan*	10–5	M	T	W	T	·	S	S
1 Feb–27 Mar*	10–5	M	T	W	T	F	S	S
28 Mar–24 Oct*	10–6	M	T	W	T	F	S	S
25 Oct–1 Nov*	10–5	M	T	W	T	F	S	S
2 Nov–31 Dec*	10–5	M	T	W	T	·	S	S
Deer-park								
1 Jan–27 Mar	6–6	M	T	W	T	F	S	S
28 Mar–24 Oct	6–9	M	T	W	T	F	S	S
25 Oct–31 Dec	6–6	M	T	W	T	F	S	S
St Mary's Church								
1 Apr–30 Sep	12–4	M	T	W	T	F	S	S

*Last admission one hour before closing. Hall, mill, shop and restaurant close half an hour earlier than Abbey and Water Garden. Studley Royal shop, Studley Royal tea-room and Abbey tea-room opening times vary. Property closed 24 and 25 December.

George Stephenson's Birthplace

near Wylam, Northumberland NE41 8HP

Map (6) G5 1949

This simple cottage, with its pretty garden, was railway pioneer George Stephenson's birthplace. You can share, with our costumed guide, in the story and challenges of a mining family living in one room and their engineering legacy, then stroll along Wylam's historic Waggonway on the banks of the River Tyne.

Eating and shopping: tea-room serving light snacks and homemade cakes, with garden seating. Souvenirs and books for sale.

Making the most of your day: **Indoors** Tiny room decorated exactly as in 1781, the year of Stephenson's birth. **Outdoors** Family-friendly walk and cycle path following the route of one of the world's first steam railways.
Dogs: welcome on leads in garden.

Access: **Birthplace** **Café** **Garden**
Parking: in village, then ½ mile along Wylam Waggonway.

George Stephenson's Birthplace, Northumberland

Finding out more: 01207 541820 or georgestephensons@nationaltrust.org.uk

George Stephenson's Birthplace		M	T	W	T	F	S	S
Cottage, tea-room and tea-garden								
5 Mar–1 Nov	11–5	·	·	·	**T**	**F**	**S**	**S**
Tea-room and tea-garden								
3 Jan–1 Mar	11–3	·	·	·	·	·	**S**	**S**
7 Nov–20 Dec	11–3	·	·	·	·	·	**S**	**S**

Open Bank Holiday Mondays.

Gibside

near Rowlands Gill, Gateshead, Tyne & Wear NE16 6BG

Map (6) H5 1974

Home to red kites, roe deer and much other rare wildlife, Gibside is great for exploring trails, meandering through woodland and gardens, soaking up the views across the Derwent Valley and discovering fascinating historic buildings and ruins. You can experience this designed landscape commissioned by George Bowes, one of the wealthiest men of his time, and discover the story of his daughter Mary Eleanor's traumatic love-life and her gardening passion. Restoration of this once grand estate is turning a neglected wilderness back to its former glory. **Note**: restoration work to the Walled Garden continues.

Eating and shopping: Gibside café. Carriage House coffee shop and second-hand books at the Stables. Kiosk at adventure play area (weekends and holidays). Gibside shop selling plants and gifts. Friday evening beer garden. Twice-monthly farmers' market.

Making the most of your day: **Indoors** Palladian chapel with unique three-tier pulpit. Gibside story and wildlife interpretation at the Stables. **Outdoors** Restoration of the Walled Garden and wider estate. Walks. Family-friendly events. Adventure play areas. **Dogs**: welcome on leads (assistance dogs only in Strawberry Castle Adventure play area).

Access: **Chapel** **Stables** **Garden**
Parking: 382 yards from café and shop (uphill walkway).

Finding out more: 01207 541820 or gibside@nationaltrust.org.uk

Gibside		M	T	W	T	F	S	S
Landscape gardens, woodlands, café and shop*								
1 Jan–1 Mar	10–4	**M**	**T**	**W**	**T**	**F**	**S**	**S**
2 Mar–1 Nov**	10–6	**M**	**T**	**W**	**T**	**F**	**S**	**S**
2 Nov–31 Dec	10–4	**M**	**T**	**W**	**T**	**F**	**S**	**S**
Chapel								
3 Jan–1 Mar	10–4	·	·	·	·	·	**S**	**S**
2 Mar–1 Nov	10–5	**M**	**T**	**W**	**T**	**F**	**S**	**S**
7 Nov–27 Dec	10–4	·	·	·	·	·	**S**	**S**

*Pub and beer garden: open 6 to 9 Fridays (excluding 26 December) and additionally on summer Saturdays. Estate: closed 24 and 25 December. Last entry: winter 3:30, summer 4:30. **Café and shop close at 5.

Restoration of Gibside, Tyne & Wear, is gradually returning this neglected wilderness to its former glory

Arts and Crafts Goddards House and Garden, North Yorkshire

Goddards House and Garden

27 Tadcaster Road, York,
North Yorkshire YO24 1GG

Map (5) H5 1984

Nestled on the edge of York racecourse, this former home of the Terry family (think Chocolate Orange) is a warm Arts and Crafts house full of memories. You can sit down, pour yourself a sherry and feel at home, then meander through garden rooms, discovering fragrant borders and hidden corners.

Eating and shopping: lunch served in the Terry's dining-room, with a view of the Arts and Crafts garden from the lavender terrace. Why not treat yourself to a chocolate souvenir to take home?

Making the most of your day: **Indoors** Curl up with a *Terry Times* in the drawing-room. Table tennis in the playroom. Everyone's welcome to leave their Terry's memories on the typewriter. **Outdoors** Croquet in the garden. **Dogs**: welcome on leads in garden.

Access: **House** **Grounds**
Sat Nav: enter 27 Tadcaster Road, York, not postcode. **Parking**: limited at weekends. On weekdays, car park used by regional office, please use city-centre car parks (1 to 2 miles) or park on nearby Knavesmire Road (off A1036).

Finding out more: 01904 771930 or goddards@nationaltrust.org.uk

Goddards		M	T	W	T	F	S	S
House, garden and dining-room								
1 Mar–1 Nov	11–5	·	·	**W**	**T**	**F**	**S**	**S**
House and dining-room								
14 Nov–20 Dec	11–3:30	·	·	·	·	·	**S**	**S**
House, garden and dining-room open Bank Holiday Mondays.								

Hadrian's Wall and Housesteads Fort

Near Bardon Mill, Hexham,
Northumberland NE47 6NN

Map (6) F5 1930

You can enjoy breathtaking views at one of the Roman Empire's best-maintained outposts in northern Europe. Here, you can walk in the footsteps of Romans and Reivers across 110 miles of World Heritage Site, where the wall and fort provide a real insight into a Roman soldier's life. **Note**: fort owned by National Trust, maintained/managed by English Heritage. ½ mile to fort from visitor centre.

Walkers following Hadrian's Wall, Northumberland

Looking towards Lindisfarne Castle, Northumberland: a former fort turned Edwardian holiday home

Eating and shopping: visitor centre offering sandwiches and snacks, ice-cream and drinks. Shop selling books, cards, gifts, souvenirs and plants. Picnics welcome.

Making the most of your day: **Indoors** Museum (not National Trust) with dressing-up clothes and video presentation. **Outdoors** Play area. Why not walk along the wall to Milecastle 37 and Sycamore Gap? Cottages for rent. **Dogs**: welcome on leads.

Access:
Visitor centre **Museum**
Parking: at Housesteads, Steel Rigg and Cawfields, not National Trust (charge including members).

Finding out more: 01434 344525 or housesteads@nationaltrust.org.uk

Hadrian's Wall and Housesteads Fort

Open every day, with limited opening over Christmas and New Year.

Lindisfarne Castle

Holy Island, Berwick-upon-Tweed, Northumberland TD15 2SH

Map (6) G1 1944

Location is the thing at Lindisfarne Castle. From a former fort to the holiday home of a wealthy Edwardian bachelor seeking a quiet retreat, the idyllic location of the castle has intrigued and inspired for centuries. Perched atop a rocky crag, this romantic castle is full of intimate spaces typical of the work of Sir Edwin Lutyens. From the upper battery you can enjoy panoramic views back across the Northumberland coast, and there are shoreline walks, the unexpected grandeur of the lime kilns and the summer-flowering garden designed by Gertrude Jekyll all waiting to be explored. **Note**: limited number of toilets. Island accessed via tidal causeway (check safe crossing times at northumberland.gov.uk).

Boat shed on Holy Island, Northumberland

Eating and shopping: souvenirs, coffee machine, water, snacks and ice-cream available. National Trust shop in village.

Making the most of your day: regular events and family trails. Kites and binoculars available to borrow. Occasional seal-spotting from the upper battery and rock-pooling events.
Dogs: welcome on leads. Assistance dogs only in castle.

Access: [symbols] **Castle** [symbols] **Grounds** [symbol]
Parking: at main island car park, 1 mile, not National Trust (charge including members). Private transfer available most days.

Finding out more: 01289 389244 or lindisfarne@nationaltrust.org.uk

Lindisfarne Castle	M	T	W	T	F	S	S
14 Feb–1 Nov	·	**T**	**W**	**T**	**F**	**S**	**S**
1 Aug–31 Aug	**M**	**T**	**W**	**T**	**F**	**S**	**S**

Opening times vary due to tides, either 10 to 3 or 12 to 5. Check times before visiting. Open Bank Holiday Mondays. Some additional Monday openings throughout season and some weekend openings in winter.

Maister House

160 High Street, Hull, East Yorkshire HU1 1NL

Map (5) J6 [symbol] 1966

A merchant family's tale of fortune and tragedy is intertwined with the intriguing history of Maister House. **Note**: staircase and entrance hall only on show. Sorry no toilet.

Finding out more: 01723 870423 or maisterhouse@nationaltrust.org.uk

Middlethorpe Hall Hotel, Restaurant and Spa

Bishopthorpe Road, York, North Yorkshire YO23 2GB

Map (5) H5 [symbols] 2008

William and Mary house, built in 1699, set in eight hectares (20 acres) of manicured gardens and parkland. **Note**: access is for paying guests, including for luncheon, afternoon tea and dinner.

Finding out more: 01904 641241. 01904 620176 (fax) or info@middlethorpe.com. middlethorpe.com

Moulton Hall

Moulton, Richmond, North Yorkshire DL10 6QH

Map (5) F2 [symbol] 1966

Elegant 17th-century tenanted manor house with a beautiful carved staircase.
Note: sorry no toilet. Visit by arrangement.

Finding out more: 01325 377227 or moultonhall@nationaltrust.org.uk

Mount Grace Priory

near Northallerton, North Yorkshire DL6 3JG

Map (5) G3 [symbol] 1953

You can discover how medieval Carthusian monks lived and explore priory ruins, garden and Arts and Crafts-style manor house rooms. **Note**: operated by English Heritage; members free, except on event days.

Finding out more: 01609 883494 or mountgracepriory@nationaltrust.org.uk

Nostell Priory and Parkland, West Yorkshire: the entrance front (above) and corner of the Top Hall (below)

Nostell Priory and Parkland

Doncaster Road, Nostell, near Wakefield, West Yorkshire WF4 1QE

Map (5) G6 1954

Nostell was home of the Winn family for more than 350 years and the grand interiors, designed by Robert Adam, contain a renowned collection of Chippendale furniture – providing an exciting window into this world of wealth and splendour. Children can find the mouse in our 18th-century doll's-house or enjoy our packed programme of family activities. Outside, our ongoing garden restoration project provides seasonal opportunities to explore the delights of the rose, kitchen and fruit gardens. You can wander through the orchard and woodland garden towards our lake, and savour the attractive views across the estate. In the parkland there are trails to discover, providing access to meadows and woodlands where you can enjoy wild flowers and birds.

Eating and shopping: Courtyard Café serving hot food and refreshments. Bite to Eat kiosk offering snacks and drinks at peak times. Shop selling gifts, souvenirs and plants. Picnics welcome in the park and gardens.

Making the most of your day: **Indoors** Year-round events, including craft fairs and family activities during school holidays. Regular tours of the house and stables, specialist talks, 'upstairs-downstairs' tour of the attics and cellars and library talks (bookable in advance). Special opening in December, when the house is decorated for Christmas. **Outdoors** Seasonal events, including open-air theatre and live music. Guided parkland walks. Geocaching and orienteering trails. Children's adventure playground, play trail and den-building. Running, walking, cycling groups and sports activities. **Dogs**: on leads in park (exercise area in car park). Assistance dogs only in gardens.

Access:
House **Grounds**
Sat Nav: use WF4 1QE. **Parking**: 500 yards.

Finding out more: 01924 863892 or nostellpriory@nationaltrust.org.uk

Nostell Priory and Parkland		M	T	W	T	F	S	S
House								
28 Feb–1 Nov*	1–5	·	·	**W**	**T**	**F**	**S**	**S**
28 Nov–13 Dec	11–3	·	·	·	·	·	**S**	**S**
Gardens, shop and tea-room**								
1 Jan–13 Feb	11–4:30	**M**	**T**	**W**	**T**	**F**	**S**	**S**
14 Feb–1 Nov	10–5:30	**M**	**T**	**W**	**T**	**F**	**S**	**S**
2 Nov–31 Dec	11–4:30	**M**	**T**	**W**	**T**	**F**	**S**	**S**
Parkland†								
Open all year	7–7	**M**	**T**	**W**	**T**	**F**	**S**	**S**

*House: open 11 to 12 for guided tours (places limited and allocated on arrival). Last admission to house 45 minutes before closing. Open Bank Holiday Mondays. **Rose Garden: may close for private functions. Property closed 25 December. †Parkland: closes dusk if earlier.

The lake at Nostell Priory and Parkland, West Yorkshire

Nunnington Hall

Nunnington, near York, North Yorkshire YO62 5UY

Map (5) H4 1953

A perfect day out for all the family, rain or shine. In the picturesque village of Nunnington, within easy reach of York and Scarborough, this welcoming and friendly family home is known for its enchanting house and beautiful gardens. You can learn about the Fife family, owners of the Hall in the 1920s and, if you're brave enough, hear the Hall's ghostly tales! The beautiful wildflower meadows in the organic gardens are great to wander through and give the best view of the house from the cherry tree avenue. Why not relax and picnic by the meandering River Rye too?

Eating and shopping: licensed waitress-service tea-rooms within atmospheric historic rooms serving dishes made using Nunnington produce. Outdoor self-service kiosk during peak times with outside seating next to the river. Picnics welcome – tables are situated around the grounds. Shop selling local ranges.

A perfectly mown grass path leads through the garden at Nunnington Hall, North Yorkshire

Making the most of your day: **Indoors** Family fun, with 1920s games, dressing-up and activity room. Carlisle collection of miniature rooms. Events and exhibitions, tours, family days, theatre and concerts. **Outdoors** Tepee glade and mud-pie kitchen. **Dogs**: welcome on leads in garden.

Access: [icons] **Building** [icons] **Grounds** [icons]
Parking: on site.

Finding out more: 01439 748283 or nunningtonhall@nationaltrust.org.uk

Nunnington Hall		M	T	W	T	F	S	S
14 Feb–22 Feb	11-5	M	T	W	T	F	S	S
24 Feb–29 Mar	11-5	·	T	W	T	F	S	S
30 Mar–12 Apr	11-5	M	T	W	T	F	S	S
14 Apr–26 Jul	11-5	·	T	W	T	F	S	S
27 Jul–6 Sep	11-5	M	T	W	T	F	S	S
8 Sep–25 Oct	11-5	·	T	W	T	F	S	S
26 Oct–1 Nov	11-4	M	T	W	T	F	S	S
7 Nov–13 Dec	11-4	·	·	·	·	·	S	S

Open Bank Holiday Mondays.

Ormesby Hall

Ladgate Lane, Ormesby, near Middlesbrough, Redcar & Cleveland TS3 0SR

Map (5) G2 [icons] 1962

Once home to the Pennyman family, the spirit of this Georgian home remains true to the kind couple who lived here last, Colonel Jim and his arts-loving wife Ruth, with the stylish legacy of Jim's ancestor, 'Wicked' Sir James, providing an intriguing backdrop.

Eating and shopping: refreshments served in servants' hall or terrace.

Making the most of your day: model railway layouts (only ones owned by the National Trust). **Dogs**: welcome on leads in the parkland.

Access: [icons] **Building** [icons] **Grounds** [icons]
Parking: on site.

Finding out more: 01642 324188 or ormesbyhall@nationaltrust.org.uk. Church Lane, Ormesby, Middlesbrough TS7 9AS

Ormesby Hall		M	T	W	T	F	S	S
1 Mar–1 Nov	10-5	·	·	·	·	·	·	S

Open Bank Holiday Mondays. Additionally open Saturday 21 March for Model Railway Weekend. Closures at short notice possible.

The laundry room at Ormesby Hall, Redcar & Cleveland

Rievaulx Terrace

Rievaulx, Helmsley, North Yorkshire YO62 5LJ

Map (5) H3 1972

There are spectacular views of Rievaulx Abbey and the valley beyond through man-made vistas, which gradually reveal more as you stroll along the terrace. Created by the Duncombe family and finished *circa* 1757, Rievaulx Terrace was designed for promenading and dining and maintains its unique feeling of grandeur and tranquility. The woods are a perfect start to your visit, giving tantalising glimpses of the terrace and the views beyond. The Tuscan Temple is revealed when you leave the woods, and as you walk down the terrace you approach the Ionic Temple, where the family dined under the magnificant painted ceiling. **Note**: no access to Rievaulx Abbey.

Eating and shopping: ice-cream, cold drinks and sweet snacks available. Picnics welcome. Shop selling gifts and souvenirs.

Making the most of your day: natural play and den-building areas for children, as well as rope swing, balance beam, stepping stones and sky glade. Ionic Temple (open regularly weekends). Family trails and activities (school holidays). **Dogs**: welcome on leads.

Access: **Visitor centre**
Temples **Grounds**
Parking: 100 yards.

Finding out more: 01439 798340 (summer). 01439 748283 (winter) or rievaulxterrace@nationaltrust.org.uk

Rievaulx Terrace		M	T	W	T	F	S	S
14 Feb–1 Nov	11–5	**M**	**T**	**W**	**T**	**F**	**S**	**S**

Last admission one hour before closing or dusk if earlier.

The Ionic Temple at Rievaulx Terrace, North Yorkshire

Some places are easy to get to on foot or by public transport. See page 3

Seaton Delaval Hall, Northumberland: Sir John Vanbrugh's masterpiece, as seen from the parterre

Seaton Delaval Hall

The Avenue, Seaton Sluice,
Northumberland NE26 4QR

Map (6) H4 2009

Welcome to the home of the Delavals, a notorious Georgian family of party-goers, actors and pranksters. They made the Hall, designed by Sir John Vanbrugh, a place of revelry and fun at the heart of the Industrial Revolution. The Hall survived a fire, military occupation and near dereliction. In its first years since acquisition, the Hall has undergone major conservation work to help secure its future, and work continues this year. There is so much to enjoy – the architecture of the central Hall, the gardens, beautiful whatever the season, the regular family activities, as well as the surrounding coastal landscape. **Note**: due to ongoing work, access arrangements may change at short notice.

Eating and shopping: refreshment kiosk in the east wing serving drinks and snacks. In fine weather, ice-cream, coffee and tea are served from the summerhouse. Picnics welcome – tables throughout the gardens and grounds. Souvenir shop in ticket hut.

Making the most of your day: Indoors Vanbrugh's architecture and stonework. Magnificent fire-damaged Hall interior and original statues. **Outdoors** 18th-century stables. Tranquil formal garden. Large play paddock and natural playscape for little ones. Family activities. **Dogs**: welcome on leads outdoors.

Access: **Hall** **Stables** **Grounds**
Parking: 500 yards.

Finding out more: 0191 237 9100 or seatondelavalhall@nationaltrust.org.uk

Seaton Delaval Hall		M	T	W	T	F	S	S
Central hall, stables and gardens								
3 Jan–22 Feb	11-3	·	·	·	·	·	S	S
28 Feb–1 Nov	11-5	M	·	·	T	F	S	S
28 Mar–19 Apr	11-5	M	T	W	T	F	S	S
18 Jul–31 Aug	11-5	M	T	W	T	F	S	S
7 Nov–27 Dec	11-3	·	·	·	·	·	S	S
West wing								
28 Feb–1 Nov	11-5	M	·	·	T	F	S	S
28 Mar–19 Apr	11-5	M	T	W	T	F	S	S
18 Jul–31 Aug	11-5	M	T	W	T	F	S	S

Last admission 45 minutes before closing. Access to west wing may be limited on certain days and sometimes by tour only.

Iconic Souter Lighthouse, Tyne & Wear, was the first purpose-built electric lighthouse in the world

Souter Lighthouse and The Leas

Coast Road, Whitburn, Sunderland, Tyne & Wear SR6 7NH

Map (6) 15 1990

Souter is an iconic beacon. Hooped in red and white it stands proud on the coastline between the Tyne and the Wear. Opened in 1871, it's the first purpose-built electric lighthouse in the world. Visitors can imagine the fascinating story of 'life in a lighthouse' and by climbing the stairs to the top will be rewarded with the lighthouse keeper's view of the world. The Leas is a stretch of magnesian limestone cliffs with a wave-cut foreshore and coastal grassland, perfect for walking. The nearby rock stacks of Marsden Bay are home to nesting kittiwakes, fulmars, cormorants, shags and guillemots.

Eating and shopping: Galley Coffee Shop serving light lunches, soup, cakes and refreshments. Local dishes Panacklety and Singin' Hinnies are a must-try. Coastal-themed gift shop.

Making the most of your day: events and family activities, including rock-pool rambles, bug hunting, birdwatching and geocaching. Pirate events and holiday crafts. Car boot sales. Outdoor play area. Foghorn demonstrations, talking telescope and wildlife garden.
Dogs: welcome on leads outdoors.

Access:
Building **Grounds**
Parking: on site.

Finding out more: 0191 529 3161 or souter@nationaltrust.org.uk

Souter Lighthouse and The Leas		M	T	W	T	F	S	S
14 Feb–22 Feb	11–5	**M**	**T**	**W**	**T**	**F**	**S**	**S**
23 Feb–29 Mar	11–5	**M**	**T**	**W**	**T**	·	**S**	**S**
30 Mar–19 Apr	11–5	**M**	**T**	**W**	**T**	**F**	**S**	**S**
20 Apr–24 May	11–5	**M**	**T**	**W**	**T**	·	**S**	**S**
25 May–31 May	11–5	**M**	**T**	**W**	**T**	**F**	**S**	**S**
1 Jun–28 Jun	11–5	**M**	**T**	**W**	**T**	·	**S**	**S**
29 Jun–31 Aug	11–5	**M**	**T**	**W**	**T**	**F**	**S**	**S**
1 Sep–25 Oct	11–5	**M**	**T**	**W**	**T**	·	**S**	**S**
26 Oct–1 Nov	11–5	**M**	**T**	**W**	**T**	**F**	**S**	**S**
2 Nov–29 Nov	11–4	**M**	**T**	**W**	**T**	·	**S**	**S**
5 Dec–20 Dec	11–4	·	·	·	·	·	**S**	**S**

Treasurer's House, York

Minster Yard, York, North Yorkshire YO1 7JL

Map (5) H5 1930

Located next to York Minster, Treasurer's House reveals wealthy industrialist Frank Green's love of furniture and interior design. In 1897 he transformed the house from a 'bug-ridden slum' into the grand house you see today. Left to the National Trust in 1930, with strict instructions not to move anything, this 14-room showcase is just as he left it. The room guides bring the house and Frank Green to life with stories of how he left his mark on the city of York – indeed the walled garden is the perfect place to enjoy views of the Minster.

A time capsule since 1930, Treasurer's House, York in North Yorkshire, boasts a popular licensed café (below right)

Eating and shopping: Below Stairs Café (licensed), enjoyed by locals and visitors alike, offers table service, morning coffee, lunch and afternoon tea. Around the corner, at 32 Goodramgate, is one of the largest National Trust gift shops.

Making the most of your day: Roman ghost tours in the cellar and family trails in the school holidays. **Dogs**: welcome on a lead, in the garden.

Access:
House **Garden**
Parking: nearest at Lord Mayor's Walk. Park and ride from city outskirts recommended.

Finding out more: 01904 624247 or treasurershouse@nationaltrust.org.uk

Treasurer's House		M	T	W	T	F	S	S
14 Feb–26 Feb*	11–3	**M**	**T**	**W**	**T**	·	**S**	**S**
28 Feb–1 Nov	11–5	**M**	**T**	**W**	**T**	·	**S**	**S**
19 Nov–20 Dec	11–4	·	·	·	**T**	**F**	**S**	**S**

*Guided tour only.

Wallington

Cambo, near Morpeth,
Northumberland NE61 4AR

Map (6) G4 1941

Gifted to you by Sir Charles Philips Trevelyan, Socialist MP and 'illogical Englishman', this 5,260-hectare (13,000-acre) estate has something for everyone. You can enjoy wild play in the West Wood, visit our family-friendly wildlife hide and spot red squirrels, then stroll by the river or refresh your mind in the tranquil Walled Garden. Visit all year to enjoy the changing seasonal colours. Further afield, there are walks to Broomhouse Farm and beyond, or you could simply spend some time in the Trevelyan's home, with its impressive collections of ceramics, curiosities and needlework. Wallington offers a relaxing day out, whether it's exploring the house and grounds, letting off steam with your family or simply walking your dog. **Note**: farm activities run in partnership with our tenant farmer. Charges may apply (including members).

Eating and shopping: Clocktower Café serving brunch, lunch and afternoon tea. Refreshments available from the Walled Garden kiosk or take 'Tea the Trevelyan Way' in the house (seasonal). New range of gifts and souvenirs for sale in our shops and garden centre.

Making the most of your day: **Indoors** Why not soak up the atmosphere in the Trevelyan's home, discovering more about this well-travelled family? Events, tours and activities, including the traditional Wallington Christmas. **Outdoors** Lady Trevelyan's beloved Walled Garden, featuring the Mary Pool and fragrant conservatory. Adventure playground, play train and fort in the West Wood. Tours and guided walks. Year-round events, including the food and craft fair. Family activities during school holidays. New this year – camping, farm experience and Rothley lake tours.
Dogs: welcome on leads.

Access:
House **Grounds**
Parking: on site.

Wallington, Northumberland (above), is home to the rare red squirrel (left)

Finding out more: 01670 773600 or wallington@nationaltrust.org.uk

Wallington		M	T	W	T	F	S	S
Walled garden, woodland and estate*								
Open all year	10–6	M	T	W	T	F	S	S
House**								
14 Feb–1 Nov	12–5	M	·	W	T	F	S	S
Shops and café								
1 Jan–13 Feb	10:30–4:30	M	T	W	T	F	S	S
14 Feb–1 Nov	10:30–5:30	M	T	W	T	F	S	S
2 Nov–23 Dec	10:30–4:30	M	T	W	T	F	S	S
27 Dec–31 Dec	10:30–4:30	M	T	W	T	·	·	S

*Woodland and estate close dusk if earlier; walled garden closes 7 in summer and 4 in winter. **House open Tuesdays for special events and tours. Last admission to house one hour before closing. Last orders in café 30 minutes before closing.

Washington Old Hall

The Avenue, Washington Village, Washington, Tyne & Wear NE38 7LE

Map (6) H5

The name Washington is very important in world history. Did you know that the capital of the US would not bear this name, if it wasn't for this little gem in North-East England? A warm and friendly welcome awaits at this historic house and tranquil garden.

Eating and shopping: tea-room also selling second-hand books and bric-a-brac (volunteer-run by the Friends of Washington Old Hall; all funds raised are used to enhance visitor facilities). Picnics welcome in the garden.

Making the most of your day: **Indoors** Christmas craft day and frost fayre. Santa Claus visits. Heritage open day. **Outdoors** July 4th Independence Day ceremony, with flag raising 11 to 12. Open-air theatre. Children's nature activities.
Dogs: welcome on leads in garden only.

Access: **Building** **Grounds**
Parking: on site (additional parking on The Avenue).

Finding out more: 0191 416 6879 or washingtonoldhall@nationaltrust.org.uk

Washington Old Hall		M	T	W	T	F	S	S
29 Mar–28 Oct	10–4	M	T	W	·	·	·	S

Also open 3 and 4 April.

Warm and friendly Washington Old Hall, Tyne & Wear

Map 4

Wales

Henrhyd Falls, Powys

Outdoors in Wales

From Snowdon's mystical lakes to Gower's golden beaches; from the temperate Celtic rainforest to the Trust's first property, the magical land of Wales awaits you.

Cemlyn and the North Anglesey Coast

Cemaes Bay, Anglesey

Map (4) D1 1971

Ruggedly beautiful, the north coast of the Isle of Anglesey has a unique coastline of rocks, small bays and headlands and is a delight for walkers. Cemlyn is recognised for its National Nature Reserve and is a designated Area of Outstanding Natural Beauty and home to the rare spotted rock rose. Renowned for its breeding colonies of Sandwich, common and Arctic terns, Cemlyn Bay is a hive of seabird activity in spring and summer. Headland paths offer dramatic land and seascapes during autumn and winter. The brackish lagoon is separated from the sea by a remarkable shingle-ridge. **Note**: nearest toilets in Cemaes Bay, 3 miles (not National Trust).

Cemlyn, Anglesey: a ridge separates the lagoon from the sea

Making the most of your day: numerous footpaths and downloadable walks to help you explore. Events, including pram walks and walking festival. Summer fair at Swtan, a restored whitewashed cottage nearby (LL65 4EU). **Dogs**: welcome under control near livestock.

Access:
Sat Nav: use LL67 0DY. **Parking**: at Bryn Aber car park, Cemlyn.

Finding out more: 01248 714795 or cemlyn@nationaltrust.org.uk

Brecon Beacons and Monmouthshire

Where the vast open spaces of mid-Wales give way to the verdant rolling countryside of the south, the area offers wonderful walks and views.

Brecon Beacons

Powys

Map (4) F8 1936

The Brecon Beacons, Sugarloaf and Skirrid have captivated visitors for hundreds of years with their mountainous peaks and tranquil valleys. With lush farmland, ancient moorland and southern Britain's highest mountain, Pen y Fan, they are perfect for hill-walking and exploring hidden streams and woodlands. By contrast, the Clytha Estate is a great place to have a picnic or take a short walk, meandering through parkland with views of Clytha House and Castle. In the heart of Wales you can discover the vast, remote moorlands of Abergwesyn Commons or ramble over the Begwns with its panoramic views of the Brecon Beacons. **Note**: only toilets at Pont ar Daf car park in the Brecon Beacons.

Making the most of your day: guided walks throughout the year. Bunkhouse near Pen y Fan. Why not visit The Kymin nearby?

Mae'r wybodaeth sydd yn y llawlyfr hwn am feddiannau'r Ymddiriedolaeth Genedlaethol yng Nghymru ar gael yn Gymraeg o Swyddfa'r Ymddiriedolaeth Genedlaethol, Tŷ Tredegar, Casnewydd, NP10 8YW, neu drwy e-bostio wa.customerenquiries@nationaltrust.org.uk

Walkers stop for a welcome break on Pen y Fan in the Brecon Beacons, Powys

Dogs: welcome on leads.

Access:
Sat Nav: use LD3 8NL. **Parking**: main car park at Pont ar Daf, off A470; alternatives not all National Trust.

Finding out more: 01874 625515 or brecon@nationaltrust.org.uk

Henrhyd Falls

Coelbren, Powys

Map (4) F8   1947

The highest waterfall in the Brecon Beacons, Henrhyd Falls plunges down into a wooded gorge – a haven for damp-loving wildlife. A pleasant walk takes you to the falls and down the Nant Llech valley, passing an old landslide and disused watermill. **Note**: sorry no toilet. Steep descent to waterfall.

Henrhyd Falls, Powys: the Brecon Beacons' highest waterfall

Making the most of your day: downloadable walk available on website. National Trust and Geopark archaeological walk leaflet available locally. Why not visit nearby Brecon Beacons and Aberdulais Falls? **Dogs**: welcome on leads.

Access:
Sat Nav: use SA10 9PH.
Parking: adjoining property.

Finding out more: 01874 625515 or henrhydfalls@nationaltrust.org.uk

Carmarthenshire

Rugged, varied and full of undiscovered gems, often off the beaten track but worth discovering for yourself. Don't pass by – spend some time exploring.

Cwmdu

Llandeilo, Carmarthenshire

Map (4) E8 1991

Georgian terrace with pub, post office, chapel and vestry. Representing a rural Welsh village of the past.
Note: pub and shop run by community.
For Sat Nav use SA19 6DY.

Finding out more: 01558 685088 or cwmdu@nationaltrust.org.uk

Dolaucothi Estate Woodland

near Pumsaint, Llanwrda, Carmarthenshire

Map (4) E7 1944

Hours of woodland walks and a multi-user trail with route information in Dolaucothi Gold Mines welcome centre; plenty to discover.
Note: for Sat Nav use SA19 8US.

Finding out more: 01558 650809 or dolaucothi@nationaltrust.org.uk

Paxton's Tower

Llanarthne, near Dryslwyn, Carmarthenshire

Map (4) D8 1965

Known as 'Golwg y Byd' (Eye of the World), Paxton's is said to give a view of seven counties. **Note**: sorry no toilet. Nearest National Trust facilities at Dinefwr in Llandeilo. For Sat Nav use SA32 8HX.

Finding out more: 01558 823902 or paxtonstower@nationaltrust.org.uk

Ceredigion

Wales's best-kept secret, with boundaries unchanged since the fifth century. Ceredigion's hidden, special, untouched qualities await discovery, exploration and pure enjoyment.

Mwnt

near Cardigan, Ceredigion

Map (4) C7 1963

Beautiful secluded bay with a sandy beach – perfect for relaxing, spotting dolphins, seals and other amazing wildlife.
Note: steep steps down to beach. Small café and shop selling snacks and beach essentials.
For Sat Nav use SA43 1QF.

Finding out more: 01545 570200 or mwnt@nationaltrust.org.uk

Penbryn

near Sarnau, Cardigan, Ceredigion

Map (4) D7 1967

One of Ceredigion's best-kept secrets, this beautifully secluded sandy cove lies down leafy lanes, edged with flower-covered banks.
Note: Cartws Café (open daily) serves a wide selection of snacks and drinks.
For Sat Nav use SA44 6QL.

Finding out more: 01545 570200 or penbryn@nationaltrust.org.uk

Gower

The UK's first designated Area of Outstanding Natural Beauty, with sandy bays, secluded coves, ancient woodland and spectacular clifftop walks.

Gower: Rhossili Shop and Visitor Centre

Coastguard Cottages, Rhossili, Gower, Swansea SA3 1PR

Map (4) D9 1933

Perched on the clifftop overlooking the spectacular Rhossili Bay (Britain's best beach: Trip Advisor Travellers' Choice Awards 2013 and 2014), Rhossili Shop and Visitor Centre offers everything you need to enjoy beautiful Gower, from local information and advice to tempting treats and gifts to remember your day. **Note**: car park is privately owned and charges apply to all (including members).

Eating and shopping: self-service refreshments and Swansea's famous Joe's ice-cream available all year.

Making the most of your day: shop offers visitor information and advice on tides and walks. Free geocaching units available (call to reserve at busy times). Free exhibitions in the Visitor Centre. **Dogs**: welcome on leads near livestock. The beach is dog friendly all year round.

Access: Visitor Centre
Grounds
Parking: 50 yards, not National Trust (charge including members).

Finding out more: 01792 390707 or rhossili.shop@nationaltrust.org.uk

Rhossili Visitor Centre		M	T	W	T	F	S	S
3 Jan–22 Feb	10:30–4	·	T	W	T	F	S	S
23 Feb–27 Mar	10:30–4	M	T	W	T	F	S	S
28 Mar–22 May	10:30–4:30	M	T	W	T	F	S	S
23 May–6 Sep*	10–5	M	T	W	T	F	S	S
7 Sep–2 Nov	10:30–4:30	M	T	W	T	F	S	S
3 Nov–23 Dec	10:30–4	M	T	W	T	F	S	S
29 Dec–31 Dec	10:30–4	·	T	W	T	·	·	·

The Visitor Centre closes 15 minutes before the shop.
*During August, the shop is open until 6 on Saturdays and Sundays only.

The wide expanses of Pennard beach in Gower, Swansea, are perfect for enjoying the last rays of the setting sun

The view from Pennard Cliffs, Gower, Swansea: worth stopping for

Pennard, Pwll Du and Bishopston Valley

near Southgate, Swansea

Map (4) E9 1954

Spectacular cliffs, caves where mammoth remains have been found, rare birds, an underground river, bat roosts, silver-lead mining, ancient woodland, smuggling and limestone quarrying are just a few of the wonders of this area. There are also numerous archaeological features and two important caves – Bacon Hole and Minchin Hole.

Eating and shopping: coffee shop, village stores, tea-rooms and a pub in Pennard (none National Trust). Picnics welcome.

Making the most of your day: Pennard provides a great starting point for a variety of walks, on which you can enjoy wild flowers and spot rare birds, such as choughs and Dartford warblers. **Dogs**: welcome, but please be aware livestock graze freely across Pennard Burrows.

Access:
Sat Nav: use SA3 2DH.
Parking: at Southgate car park.

Finding out more: 01792 390636 or pennard@nationaltrust.org.uk

Llŷn Peninsula

This is a hidden jewel of Wales. It's an ancient land, rich in culture and history, all set in a dramatic, beautiful coastal environment.

Llanbedrog Beach

Llanbedrog, Gwynedd

Map (4) D4 2000

Best known for its colourful beach huts, this wonderful stretch of sand has been enjoyed by generations. Its sheltered waters, fantastic views over Cardigan Bay and adjacent wooded and craggy landscape make this a real gem of Llŷn. **Note**: toilet (not National Trust).

Eating and shopping: shops and cafés at Llanbedrog and at nearby Pwllheli and Abersoch (not National Trust).

Making the most of your day: events during summer months. Maps and guides available at car park welcome cabin. Beach huts available to hire. **Dogs**: welcome.

Access:
Sat Nav: use LL53 7TT. **Parking**: on site.

Finding out more: 01758 760469 or llanbedrog@nationaltrust.org.uk

Sheltered waters lap Llanbedrog Beach in Gwynedd

Porth Meudwy

near Aberdaron, Gwynedd

Map (4) C4 [icon] 1990

Nowhere expresses the essence of the area better than this sheltered cove on the wild and rocky coastline west of Aberdaron. It was from here that pilgrims set out to Ynys Enlli (Bardsey Island). Today fishermen still bring the daily catch in to the cove. **Note**: sorry no toilet.

Eating and shopping: in Aberdaron village (not National Trust).

Making the most of your day: the Wales Coast Path – a birdwatchers' paradise – runs dramatically along the clifftop. **Dogs**: welcome.

Access: [icon]
Sat Nav: use LL53 8DA. **Parking**: ½ mile.

Finding out more: 01758 760469 or porthmeudwy@nationaltrust.org.uk

Picturesque Porth Meudwy (below) and Porthdinllaen (top right), both in Gwynedd

Porthdinllaen

Morfa Nefyn, Gwynedd

Map (4) D3 [icon] 1994

An old fishing village perched on the end of a thin ribbon of land stretching into the Irish Sea, with its clear sheltered waters lapping against stout stone houses, Porthdinllaen really is a jewel. You can watch fishermen bring in the daily catch while relaxing with a drink at the Tŷ Coch Inn. **Note**: nearest toilet in village (not National Trust). Steps from car park down to beach.

Eating and shopping: refreshments available at Tŷ Coch Inn (not National Trust).

Making the most of your day: events during summer for all the family. Wonderful walking on the coastal path – maps and guides available at car park welcome cabin. Find out about village history at 'Caban Gruff'. **Dogs**: welcome.

Access: [icons]
Sat Nav: use LL53 6DB. **Parking**: on site for beach; 1 mile from village.

Finding out more: 01758 760469 or porthdinllaen@nationaltrust.org.uk

Low tide reveals the perfect sand at Porthor in Gwynedd

Pembrokeshire

Dramatically unspoilt, Pembrokeshire offers a world-class coastal landscape, where choughs, seals and otters are wildlife stars of the 60 miles the Trust cares for.

Marloes Sands

Marloes, Pembrokeshire

Map (4) B8/9 1941

Laze on this long sandy beach or explore its interesting rock formations and rock pools. Take in the inland mere for its birdlife. **Note**: nearest toilets by Runwayskiln Youth Hostel.

Porthor

Aberdaron, Gwynedd

Map (4) C3 1981

This wonderful beach is famous for its 'whistling sands' and glistening waters. If the joys of sandcastles and sunbathing are not enough for you, then why not have a go at surfing? The sea here is perfect. In addition, the Wales Coast Path runs in both directions from the car park. **Note**: nearest toilet in car park.

Eating and shopping: beachside café and shop offering everything from lunch to sun cream.

Making the most of your day: famous beach and glorious clifftop coast path to explore. Children's adventure pack available from car park. **Dogs**: seasonal restrictions on beach apply from 1 April to 30 September.

Access:
Sat Nav: use LL53 8LG. **Parking**: on site.

Finding out more: 01758 760469 or porthor@nationaltrust.org.uk

Eating and shopping: National Trust information point at Martin's Haven. Shop, café and pub in nearby Marloes village (not National Trust).

Making the most of your day: nature discovery Tracker Packs, available from car park, for rock-pooling, birdwatching and getting closer to nature. **Dogs**: welcome under close control.

Access:
Sat Nav: use SA62 3BH. **Parking**: on site.

Finding out more: 01348 837860 or marloessands@nationaltrust.org.uk

Martin's Haven

near Marloes, Pembrokeshire

Map (4) B8 1981

The gateway to Skomer Island and a fabulously wild headland with fine panoramic views of St Bride's Bay. Combine spotting marine wildlife with traces of ancient settlements. **Note**: nearest toilets by the slipway.

Eating and shopping: National Trust information point at Martin's Haven. Shop, café and pub in nearby Marloes village (not National Trust).

Making the most of your day: nature discovery Tracker Packs, available from car park, for rock-pooling, birdwatching and getting closer to nature. **Dogs**: welcome under close control.

Access:
Sat Nav: use SA62 3BJ.
Parking: on site.

Finding out more: 01348 837860 or martinshaven@nationaltrust.org.uk

Perfecting ball skills on Marloes Sands (opposite) and tackling the coastal path at St David's Head (top right), both in Pembrokeshire

St David's Visitor Centre and Shop

Captain's House, High Street, St David's, Pembrokeshire SA62 6SD

Map (4) A8 1974

Overlooking the Celtic Old Cross in the centre of St David's, Wales's smallest historic city, the visitor centre and well-stocked shop is open all year. For a complete guide to the National Trust in Pembrokeshire, visitors can take a tour of our special places, beaches and walks using interactive technology. **Note**: sorry no toilet.

Eating and shopping: books, cards, maps, wide range of gifts and local produce. Walks leaflets available.

Making the most of your day: guided walks, evening talks and events. St David's Head, Porth Clais, Solva and Abereiddi nearby.

Access: **Building**
Parking: none on site.

Finding out more: 01437 720385 or stdavidsshop@nationaltrust.org.uk

St David's Visitor Centre		M	T	W	T	F	S	S
2 Jan–21 Mar	10–4	**M**	**T**	**W**	**T**	**F**	**S**	
22 Mar–31 Dec	10–5	**M**	**T**	**W**	**T**	**F**	**S**	**S**

Closes 4 on Sundays. Closed 1 January, 25 and 27 December.

The quay at Stackpole in Pembrokeshire

Making the most of your day: guided kayak and coasteering trips. Guided walks. Beach activity days. Coarse fishing. Theatre and music concerts. Wild camping with Rangers. Stay at holiday cottages or the Outdoor Learning Centre. **Dogs**: under close control on the estate.

Access: **Building** **Grounds**
Sat Nav: for Stackpole Quay use SA71 5LS; Broadhaven South SA71 5DZ; Bosherston Lakes SA71 5DR. **Parking**: at Stackpole Quay, Broadhaven South, Bosherston Lakes and Stackpole Court.

Finding out more: 01646 661359 or stackpole@nationaltrust.org.uk

Stackpole		M	T	W	T	F	S	S
Estate								
Open all year	Dawn–dusk	**M**	**T**	**W**	**T**	**F**	**S**	**S**
Boathouse tea-room								
14 Feb–22 Feb	11–4	**M**	**T**	**W**	**T**	**F**	**S**	**S**
28 Feb–22 Mar	11–4	·	·	·	·	·	**S**	**S**
28 Mar–1 Nov	10–5	**M**	**T**	**W**	**T**	**F**	**S**	**S**
7 Nov–13 Dec	11–4	·	·	·	·	·	**S**	**S**
19 Dec–30 Dec	11–4	**M**	**T**	**W**	**T**	**F**	**S**	**S**

Boathouse tea-room closed 24 and 25 December.

Stackpole

near Pembroke, Pembrokeshire

Map (4) B9 1976

A former grand estate stretching down to some of the most beautiful coastline in the world, including Broadhaven South, Barafundle and Stackpole Quay. Today Bosherston Lakes, famous for their superb display of lilies, and the dramatic cliffs of Stackpole Head are a National Nature Reserve. The former site of the grand Stackpole Court and nearby Lodge Park Woods give the historical background to this magnificent estate and reveal the story behind the designed landscape.

Eating and shopping: The Boathouse at Stackpole Quay serving fresh locally sourced food, including homemade cakes and scones, local seafood and Pembrokeshire heathland beef. Estate-grown produce for sale at Mencap walled gardens.

Stackpole Outdoor Learning Centre

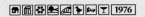

Old Home Farm Yard, Stackpole, near Pembroke, Pembrokeshire SA71 5DQ

Map (4) B9 1976

Located in the heart of the Stackpole Estate, our eco award-winning centre provides residents with easy access to Bosherston Lakes, Stackpole Quay and award-winning beaches – including Barafundle and Broadhaven South – as well as the historic site of Stackpole Court. The recently refurbished centre can house up to 140 guests and offers flexible accommodation with modern facilities, including a theatre, meeting and classroom space. It is ideal for groups, corporate clients, celebrations, family holidays and couples' getaways. We also offer special interest breaks, covering subjects as wide-ranging as photography, health, well-being and wildlife identification.

Canoeing lesson at Stackpole Outdoor Learning Centre, Pembrokeshire

Note: contact the centre for activity programmes, prices and availability.

Eating and shopping: self-catering or chef-catered options. Meals provided by inhouse National Trust catering team and made using locally sourced seasonal produce, including Pembrokeshire heathland beef. Full entertainment licence for events with bar. Residents' barbecue area. Shop and information hub.

Making the most of your day: events, including rock-pool rambles, wild camping, guided walks, open-air theatre and concerts. Hire one of our bikes to explore the area or join our kayaking or coasteering guided tours! **Dogs**: assistance dogs only.

Access:
Sat Nav: do not use, instead follow brown signs. **Parking**: free for guests.

Finding out more: 01646 661425 (reception). 01646 661359 (estate office) or stackpoleoutdoorlearning @nationaltrust.org.uk

Stackpole Outdoor Centre
Please contact the centre for more information on residential group bookings, courses and activities.

Snowdonia

From the mountainous terrain of the Carneddau massif to the delightful remote property that is Tŷ Mawr Wybrnant. Snowdonia has beauty, excitement and tranquility.

Carneddau and Glyderau

Nant Ffrancon, Bethesda, Gwynedd

Map (4) E2 1951

This 8,498-hectare (21,000-acre) mountainous area includes Cwm Idwal Nature Reserve, renowned for its geology and Arctic-Alpine plants, such as the rare Snowdon lily. There are eight tenanted upland farms here and nine peaks over 3,000 feet, including the famous Tryfan, where Edmund Hilary trained for his ascent of Everest. The area is home to a variety of wildlife, including otters, feral ponies and rare birds such as dotterel and peregrine. The 60 miles of footpaths attract 500,000 walkers each year, while the bleak, photogenic landscapes have proved popular with artists. **Note**: mountainous and difficult terrain – please come well equipped and check the weather. Charges apply in the National Park car parks.

Mysterious Carneddau in Snowdonia, Gwynedd

Eating and shopping: facilities at Ogwen visitor centre, including food kiosk (not National Trust) and a warden centre run in partnership with Snowdonia National Park and Natural Resources Wales.

Making the most of your day: easy walk to Cwm Idwal allows visitors to enjoy Snowdonia at its most dramatic and follow in the footsteps of Charles Darwin, who 'discovered' glaciation here. **Dogs**: on a lead at all times.

Access: [access icon]
Sat Nav: use LL57 3LZ. **Parking**: at Ogwen lake (not National Trust).

Finding out more: 01248 600954 or carneddau@nationaltrust.org.uk

Craflwyn and Beddgelert

near Beddgelert, Gwynedd

Map (4) E3 1994

The 81-hectare (200-acre) Craflwyn Estate is set in the heart of beautiful Snowdonia, within a landscape steeped in history and legend. There is a network of paths and woodland walks to explore and tumbling waterfalls to discover. At Craflwyn you can learn about the Princes of Gwynedd before venturing up to nearby Dinas Emrys, the legendary birthplace of Wales's national emblem, the red dragon. Within a couple of miles of Craflwyn, there are great walks for all abilities, from a village stroll at pretty Beddgelert to the rugged Fisherman's Path down the spectacular Aberglaslyn Pass. **Note**: Craflwyn Hall is run and managed by HF Holidays (surrounding land open to the public).

Eating and shopping: picnics welcome at Craflwyn. Local crafts on offer in Tŷ Isaf shop in Beddgelert. The village also has a selection of restaurants, cafés, taverns and hotels (not National Trust).

Making the most of your day: you can discover the story of Prince Llywelyn's failthful hound by visiting Gelert's Grave. Maps and guides available from Tŷ Isaf shop. Guided walks and events. **Dogs**: welcome under control near livestock.

Access: [access icon]
Sat Nav: use LL55 4NG. **Parking**: in Craflwyn.

Finding out more: 01766 510120 or craflwyn@nationaltrust.org.uk

Dolmelynllyn Estate

near Dolgellau, Gwynedd

Map (4) E4 1936

Dolmelynllyn Estate covers 696 hectares (1,719 acres) and comprises two tenanted farms, with the remaining woodland managed by the Trust. Dolmelynllyn Hall is Grade II listed, with well-preserved formal gardens, walled kitchen garden, Britain's largest bee-bole wall, ornamental lake and parkland. **Note**: Dolmelynllyn Hall is a privately run hotel, not a pay-to-enter property.

The path to the 'grave' of Gelert in Beddgelert, Gwynedd

The beautiful Dolmelynllyn Estate and rugged Hafod y Llan (above left and right), both in Gwynedd

Eating and shopping: two National Trust-owned but tenanted hotels on the estate offering refreshments and light meals. Picnic site.

Making the most of your day: estate walks leaflet guides visitors around the more interesting parts of the estate, such as Rhaeadr Ddu waterfall, Cefn Coch gold mines and the wildlife-rich oak woodlands.
Dogs: welcome on leads.

Access: [walking icon]
Sat Nav: use LL40 2TF. **Parking**: on site.

Finding out more: 01341 440238 or dolmelynllyn@nationaltrust.org.uk

Hafod y Llan

near Beddgelert, Gwynedd

Map (4) E3 [icons] 1998

Hafod y Llan, in the beautiful Nantgwynant Valley, is the largest farm run by the National Trust, part of which is designated a National Nature Reserve and a Site of Special Scientific Interest. It extends from the valley floor to the summit of Snowdon and visitors are free to wander the many paths which cross this unique landscape. **Note**: as this is a working farm, access to the farmyard is by foot only.

Eating and shopping: refreshments available at nearby Caffi Gwynant (not National Trust).

Making the most of your day: network of paths cross Hafod y Llan, including the Watkin Path leading to the summit of Snowdon.
Dogs: welcome on leads.

Access: [walking icon]
Parking: on farm for campsite only. Car park near farm entrance (not National Trust).

Finding out more: 01766 890473 or hafodyllan@nationaltrust.org.uk

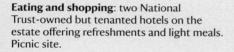

Additional coastal and countryside car parks in Wales

Ceredigion	
Mwnt	SM 193 519
Penbryn	SM 296 520
Llŷn Peninsula	
Uwchmynydd	SH 155 264
Pembrokeshire	
Broadhaven	SR 977 938
Bosherston	SR 968 947
Porthclais	SM 741 242
Snowdonia	
Cregennan	SH 660 140
Nantmor	SH 597 463

Aberconwy House, Conwy: rare survivor of turbulent times

Aberconwy House

Castle Street, Conwy LL32 8AY

Map (4) E2 1934

This is the only medieval merchant's house in Conwy to have survived the turbulent history of the walled town over seven centuries. Furnished rooms and helpful volunteers bring different periods in its history alive. **Note**: nearest toilets 50 yards. Steps to all parts of property.

Eating and shopping: gift shop.

Making the most of your day: Easter and Hallowe'en activities. Father Christmas visits. Living history events. **Dogs**: assistance dogs only.

Access: Building

Parking: none on site.

Finding out more: 01492 592246 or aberconwyhouse@nationaltrust.org.uk

Aberconwy House		M	T	W	T	F	S	S
House								
7 Mar–1 Nov	11–5	M	T	W	T	F	S	S
21 Nov–20 Dec	10–4	·	·	·	·	·	S	S
Shop								
1 Jan–1 Mar	11–5	·	T	W	T	F	S	S
2 Mar–1 Nov	10–5	M	T	W	T	F	S	S
2 Nov–31 Dec	11–5	M	T	W	T	F	S	S

House and shop closed 25 December.

Aberdulais Tin Works and Waterfall

Aberdulais, Neath, Neath Port Talbot SA10 8EU

Map (4) E9 1980

If you like archaeology, you'll love some of the secrets that have been uncovered here at Aberdulais – one of Britain's oldest tin works. As you wander through the site, you'll find yourself at the very heart of the earliest industry in Britain. You'll also discover how Aberdulais played its part in shaping the world as we know it today. If you think you've seen Aberdulais before, think again – we've made new discoveries and we're dying to share them with you. We aim to enthral and fascinate all ages… Whoever thought history could be so much fun? **Note**: waterwheel and turbine subject to water levels and conservation work.

Aberdulais Tin Works and Waterfall, Neath Port Talbot (below and top right): one of Britain's oldest tin works

Eating and shopping: Old School House tea-room serving light lunches, soup, cakes and refreshments. Gift shop and second-hand bookshop.

Making the most of your day: activities, including Conservation in Action. Demonstrations and family Tin Detectives Packs. Archaeology days. **Dogs**: welcome on leads.

Access: **Stable and Tin Exhibition** **Turbine House** **Grounds**
Sat Nav: follow brown signs. **Parking**: 50 yards.

Finding out more: 01639 636674 or aberdulais@nationaltrust.org.uk

Aberdulais		M	T	W	T	F	S	S
3 Jan–15 Feb	11–4	·	·	·	·	·	**S**	**S**
16 Feb–22 Feb	11–4	**M**	**T**	**W**	**T**	**F**	**S**	**S**
28 Feb–1 Mar	11–4	·	·	·	·	·	**S**	**S**
2 Mar–27 Mar	11–4	**M**	**T**	**W**	**T**	**F**	**S**	**S**
28 Mar–6 Sep	10:30–5	**M**	**T**	**W**	**T**	**F**	**S**	**S**
7 Sep–1 Nov	11–4	**M**	**T**	**W**	**T**	**F**	**S**	**S**
6 Nov–20 Dec	11–4	·	·	·	·	**F**	**S**	**S**

Tea-room opening times vary from main property. Contact property for detailed times.

Bodnant Garden

Tal-y-Cafn, near Colwyn Bay, Conwy LL28 5RE

Map (4) F2 1949

A breathtaking garden with grand terraces and views of Snowdonia, a valley of giant conifers and cascading water, open grassy wildflower glades and shrub borders of dappled sunlight filled with plants from all over the world. Created by five generations of one family, this garden sits perfectly within its dramatic North Wales landscape. Rhododendrons, magnolias and camellias, grown from seed and cuttings gathered by plant hunters more than a century ago, light up the garden in spring, while summer herbaceous borders, fiery autumn-coloured shrubs, trees and a winter garden provide interest throughout the year. A new area opens in March. **Note**: garden and tea-rooms managed on behalf of the National Trust by Michael McLaren.

Eating and shopping: Pavilion tea-room serving lunch, Magnolia tea-room offering coffee and cake, and al fresco dining available in the Dell. Cakes, pies and bread made on site by our baker. Garden centre (not National Trust) adjacent. Picnics welcome in specially selected areas.

Breathtaking Bodnant Garden in Conwy

Making the most of your day: varied events, including walks and talks. Family events and activities, explorer backpacks and adventure playground. **Dogs**: welcome on leads Thursday to Saturday (January/February, November/December); Wednesdays from 5 (May to August).

Access: [access symbols] **Grounds** [access symbols]
Parking: 150 yards.

Finding out more: 01492 650460 or bodnantgarden@nationaltrust.org.uk

Bodnant Garden		M	T	W	T	F	S	S
1 Jan–28 Feb	10–4	M	T	W	T	F	S	S
1 Mar–31 Oct	10–5	M	T	W	T	F	S	S
1 Nov–23 Dec	10–4	M	T	W	T	F	S	S
27 Dec–31 Dec	10–4	M	T	W	T	·	·	S

Garden open until 8 on Wednesdays from May to August.

Bodysgallen Hall Hotel, Restaurant and Spa

The Royal Welsh Way, Llandudno, Conwy LL30 1RS

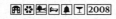

Map (4) F2 [symbols] 2008

This Grade I listed 17th-century house, set within 89 hectares (220 acres) of parkland, has the most spectacular views towards Conwy Castle and Snowdonia. The romantic gardens, which have won awards for their restoration, include a rare parterre filled with sweet-smelling herbs, as well as several follies, cascade, walled garden and formal rose gardens. Beyond, the hotel's parkland offers miles of stunning walks and views to the coastline. **Note**: access is for paying guests of the hotel, including for luncheon, afternoon tea and dinner, and the Spa.

Finding out more: 01492 584466. 01492 582519 (fax) or info@bodysgallen.com bodysgallen.com

Chirk Castle

Chirk, Wrexham LL14 5AF

Map (4) G3 [symbols] 1981

Completed in 1310, Chirk is the last Welsh castle from the reign of Edward I still lived in today. Features from its 700 years include the medieval tower and dungeon, 17th-century Long Gallery, grand 18th-century state apartments, servants' hall and historic laundry. The newly refurbished east wing depicts the life of Lord Howard de Walden during the 1930s. The award-winning gardens contain clipped yews, herbaceous borders, shrub and rock gardens. A terrace with far-reaching views looks out over the Cheshire and Shropshire plains, while the parkland provides a habitat for rare invertebrates and wild flowers, and contains many mature trees.

Eating and shopping: tea-room and coffee shop serving home-grown produce. Gift shops with plant sales and second-hand books.

Making the most of your day: our leaflets tell you all about the many places to explore (including the fortress, gardens and woods), plus fascinating stories about servants' lives and the Myddelton family home.

Completed in 1310, Chirk Castle in Wrexham is everything a castle should be, and more

Dogs: welcome on leads, assistance dogs only in formal gardens.

Access:
State rooms **Adam Tower**
Gardens
Parking: at home farm, 200 yards (via steep hill).

Finding out more: 01691 777701 or chirkcastle@nationaltrust.org.uk

Chirk Castle		M	T	W	T	F	S	S
Estate								
Open all year*	7-7	M	T	W	T	F	S	S
Garden, tower, shops and tea-rooms								
31 Jan-31 Mar	10-4	M	T	W	T	F	S	S
1 Apr-30 Sep**	10-5	M	T	W	T	F	S	S
1 Oct-1 Nov	10-4	M	T	W	T	F	S	S
7 Nov-29 Nov	10-4	·	·	·	·	·	S	S
12 Dec-24 Dec	11-4	M	T	W	T	F	S	S
26 Dec-31 Dec†	11-4	M	T	W	T	·	S	S
State rooms								
28 Feb-31 Mar††	12-4	M	T	W	T	F	S	S
1 Apr-30 Sep††	12-5	M	T	W	T	F	S	S
1 Oct-1 Nov††	12-4	M	T	W	T	F	S	S
12 Dec-24 Dec	11-4	M	T	W	T	F	S	S

*Estate open until 9, June to August. **Garden open until 6. †Garden and Home Farm kiosk only. ††Guided state room tours 11 to 12 (places limited).

Cilgerran Castle

near Cardigan, Pembrokeshire SA43 2SF

Map (4) C7 1938

13th-century castle overlooking the Teifi Gorge – the perfect location to repel attackers. Walk the walls and admire the stunning views. **Note**: in the guardianship of Cadw – Welsh Government's historic environment service. Dogs on leads allowed.

Finding out more: 01239 621339 or cilgerrancastle@nationaltrust.org.uk

Colby Woodland Garden

near Amroth, Pembrokeshire SA67 8PP

Map (4) C8 1980

A short walk from the beach, this hidden wooded valley, with its secret garden and industrial past, is a place for play. There are fallen trees to climb, rope swings and playful surprises everywhere. Spring brings bluebells, camellias, rhododendrons and azaleas, while the walled garden gives year-round colour, peace and seclusion. There are woodland walks, meandering streams and ponds with stepping stones and log bridges in the wildflower meadow, and the whole valley teems with wildlife. Fun learning activities and exploration packs are available, and there are picnic and campfire spots in the meadow and free games to borrow. **Note**: house not open.

Eating and shopping: shop, plant sales and second-hand books. Bothy tea-room (concession). Gallery selling Pembrokeshire arts and crafts. Picnics welcome.

Making the most of your day: rope swings, den- and dam-building, pond-dipping, camp fires, duck racing, activity sheets, exploration packs and games equipment. Virtual tour and film. Easter trails, wildlife events and holiday activities.

Duck race at Colby Woodland Garden, Pembrokeshire

Dogs: under control in estate woodlands. On leads in garden and meadow.

Access: [access symbols]
Grounds [access symbols]
Parking: 50 yards.

Finding out more: 01834 811885 or colby@nationaltrust.org.uk

Colby Woodland Garden		M	T	W	T	F	S	S
Woodland and walled gardens and bothy exhibition								
2 Jan–13 Feb	10–3	M	T	W	T	F	S	S
2 Nov–24 Dec	10–3	M	T	W	T	F	S	S
Woodland and walled gardens, shop and bothy exhibition								
14 Feb–1 Nov	10–5	M	T	W	T	F	S	S
Gallery and tea-room								
28 Mar–1 Nov	10–4:30	M	T	W	T	F	S	S

Car park open as woodland and walled gardens.
Closed 1 January, 24 to 31 December.

Conwy Suspension Bridge

Conwy LL32 8LD

Map (4) E2 1965

Designed in the 1820s by Thomas Telford, this graceful bridge with its beautifully restored tiny toll-keeper's house has stunning views over the Conwy Estuary. Kept open by a husband and wife at a time when trade and travel brought Conwy to life, it never closed, whatever the weather. **Note**: sorry no toilet.

Eating and shopping: bring your own picnic to enjoy on the grassed area.

Making the most of your day: superb views of the river and castle. **Dogs**: allowed.

Access: **Building** [access symbol] **Grounds** [access symbol]
Parking: none on site.

Finding out more: 01492 573282 or conwybridge@nationaltrust.org.uk

Conwy Suspension Bridge

Open 7 March to 1 November. Toll House opening times available at Aberconwy House (01492 592246).

Looking along Conwy Suspension Bridge, Conwy

Some places are easy to get to on foot or by public transport. See page 3

Dinefwr

Llandeilo, Carmarthenshire SA19 6RT

Map (4) E8 1990

A place of legends and folklore, Dinefwr's long history has featured power, glory, downfall and loss. There is even a direct link with the past through our iconic White Park cattle, which have been kept here for 1,000 years. Walks lead through ancient woods, with gnarled veteran trees, and you can seek the inhabitants of the Bogwood and Mill Pond and walk in the footsteps of medieval princes – viewing 'your kingdom' from the castle on the hill. After exploring the tranquil countryside, you can continue your adventure in atmospheric Newton House, discovering the many changes the years have wrought. **Note**: Dinefwr Castle is owned by the Wildlife Trust and is in the guardianship of Cadw.

Eating and shopping: Billiard Room licensed restaurant (concession) in Newton House serving a local Welsh menu. Inner Courtyard with a gift shop and plant sales, plus a pre-loved bookshop offering coffee. China Passage art gallery showcasing local artwork, all for sale.

Making the most of your day: **Indoors** Daily tours of Newton House. **Outdoors** Seasonal tours of the National Nature Reserve, with its fallow deer. Trailer tours of estate. School holiday and family activities. Events. Holiday cottages. **Dogs**: welcome in outer park on leads (cattle/sheep grazing).

Access: **Newton House** **Castle** **Estate**
Sat Nav: do not use. **Parking**: 50 yards.

Finding out more: 01558 824512 or dinefwr@nationaltrust.org.uk

Dinefwr		M	T	W	T	F	S	S
Parkland, boardwalk and deer-park*								
1 Jan–29 Mar	10–4	M	T	W	T	F	S	S
30 Mar–1 Nov	10–6	M	T	W	T	F	S	S
2 Nov–31 Dec	10–4	M	T	W	T	F	S	S
Newton House, gift shop, plant sales and gallery†								
2 Jan–29 Mar	11–4	·	·	·	·	F	S	S
30 Mar–1 Nov	11–6	M	T	W	T	F	S	S
6 Nov–27 Dec	11–4	·	·	·	·	F	S	S
Billiard Room Restaurant**								
2 Jan–29 Mar	11–3:30	·	·	·	·	F	S	S
30 Mar–1 Nov	11–5:30	M	T	W	T	F	S	S
6 Nov–27 Dec	11–3:30	·	·	·	·	F	S	S
Dinefwr Castle (Cadw managed)								
2 Jan–31 Dec	10–4	M	T	W	T	F	S	S

*Boardwalk and deer-park close one hour earlier.
†Last admission to Newton House one hour before closing.
**Billiard Room Restaurant last orders 30 minutes after last admission to Newton House. Cadw manages Dinefwr Castle and may alter opening times. Property closed 24 and 25 December. Whole property open all other Bank Holidays.

A view of the landscape park surrounding Newton House and Dinefwr in Carmarthenshire

Dolaucothi Gold Mines

Pumsaint, Llanwrda,
Carmarthenshire SA19 8US

Map (4) E7 1941

Not your average National Trust visit, this hidden gem reveals the story of the quest for gold more than 2,000 years ago. You too can try your luck by panning for gold, and anything you find you keep. Or you can venture on an overground tour of the Roman archaeology, go underground to experience the harsh conditions of Victorian times and listen to what 1930s miners had to say in their very own words about their final efforts to search for gold. Why not join us for the ultimate adventure and discover centuries of stories in just one day? **Note**: steep slopes, stout enclosed footwear essential. Minimum height on underground tours; no carried children. Caravan park on site; pitch charges (including members).

Eating and shopping: tea-room (concession) offering light refreshments. Shop specialising in Welsh gold jewellery (also available online) and gifts. Dolaucothi Arms (tenant-run) offering food and accommodation. Picnic tables in the mineyard.

Making the most of your day: **Indoors** Underground tours throughout day. 1930s machinery sheds. **Outdoors** Overground self-guided audio tour of Roman adits. Walks around woodland estate. **Dogs**: welcome on leads in mineyard.

Access: **Office** **Machinery sheds** **Yard**
Parking: on site; overflow car park opposite main entrance.

Finding out more: 01558 650809 or dolaucothi@nationaltrust.org.uk

Dolaucothi Gold Mines		M	T	W	T	F	S	S
Gold mines, gift shop and tea-room								
20 Mar–30 Jun	11–5	M	T	W	T	F	S	S
1 Jul–31 Aug	10–6	M	T	W	T	F	S	S
1 Sep–1 Nov	11–5	M	T	W	T	F	S	S
Dolaucothi Arms								
Open all year	12–11*		T	W	T	F	S	S

Caravan site: open daily 19 March to 31 October, dawn to dusk. Last admission to the mine yard one hour before closing. Peak season: Victorian tour 11, 12, 1, 1:30, 2:30, 3 and 4:30. Roman tour 12:30, 2 and 3:30. Off-peak season: Victorian tour 11:30, 12:30, 2:30 and 3:30. Roman tour 12:30, 2 and 3:30. *Open Tuesdays 6 to 11, Sundays 12 to 10 and Bank Holidays.

Exploring Dolaucothi Gold Mines, Carmarthenshire: not your average National Trust visit

The botanical collection at Dyffryn Gardens in the Vale of Glamorgan is among the best in Wales

Dyffryn Gardens

St Nicholas, Vale of Glamorgan CF5 6SU

Map (4) G10 2012

A garden for all seasons, celebrated for its botanical collection, among the best in Wales. Meandering through the gardens, you will discover intimate garden rooms, formal lawns, an extensive arboretum and re-instated glasshouse in the kitchen garden, housing an impressive collection of cacti and orchids. Designed by the eminent landscape architect Thomas Mawson, the gardens are the early 20th-century vision of Reginald Cory. Dyffryn House stands at the heart of the garden, and this Grade II* listed house is built as a gallery from which to view the landscape. Recently restored as a blank canvas to interpret Cory family history.

Eating and shopping: tea-room serving kitchen garden produce, including an edible flower menu in the summer and hearty soups in the autumn. Shop selling plants and gifts.

Making the most of your day: network of garden rooms and champion trees in the arboretum to discover. Family events and play area. Tredegar House nearby. **Dogs**: welcome on short leads.

Access: **House**
Grounds
Sat Nav: do not use. **Parking**: on site.

Finding out more: 02920 593328 or dyffryn@nationaltrust.org.uk

Dyffryn Gardens		M	T	W	T	F	S	S
Gardens, tea-room and shop*								
1 Jan–1 Mar	10–4	M	T	W	T	F	S	S
2 Mar–29 Mar	10–5	M	T	W	T	F	S	S
30 Mar–27 Sep	10–6	M	T	W	T	F	S	S
28 Sep–1 Nov	10–5	M	T	W	T	F	S	S
2 Nov–31 Dec	10–4	M	T	W	T	F	S	S
House								
3 Jan–1 Feb	12–3	·	·	·	·	·	S	S
5 Feb–1 Mar	12–4	·	·	·	T	F	S	S
2 Mar–27 Sep	12–4	M	T	W	T	F	S	S
1 Oct–1 Nov	12–4	·	·	·	T	F	S	S
7 Nov–27 Dec*	12–3	·	·	·	·	·	S	S

Last admission to gardens one hour before closing.
*Closed 25 and 26 December.

The pleached lime avenue at Erddig, Wrexham, is just one of the delights of this lovely house's 18th-century garden

Erddig

Wrexham LL13 0YT

Map (4) H3 1973

Erddig tells the 250-year story of a gentry family's relationship with its servants. A large collection of servants' portraits and carefully preserved rooms capture their lives in the early 20th century. Upstairs is a treasure trove of fine furniture, textiles and wallpapers, while outdoors you can explore the 18th-century formal garden with grand lawns, avenues of pleached limes and a Victorian parterre. The 486-hectare (1,200-acre) landscape pleasure-park, designed by William Eames, is a haven of peace and natural beauty, perfect for riverside picnics. The 'romantic walk' was recently included in the National Trust's top ten 'secret' walks.

Eating and shopping: second-hand bookshop and gift shop selling crafts, sweet treats and plants. Restaurant serving light lunches, cakes and cream teas. Café and tea-garden offering Welsh ingredients, including Erddig apples, herbs, honey and cider. Picnics welcome.

Making the most of your day: **Indoors** Themed tours. Christmas event. You are welcome to play the piano. **Outdoors** Open-air theatre, Easter trail and Christmas programme. Orienteering and walking maps. Wolf's Den natural play area. **Dogs**: welcome in country park.

Access:
Building **Grounds**
Sat Nav: do not use; follow brown signs.
Parking: 200 yards.

Finding out more: 01978 355314 or erddig@nationaltrust.org.uk

Erddig		M	T	W	T	F	S	S
House								
2 Feb–6 Mar††	11:30–2:30	M	T	W	T	F	S	S
7 Mar–24 Oct	12:30–3:30	M	T	W	T	F	S	S
25 Oct–31 Dec**	11:30–2:30	M	T	W	T	F	S	S
Garden, natural play area, restaurant and shop								
3 Jan–25 Jan*	11–3	·	·	·	·	·	S	S
31 Jan–28 Mar	11–4	M	T	W	T	F	S	S
29 Mar–24 Oct	10–6†	M	T	W	T	F	S	S
25 Oct–31 Dec	11–4	M	T	W	T	F	S	S

***House closed until 2 February.** ††Limited house opening for fireside chats and selected highlight tours. **Ground-floor servants' quarters only, by guided tour. †Open until 9 every Thursday, May to September. Property closed 25 December. Timed tickets operate on Bank Holidays and during busy periods.

 Some places are easy to get to on foot or by public transport. See page 3

The Kymin

Monmouth, Monmouthshire NP25 3SF

Map (4) H8 1902

Lord Nelson and Lady Hamilton were delighted with this Georgian banqueting house and Naval Temple when they visited in 1802. The Kymin is still a great spot from which to enjoy panoramic views of the Brecon Beacons and Wye Valley. The woods and pleasure grounds are also perfect for picnics.

Eating and shopping: refreshments and snacks available (when Round House open). Picnics welcome.

Making the most of your day: self-guided walks, including bluebell walks in spring. Garden games available to hire (when Round House open). Special events throughout the year. **Dogs**: welcome in house and grounds.

Access: **Round House** **Naval Temple** **Grounds**
Parking: limited.

Finding out more: 01600 719241 or kymin@nationaltrust.org.uk

The Kymin		M	T	W	T	F	S	S
Round House								
28 Mar–26 Oct	11-4	**M**	·	·	·	·	**S**	**S**
Grounds								
Open all year	7-9	**M**	**T**	**W**	**T**	**F**	**S**	**S**

Open Good Friday. Car park open during daylight hours only.

Llanerchaeron

Ciliau Aeron, near Aberaeron, Ceredigion SA48 8DG

Map (4) D6 1989

Totally self-sufficient 18th-century Welsh minor gentry estate. The villa, designed in the 1790s, is the most complete example of the early work of John Nash. It has its own service courtyard with dairy, laundry, brewery and salting house, giving a full 'upstairs downstairs' experience. The walled kitchen gardens, pleasure grounds, ornamental lake and parkland offer peaceful walks, while the Home Farm complex has an impressive range of traditional, atmospheric outbuildings. A working farm, there are Welsh Black cattle, Llanwenog sheep and rare Welsh pigs as well as chickens, geese and doves. Woodland walks available.

Eating and shopping: café serving light meals and cakes (not National Trust). Picnic site. Fresh garden produce and plants, farm meat, local crafts, art, gifts and books for sale. Second-hand bookshop.

Making the most of your day: activities during local school holidays, including crafts, gardening, nature activities and self-led trails. Special events days. Cycle hire. **Dogs**: welcome on the woodland walks and in the parkland on leads.

Access: **Visitor building** **Villa** **Grounds**
Parking: 50 yards.

The Kymin, Monmouthshire (below left), Georgian banqueting house, and the kitchen garden at Llanerchaeron, Ceredigion

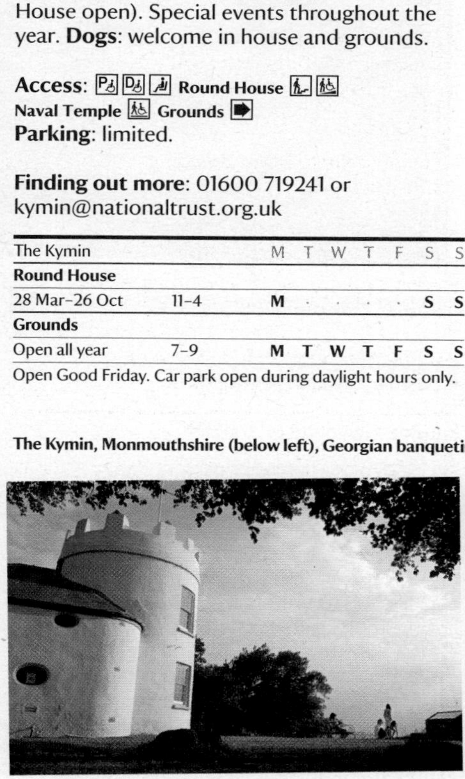

A riot of colour at Llanerchaeron in Ceredigion

Finding out more: 01545 570200 or
llanerchaeron@nationaltrust.org.uk

Llanerchaeron		M	T	W	T	F	S	S
Entire property								
14 Feb–22 Feb	11:30–3:30	**M**	**T**	**W**	**T**	**F**	**S**	**S**
21 Mar–1 Nov	10:30–5*	**M**	**T**	**W**	**T**	**F**	**S**	**S**
Farm, garden, woodland walks and shop only								
1 Jan–4 Jan	11:30–3:30	·	·	·	**T**	**F**	**S**	**S**
10 Jan–8 Feb	11:30–3:30	·	·	·	·	·	**S**	**S**
28 Feb–15 Mar	11:30–3:30	·	·	·	·	·	**S**	**S**
2 Nov–31 Dec**	11:30–3:30	**M**	**T**	**W**	**T**	**F**	**S**	**S**
Christmas Fair								
5 Dec–6 Dec	11–4	·	·	·	·	·	**S**	**S**

Last admission one hour before closing. *Villa opens 11:30. **Closed 24 and 25 December. Geler Jones Rural Life Collection open Wednesday and Friday 12 to 4, 21 March to 1 November. Parkland and woodland walks open daily.

Penrhyn Castle

Bangor, Gwynedd LL57 4HN

Map (4) E2 1951

Penrhyn was built to be remembered – whether for its commanding position, the luxurious decoration, or simply the vast principal rooms, and since 1830 visitors have come away with a lasting impression. Presented at the time of the visit of Edward, Prince of Wales, in 1894, you can experience not only the parts of the castle the family guests would have seen – the grand dining-room, the finest art collection in North Wales and the opulent bedrooms – but also the 'below stairs' areas, including the butler's

Please display your current sticker for free parking

Commanding Penrhyn Castle, Gwynedd (centre): so much to discover both inside and out

pantry and Victorian kitchens. An essential part of any visit is a walk around the parkland, where you can admire breathtaking views and enjoy the tranquility of the walled garden.

Eating and shopping: light meals and homemade cakes available in our new coffee shop; lunches in the tea-room. Gift shop in the heart of the castle. New Stables shop and second-hand bookshop.

Making the most of your day: **Indoors** Events, including summer fun days. Tours to hidden parts of the castle most days. You can climb aboard an engine or explore local industrial history in the Railway Museum. Art collection displayed in cathedral-like interiors. **Outdoors** Woodland walks and hidden parts of garden to discover. **Dogs**: welcome on leads in grounds. Assistance dogs only in castle and walled garden.

Access:
Castle **Stableblock** **Grounds**
Sat Nav: use LL57 4HT. **Parking**: 500 yards.

Finding out more: 01248 363219 (Infoline). 01248 353084 or penrhyncastle@nationaltrust.org.uk

Penrhyn Castle		M	T	W	T	F	S	S
Castle, shop, tea-room and Victorian kitchens								
28 Feb–1 Nov	12–5	M	T	W	T	F	S	S
Garden, parkland, railway museum, coffee shop and shop								
1 Jan–27 Feb	12–3	M	T	W	T	F	S	S
28 Feb–1 Nov	11–5	M	T	W	T	F	S	S
2 Nov–31 Dec	12–3	M	T	W	T	F	S	S

Castle taster tours offered whenever possible.
Selected areas of the castle open for winter weekend and guided tours. Closed 25 December.

Plas Newydd House and Gardens

Llanfairpwll, Anglesey LL61 6DQ

Map (4) D2 1976

This enchanting 18th-century mansion sits on the shores of the Menai Strait, with breathtaking views of Snowdonia. The surrounding gardens include an Australasian arboretum, formal Italianate terraces and an important rhododendron collection. There are superb woodland walks and a fabulous hand-crafted tree house to visit. Dairy Wood offers a great adventure playground and fun Frisbee™ Golf course. A military museum contains relics belonging to the 1st Marquess of Anglesey, who commanded the cavalry at the Battle of Waterloo. At the heart of the 1930s interior of the Marquess of Anglesey's ancestral family home, is Rex Whistler's 58-foot fantasy landscape mural.

Plas Newydd House and Gardens, Anglesey (above and below)

Eating and shopping: tea-room at the old dairy. Visitor centre and gift shop. Lord A's coffee shop, second-hand bookshop and another gift shop in the mansion.

Making the most of your day: **Indoors** Christmas food and craft fair. **Outdoors** Specialist garden 'walks and talks'. Events, including Easter fun weekend and summer fair. **Dogs**: welcome on short leads in designated woodland areas.

Access:
Building **Grounds**
Parking: 400 yards from main entrance.

Finding out more: 01248 714795 or plasnewydd@nationaltrust.org.uk

Plas Newydd		M	T	W	T	F	S	S
House								
28 Feb–8 Mar*	11-3	·	·	·	·	·	**S**	**S**
14 Mar–4 Nov**	12-4:30	**M**	**T**	**W**	·	·	**S**	**S**
Garden								
3 Jan–22 Feb	11-3	·	·	·	·	·	**S**	**S**
28 Feb–28 Jun†	10:30-5:30	**M**	**T**	**W**	**T**	·	**S**	**S**
29 Jun–30 Aug	10:30-5:30	**M**	**T**	**W**	**T**	**F**	**S**	**S**
31 Aug–4 Nov	10:30-5:30	**M**	**T**	**W**	**T**	·	**S**	**S**
5 Nov–20 Dec	11-3	**M**	**T**	**W**	**T**	·	**S**	**S**
26 Dec–31 Dec	11-3	**M**	**T**	**W**	**T**	·	**S**	**S**
Shop, tea-room, playground and Frisbee™ Golf course								
3 Jan–8 Mar	11-3	·	·	·	·	·	**S**	**S**
14 Mar–4 Nov	10:30-5:30	**M**	**T**	**W**	**T**	**F**	**S**	**S**
5 Nov–20 Dec	11-3	**M**	**T**	**W**	**T**	**F**	**S**	**S**
26 Dec–31 Dec	11-3	**M**	**T**	**W**	**T**	·	**S**	**S**

*Taster tours only, no free-flow. **Specialist tours 11 to 12, places limited. **Coffee shop and second-hand bookshop 11:30 to 5. †Gardens open Friday 29 May. Closed 21 to 25 December.

Plas yn Rhiw

Rhiw, Pwllheli, Gwynedd LL53 8AB

Map (4) C4 1952

The house was rescued from neglect and lovingly restored by the three Keating sisters, who bought it in 1938. The views from the grounds and gardens across Cardigan Bay are among the most spectacular in Britain. The house is 16th-century with Georgian additions, and the garden contains many beautiful flowering trees and shrubs, with beds framed by box hedges and grass paths. It's stunning whatever the season.

Eating and shopping: tea-room serving a selection of fresh sandwiches, soup, cakes and drinks. Shop selling gifts, plants, books and prints of Honora Keating's landscapes. Hot or cold drinks and ice-cream also available in the shop.

Making the most of your day: woodland walks and a native-apple orchard. Guided tours available by arrangement. Three holiday cottages within walking distance of Plas yn Rhiw. **Dogs**: on woodland walk below shop only (on leads).

Access: **Building** **Grounds**
Parking: 100 yards (narrow lanes).

Finding out more: 01758 780219 or plasynrhiw@nationaltrust.org.uk

Plas yn Rhiw		M	T	W	T	F	S	S
26 Mar–25 May*	12–5	M	·	·	T	F	S	S
27 May–13 Jul*	12–5	M	·	W	T	F	S	S
15 Jul–7 Sep*	12–5	M	T	W	T	F	S	S
10 Sep–28 Sep*	12–5	M	·	·	T	F	S	S
1 Oct–1 Nov**	12–4	·	·	·	T	F	S	S

Garden and snowdrop wood open occasionally at weekends in January and February. *Tea-room open same dates as property, 11 to 4:30. **Tea-room open as property but from 11 to 3:30.

A corner of one of the Keating sisters' bedrooms at Plas yn Rhiw, Gwynedd. The sisters rescued and lovingly restored the house

Porth y Swnt

Henfaes, Aberdaron, Pwllheli, Gwynedd LL53 8BE

Map (4) C4 2010

This exciting interpretation centre, at the heart of the beautiful fishing village of Aberdaron, shines a light on Llŷn's unique culture, heritage and environment. You can experience Bardsey Island's retired lighthouse optic up close, follow in the footsteps of pilgrims for a journey across the Sound in the video pod, catch up on what Llŷn's rangers are up to and form your reflective thoughts in the Sea of Words. If you want to stay longer, our Henfaes holiday apartments are also in the centre of the village.

Eating and shopping: gift shop in visitor centre. Cafés, pubs and convenience stores in village (none National Trust).

Porth y Swnt, Gwynedd: fun on the beach at Aberdaron

Making the most of your day: walks, including access to Wales Coast Path from Aberdaron and nearby beaches Porthor, Porthdinllaen, Llanbedrog. Llŷn Coast Festival and events, including beach fun days, seafood festival and guided walks. **Dogs**: beach access restricted during summer.

Access: **Car park**
Parking: on site.

Finding out more: 01758 703810 or porthyswnt@nationaltrust.org.uk

Porth y Swnt		M	T	W	T	F	S	S
1 Jan–31 Mar	10–4	**M**	**T**	**W**	**T**	**F**	**S**	**S**
1 Apr–30 Jun	10–5	**M**	**T**	**W**	**T**	**F**	**S**	**S**
1 Jul–31 Aug	10–6	**M**	**T**	**W**	**T**	**F**	**S**	**S**
1 Sep–30 Sep	10–5	**M**	**T**	**W**	**T**	**F**	**S**	**S**
1 Oct–30 Dec	10–4	**M**	**T**	**W**	**T**	**F**	**S**	**S**

Closed 25, 26 and 31 December.

Powis Castle and Garden

Welshpool, Powys SY21 8RF

Map (4) G5 1952

The Herbert family spent more than 400 years transforming a medieval fortress into the comfortable family home you see today. Furnished with sumptuous fabrics and exquisite works of art from around the world, the interior reflects the Elizabethan to Edwardian periods. The UK's largest private collection of Indian treasures is housed in the Clive Museum. From weaponry to a gold bejewelled tiger's head, the collection is unique. The world-renowned gardens are an eclectic mix of Italianate terraces filled with herbaceous borders, a formal garden with clipped yews and a woodland area which boasts a number of champion trees.

Eating and shopping: restaurant (licensed) and garden coffee shop. Gift shop and plant sales.

Making the most of your day: Indoors
Themed tours and daily introductory talks about the castle. Family fun trails.

Two views of the Italianate terraces (above and below) at Powis Castle and Garden, Powys

Outdoors Talks on the garden every day. Children's activities during school holidays and family trails. **Dogs**: assistance dogs only.

Access: [access symbols]
Building [symbol] **Grounds** [symbols]
Parking: on site.

Finding out more: 01938 551944 (Infoline). 01938 551929 or powiscastle@nationaltrust.org.uk

Powis Castle and Garden		M	T	W	T	F	S	S
Castle and Clive Museum*								
3 Jan–28 Feb	12–4	·	·	·	·	·	S	S
1 Mar–27 Mar	11–4	M	T	W	T	F	S	S
28 Mar–30 Sep	11–5	M	T	W	T	F	S	S
1 Oct–23 Dec	11–4	M	T	W	T	F	S	S
Garden								
1 Jan–27 Mar	11–4	M	T	W	T	F	S	S
28 Mar–30 Sep	10–6	M	T	W	T	F	S	S
1 Oct–31 Dec	10–4	M	T	W	T	F	S	S
Restaurant**								
1 Mar–27 Mar	10–4	M	T	W	T	F	S	S
28 Mar–30 Sep	10–5	M	T	W	T	F	S	S
1 Oct–31 Dec	10–4	M	T	W	T	F	S	S
Gift shop								
3 Jan–28 Feb	11–4	·	·	·	·	·	S	S
1 Mar–27 Mar†	11–4	M	T	W	T	F	S	S
28 Mar–30 Sep†	11–5	M	T	W	T	F	S	S
1 Oct–31 Dec†	11–4	M	T	W	T	F	S	S

*Reduced number of state rooms open 3 January to 28 February and 2 November to 23 December.
**Garden coffee shop open from 1 March to 31 October (opening times vary). Limited catering offer in January and February. †Garden shop also open. Property closed 25 December.

Segontium

Caernarfon, Gwynedd

Map (4) D2 1937

Fort built to defend the Roman Empire against rebellious tribes. **Note**: in the guardianship of Cadw – Welsh Government's historic environment service. Museum not National Trust. For Sat Nav use LL55 2LN.

Finding out more: 01443 336000 or segontium@nationaltrust.org.uk

Skenfrith Castle

Skenfrith, near Abergavenny, Monmouthshire NP7 8UH

Map (4) H8 1936

Remains of early 13th-century castle, built beside the River Monnow to command one of the main routes from England. **Note**: in the guardianship of Cadw – Welsh Government's historic environment service.

Finding out more: 01874 625515 or skenfrithcastle@nationaltrust.org.uk

Tredegar House

Newport, NP10 8YW

Map (4) G9 2012

For centuries, the flamboyant Morgan family called this Grade I listed 17th-century Restoration house their home. With tales of giant birds' nests, riotous parties, dark arts, war heroism and animal menageries, the Morgan's was certainly no ordinary household. You can hear about the lives of their servants, well looked after by the family, meet the newest 'family' – today's team – and be part of this latest chapter at Tredegar House. Outside, as you meander through the formal walled gardens you will see the original Tudor house, distinctive parterre garden, the Sir Briggs monument and impressive Grade I listed stables – all set within a 36-hectare (90-acre) park, with an avenue of veteran oak trees, woodland walks, open parkland and lake. **Note**: trialling new ways of opening the house as part of the 'Changing Rooms' project.

Eating and shopping: tea-room serving light lunches, homemade cakes and homemade dog biscuits. Tredegar House gifts, books and local food for sale in the shop.

Kitchen utensils (top right) at Tredegar House, Newport (main picture), were put to good use by the flamboyant Morgans. Young visitors (right)

Making the most of your day: **Indoors** Introductory talks about the house and family. You can go 'below stairs' and find out about the people who worked here. Traditional Christmas experience. **Outdoors** Lakeside walks. Events, including Easter trail and Pirate Day. Summer family activities. Impressive stables to discover. Dyffryn Gardens nearby. **Dogs**: welcome in the garden, park and tea-room.

Access: **House** **Reception** **Grounds**
Parking: on site.

Finding out more: 01633 815880 or tredegar@nationaltrust.org.uk

Tredegar House		M	T	W	T	F	S	S
House and garden**								
14 Feb–27 Mar*	11–4	**M**	**T**	**W**	**T**	**F**	**S**	**S**
28 Mar–1 Nov*	11–5	**M**	**T**	**W**	**T**	**F**	**S**	**S**
28 Nov–20 Dec	11–5	·	·	·	·	·	**S**	**S**
Tea-room and shop								
10 Jan–8 Feb	10–4	·	·	·	·	·	**S**	**S**
14 Feb–27 Mar	10–4	**M**	**T**	**W**	**T**	**F**	**S**	**S**
28 Mar–1 Nov	10–5	**M**	**T**	**W**	**T**	**F**	**S**	**S**
7 Nov–22 Nov	10–4	·	·	·	·	·	**S**	**S**
28 Nov–20 Dec	10–5	·	·	·	·	·	**S**	**S**
Park								
Open all year	Dawn–dusk	**M**	**T**	**W**	**T**	**F**	**S**	**S**

*Gardens open 10:30. House: 14 February to 1 March 'below-stairs' only with tours to ground floor. 2 March to 27 March 'below-stairs' and ground floor only, tours to second floor. 28 March to 1 November house fully open.
**Last admission to house one hour before closing.

Hands on at Tudor Merchant's House in Pembrokeshire

Tudor Merchant's House

Quay Hill, Tenby, Pembrokeshire SA70 7BX

Map (4) C9 1937

Over 500 years ago when Tenby was a busy trading port, a merchant built this three-storey house to live in and trade from. Today, this unaltered house and shop have been furnished with exquisitely carved replicas and brightly coloured wall-hangings which re-create the atmosphere of life in Tudor Tenby.
Note: sorry no toilet.

Eating and shopping: shop range includes specially made Tudor-style pottery (design based on finds at the house), pewterware, horn cups, glass, beeswax candles and books about the Tudors.

Making the most of your day: Tudor Family Fortunes game, superstitions scrolls, lay the high table, costumes to try on and replica toys. Easter, Hallowe'en and Tudor-themed family events. Colby Woodland Garden and Stackpole nearby. **Dogs**: assistance dogs only.

Access: Building
Parking: very limited on-street parking. July to August: pay-and-display car parks or park and ride (charge including members).

Finding out more: 01834 842279 or tudormerchantshouse@nationaltrust.org.uk

Tudor Merchant's House		M	T	W	T	F	S	S
14 Feb–22 Feb	11-3	M	T	W	T	F	S	S
28 Feb–22 Mar	11-3	·	·	·	·	·	S	S
28 Mar–19 Jul	11-5	M	·	W	T	F	S	S
20 Jul–6 Sep	11-5*	M	T	W	T	F	S	S
7 Sep–1 Nov	11-5	M	·	W	T	F	S	S
7 Nov–20 Dec	11-3	·	·	·	·	·	S	S

Open Tuesdays of Bank Holiday weeks, 11 to 5. *Open until 7 on Tuesdays and Wednesdays 21 July to 26 August.

Tŷ Mawr Wybrnant

Penmachno, Betws-y-Coed, Conwy LL25 0HJ

Map (4) E3 1951

Hidden in the beautiful Conwy Valley, this traditional upland farmhouse was the birthplace of Bishop William Morgan, who first translated the Bible into Welsh. This is one of the most important houses in the history of the Welsh language. An original rare copy of William Morgan's Bible is on display.

Eating and shopping: picnics welcome.

Making the most of your day: **Indoors** Introductory talks and exhibition room. Virtual tours available. **Outdoors** Tudor kitchen garden, woodland walks and two animal puzzle trails. **Dogs**: under close control.

Access: **Building** **Grounds**
Sat Nav: no access from the A470.
Parking: 500 yards.

Finding out more: 01690 760213 or tymawrwybrnant@nationaltrust.org.uk

Tŷ Mawr Wybrnant		M	T	W	T	F	S	S
26 Mar–27 Sep	12–5	·	·	·	T	F	S	S
1 Oct–1 Nov	12–4	·	·	·	T	F	S	S

Open Bank Holiday Mondays.

Tŷ Mawr Wybrnant, Conwy: traditional upland farmhouse

Map 7

Northern Ireland

Portstewart Strand, County Londonderry

Outdoors in Northern Ireland

Famed throughout the world for our coastline, we also have wild mountains, peaceful lakes and huge stretches of idyllic countryside for you to enjoy.

Divis and the Black Mountain

Hannahstown, near Belfast, County Antrim

Map (7) E6 2004

Sitting in the heart of the Belfast Hills, this 809-hectare (2,000-acre) mosaic of upland heath and blanket bog is a great place for a wild countryside experience. There are four walking trails to explore, affording panoramic views across Belfast and a wealth of flora, fauna and archaeological remains to discover.
Note: cattle roam freely during summer months. Mountain environment and weather conditions can change rapidly.

Eating and shopping: tea, coffee and light refreshments available in The Barn (seasonal opening).

Making the most of your day: guided walks on biodiversity and archaeology. **Dogs**: welcome, but please note cattle roam freely during summer.

Access: Visitor centre Mountain
Sat Nav: use BT17 0NG. **Parking**: on Divis Road, opposite Divis Mountain gates.

Finding out more: 028 9082 5434 or divis@nationaltrust.org.uk

Islandmagee

near Larne, County Antrim

Map (7) E5 1996

Once the site of smuggling and home to an ancient monastery and a groundbreaking suspended cliff path (below), Islandmagee peninsula's coastline is steeped in history. An Area of Special Scientific Interest, it has some of Northern Ireland's largest colonies of cliff-nesting seabirds and offers views of the famous Antrim Coast. **Note**: paths uneven and steep in places.

Eating and shopping: Chapter 1 café in Mullaghboy village serving food, tea and coffee and The Rinkha (neither National Trust) in Ballystrudder village offering famous ice-cream. Picnics welcome.

Making the most of your day: coastal walks and yearly guided walk at Portmuck.
Dogs: on leads only.

Access: Portmuck and Skernaghan
Parking: at Portmuck and Skernaghan Point (not National Trust).

Finding out more: 028 9064 7787 or islandmagee@nationaltrust.org.uk

Lisnabreeny

near Belfast, County Down

Map (7) E6 1938

The path (below) through this easily overlooked haven on the edge of Belfast climbs along a tumbling stream through a wooded glen and across rolling farmland to emerge at a hilltop rath at the summit of the Castlereagh Hills. This picturesque setting affords sweeping views across the city and beyond. **Note**: sorry no toilet. Uneven paths and steep steps.

Making the most of your day: viewpoint and Second World War memorial commemorating US servicemen who died in Northern Ireland. Walks through glen, woodlands and ancient rath. Yearly guided walk. **Dogs**: welcome on leads.

Access: Glen
Sat Nav: use BT8 6SA. **Parking**: on Lisnabreeny Road (no parking on Manse Road).

Finding out more: 028 9064 7787 or lisnabreeny@nationaltrust.org.uk

Minnowburn

near Belfast, County Down

Map (7) E6 1952

Just a few miles from Belfast city centre yet in the heart of the country, this 52-hectare (128-acre) naturally mixed countryside is a paradox all of its own. Nestled in the heart of the Lagan Valley Regional Park, it has riverside, meadow and woodland walks and is rich in wildlife. **Note**: sorry no toilet. Trails are uneven and steep in places.

Eating and shopping: Piccolo Mondo catering van (not National Trust) serves food, tea and coffee in car park at weekends. Lock Keeper's Inn (not National Trust) serving food, tea and coffee, ¾-mile along riverside path. Picnic tables in Terrace Hill garden.

Making the most of your day: guided walks, including heritage, history and woodlands. Waymarked walks, including the Giant's Ring Trail. Sculpture trail. Riverside and pond walks. Terrace Hill Garden, venue for 'Gig in the Garden' event. **Dogs**: on leads only.

Access:
Sat Nav: use BT8 8LD. **Parking**: on site.

Finding out more: 028 9064 7787 or minnowburn@nationaltrust.org.uk

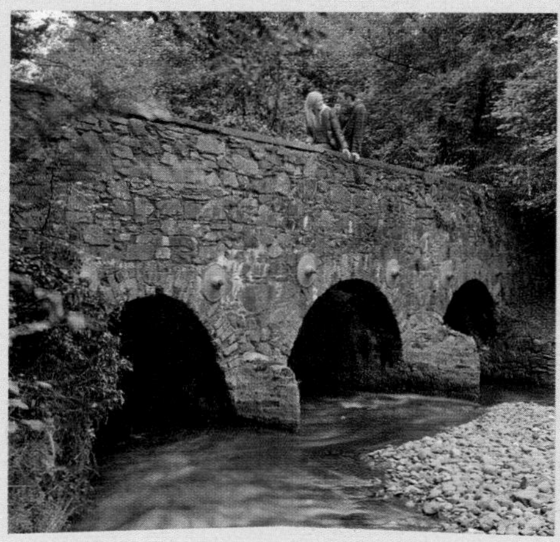

The Mournes

near Newcastle, County Down

Map (7) E8 1992

These famous wildlife-rich mountains are criss-crossed by well-marked coastal and mountain paths. Great for exploring, the National Trust-maintained paths stretch from the shore into the heart of the Mournes, offering views over Dundrum Bay – as far as the Isle of Man on a clear day.

Eating and shopping: picnics welcome. Nearest shops, restaurants and cafés in Newcastle (none National Trust).

Making the most of your day: outstanding views from Bloody Bridge. Coastal path to St Mary's Chapel ruins. Bird-watching. **Dogs**: welcome under control.

Access:
Sat Nav: use BT33 0EU for Slieve Donard and BT33 0LA for Bloody Bridge.
Parking: for Slieve Donard, park in Newcastle; for Bloody Bridge, park on A2.

Finding out more: 028 437 51467 or mournes@nationaltrust.org.uk

Murlough National Nature Reserve

near Dundrum, County Down

Map (7) E8 1967

Home to seals, Neolithic sites and Ireland's first nature reserve, Murlough is one of the most extensive examples of dune landscape in Ireland. A network of paths and boardwalks through these ancient dunes, woodland and heath makes it ideal for relaxed walks and spotting a wonderland of wildlife.
Note: limited toilet facilities.

Eating and shopping: beach café (seasonal opening). Picnics welcome on beach or in car park.

Making the most of your day: self-guided nature walk and series of guided walks. Volunteer events and family activities throughout year. **Dogs**: welcome on leads, restrictions apply when ground-nesting birds breeding or cattle grazing.

Access: **Grounds**
Sat Nav: use BT33 0NQ. **Parking**: on site.

Finding out more: 028 4375 1467 or murlough@nationaltrust.org.uk

Murlough		M	T	W	T	F	S	S
Facilities								
14 Mar–29 Mar	10–6	·	·	·	·	·	**S**	**S**
3 Apr–12 Apr	10–6	**M**	**T**	**W**	**T**	**F**	**S**	**S**
18 Apr–31 May	10–6	·	·	·	·	·	**S**	**S**
1 Jun–31 Aug	10–6	**M**	**T**	**W**	**T**	**F**	**S**	**S**
5 Sep–27 Sep	10–6	·	·	·	·	·	**S**	**S**

Open Bank Holiday Mondays, dawn to dusk, and all other public holidays in Northern Ireland.

With its sweep of golden sand, Portstewart Strand in County Londonderry is one of Northern Ireland's finest beaches

Portstewart Strand

near Portstewart, County Londonderry

Map (7) C3 1981

Sweeping along the edge of the North Coast, this 2-mile stretch of golden sand is one of Northern Ireland's finest beaches and affords uninterrupted views of the coastline. It's an ideal place for lazy picnics, Quad Pod rides, surfing, slacklining and long walks into the wildlife-rich sand dunes.

Eating and shopping: Harry's Shack on site with great new catering offer. New mobile beach retail and information service.

Making the most of your day: waymarked nature trail. Barmouth Estuary bird hide. Events during peak season. **Dogs**: on leads only.

Access: Café Beach
Sat Nav: use BT55 7PG. **Parking**: on beach.

Finding out more: 028 7083 6396 or portstewart@nationaltrust.org.uk

Portstewart Strand		M	T	W	T	F	S	S
Facilities								
28 Mar–3 Apr	10–5	M	T	W	T	F	S	S
4 Apr–30 Apr	10–6	M	T	W	T	F	S	S
1 May–31 Aug	10–7	M	T	W	T	F	S	S
1 Sep–13 Sep	10–5	M	T	W	T	F	S	S
Beach								
Open all year	Dawn–dusk	M	T	W	T	F	S	S

Barrier to beach closes two hours after facilities close.
Open Bank Holiday Mondays and all other public holidays in Northern Ireland. Closed 24, 25 and 26 December.
Facilities may open at other times, weather permitting.

Strangford Lough

County Down

Map ⑦ F7 1969

The tidal treasures of Britain's largest sea lough (above) and one of Europe's key wildlife habitats await discovery. This delicately balanced landscape is rich in natural and built heritage. Northern Ireland's first Marine Conservation Zone and the winter home for over 90 per cent of the world's light-bellied brent geese.

Eating and shopping: tea-rooms at Mount Stewart and Castle Ward. Also numerous restaurants serving dishes made from local produce, including meat produced on the surrounding land and seafood from the lough, and arts and crafts shops (none National Trust).

Making the most of your day: birdwatching (some of the best in UK and Ireland), rock-pooling and geocaching. Red squirrels and seals to spot. Canoe and cycle trail.

Access:
Sat Nav: use BT22 1RG. **Parking**: small car park at Ballyquintin or parking around Lough (not all National Trust).

Finding out more: 028 4278 7769 or strangford@nationaltrust.org.uk

White Park Bay

near Ballintoy, County Antrim

Map ⑦ D3 1939

Embraced by ancient dunes, Neolithic settlements and passage tombs, this arc of white sand nestles between two headlands on the North Antrim Coast. Home to a range of rich habitats for a myriad of wildlife, its secluded location makes it ideal for quiet relaxation and peaceful walks.

Eating and shopping: shops, restaurants and cafés in nearby towns (not National Trust). Picnics welcome.

Making the most of your day: *50 things to do before you're 11¾* events. Part of the Causeway Coast Way and the Ulster Way.

Access:
Sat Nav: use BT54 6NH. **Parking**: on site.

Finding out more: 028 2073 3320 or whiteparkbay@nationaltrust.org.uk

Ardress House, County Armagh: this 17th-century farmhouse boasts fine Georgian interiors, a traditional cobbled farmyard, as well as orchards, woodlands and walks

Ardress House

64 Ardress Road, Annaghmore, Portadown, County Armagh BT62 1SQ

Map (7) D7 1959

Nestling in 40 hectares (100 acres) of rolling countryside, this 17th-century farmhouse is an elegant example of 18th-century remodelling, with detailed plasterwork and fine Georgian interiors. The cobbled farmyard is the perfect spot for children to feed the resident chickens, and the nearby apple orchards are great for exploring.

Eating and shopping: takeaway hot and cold drinks and ice-cream available. Picnics welcome in the garden or woodlands.

Making the most of your day: miniature Shetland ponies, pygmy goats, Soay sheep, ducks and chickens. Children's play area. Events, including Easter Egg trail, Apple Blossom Day and Apple Press Day.
Dogs: on leads in garden only.

Access: **Building** **Grounds**
Parking: 10 yards.

Finding out more: 028 8778 4753 or ardress@nationaltrust.org.uk

Ardress House		M	T	W	T	F	S	S
Farmyard and house								
14 Feb–17 Feb	12–5	**M**	**T**	·	·	·	**S**	**S**
14 Mar–29 Mar	1–6	·	·	·	·	·	**S**	**S**
3 Apr–12 Apr	1–6	**M**	**T**	**W**	**T**	**F**	**S**	**S**
18 Apr–28 Jun	1–6	·	·	·	·	·	**S**	**S**
2 Jul–30 Aug	1–6	·	·	·	**T**	**F**	**S**	**S**
5 Sep–27 Sep	1–6	·	·	·	·	·	**S**	**S**
Lady's Mile Walk								
Open all year	Dawn–dusk	**M**	**T**	**W**	**T**	**F**	**S**	**S**

House: admission by guided tour, last tour one hour before closing. Open Bank Holiday Mondays and all other public holidays in Northern Ireland.

The Argory

144 Derrycaw Road, Moy, Dungannon, County Armagh BT71 6NA

Map (7) C7 1979

From Georgian beginnings to the home of a Victorian hero, this Irish gentry house can trace more than 190 years of history. Built in the 1820s for the MacGeough Bond family, the house and surrounding 130-hectare (320-acre) wooded riverside estate came into existence due to a quirky stipulation in a will. The interior of this Neo-classical building still evokes the eclectic tastes and interests of the family, and guides bring history to life, recounting tales of Captain Shelton's heroism at sea. The rose garden, with its unusual sundial, colourful courtyard exhibitions and wooded riverside walks are ideal for exploring.

Eating and shopping: Courtyard Coffee Shop serving home-baked scones, sandwiches, paninis and cakes. Gift shop offering a wide range of products: jewellery, books and items for the home and garden. Bookshop with second-hand books for all tastes and interests. Picnics welcome.

The Argory in County Armagh (above and below) is perfect for exploring, both inside and out

Making the most of your day: **Indoors** Guided tours. Interactive room. Events, such as country and Christmas fairs. Santa's Grotto. **Outdoors** Variety of walks and trails, including snowdrop walk (February). Play area and Easter Egg trails. **Dogs**: on leads in grounds and garden only.

Access: Grounds

Parking: 100 yards.

Finding out more: 028 8778 4753 or argory@nationaltrust.org.uk

The Argory		M	T	W	T	F	S	S
Courtyard, café and shop								
7 Feb–1 Mar	12–5	·	·	·	·	·	S	S
16 Feb–17 Feb	12–5	M	T	·	·	·	·	·
House, courtyard, café and shop								
14 Mar–29 Mar	12–5	·	·	·	T	F	S	S
30 Mar–12 Apr	12–5	M	T	W	T	F	S	S
16 Apr–31 May	12–5	·	·	·	T	F	S	S
3 Jun–28 Jun	12–5	·	·	W	T	F	S	S
1 Jul–31 Aug	12–5	M	T	W	T	F	S	S
5 Sep–27 Sep	12–5	·	·	·	T	F	S	S
3 Oct–1 Nov	12–4	·	·	·	·	·	S	S
26 Oct–30 Oct	12–4	M	T	W	T	F	·	·
Grounds								
Open all year	10–5	M	T	W	T	F	S	S

House: admission by guided tour, last tour one hour before closing. Open Bank Holiday Mondays and all other public holidays in Northern Ireland. Closed 25, 26, 27 and 28 December.

 For other ways to get involved go to nationaltrust.org.uk/get-involved/volunteer

Belmont Tower

82 Belmont Church Road, Belfast,
County Antrim BT4 3FG

Map ⑦ E6 [2013]

For more than 100 years this prominent Gothic-style late-Victorian building buzzed to the sound of children playing and learning in its former life as Belmont Primary School. Today this inspirational space has been restored and adapted to offer classes, conference facilities, a coffee shop and C. S. Lewis exhibition.

Eating and shopping: freshly prepared food and delicious scones at Belmont Tower Café.

Making the most of your day: community groups, such as Belfast Historical Society, baby sensory and wine-making. Exhibition on the life of C. S. Lewis. **Dogs**: assistance dogs only.

Access:
Parking: on site and on street at Belmont Road and Belmont Church Road.

Finding out more: 028 9065 3338 or belmonttower@nationaltrust.org.uk

Belmont Tower		M	T	W	T	F	S	S
Open all year	9–4*	**M**	**T**	**W**	**T**	**F**	**S**	·

*Saturday closes at 3. Also open in evenings and other times for booked classes and events. Closed 1 January, 3 to 7 April, 12 and 13 July, 25 and 26 December.

Belmont Tower, County Antrim, dates from the late-Victorian period

Carrick-a-Rede

Ballintoy, County Antrim BT54 6LS

Map (7) D3 1967

Connected to the cliffs by a rope bridge across the Atlantic Ocean (left), this rocky island is the ultimate clifftop experience. Jutting out from the rugged North Antrim Coast Road, the 30 metre-deep and 20 metre-wide chasm separating Carrick-a-Rede from the mainland is traversed by an amazing rope bridge that was traditionally erected by salmon fishermen. If you are bold enough to make the crossing, there is unique geology and wildlife as well as uninterrupted vistas across the seas of Moyle to Rathlin Island and beyond to the Scottish islands to enjoy. It offers windswept coastal scenery and clifftop birdwatching. **Note**: eight people maximum on bridge (open weather permitting). Entrance at 119a Whitepark Road.

Eating and shopping: Weighbridge tea-room and gift shop offering hot food, snacks, sweets, gifts and souvenirs.

Making the most of your day: coastal path – part of the Causeway Coast Way from Portstewart to Ballycastle and the Ulster Way. Birdwatching and coastal scenery. Unique flora and fauna. Guided tours (by prior arrangement). **Dogs**: on leads (not permitted to cross bridge).

Access: **Grounds**
Parking: on site.

Finding out more: 028 2076 9839 or carrickarede@nationaltrust.org.uk

Carrick-a-Rede		M	T	W	T	F	S	S
Bridge								
1 Jan–22 Feb	9:30–3:30	**M**	**T**	**W**	**T**	**F**	**S**	**S**
23 Feb–29 Mar	9:30–6	**M**	**T**	**W**	**T**	**F**	**S**	**S**
30 Mar–12 Apr	9:30–7:00	**M**	**T**	**W**	**T**	**F**	**S**	**S**
13 Apr–24 May	9:30–6	**M**	**T**	**W**	**T**	**F**	**S**	**S**
25 May–30 Aug	9:30–7:00	**M**	**T**	**W**	**T**	**F**	**S**	**S**
31 Aug–25 Oct	9:30–6	**M**	**T**	**W**	**T**	**F**	**S**	**S**
26 Oct–31 Dec	9:30–3:30	**M**	**T**	**W**	**T**	**F**	**S**	**S**

Last entry to rope bridge 45 minutes before closing. Car park and North Antrim coastal path open all year. Bridge open weather permitting. Closed 24, 25 and 26 December.

 Some places are easy to get to on foot or by public transport. See page 3

Castle Coole

Enniskillen, County Fermanagh BT74 6JY

Map (7) A7 1951

You can glimpse what 18th-century life was like in the stately home of the Earls of Belmore through the story of the people who lived and worked here. Widely recognised as one of the finest Neo-classical houses in Ireland, Castle Coole sits grandly in wooded parklands that change with the seasons and are ideal for family walks. Showcasing fine architecture and opulent Regency interiors, guided tours reveal life 'below stairs' in the suite of servants' rooms and service quarters. Located on the edge of Enniskillen the estate affords sweeping views from the shores of Lough Coole.

Eating and shopping: Tallow House tea-room. Gift shop selling souvenirs and second-hand bookshop (volunteer-run).

The opulent interiors (above) of Castle Coole, County Fermanagh, match the grandeur of its exterior (top right)

Making the most of your day: **Indoors** Musical events throughout year. Guided tours of historic basement. Castle Coole Gallery. **Outdoors** Events, including Easter Sunday treasure trails. Trails and walks. **Dogs**: on leads in grounds only.

Access:
Building **Grounds**
Parking: 150 yards.

Finding out more: 028 6632 2690 or castlecoole@nationaltrust.org.uk

Castle Coole		M	T	W	T	F	S	S
Grounds								
1 Jan–28 Feb	10–4	**M**	**T**	**W**	**T**	**F**	**S**	**S**
1 Mar–1 Nov	10–7	**M**	**T**	**W**	**T**	**F**	**S**	**S**
2 Nov–31 Dec	10–4	**M**	**T**	**W**	**T**	**F**	**S**	**S**
House, tea-room and shop								
14 Mar–29 Mar	11–5	·	·	·	·	·	**S**	**S**
3 Apr–12 Apr	11–5	**M**	**T**	**W**	**T**	**F**	**S**	**S**
18 Apr–26 Apr	11–5	·	·	·	·	·	**S**	**S**
1 May–31 May	11–5	**M**	·	**W**	**T**	**F**	**S**	**S**
1 Jun–31 Aug	11–5	**M**	**T**	**W**	**T**	**F**	**S**	**S**
2 Sep–30 Sep	11–5	**M**	·	**W**	**T**	**F**	**S**	**S**

House: admission by guided tour (last tour one hour before closing). Open Bank Holiday Mondays and all other public holidays in Northern Ireland.

Castle Ward

Strangford, Downpatrick,
County Down BT30 7LS

Map (7) F7 1953

High on a hillside, with views across the tranquil waters of Strangford Lough, the distinctly different styles of Gothic and classical collide at Castle Ward. This eccentric 18th-century mansion within an 332-hectare (820-acre) walled demesne is one of the most peculiar architectural compromises between two people. The former home of the Viscounts Bangor, guided tours reveal the history of the different façades. In the Farmyard Craft Village and gardens you can browse and stroll among handmade pottery, flowers and subtropical plants, while the extensive grounds are criss-crossed by a 21-mile network of family-friendly multi-use trails. The impressive laundry, tack room, children's Victorian play centre and adventure playground provide further opportunities to explore the demesne. **Note**: 1 March to 30 November visitor access to livestock grazing areas may be restricted.

Eccentric Castle Ward in County Down (bottom), overlooks tranquil Strangford Lough (right) and sits within extensive grounds

Eating and shopping: Coach House tea-room. Gift shop selling local produce and souvenirs. Second-hand bookshop.

Making the most of your day: **Indoors** Guided house tours. **Outdoors** Network of multi-use trails. Bicycles for hire. Farmyard with animals. Victorian play centre, adventure playground. Tracker Packs and children's activities. Events, including Easter Fair, Pumpkinfest, Jazz in the Grounds and Santa's House. Caravan park and pods available for hire. **Dogs**: on leads in grounds only (livestock grazing areas out of bounds).

Access: **Building**
Grounds
Sat Nav: follow brown signs. **Parking**: on site.

Finding out more: 028 4488 1204 or castleward@nationaltrust.org.uk

Castle Ward		M	T	W	T	F	S	S
Parkland, woodland and garden								
1 Jan–29 Mar	10–4	**M**	**T**	**W**	**T**	**F**	**S**	**S**
30 Mar–27 Sep	10–8	**M**	**T**	**W**	**T**	**F**	**S**	**S**
28 Sep–31 Dec	10–4	**M**	**T**	**W**	**T**	**F**	**S**	**S**
House, laundry and pastimes centre								
14 Mar–29 Mar	12–5	·	·	·	·	·	**S**	**S**
3 Apr–12 Apr	12–5	**M**	**T**	**W**	**T**	**F**	**S**	**S**
18 Apr–31 May	12–5	·	·	·	·	·	**S**	**S**
6 Jun–28 Jun	12–5	·	·	**W**	**T**	**F**	**S**	**S**
29 Jun–30 Aug	12–5	**M**	**T**	**W**	**T**	**F**	**S**	**S**
5 Sep–1 Nov	12–5	·	·	·	·	·	**S**	**S**
Coach House tea-room, shop and second-hand bookshop								
10 Jan–8 Mar	12–4	·	·	·	·	·	**S**	**S**
14 Mar–29 Mar	12–5	·	·	**W**	**T**	**F**	**S**	**S**
1 Apr–12 Apr	12–5	**M**	**T**	**W**	**T**	**F**	**S**	**S**
15 Apr–28 Jun	12–5	·	·	**W**	**T**	**F**	**S**	**S**
29 Jun–30 Aug	11–5	**M**	**T**	**W**	**T**	**F**	**S**	**S**
2 Sep–20 Dec	12–5	·	·	**W**	**T**	**F**	**S**	**S**

Last admission to house one hour before closing. Timed tickets apply to guided house tours. Open Bank Holiday Mondays and all other public holidays in Northern Ireland. Trailhead and refreshments: open daily 29 June to 30 August, 12 to 5. Tea-room, shop and second-hand bookshop also open 16 to 20 February, 12 to 4, and 26 to 30 October, 12 to 5. The Barn is open when primary schools are closed. The corn mill operates on Sundays from Easter to September, 2 to 5.

Peaceful Crom in County Fermanagh offers an escape to a slower, quieter world

Crom

Upper Lough Erne, Newtownbutler, County Fermanagh BT92 8AP

Map (7) A8 1987

Home to islands, ancient woodland and historical ruins, this 810-hectare (2,000-acre) demesne sits in a tranquil landscape on the peaceful southern shores of Upper Lough Erne. One of Ireland's most important conservation areas, it has many rare species and is great for relaxing walks, cycling and boat trips. **Note**: 19th-century castle not open to public.

Eating and shopping: afternoon tea, gifts and souvenirs available in visitor centre. Convenience goods and outdoor clothing also for sale.

Making the most of your day: regular guided walks. Historic castle ruins. Cot trips (Bank Holiday Mondays). Holiday cottages and campsite. **Dogs**: on leads only.

Access: **Building** **Grounds**
Sat Nav: GPS coordinates N54 10.397, W7 25.527. **Parking**: 100 yards.

Finding out more: 028 6773 8118 or crom@nationaltrust.org.uk

Crom		M	T	W	T	F	S	S
Grounds								
14 Mar–31 May	10–6	M	T	W	T	F	S	S
1 Jun–31 Aug	10–7	M	T	W	T	F	S	S
1 Sep–1 Nov	10–6	M	T	W	T	F	S	S
Visitor centre								
14 Mar–30 Sep	11–5	M	T	W	T	F	S	S
3 Oct–1 Nov	11–5	·	·	·	·	·	S	S

Open Bank Holiday Mondays and all other public holidays in Northern Ireland. Last admission one hour before closing. Tea-room open as visitor centre (but closed October).

The Crown Bar

46 Great Victoria Street, Belfast, County Antrim BT2 7BA

Map (7) E6 1978

Belfast's most famous pub remains one of the finest examples of a high-Victorian gin palace complete with period features. **Note**: run by Mitchells & Butlers.

Finding out more: 028 9024 3187 or info@crownbar.com

Derrymore House

Bessbrook, Newry, County Armagh BT35 7EF

Map (7) D8 1953

Resting peacefully in a landscape demesne, this 18th-century thatched cottage is historically rich and a great place for walks.
Note: sorry no toilet.

Finding out more: 028 8778 4753 or derrymore@nationaltrust.org.uk

Downhill Demesne and Hezlett House

Mussenden Road, Castlerock, County Londonderry BT51 4RP

Map (7) C3 1949

The sheltered gardens, cliff-edge landmark and striking ruins of a grand headland mansion bear testament to the eccentricity of the Earl Bishop who once made this 18th-century demesne his home. Mussenden Temple, perched atop sheer cliffs, offers panoramic views of the famous Antrim coastline and is a great place for walking and kite-flying. Nearby at Hezlett House, life in a rural 17th-century cottage is told through the people who once lived there. One of the oldest thatched cottages left standing in Northern Ireland, it boasts a rare cruck frame and houses the Downhill Marble Collection.

Mussenden Temple (above) on the Downhill Demesne and 17th-century Hezlett House (below), County Londonderry

Eating and shopping: tea and coffee facilities at Hezlett House. Picnics welcome in gardens.

Making the most of your day: **Indoors** Hallowe'en and Christmas at Hezlett House. Guided tours on request (booking essential). **Outdoors** Numerous events throughout year, including Easter Egg trails and a Kite Festival. **Dogs**: on leads only.

Access: **Building** **Grounds**
Parking: at Lion's Gate.

Finding out more: 028 7084 8728 or downhilldemesne@nationaltrust.org.uk Hezlett House, 107 Sea Road, Castlerock, County Londonderry BT51 4TW

Downhill and Hezlett		M	T	W	T	F	S	S
Downhill Demesne grounds								
Open all year	Dawn–dusk	M	T	W	T	F	S	S
Hezlett House and facilities								
14 Mar–17 Mar	10–5	M	T	·	·	·	S	S
21 Mar–22 Mar	10–5	·	·	·	·	·	S	S
28 Mar–13 Sep	10–5	M	T	W	T	F	S	S
14 Sep–28 Sep	10–5	M	·	·	T	F	S	S

Open Bank Holiday Mondays and all other public holidays in Northern Ireland. Closed 24, 25 and 26 December.

Florence Court

Enniskillen, County Fermanagh BT92 1DB

Map (7) A7 1954

Sitting peacefully in West Fermanagh, against a backdrop of mountains and forests, the former home of the Earls of Enniskillen has a tall story or two to tell. This three-storeyed Georgian mansion is the creation of six successive generations of the Cole family and contains Rococo plasterwork and a collection of 18th-century furniture. Informative guided tours bring this classical Irish house to life and recount stories of its patchwork history. Beyond, the extensive gardens are ideal for a stroll – the Yew Tree Trail through the 3,500-hectare (8,649-acre) forest park leads to the 'mother' of all Irish yew trees.

Eating and shopping: Stables restaurant. Coach House gift shop.

Making the most of your day: events throughout year. Children's Tracker Packs.

Florence Court, County Fermanagh (above and below), sits against a backdrop of mountains and forests

Dogs: on leads in garden and grounds only.

Access:
Building **Grounds**
Parking: 200 yards.

Finding out more: 028 6634 8249 or florencecourt@nationaltrust.org.uk

Florence Court		M	T	W	T	F	S	S
Gardens and park								
1 Jan–28 Feb	10–4	M	T	W	T	F	S	S
1 Mar–1 Nov	10–7	M	T	W	T	F	S	S
2 Nov–31 Dec	10–4	M	T	W	T	F	S	S
House, tea-room and shop								
14 Mar–29 Mar	11–5	·	·	·	·	·	S	S
3 Apr–12 Apr	11–5	M	T	W	T	F	S	S
18 Apr–26 Apr	11–5	·	·	·	·	·	S	S
2 May–31 May	11–5	M	T	W	T	·	S	S
1 Jun–31 Aug	11–5	M	T	W	T	F	S	S
1 Sep–30 Sep	11–5	M	T	W	T	·	S	S
3 Oct–1 Nov	11–5	·	·	·	·	·	S	S

House: admission by guided tour, last tour one hour before closing. Open Bank Holiday Mondays and all other public holidays in Northern Ireland. Open Irish Bank Holiday 26 October.

A geological wonder, Giant's Causeway in County Antrim is steeped in legend and mythology

Giant's Causeway

44 Causeway Road, Bushmills,
County Antrim BT57 8SU

Map (7) D3 1962

You can follow in the legendary footsteps of giants at Northern Ireland's iconic World Heritage Site. The famous basalt stone columns and fancifully named formations of the Causeway landscape, left by volcanic eruptions 60 million years ago, are great for exploration and are home to more than Finn McCool. Its nooks and crannies are dotted with dainty sea campion, and defensive fulmars protect their rocky cliff nests. Four windswept walking trails wind through this Area of Outstanding Natural Beauty with an all-accessible walk at Runkerry Head and more challenging terrain along the Causeway Coast Way and Ulster Way. The interactive exhibition in the Visitor Centre and innovative audio-guides unlock the secrets of the landscape and regale visitors with legends of giants.

Eating and shopping: light lunches and snacks available in Visitor Centre. Lunch and evening meals in the Causeway Hotel. Gift shop.

Making the most of your day: **Indoors** Interactive exhibition brings the science and stories of the Causeway to life. **Outdoors** Audio-guides (in a range of languages) reveal the many secrets of the landscape. Colour-coded walking trails, including the coastal path which extends 11 miles to Carrick-a-Rede Rope Bridge and a ½-mile all-accessible trail to the viewpoint and picnic area at Runkerry Head. Geology, flora and fauna of international importance. Guided tours available. Range of events and family activities throughout the year. **Dogs**: on leads only.

Access: Visitor Centre
Causeway Hotel Grounds
Parking: on site and park and ride in Bushmills village.

Finding out more: 028 2073 1855 or giantscauseway@nationaltrust.org.uk

Giant's Causeway		M	T	W	T	F	S	S
Stones and coastal path								
Open all year	Dawn–dusk	M	T	W	T	F	S	S
Visitor Centre								
1 Jan–31 Jan	9–5	M	T	W	T	F	S	S
1 Feb–31 Mar	9–6	M	T	W	T	F	S	S
1 Apr–30 Sep	9–7	M	T	W	T	F	S	S
1 Oct–31 Oct	9–6	M	T	W	T	F	S	S
1 Nov–31 Dec	9–5	M	T	W	T	F	S	S

Last admission to Visitor Centre is one hour before closing. Closed 24, 25 and 26 December.

The Visitor Centre at Giant's Causeway, County Antrim

Gray's Printing Press

49 Main Street, Strabane,
County Tyrone BT82 8AU

Map 7 B5 1966

The indelible story of printing is told behind this Georgian shop front in Strabane, once reputed as Ireland's printing capital.

Finding out more: 028 8674 8210 or grays@nationaltrust.org.uk

Mount Stewart

Portaferry Road, Newtownards,
County Down BT22 2AD

Map 7 F6 1976

Voted one of the world's top ten gardens, Mount Stewart reflects a rich tapestry of design and planting artistry bearing the hallmark of its creator. Edith, Lady Londonderry's passion for bold planting schemes, coupled with the mild climate of Strangford Lough, means rare and tender plants from across the globe thrive in this celebrated garden, with the formal gardens exuding a distinct character and appeal. The Londonderry's family home re-opens this April after a three-year £7 million restoration programme. You can see how this transformation has changed the house, including new rooms on show, the opportunity to see internationally significant Lawrence portraits, stunning silver collection and other family treasures. More rooms will be opened throughout the year.

Eating and shopping: locally sourced gifts and crafts sold in our gift shop. Garden shop selling a range of garden tools and plants specially propagated from plants grown in this world-class garden. Award-winning Bay Restaurant.

The garden at Mount Stewart, County Down (below and opposite), has been voted one of the world's top ten

Making the most of your day: **Indoors** You can explore the recently restored family home and discover a wealth of new treasures. Key centenary celebrations, seasonal events and continuing conservation in action. **Outdoors** Why not stroll around the walled garden, discover interesting new walks and join a garden tour? Don't miss the lakeside walk, where the colours and smells vary from season to season. In the formal gardens look out for the creation of a 14-foot-high Irish yew topiary statue depicting a Formorian – a half-human, half-demon associated with Strangford Lough. **Dogs**: welcome on short leads in all areas.

Access: **Building** **Grounds**
Parking: 200 yards.

Finding out more: 028 4278 8387 or mountstewart@nationaltrust.org.uk

Mount Stewart		M	T	W	T	F	S	S
Formal and lakeside gardens, restaurant and shop								
1 Jan–6 Mar	10–4*	**M**	**T**	**W**	**T**	**F**	**S**	**S**
7 Mar–1 Nov	10–5	**M**	**T**	**W**	**T**	**F**	**S**	**S**
2 Nov–31 Dec	10–4*	**M**	**T**	**W**	**T**	**F**	**S**	**S**
House								
3 Apr–1 Nov	11–5	**M**	**T**	**W**	**T**	**F**	**S**	**S**
7 Nov–19 Dec	12–3	·	·	·	·	·	**S**	**S**

Temple of the Winds: open 8 March to 1 November, 2 to 5 (Sundays only). *Restaurant and shop close at 5 on Saturday and Sunday, Bank Holidays and public holidays. House: admission by free-flow with guided tours on selected days. Last admission to garden one hour before closing. Open Bank Holiday Mondays and all other public holidays in Northern Ireland. Formal and lakeside gardens, restaurant and shop closed 25 and 26 December.

Working the forge at Patterson's Spade Mill, County Antrim

Patterson's Spade Mill

751 Antrim Road, Templepatrick, County Antrim BT39 0AP

Map (7) E6 1991

Travel back in time and witness history literally forged in steel at the last working water-driven spade mill in daily use in the British Isles. Dig up the history and culture of the humble spade and visit bygone life fashioning steel into spades during the industrial era.

Eating and shopping: handcrafted spades on sale and made to specification. Tea and coffee available from drinks machine.

Making the most of your day: guided tours and demonstrations for all the family. Ulster Scots event in June. **Dogs**: on leads only.

Access: **Building** **Grounds**
Parking: 50 yards.

Finding out more: 028 9443 3619 or pattersons@nationaltrust.org.uk

Patterson's Spade Mill		M	T	W	T	F	S	S
3 Apr–12 Apr	12–4	**M**	**T**	**W**	**T**	**F**	**S**	**S**
2 May–31 May	12–4	·	·	·	·	·	**S**	**S**
1 Jun–30 Aug	12–4	**M**	**T**	**W**	·	·	**S**	**S**
5 Sep–27 Sep	12–4	·	·	·	·	·	**S**	**S**

Admission by guided tour, last tour one hour before closing. Open Bank Holiday Mondays and all other public holidays in Northern Ireland from 3 April to 27 September.

Rowallane Garden

Saintfield, County Down BT24 7LH

Map (7) E7 1956

Carved into the County Down drumlin landscape since the mid-1860s, this inspirational 21-hectare (52-acre) garden is 'a world apart'. The passion and shared vision of the Reverend John Moore, and later his nephew Hugh Armytage Moore, created a garden where you can leave the outside world behind and immerse yourself in nature's beauty. The formal and informal garden spaces are home to magical features mingled with native and exotic plants, such as drifts of rare rhododendrons. It is a great place for a leisurely walk or just to relax on a seat and soak up the atmosphere.

Eating and shopping: garden café with stunning views across the gardens. Shop offering garden and outdoor products. Second-hand bookshop. Pottery providing unique Rowallane Garden items and garden pots.

Making the most of your day: events, including spring and autumn plant fair, Ghosts and Gourds and Yuletide market. Children's activity sheets. **Dogs**: on leads in garden only.

Access: **Grounds**
Parking: on site.

Finding out more: 028 9751 0131 or rowallane@nationaltrust.org.uk

Rowallane Garden		M	T	W	T	F	S	S
Garden								
1 Jan–28 Feb	10–4	**M**	**T**	**W**	**T**	**F**	**S**	**S**
1 Mar–30 Apr	10–6	**M**	**T**	**W**	**T**	**F**	**S**	**S**
1 May–31 Aug	10–8	**M**	**T**	**W**	**T**	**F**	**S**	**S**
1 Sep–31 Oct	10–6	**M**	**T**	**W**	**T**	**F**	**S**	**S**
1 Nov–31 Dec	10–4	**M**	**T**	**W**	**T**	**F**	**S**	**S**
Café and shop								
3 Jan–28 Feb	11–3:30	·	·	·	·	·	**S**	**S**
1 Mar–5 Apr	11–4	·	·	·	**T**	**F**	**S**	**S**
6 Apr–12 Apr	11–4	**M**	**T**	**W**	**T**	**F**	**S**	**S**
15 Apr–30 Apr	11–4	·	·	**W**	**T**	**F**	**S**	**S**
1 May–30 Aug	11–5	**M**	**T**	**W**	**T**	**F**	**S**	**S**
2 Sep–31 Oct	11–4	·	·	**W**	**T**	**F**	**S**	**S**
1 Nov–27 Dec	11–3:30	·	·	·	·	·	**S**	**S**

Open Bank Holiday Mondays and all other public holidays in Northern Ireland. Closed 25 and 26 December.

Home to native and exotic plants and interspersed with magical features, the formal and informal spaces at Rowallane Garden, County Down, are inspirational

Springhill

20 Springhill Road, Moneymore, Magherafelt, County Londonderry BT45 7NQ

Map (7) C6 1957

Hundreds of years ago the Lenox-Conyngham family chose this bucolic spot to build their home and, after ten generations, this 17th-century 'Plantation' house is still regarded as 'one of the prettiest houses in Ulster'. The welcoming family home they created is brought to life on enlightening guided tours of its portraits, furniture and decorative arts. The old laundry houses Springhill's celebrated Costume Collection of 18th- to 20th-century pieces that capture its enthralling past. There is a new Visitor Centre, a new natural play trail and short walks around the estate that are perfect for a leisurely stroll.

Eating and shopping: takeaway drinks, snacks and ice-cream available from the Visitor Centre. Tea-room serving homemade scones and cakes. Retail area with a range of items for the home and garden. Bookshop with second-hand books for all tastes and interests.

Making the most of your day: events, including Easter Egg trails and country fairs. Walks and new natural play trail.
Dogs: on leads in grounds only.

Access: **Building**
Parking: 50 yards.

Finding out more: 028 8674 8210 or springhill@nationaltrust.org.uk

Springhill		M	T	W	T	F	S	S
Visitor centre								
7 Feb–1 Mar	12–5	·	·	·	·	·	**S**	**S**
16 Feb–17 Feb	12–5	**M**	**T**	·	·	·	·	·
4 Oct–25 Oct	12–4	·	·	·	·	·	·	**S**
Visitor centre, house and costume collection								
14 Mar–29 Mar	12–5	·	·	·	·	·	**S**	**S**
30 Mar–12 Apr	12–5	**M**	**T**	**W**	**T**	**F**	**S**	**S**
18 Apr–26 Apr	12–5	·	·	·	·	·	**S**	**S**
1 May–31 May	12–5	·	·	·	·	**F**	**S**	**S**
4 Jun–28 Jun	12–5	·	·	·	**T**	**F**	**S**	**S**
1 Jul–31 Aug	12–5	**M**	**T**	**W**	**T**	**F**	**S**	**S**
5 Sep–27 Sep	12–5	·	·	·	·	·	**S**	**S**
Grounds								
Open all year	10–5	**M**	**T**	**W**	**T**	**F**	**S**	**S**

House: admission by guided tour, last tour one hour before closing. Open Bank Holiday Mondays and all other public holidays in Northern Ireland. Closed 25, 26, 27 and 28 December. Visitor centre has refreshment area and shop. Servants' Hall tea-room also open at weekends when visitor centre is open.

A 17th-century 'Plantation' home, Springhill in County Londonderry is both welcoming and enthralling

Wellbrook Beetling Mill

20 Wellbrook Road, Corkhill, Cookstown, County Tyrone BT80 9RY

Map (7) C6 1968

You can step back in time and discover how yarn was spun at Northern Ireland's last working water-powered linen beetling mill. Hands-on demonstrations reveal the importance of the linen industry in 19th-century Ireland. The glen is ideal for relaxing walks and perfect for a picnic by the Ballinderry River.

Eating and shopping: tea and coffee available on request. Small cottage shop. Picnic tables near river.

Making the most of your day: **Indoors** Tours of the mill, covering history and linen-making processes. **Outdoors** Walks up to the head-race. **Dogs**: on leads in grounds only.

Access: **Building** **Grounds**
Parking: 10 yards.

Finding out more: 028 8675 1735 or wellbrook@nationaltrust.org.uk

Wellbrook Beetling Mill		M	T	W	T	F	S	S
14 Mar–27 Sep	2–5	·	·	·	·	·	**S**	**S**

Admission by guided tour (last admission one hour before closing). Open Bank Holiday Mondays and all other public holidays in Northern Ireland.

Wellbrook Beetling Mill, County Tyrone: step back in time

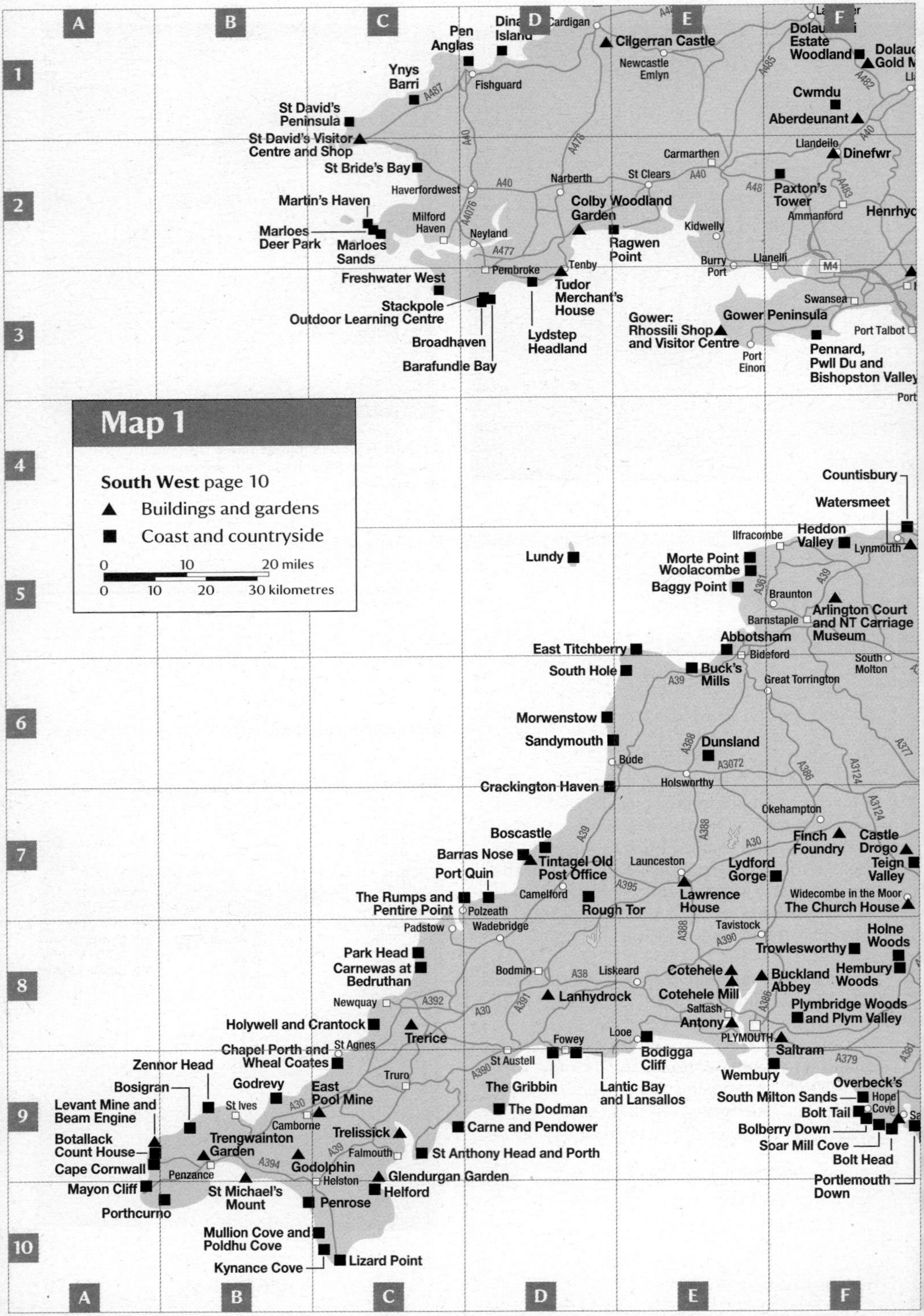
Map 1
South West page 10
Buildings and gardens
Coast and countryside
0 10 20 miles
0 10 20 30 kilometres
A
B
C
D
E
F
1
2
3
4
5
6
7
8
9
10
Pen Anglas
Cardigan
Cilgerran Castle
Newcastle Emlyn
Dolau
Estate Woodland
Gold
Ynys Barri
Fishguard
A487
A485
A482
Cwmdu
Aberdeunant
St David's Peninsula
St David's Visitor Centre and Shop
A40
A478
Llandeilo
Dinefwr
Carmarthen
St Bride's Bay
Haverfordwest
A40
Narberth
St Clears
A40
A48
Paxton's Tower
A483
Martin's Haven
Milford Haven
A4076
Colby Woodland Garden
Kidwelly
Ammanford
Henrhyd
Marloes Deer Park
Marloes Sands
Neyland
A477
Ragwen Point
Burry Port
Llanelli
M4
Pembroke
Tenby
Freshwater West
Tudor Merchant's House
Swansea
Stackpole Outdoor Learning Centre
Gower: Rhossili Shop and Visitor Centre
Gower Peninsula
Port Talbot
Broadhaven
Lydstep Headland
Port Einon
Pennard, Pwll Du and Bishopston Valley
Barafundle Bay
Countisbury
Watersmeet
Ilfracombe
Heddon Valley
Lynmouth
Lundy
Morte Point
Woolacombe
Baggy Point
A361
A39
Braunton
Arlington Court and NT Carriage Museum
Barnstaple
East Titchberry
Abbotsham
Bideford
South Molton
South Hole
Buck's Mills
A39
Great Torrington
Morwenstow
Sandymouth
Dunsland
A388
A3072
A377
A386
A3124
Bude
Crackington Haven
Holsworthy
Okehampton
Boscastle
A39
A388
A30
Finch Foundry
Castle Drogo
Barras Nose
Tintagel Old Post Office
Launceston
Lydford Gorge
Teign Valley
Port Quin
A395
The Rumps and Pentire Point
Polzeath
Camelford
Rough Tor
Lawrence House
Widecombe in the Moor
The Church House
Padstow
Wadebridge
Tavistock
Holne Woods
A388
A390
Trowlesworthy
Park Head
Carnewas at Bedruthan
Bodmin
A38
Liskeard
Cotehele
Buckland Abbey
Hembury Woods
Lanhydrock
Cotehele Mill
Newquay
A392
A30
A391
A386
Plymbridge Woods and Plym Valley
Saltash
Holywell and Crantock
Antony
Trerice
Looe
PLYMOUTH
Saltram
Chapel Porth and Wheal Coates
St Agnes
Fowey
Bodigga Cliff
A379
A381
Zennor Head
St Austell
A390
Wembury
Truro
The Gribbin
Lantic Bay and Lansallos
Overbeck's
Bosigran
Godrevy
East Pool Mine
Hope Cove
South Milton Sands
Levant Mine and Beam Engine
St Ives
A30
The Dodman
Bolt Tail
Camborne
Trelissick
Carne and Pendower
Bolberry Down
Botallack Count House
Trengwainton Garden
A39
Soar Mill Cove
A394
Falmouth
St Anthony Head and Porth
Bolt Head
Cape Cornwall
Godolphin
Penzance
Helston
Glendurgan Garden
Portlemouth Down
Mayon Cliff
St Michael's Mount
Helford
Porthcurno
Penrose
Mullion Cove and Poldhu Cove
Kynance Cove
Lizard Point

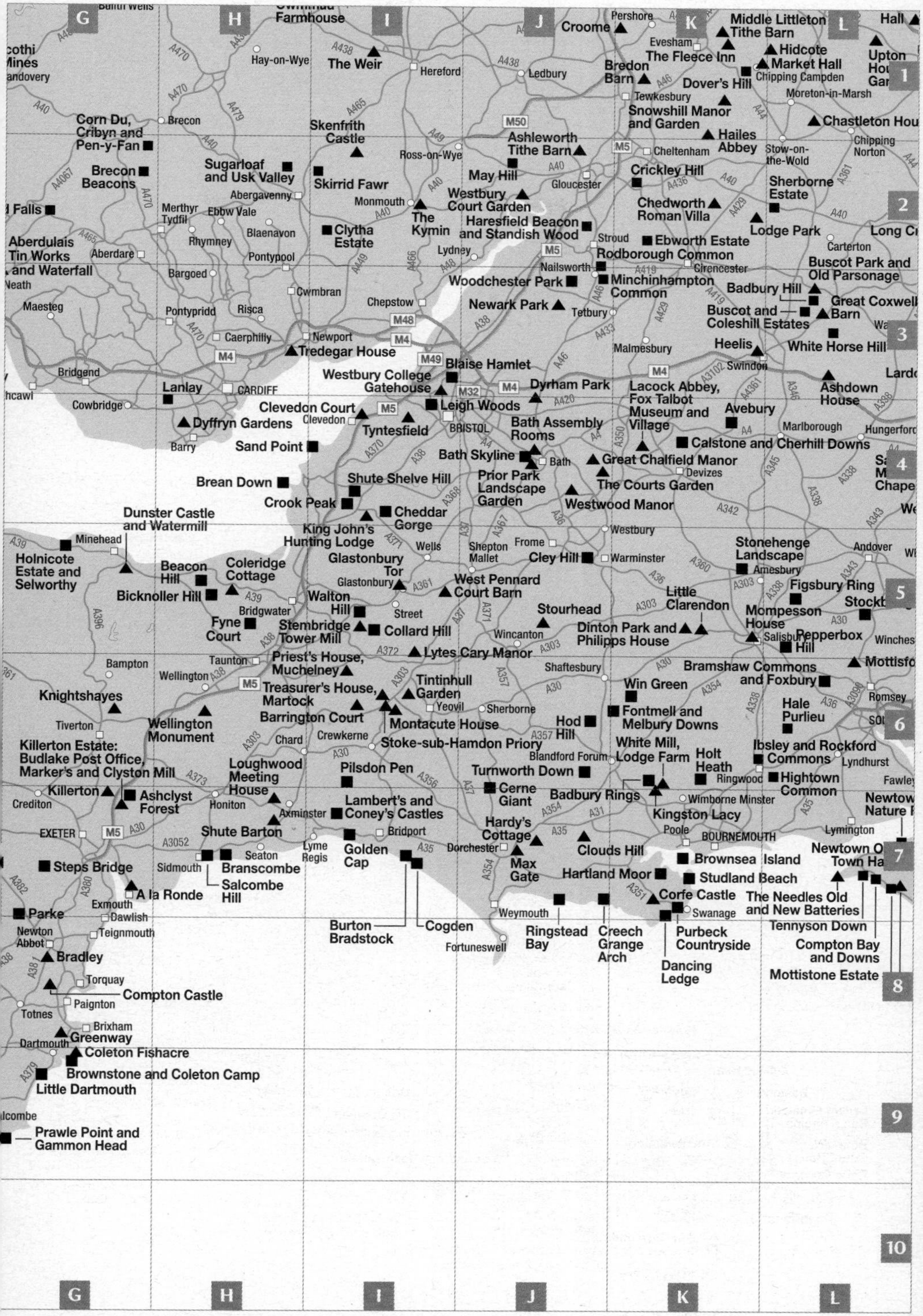

G
H
I
J
K
L
1
2
3
4
5
6
7
8
9
10
Builth Wells
Cwmmau Farmhouse
Croome
Pershore
Middle Littleton Tithe Barn
Hall
Hidcote
Upton House and Garden
Evesham
The Fleece Inn
Market Hall
Chipping Campden
Bredon Barn
Dover's Hill
Moreton-in-Marsh
Tewkesbury
Snowshill Manor and Garden
Chastleton House
Hailes Abbey
Stow-on-the-Wold
Chipping Norton
Cheltenham
Ashleworth Tithe Barn
Dolaucothi Gold Mines
Llandovery
Hay-on-Wye
The Weir
Hereford
Ledbury
Corn Du, Cribyn and Pen-y-Fan
Brecon
Skenfrith Castle
Ross-on-Wye
Brecon Beacons
Sugarloaf and Usk Valley
Skirrid Fawr
May Hill
Gloucester
Crickley Hill
Sherborne Estate
Abergavenny
Westbury Court Garden
Chedworth Roman Villa
Henrhyd Falls
Merthyr Tydfil
Ebbw Vale
Monmouth
The Kymin
Haresfield Beacon and Standish Wood
Lodge Park
Long Crendon
Blaenavon
Clytha Estate
Stroud
Ebworth Estate
Carterton
Aberdulais Tin Works and Waterfall
Aberdare
Rhymney
Pontypool
Lydney
Rodborough Common
Buscot Park and Old Parsonage
Neath
Bargoed
Nailsworth
Minchinhampton Common
Cirencester
Cwmbran
Woodchester Park
Badbury Hill
Great Coxwell Barn
Maesteg
Pontypridd
Risca
Chepstow
Newark Park
Tetbury
Buscot and Coleshill Estates
Caerphilly
Newport
Heelis
White Horse Hill
Tredegar House
Malmesbury
Swindon
Bridgend
Blaise Hamlet
Westbury College Gatehouse
Lanlay
CARDIFF
Dyrham Park
Lacock Abbey, Fox Talbot Museum and Village
Ashdown House
Porthcawl
Cowbridge
Clevedon Court
Leigh Woods
Avebury
Clevedon
Dyffryn Gardens
Tyntesfield
BRISTOL
Bath Assembly Rooms
Marlborough
Hungerford
Barry
Sand Point
Bath Skyline
Calstone and Cherhill Downs
Bath
Great Chalfield Manor
Shute Shelve Hill
Prior Park Landscape Garden
Devizes
Brean Down
The Courts Garden
Crook Peak
Cheddar Gorge
Westwood Manor
Dunster Castle and Watermill
King John's Hunting Lodge
Westbury
Minehead
Wells
Shepton Mallet
Frome
Stonehenge Landscape
Andover
Holnicote Estate and Selworthy
Glastonbury Tor
Cley Hill
Warminster
Amesbury
Beacon Hill
Coleridge Cottage
Glastonbury
West Pennard Court Barn
Figsbury Ring
Bicknoller Hill
Walton Hill
Little Clarendon
Stockbridge Down
Bridgwater
Street
Stourhead
Mompesson House
Fyne Court
Stembridge Tower Mill
Collard Hill
Dinton Park and Philipps House
Pepperbox Hill
Winchester
Wincanton
Salisbury
Taunton
Priest's House, Muchelney
Lytes Cary Manor
Bampton
Wellington
Shaftesbury
Bramshaw Commons and Foxbury
Mottisfont
Treasurer's House, Martock
Tintinhull Garden
Win Green
Romsey
Knightshayes
Yeovil
Sherborne
Fontmell and Melbury Downs
Hale Purlieu
Wellington Monument
Barrington Court
Tiverton
Montacute House
Hod Hill
Southampton
Chard
Crewkerne
Stoke-sub-Hamdon Priory
White Mill, Lodge Farm
Ibsley and Rockford Commons
Killerton Estate: Budlake Post Office, Marker's and Clyston Mill
Blandford Forum
Holt Heath
Lyndhurst
Loughwood Meeting House
Pilsdon Pen
Turnworth Down
Ringwood
Hightown Common
Fawley
Killerton
Ashclyst Forest
Honiton
Cerne Giant
Badbury Rings
Crediton
Lambert's and Coney's Castles
Wimborne Minster
Newtown Nature Reserve
Axminster
Kingston Lacy
Hardy's Cottage
EXETER
Shute Barton
Bridport
Poole
BOURNEMOUTH
Lymington
Lyme Regis
Golden Cap
Dorchester
Clouds Hill
Newtown Old Town Hall
Seaton
Max Gate
Brownsea Island
Steps Bridge
Sidmouth
Branscombe
Hartland Moor
Studland Beach
Salcombe Hill
A la Ronde
Corfe Castle
The Needles Old and New Batteries
Exmouth
Swanage
Parke
Dawlish
Weymouth
Burton Bradstock
Cogden
Ringstead Bay
Creech Grange Arch
Purbeck Countryside
Tennyson Down
Newton Abbot
Teignmouth
Fortuneswell
Compton Bay and Downs
Bradley
Dancing Ledge
Mottistone Estate
Torquay
Compton Castle
Paignton
Totnes
Brixham
Greenway
Dartmouth
Coleton Fishacre
Brownstone and Coleton Camp
Little Dartmouth
Salcombe
Prawle Point and Gammon Head
M4
M5
M32
M48
M49
M50

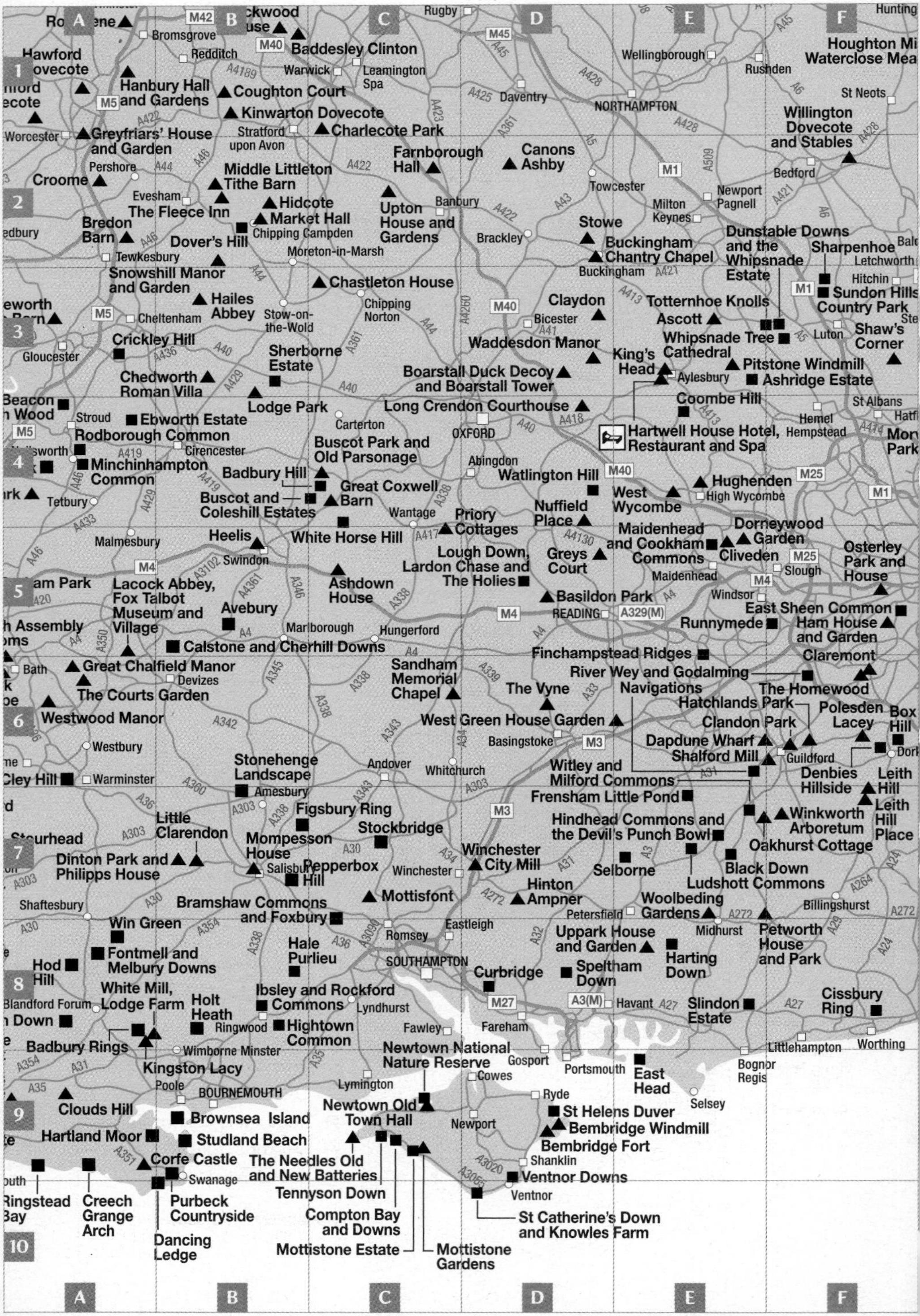

A
B
C
D
E
F
1
2
3
4
5
6
7
8
9
10
M42
M40
M45
M5
M1
M4
M25
M3
M27
A3(M)
A329(M)
Rugby
Hunting
Bromsgrove
Redditch
Baddesley Clinton
Hawford Dovecote
Hanbury Hall and Gardens
Coughton Court
Warwick
Leamington Spa
Wellingborough
Houghton Mi
Waterclose Mea
Rushden
Daventry
NORTHAMPTON
St Neots
Kinwarton Dovecote
Charlecote Park
Greyfriars' House and Garden
Worcester
Stratford upon Avon
Willington Dovecote and Stables
Pershore
Middle Littleton Tithe Barn
Farnborough Hall
Canons Ashby
Bedford
Croome
Evesham
Hidcote
Market Hall
Chipping Campden
Upton House and Gardens
Banbury
Towcester
Milton Keynes
Newport Pagnell
The Fleece Inn
Bredon Barn
Dover's Hill
Tewkesbury
Moreton-in-Marsh
Brackley
Stowe
Buckingham Chantry Chapel
Buckingham
Dunstable Downs and the Whipsnade Estate
Sharpenhoe
Letchworth
Hitchin
Snowshill Manor and Garden
Hailes Abbey
Chastleton House
Chipping Norton
Stow-on-the-Wold
Cheltenham
Claydon
Bicester
Totternhoe Knolls
Ascott
Sundon Hills Country Park
Luton
Shaw's Corner
Gloucester
Crickley Hill
Sherborne Estate
Waddesdon Manor
King's Head
Whipsnade Tree Cathedral
Pitstone Windmill
Ashridge Estate
Chedworth Roman Villa
Boarstall Duck Decoy and Boarstall Tower
Aylesbury
Lodge Park
Long Crendon Courthouse
Coombe Hill
St Albans
Hemel Hempstead
Stroud
Ebworth Estate
Carterton
Rodborough Common
OXFORD
Hartwell House Hotel, Restaurant and Spa
Cirencester
Buscot Park and Old Parsonage
Minchinhampton Common
Abingdon
Watlington Hill
Badbury Hill
Great Coxwell Barn
Tetbury
Buscot and Coleshill Estates
Hughenden
High Wycombe
West Wycombe
Nuffield Place
Priory Cottages
Wantage
Malmesbury
Heelis
White Horse Hill
Dorneywood Garden
Maidenhead and Cookham Commons
Cliveden
Greys Court
Lough Down, Lardon Chase and The Holies
Swindon
Osterley Park and House
Slough
Maidenhead
Windsor
Lacock Abbey, Fox Talbot Museum and Village
Ashdown House
Basildon Park
Avebury
READING
East Sheen Common
Runnymede
Ham House and Garden
Marlborough
Hungerford
Calstone and Cherhill Downs
Finchampstead Ridges
Bath
Great Chalfield Manor
Devizes
Sandham Memorial Chapel
Claremont
River Wey and Godalming Navigations
The Courts Garden
The Vyne
The Homewood
Hatchlands Park
Polesden Lacey
Box Hill
Westwood Manor
West Green House Garden
Clandon Park
Dapdune Wharf
Shalford Mill
Basingstoke
Guildford
Westbury
Stonehenge Landscape
Andover
Whitchurch
Witley and Milford Commons
Denbies Hillside
Leith Hill
Warminster
Amesbury
Frensham Little Pond
Leith Hill Place
Little Clarendon
Figsbury Ring
Winkworth Arboretum
Hindhead Commons and the Devil's Punch Bowl
Stourhead
Stockbridge
Mompesson House
Oakhurst Cottage
Dinton Park and Philipps House
Winchester City Mill
Salisbury
Pepperbox Hill
Winchester
Selborne
Black Down
Ludshott Commons
Hinton Ampner
Mottisfont
Shaftesbury
Bramshaw Commons and Foxbury
Woolbeding Gardens
Billingshurst
Petersfield
Midhurst
Win Green
Eastleigh
Romsey
Uppark House and Garden
Petworth House and Park
Fontmell and Melbury Downs
Hale Purlieu
Harting Down
Hod Hill
SOUTHAMPTON
Speltham Down
Curbridge
White Mill, Lodge Farm
Blandford Forum
Holt Heath
Ibsley and Rockford Commons
Lyndhurst
Havant
Slindon Estate
Cissbury Ring
Ringwood
Hightown Common
Fawley
Fareham
Badbury Rings
Wimborne Minster
Newtown National Nature Reserve
Gosport
Littlehampton
Worthing
Kingston Lacy
Portsmouth
East Head
Bognor Regis
Cowes
Poole
BOURNEMOUTH
Lymington
Ryde
Selsey
Clouds Hill
Newtown Old Town Hall
Brownsea Island
Newport
St Helens Duver
Bembridge Windmill
Hartland Moor
Studland Beach
Bembridge Fort
Corfe Castle
The Needles Old and New Batteries
Shanklin
Swanage
Ventnor Downs
Ventnor
Ringstead Bay
Creech Grange Arch
Purbeck Countryside
Tennyson Down
Compton Bay and Downs
St Catherine's Down and Knowles Farm
Dancing Ledge
Mottistone Estate
Mottistone Gardens

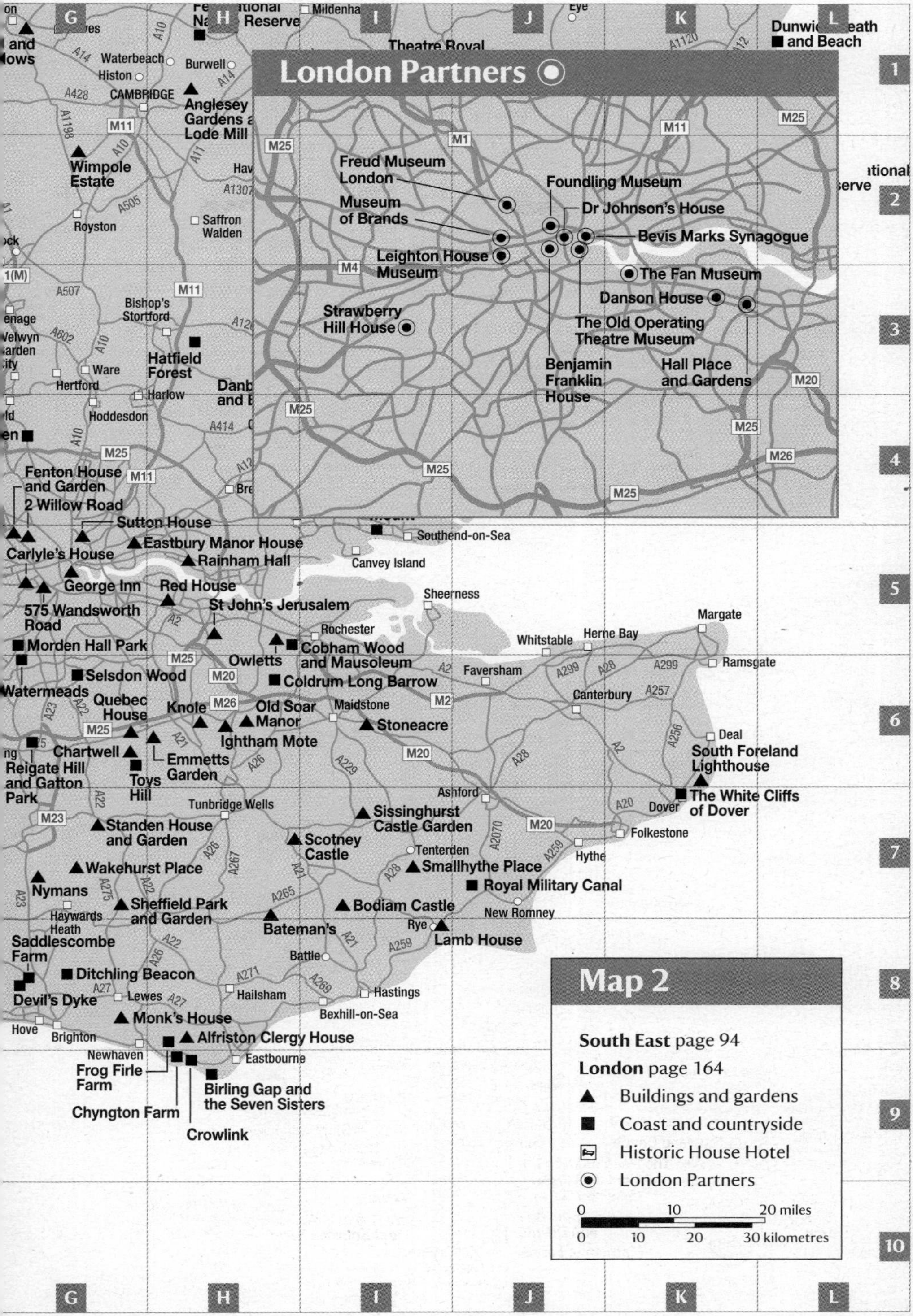
London Partners
Freud Museum London
Museum of Brands
Leighton House Museum
Strawberry Hill House
Foundling Museum
Dr Johnson's House
Bevis Marks Synagogue
The Fan Museum
Danson House
The Old Operating Theatre Museum
Benjamin Franklin House
Hall Place and Gardens
M25
M1
M11
M4
M20
M26
Theatre Royal
Dunwich Heath and Beach
Waterbeach
Histon
Burwell
CAMBRIDGE
Anglesey Abbey Gardens and Lode Mill
Wimpole Estate
Royston
Saffron Walden
Bishop's Stortford
Hatfield Forest
Ware
Hertford
Harlow
Hoddesdon
Fenton House and Garden
2 Willow Road
Sutton House
Eastbury Manor House
Rainham Hall
Carlyle's House
George Inn
Red House
575 Wandsworth Road
St John's Jerusalem
Morden Hall Park
Owletts
Cobham Wood and Mausoleum
Coldrum Long Barrow
Selsdon Wood
Watermeads
Quebec House
Knole
Old Soar Manor
Ightham Mote
Stoneacre
Chartwell
Emmetts Garden
Reigate Hill and Gatton Park
Toys Hill
Southend-on-Sea
Canvey Island
Sheerness
Rochester
Maidstone
Whitstable
Herne Bay
Margate
Faversham
Ramsgate
Canterbury
Deal
South Foreland Lighthouse
The White Cliffs of Dover
Dover
Folkestone
Hythe
Ashford
Tunbridge Wells
Standen House and Garden
Sissinghurst Castle Garden
Scotney Castle
Tenterden
Smallhythe Place
Royal Military Canal
New Romney
Wakehurst Place
Nymans
Haywards Heath
Sheffield Park and Garden
Bateman's
Bodiam Castle
Rye
Lamb House
Saddlescombe Farm
Ditchling Beacon
Devil's Dyke
Battle
Hailsham
Hastings
Bexhill-on-Sea
Lewes
Monk's House
Hove
Brighton
Alfriston Clergy House
Newhaven
Frog Firle Farm
Eastbourne
Birling Gap and the Seven Sisters
Chyngton Farm
Crowlink
Map 2
South East page 94
London page 164
Buildings and gardens
Coast and countryside
Historic House Hotel
London Partners
0 10 20 miles
0 10 20 30 kilometres
G H I J K L
1 2 3 4 5 6 7 8 9 10

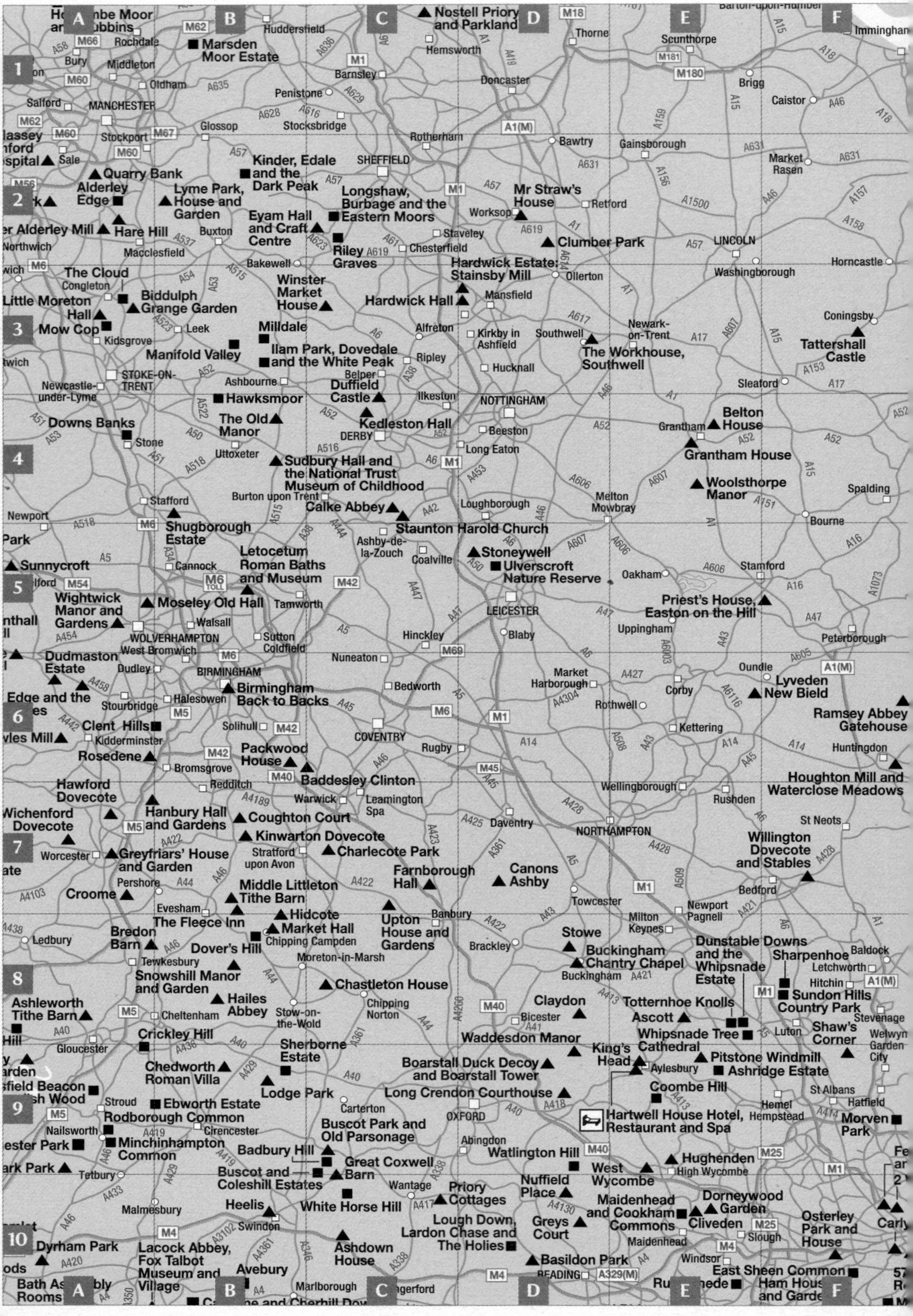
A
B
C
D
E
F
1
2
3
4
5
6
7
8
9
10
Rochdale
Bury
Middleton
Oldham
Salford
MANCHESTER
Stockport
Sale
Marsden Moor Estate
Huddersfield
Nostell Priory and Parkland
Hemsworth
Barnsley
Penistone
Stocksbridge
Glossop
Doncaster
Thorne
Scunthorpe
Brigg
Caistor
Immingham
Rotherham
SHEFFIELD
Bawtry
Gainsborough
Market Rasen
Quarry Bank
Alderley Edge
Lyme Park, House and Garden
Kinder, Edale and the Dark Peak
Longshaw, Burbage and the Eastern Moors
Eyam Hall and Craft Centre
Riley Graves
Mr Straw's House
Worksop
Retford
Alderley Mill
Hare Hill
Buxton
Macclesfield
Northwich
Staveley
Chesterfield
Clumber Park
LINCOLN
Washingborough
Horncastle
Bakewell
The Cloud
Congleton
Biddulph Grange Garden
Little Moreton Hall
Mow Cop
Kidsgrove
Leek
Winster Market House
Hardwick Hall
Hardwick Estate: Stainsby Mill
Ollerton
Mansfield
Milldale
Ilam Park, Dovedale and the White Peak
Manifold Valley
Alfreton
Kirkby in Ashfield
Southwell
The Workhouse, Southwell
Newark-on-Trent
Coningsby
Tattershall Castle
STOKE-ON-TRENT
Newcastle-under-Lyme
Ashbourne
Belper
Ripley
Hucknall
Duffield Castle
Ilkeston
NOTTINGHAM
Sleaford
Hawksmoor
The Old Manor
Kedleston Hall
DERBY
Beeston
Grantham
Belton House
Grantham House
Downs Banks
Stone
Uttoxeter
Long Eaton
Sudbury Hall and the National Trust Museum of Childhood
Woolsthorpe Manor
Melton Mowbray
Spalding
Stafford
Burton upon Trent
Calke Abbey
Loughborough
Bourne
Newport
Shugborough Estate
Staunton Harold Church
Ashby-de-la-Zouch
Coalville
Stoneywell
Ulverscroft Nature Reserve
Oakham
Stamford
Sunnycroft
Cannock
Letocetum Roman Baths and Museum
Wightwick Manor and Gardens
Moseley Old Hall
Tamworth
Walsall
WOLVERHAMPTON
LEICESTER
Priest's House, Easton on the Hill
Uppingham
Hinckley
Blaby
Sutton Coldfield
West Bromwich
Peterborough
Dudmaston Estate
Dudley
BIRMINGHAM
Nuneaton
Market Harborough
Oundle
Lyveden New Bield
Birmingham Back to Backs
Bedworth
Corby
Halesowen
Stourbridge
Rothwell
Clent Hills
Kidderminster
Solihull
COVENTRY
Rugby
Kettering
Ramsey Abbey Gatehouse
Huntingdon
Rosedene
Bromsgrove
Packwood House
Baddesley Clinton
Houghton Mill and Waterclose Meadows
Hawford Dovecote
Redditch
Warwick
Leamington Spa
Wellingborough
Rushden
Wichenford Dovecote
Hanbury Hall and Gardens
Coughton Court
Kinwarton Dovecote
Daventry
NORTHAMPTON
St Neots
Willington Dovecote and Stables
Worcester
Greyfriars' House and Garden
Stratford upon Avon
Charlecote Park
Farnborough Hall
Canons Ashby
Pershore
Croome
Middle Littleton Tithe Barn
Bedford
Evesham
Hidcote
Market Hall
Chipping Campden
Upton House and Gardens
Banbury
Towcester
Milton Keynes
Newport Pagnell
Ledbury
The Fleece Inn
Bredon Barn
Tewkesbury
Dover's Hill
Moreton-in-Marsh
Brackley
Stowe
Buckingham Chantry Chapel
Buckingham
Dunstable Downs and the Whipsnade Estate
Sharpenhoe
Baldock
Letchworth
Hitchin
Snowshill Manor and Garden
Chastleton House
Chipping Norton
Sundon Hills Country Park
Ashleworth Tithe Barn
Cheltenham
Hailes Abbey
Stow-on-the-Wold
Claydon
Totternhoe Knolls
Ascott
Stevenage
Crickley Hill
Bicester
Whipsnade Tree Cathedral
Luton
Shaw's Corner
Welwyn Garden City
Gloucester
Sherborne Estate
Waddesdon Manor
King's Head
Chedworth Roman Villa
Boarstall Duck Decoy and Boarstall Tower
Pitstone Windmill
Aylesbury
Ashridge Estate
Lodge Park
Long Crendon Courthouse
Coombe Hill
St Albans
Hatfield
Stroud
Ebworth Estate
Carterton
Hemel Hempstead
Rodborough Common
OXFORD
Hartwell House Hotel, Restaurant and Spa
Morven Park
Nailsworth
Cirencester
Buscot Park and Old Parsonage
Abingdon
Minchinhampton Common
Badbury Hill
Watlington Hill
Great Coxwell Barn
West Wycombe
Hughenden
High Wycombe
Tetbury
Buscot and Coleshill Estates
Nuffield Place
Dorneywood Garden
Wantage
Priory Cottages
Malmesbury
Heelis
White Horse Hill
Maidenhead and Cookham Commons
Cliveden
Osterley Park and House
Swindon
Lough Down, Lardon Chase and The Holies
Greys Court
Slough
Maidenhead
Dyrham Park
Lacock Abbey, Fox Talbot Museum and Village
Ashdown House
Basildon Park
Windsor
Avebury
East Sheen Common
READING
Ham House and Garden
Marlborough
M62
M66
M60
M67
M56
M18
M1
M181
M180
A1(M)
M6
M54
M6 TOLL
M42
M69
M5
M45
M40
M25
M4
A329(M)

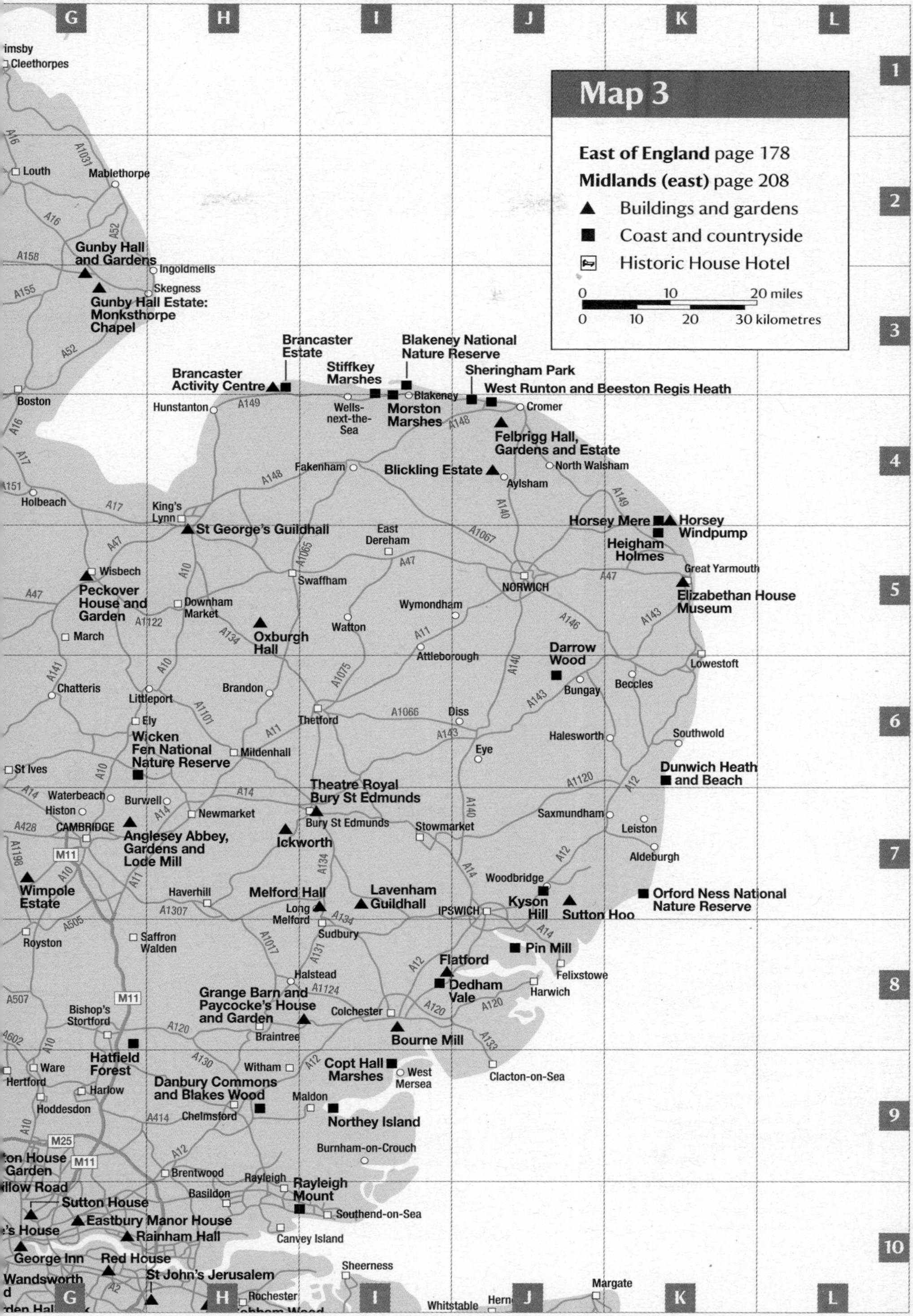

Map 3
East of England page 178
Midlands (east) page 208
Buildings and gardens
Coast and countryside
Historic House Hotel
0 10 20 miles
0 10 20 30 kilometres
G
H
I
J
K
L
1
2
3
4
5
6
7
8
9
10
Cleethorpes
Louth
Mablethorpe
Gunby Hall and Gardens
Ingoldmells
Skegness
Gunby Hall Estate: Monksthorpe Chapel
Boston
Brancaster Estate
Brancaster Activity Centre
Stiffkey Marshes
Blakeney National Nature Reserve
Sheringham Park
West Runton and Beeston Regis Heath
Blakeney
Cromer
Hunstanton
Wells-next-the-Sea
Morston Marshes
Felbrigg Hall, Gardens and Estate
North Walsham
Fakenham
Blickling Estate
Aylsham
Holbeach
King's Lynn
St George's Guildhall
East Dereham
Horsey Mere
Horsey Windpump
Heigham Holmes
Great Yarmouth
Elizabethan House Museum
Wisbech
Swaffham
NORWICH
Peckover House and Garden
Downham Market
Wymondham
March
Oxburgh Hall
Watton
Attleborough
Darrow Wood
Lowestoft
Chatteris
Littleport
Brandon
Bungay
Beccles
Ely
Thetford
Diss
Wicken Fen National Nature Reserve
Mildenhall
Halesworth
Southwold
Eye
St Ives
Dunwich Heath and Beach
Theatre Royal Bury St Edmunds
Waterbeach
Burwell
Histon
Newmarket
Bury St Edmunds
Saxmundham
Leiston
CAMBRIDGE
Anglesey Abbey, Gardens and Lode Mill
Ickworth
Stowmarket
Aldeburgh
Wimpole Estate
Woodbridge
Haverhill
Melford Hall
Lavenham Guildhall
Kyson Hill
Sutton Hoo
Orford Ness National Nature Reserve
Long Melford
IPSWICH
Sudbury
Royston
Saffron Walden
Pin Mill
Flatford
Felixstowe
Halstead
Dedham Vale
Harwich
Grange Barn and Paycocke's House and Garden
Bishop's Stortford
Colchester
Bourne Mill
Braintree
Hatfield Forest
Ware
Witham
Copt Hall Marshes
West Mersea
Clacton-on-Sea
Hertford
Harlow
Danbury Commons and Blakes Wood
Maldon
Hoddesdon
Chelmsford
Northey Island
Burnham-on-Crouch
Brentwood
Rayleigh
Rayleigh Mount
Basildon
Sutton House
Southend-on-Sea
Eastbury Manor House
Rainham Hall
Canvey Island
George Inn
Red House
Sheerness
St John's Jerusalem
Wandsworth
Rochester
Margate
Whitstable
A16
A1031
A52
A158
A155
A149
A148
A17
A47
A10
A1065
A1067
A140
A146
A143
A1122
A134
A11
A1075
A141
A1101
A1066
A12
A1120
A14
A428
A1198
M11
A505
A1307
A1017
A131
A1124
A120
A133
A507
A602
A130
A414
M25
A2

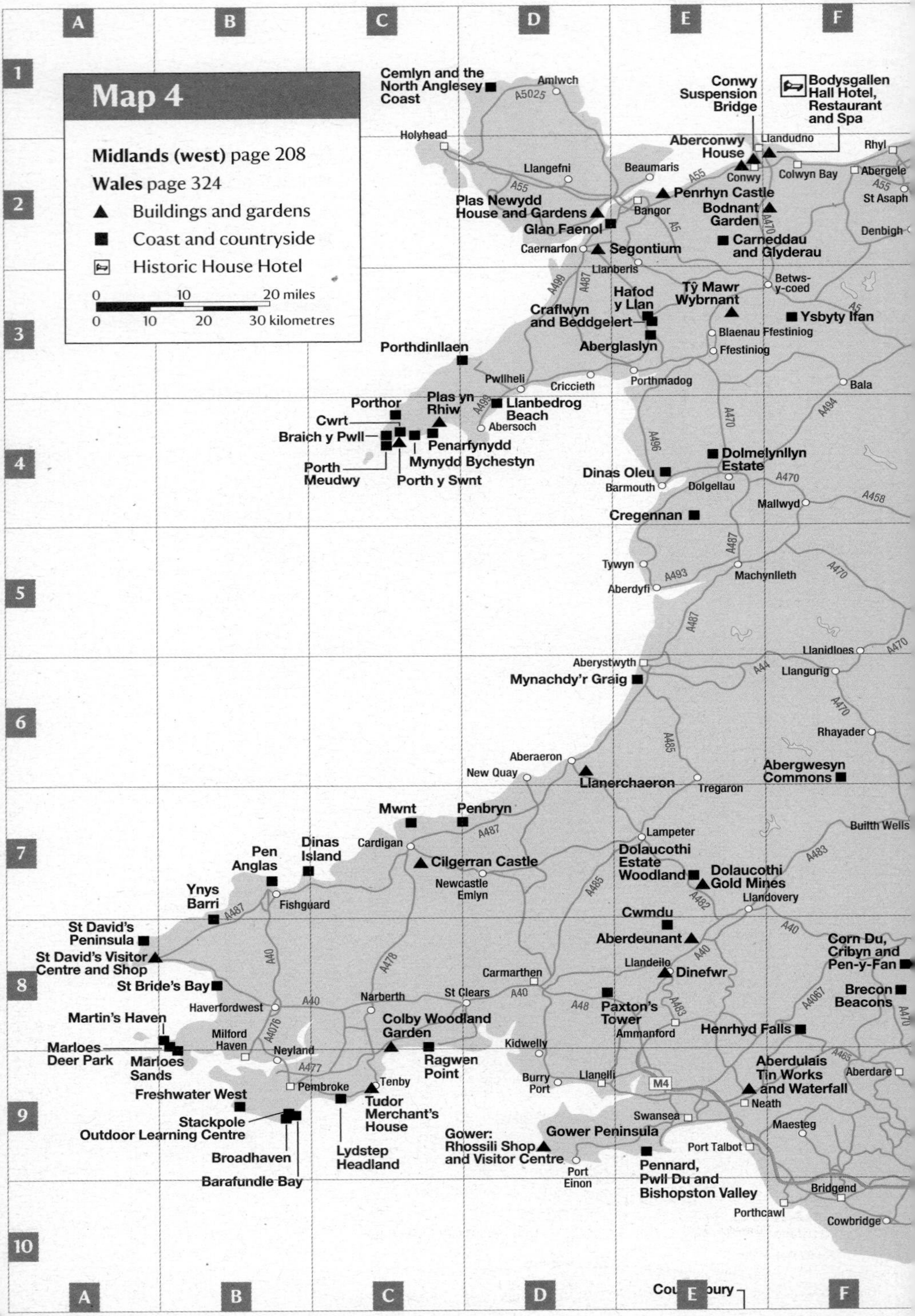

Map 4
Midlands (west) page 208
Wales page 324
Buildings and gardens
Coast and countryside
Historic House Hotel
0 10 20 miles
0 10 20 30 kilometres
A B C D E F
1 2 3 4 5 6 7 8 9 10
Cemlyn and the North Anglesey Coast
Amlwch
A5025
Holyhead
Llangefni
Beaumaris
A55
Conwy Suspension Bridge
Bodysgallen Hall Hotel, Restaurant and Spa
Aberconwy House
Llandudno
Rhyl
Conwy
Colwyn Bay
Abergele
St Asaph
Penrhyn Castle
Plas Newydd House and Gardens
Bangor
Bodnant Garden
A470
Glan Faenol
A5
Denbigh
Carneddau and Glyderau
Caernarfon
Segontium
Llanberis
A499
A487
Hafod y Llan
Tŷ Mawr Wybrnant
Betws-y-coed
Craflwyn and Beddgelert
Ysbyty Ifan
Blaenau Ffestiniog
Aberglaslyn
Ffestiniog
Porthdinllaen
Pwllheli
Criccieth
Porthmadog
Bala
Porthor
Plas yn Rhiw
A499
Llanbedrog Beach
Cwrt
Abersoch
A494
Braich y Pwll
Penarfynydd
A496
Mynydd Bychestyn
Porth Meudwy
Porth y Swnt
Dolmelynllyn Estate
Dinas Oleu
Barmouth
Dolgellau
A470
Mallwyd
A458
Cregennan
A487
Tywyn
A493
Aberdyfi
Machynlleth
A470
A487
Llanidloes
A470
Aberystwyth
A44
Llangurig
Mynachdy'r Graig
A470
A485
Rhayader
Aberaeron
New Quay
Llanerchaeron
Tregaron
Abergwesyn Commons
Mwnt
Penbryn
A487
Builth Wells
Lampeter
Cardigan
Dinas Island
Pen Anglas
Cilgerran Castle
Dolaucothi Estate Woodland
Dolaucothi Gold Mines
A483
Newcastle Emlyn
A485
Ynys Barri
Fishguard
A482
Llandovery
A487
Cwmdu
St David's Peninsula
Aberdeunant
A40
Corn Du, Cribyn and Pen-y-Fan
St David's Visitor Centre and Shop
A40
A478
Llandeilo
Dinefwr
Carmarthen
St Bride's Bay
Brecon Beacons
Narberth
St Clears
A40
Paxton's Tower
A4067
Haverfordwest
A40
A48
A483
A470
Martin's Haven
Milford Haven
A4076
Colby Woodland Garden
Ammanford
Henrhyd Falls
Marloes Deer Park
Neyland
Kidwelly
Marloes Sands
A477
Ragwen Point
Aberdulais Tin Works and Waterfall
A465
Aberdare
Tenby
Burry Port
Llanelli
M4
Pembroke
Freshwater West
Tudor Merchant's House
Neath
Stackpole Outdoor Learning Centre
Swansea
Gower Peninsula
Maesteg
Gower: Rhossili Shop and Visitor Centre
Port Talbot
Broadhaven
Lydstep Headland
Pennard, Pwll Du and Bishopston Valley
Port Einon
Barafundle Bay
Bridgend
Porthcawl
Cowbridge
Cou[E]bury

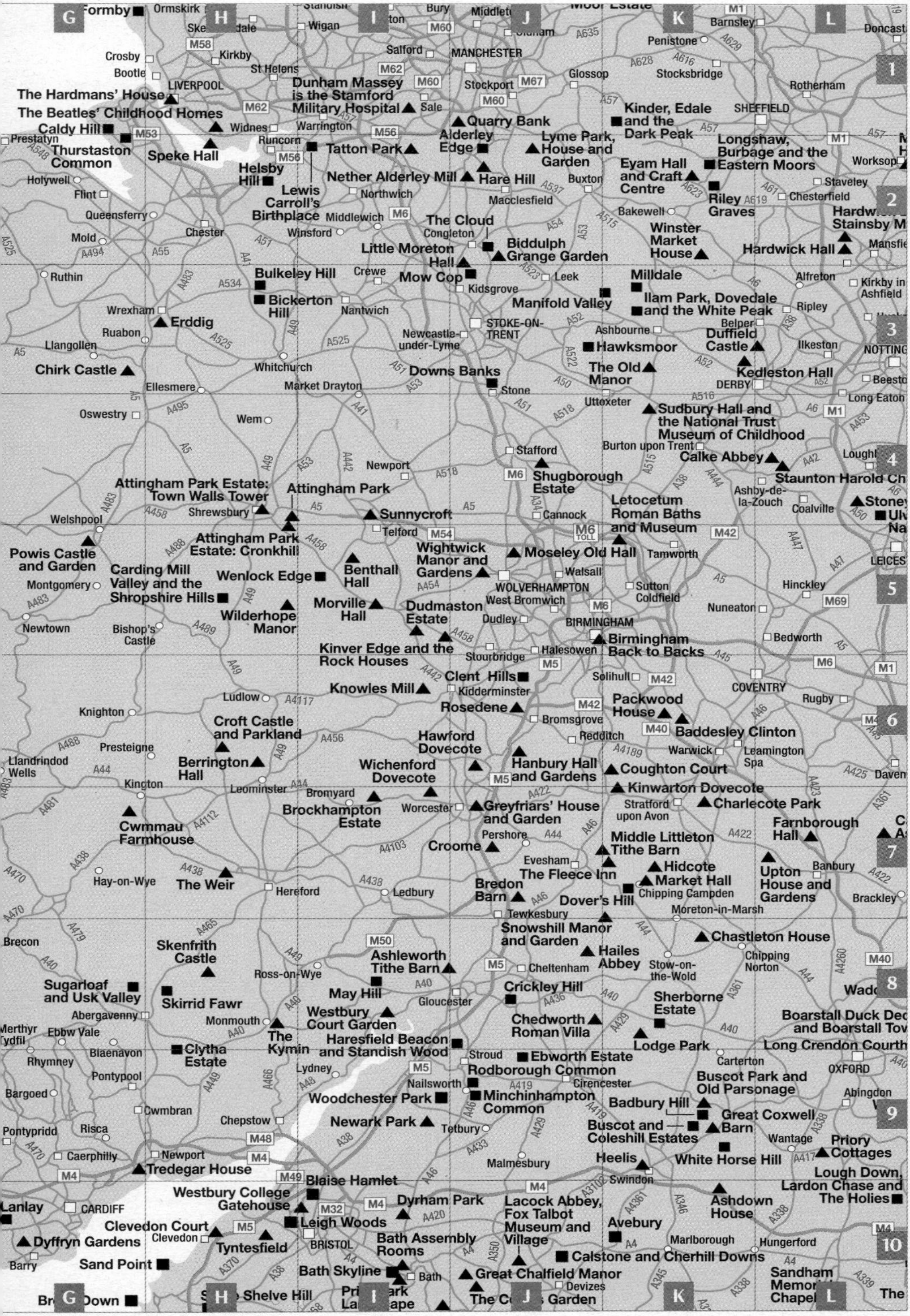

G
H
I
J
K
L
Formby
Ormskirk
Wigan
Bury
Middleton
Barnsley
Doncaster
M60
M1
A635
Penistone
A629
Crosby
Kirkby
M58
Salford
MANCHESTER
A628
A616
Stocksbridge
1
Bootle
St Helens
M62
LIVERPOOL
Dunham Massey is the Stamford Military Hospital
M60
Stockport
M67
Glossop
Rotherham
The Hardmans' House
M60
Sale
A57
Kinder, Edale and the Dark Peak
SHEFFIELD
The Beatles' Childhood Homes
M62
Quarry Bank
Caldy Hill
Widnes
Warrington
Prestatyn
M53
Runcorn
M56
Alderley Edge
Lyme Park, House and Garden
A57
Longshaw, Burbage and the Eastern Moors
M1
Thurstaston Common
Speke Hall
Tatton Park
Worksop
A548
M56
Helsby Hill
Eyam Hall and Craft Centre
Holywell
Nether Alderley Mill
Hare Hill
Buxton
Staveley
Lewis Carroll's Birthplace
Northwich
A537
A623
A61
Riley Graves
A619
Chesterfield
2
Flint
Macclesfield
Queensferry
Middlewich
M6
The Cloud
Bakewell
A515
Chester
Winsford
Congleton
A54
A53
Winster Market House
Mold
A51
Biddulph Grange Garden
Hardwick Hall
Mansfield
A525
A494
A55
Little Moreton Hall
A41
A523
Ruthin
Bulkeley Hill
Crewe
Mow Cop
Leek
Milldale
Alfreton
Kirkby in Ashfield
A483
A534
Kidsgrove
A6
Bickerton Hill
Manifold Valley
Ilam Park, Dovedale and the White Peak
Ripley
Wrexham
Erddig
Nantwich
A49
STOKE-ON-TRENT
A52
Belper
A38
Ruabon
A525
A525
Newcastle-under-Lyme
Ashbourne
Duffield Castle
3
Llangollen
Hawksmoor
Ilkeston
NOTTINGHAM
A5
A522
Chirk Castle
Whitchurch
A51
Downs Banks
The Old Manor
A52
Kedleston Hall
Ellesmere
Market Drayton
A53
A50
DERBY
Beeston
A52
A5
A41
Stone
A516
Long Eaton
A495
A51
Uttoxeter
A518
Sudbury Hall and the National Trust Museum of Childhood
A6
M1
Oswestry
A453
Wem
A5
A442
Stafford
Burton upon Trent
Calke Abbey
A515
Loughborough
4
A49
A53
Newport
A518
M6
Shugborough Estate
A38
A444
A42
Attingham Park Estate: Town Walls Tower
Attingham Park
Staunton Harold Church
Ashby-de-la-Zouch
A483
A34
Letocetum Roman Baths and Museum
Stoney
Coalville
A458
Shrewsbury
A5
A5
A50
Ulverscroft Nature Reserve
Welshpool
Sunnycroft
Cannock
A6
Telford
M54
M6 TOLL
M42
A447
Powis Castle and Garden
Attingham Park Estate: Cronkhill
A488
A458
Wightwick Manor and Gardens
Moseley Old Hall
Tamworth
LEICESTER
Carding Mill Valley and the Shropshire Hills
Wenlock Edge
Benthall Hall
Walsall
A47
Montgomery
A454
WOLVERHAMPTON
Sutton Coldfield
A5
Hinckley
5
A483
A49
West Bromwich
M6
Morville Hall
Dudmaston Estate
Nuneaton
M69
Wilderhope Manor
Dudley
Newtown
Bishop's Castle
A489
BIRMINGHAM
A458
Birmingham Back to Backs
Bedworth
Kinver Edge and the Rock Houses
A5
A49
Stourbridge
Halesowen
A45
M5
M6
A442
Clent Hills
Solihull
M42
M1
COVENTRY
Knowles Mill
Ludlow
A4117
Kidderminster
M42
Packwood House
Rugby
Knighton
Rosedene
A46
6
Croft Castle and Parkland
Bromsgrove
M40
Baddesley Clinton
M45
A456
A488
Hawford Dovecote
Redditch
Presteigne
A49
A4189
Warwick
Leamington Spa
Llandrindod Wells
Berrington Hall
Wichenford Dovecote
Hanbury Hall and Gardens
Coughton Court
A44
M5
A425
Daventry
A483
Kington
Leominster
A44
Kinwarton Dovecote
A423
Bromyard
A422
A361
A481
Worcester
Greyfriars' House and Garden
Stratford upon Avon
Charlecote Park
Brockhampton Estate
A4112
Farnborough Hall
Cwmmau Farmhouse
Pershore
A44
A46
Middle Littleton Tithe Barn
A422
A4103
Croome
7
A438
A438
Evesham
Hidcote
Banbury
A470
Hay-on-Wye
The Weir
The Fleece Inn
Market Hall
Upton House and Gardens
A422
A438
Bredon Barn
Chipping Campden
Hereford
Ledbury
A46
Dover's Hill
Brackley
A470
Tewkesbury
Moreton-in-Marsh
A479
A465
Snowshill Manor and Garden
A44
Chastleton House
Brecon
Skenfrith Castle
M50
Chipping Norton
A4260
A49
Ashleworth Tithe Barn
Hailes Abbey
Stow-on-the-Wold
M40
A40
M5
Cheltenham
A361
A44
Sugarloaf and Usk Valley
Skirrid Fawr
Ross-on-Wye
A40
Crickley Hill
Waddesdon
8
May Hill
Gloucester
A436
A40
Sherborne Estate
Abergavenny
A48
Westbury Court Garden
Boarstall Duck Decoy and Boarstall Tower
Merthyr Tydfil
Ebbw Vale
Monmouth
The Kymin
Chedworth Roman Villa
A429
A40
A40
Haresfield Beacon and Standish Wood
Lodge Park
Long Crendon Courthouse
Clytha Estate
Blaenavon
Rhymney
Stroud
Ebworth Estate
Carterton
A40
A449
A466
Lydney
M5
Rodborough Common
OXFORD
Pontypool
A48
Nailsworth
A419
Cirencester
Buscot Park and Old Parsonage
Bargoed
Woodchester Park
Minchinhampton Common
Badbury Hill
Abingdon
Cwmbran
A46
A419
Great Coxwell Barn
9
Chepstow
Newark Park
A429
Buscot and Coleshill Estates
Pontypridd
Risca
Tetbury
A338
Wantage
Priory Cottages
A470
M48
A38
A433
Newport
Caerphilly
M4
Heelis
White Horse Hill
A417
Tredegar House
Malmesbury
Lough Down, Lardon Chase and The Holies
M4
M49
Blaise Hamlet
A46
M4
Swindon
A3102
Westbury College Gatehouse
Dyrham Park
Lacock Abbey, Fox Talbot Museum and Village
A4361
A346
Ashdown House
Lanlay
CARDIFF
M32
M4
A420
A338
Clevedon Court
M5
Leigh Woods
Avebury
M4
Dyffryn Gardens
Clevedon
Tyntesfield
BRISTOL
Bath Assembly Rooms
A350
A4
Marlborough
Hungerford
10
Sand Point
A370
A4
Calstone and Cherhill Downs
A4
Barry
A38
Bath Skyline
Bath
Great Chalfield Manor
Devizes
A345
A338
Sandham Memorial Chapel
A339
Shelve Hill
Prior Park Landscape
The Courts Garden

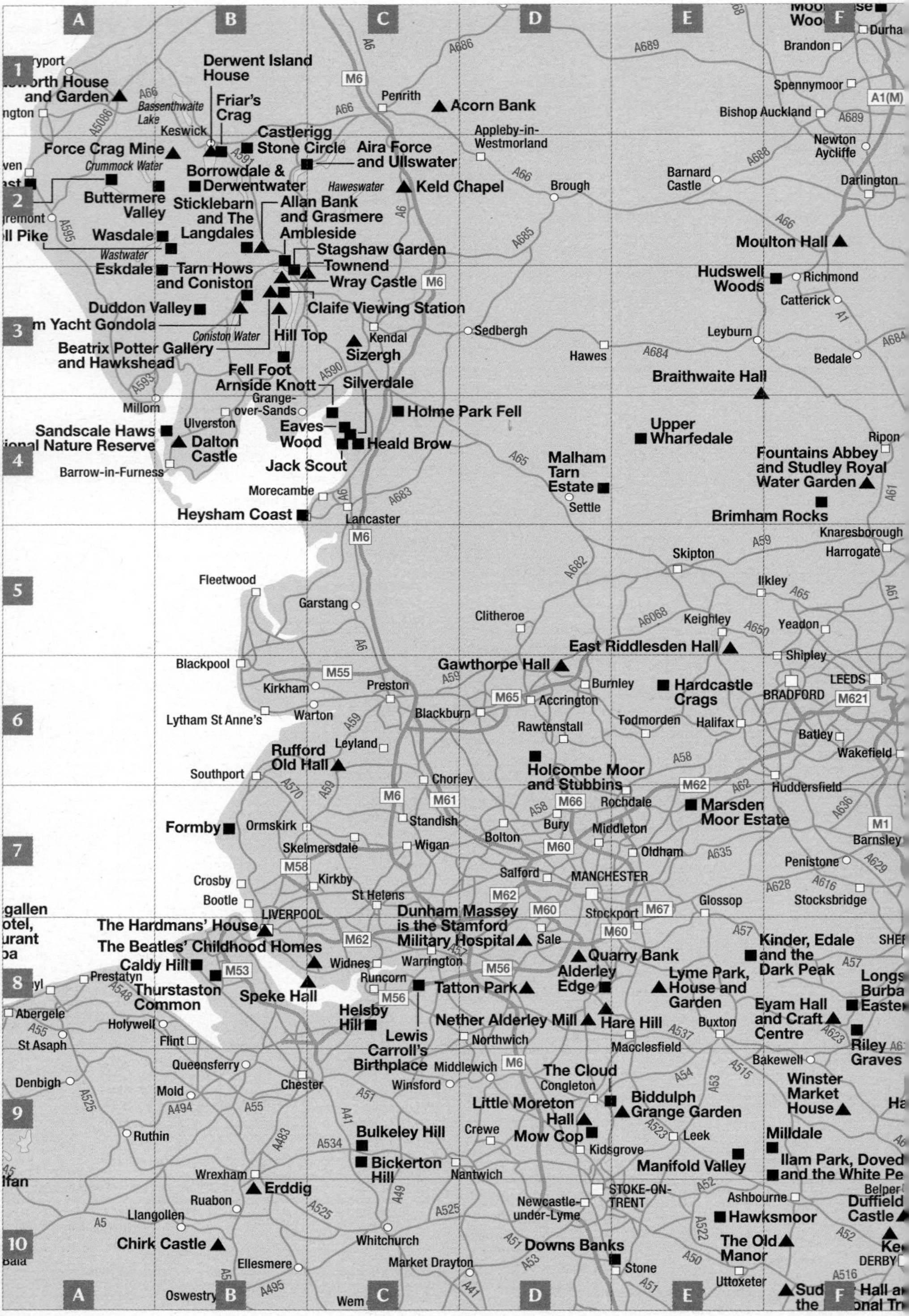

A
B
C
D
E
F
1
2
3
4
5
6
7
8
9
10
Derwent Island House
and Garden
Bassenthwaite Lake
Friar's Crag
Keswick
Castlerigg Stone Circle
Force Crag Mine
Crummock Water
Borrowdale & Derwentwater
Aira Force and Ullswater
Haweswater
Keld Chapel
Buttermere Valley
Sticklebarn and The Langdales
Allan Bank and Grasmere
Ambleside
Wasdale
Wastwater
Eskdale
Tarn Hows and Coniston
Stagshaw Garden
Townend
Wray Castle
Duddon Valley
Claife Viewing Station
Yacht Gondola
Coniston Water
Hill Top
Beatrix Potter Gallery and Hawkshead
Sizergh
Kendal
Fell Foot
Arnside Knott
Silverdale
Grange-over-Sands
Millom
Ulverston
Sandscale Haws
Dalton Castle
Eaves Wood
Heald Brow
Holme Park Fell
Jack Scout
Barrow-in-Furness
Morecambe
Heysham Coast
Lancaster
Penrith
Acorn Bank
Appleby-in-Westmorland
Brough
Sedbergh
Hawes
Malham Tarn Estate
Settle
Upper Wharfedale
Braithwaite Hall
Brandon
Spennymoor
Bishop Auckland
Newton Aycliffe
Barnard Castle
Darlington
Moulton Hall
Hudswell Woods
Richmond
Catterick
Leyburn
Bedale
Ripon
Fountains Abbey and Studley Royal Water Garden
Brimham Rocks
Knaresborough
Harrogate
Skipton
Ilkley
Keighley
Yeadon
Shipley
East Riddlesden Hall
Fleetwood
Garstang
Clitheroe
Blackpool
Kirkham
Preston
Gawthorpe Hall
Burnley
Hardcastle Crags
LEEDS
BRADFORD
Lytham St Anne's
Warton
Blackburn
Accrington
Rawtenstall
Todmorden
Halifax
Batley
Wakefield
Leyland
Rufford Old Hall
Southport
Chorley
Holcombe Moor and Stubbins
Huddersfield
Formby
Ormskirk
Standish
Bolton
Bury
Rochdale
Middleton
Marsden Moor Estate
Skelmersdale
Wigan
Oldham
Barnsley
Penistone
Crosby
Kirkby
Salford
MANCHESTER
Bootle
St Helens
Stockport
Glossop
Stocksbridge
LIVERPOOL
The Hardmans' House
The Beatles' Childhood Homes
Dunham Massey is the Stamford Military Hospital
Sale
Quarry Bank
Kinder, Edale and the Dark Peak
Caldy Hill
Widnes
Warrington
Alderley Edge
Lyme Park, House and Garden
Prestatyn
Thurstaston Common
Speke Hall
Runcorn
Tatton Park
Abergele
Helsby Hill
Eyam Hall and Craft Centre
Holywell
Lewis Carroll's Birthplace
Nether Alderley Mill
Hare Hill
Buxton
Flint
St Asaph
Northwich
Macclesfield
Riley Graves
Queensferry
Middlewich
The Cloud
Bakewell
Denbigh
Chester
Winsford
Congleton
Winster Market House
Mold
Little Moreton Hall
Biddulph Grange Garden
Ruthin
Crewe
Mow Cop
Leek
Bulkeley Hill
Kidsgrove
Milldale
Bickerton Hill
Manifold Valley
Ilam Park, Dovedale and the White Peak
Wrexham
Nantwich
STOKE-ON-TRENT
Erddig
Ashbourne
Ruabon
Newcastle-under-Lyme
Hawksmoor
Llangollen
The Old Manor
Whitchurch
Chirk Castle
Downs Banks
Ellesmere
Market Drayton
Stone
Oswestry
Uttoxeter
Wem
DERBY
M6
M55
M65
M61
M62
M66
M60
M58
M67
M56
M53
M621
M1
A1(M)
A66
A595
A591
A590
A593
A6
A686
A689
A688
A685
A684
A1
A65
A683
A682
A59
A6068
A650
A61
A58
A570
A62
A636
A635
A629
A628
A616
A57
A548
A55
A537
A623
A525
A494
A483
A41
A534
A54
A53
A515
A523
A52
A49
A5
A495
A51
A50
A522
A516

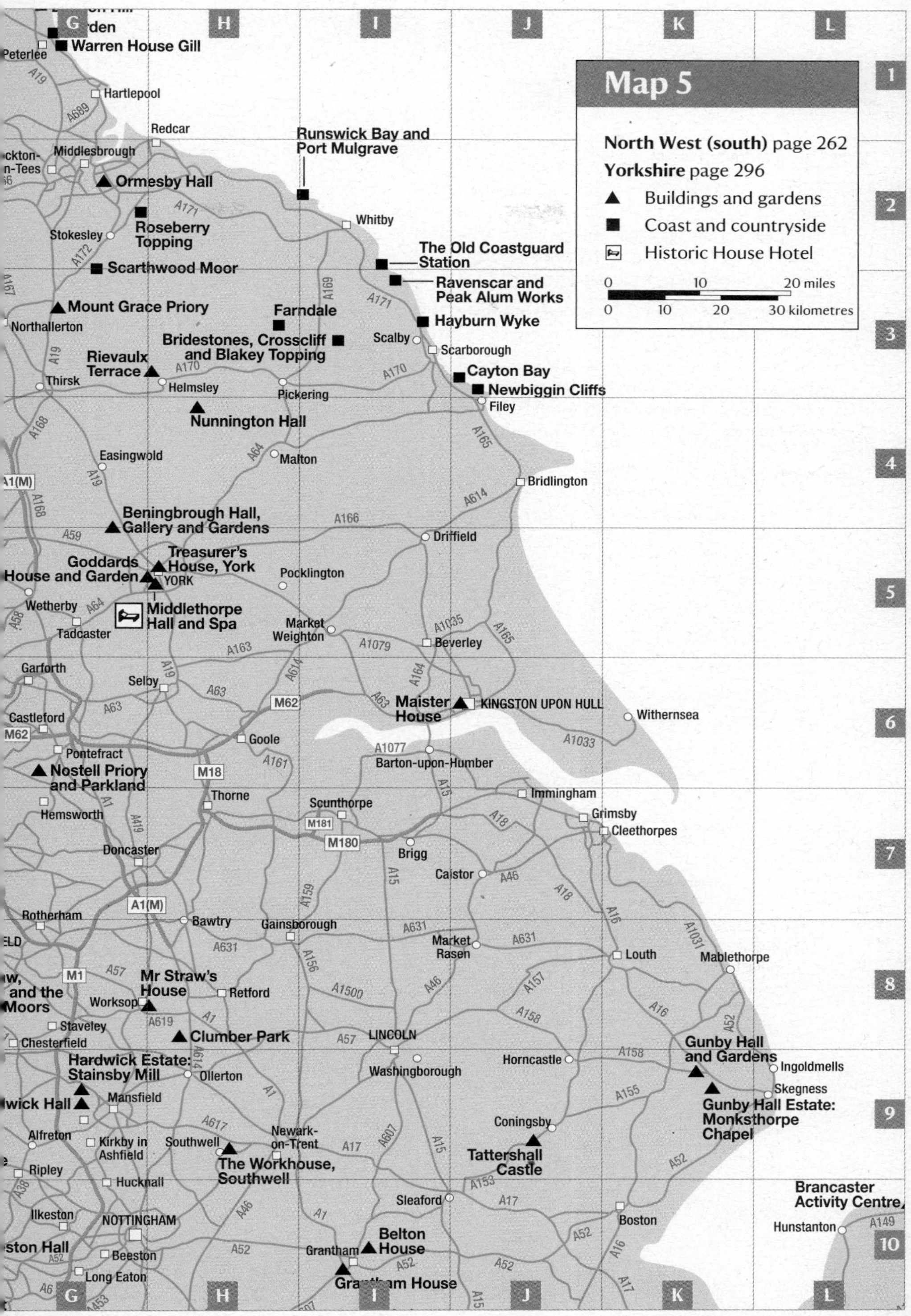

Map 5
North West (south) page 262
Yorkshire page 296
Buildings and gardens
Coast and countryside
Historic House Hotel
0 10 20 miles
0 10 20 30 kilometres
G
H
I
J
K
L
1
2
3
4
5
6
7
8
9
10
Warren House Gill
Peterlee
Hartlepool
Redcar
Middlesbrough
Ormesby Hall
Roseberry Topping
Stokesley
Scarthwood Moor
Mount Grace Priory
Northallerton
Runswick Bay and Port Mulgrave
Whitby
The Old Coastguard Station
Ravenscar and Peak Alum Works
Hayburn Wyke
Farndale
Bridestones, Crosscliff and Blakey Topping
Scalby
Scarborough
Rievaulx Terrace
Thirsk
Helmsley
Pickering
Cayton Bay
Newbiggin Cliffs
Filey
Nunnington Hall
Easingwold
Malton
Bridlington
Beningbrough Hall, Gallery and Gardens
Driffield
Treasurer's House, York
Goddards House and Garden
YORK
Pocklington
Wetherby
Middlethorpe Hall and Spa
Tadcaster
Market Weighton
Beverley
Garforth
Selby
Maister House
KINGSTON UPON HULL
Withernsea
Castleford
Goole
Pontefract
Barton-upon-Humber
Nostell Priory and Parkland
Thorne
Immingham
Hemsworth
Scunthorpe
Grimsby
Cleethorpes
Doncaster
Brigg
Caistor
Rotherham
Bawtry
Gainsborough
Market Rasen
Louth
Mablethorpe
Mr Straw's House
Retford
Worksop
Staveley
Clumber Park
Chesterfield
LINCOLN
Hardwick Estate: Stainsby Mill
Ollerton
Washingborough
Horncastle
Gunby Hall and Gardens
Ingoldmells
Skegness
Mansfield
Gunby Hall Estate: Monksthorpe Chapel
Coningsby
Alfreton
Kirkby in Ashfield
Southwell
Newark-on-Trent
Tattershall Castle
Ripley
The Workhouse, Southwell
Hucknall
Sleaford
Brancaster Activity Centre
Ilkeston
NOTTINGHAM
Boston
Hunstanton
Beeston
Grantham
Belton House
Long Eaton
Grantham House
A19
A689
A171
A172
A169
A170
A168
A64
A165
A614
A166
A59
A1(M)
A1079
A1035
A163
A63
M62
A164
A1033
A1077
A161
M18
A15
A18
A1
M181
M180
A159
A46
A16
A1031
A631
A156
A57
A1500
A157
A158
M1
A619
A614
A52
A617
A155
A17
A607
A153
A149
A6
A453

the National Trust
for Scotland

a place for everyone

Members of the National Trust are also admitted free of charge to properties of the National Trust for Scotland (NTS), a separate charity with similar responsibilities.

NTS properties include the famous Inverewe Garden, Bannockburn, Culloden and Robert Adam's masterpiece, Culzean Castle.

Full details are contained in *The National Trust for Scotland Guide to Properties*, which can be obtained by contacting the NTS Customer Service Centre, telephone 0131 458 0200. Information is also available on the Internet at **www.nts.org.uk**

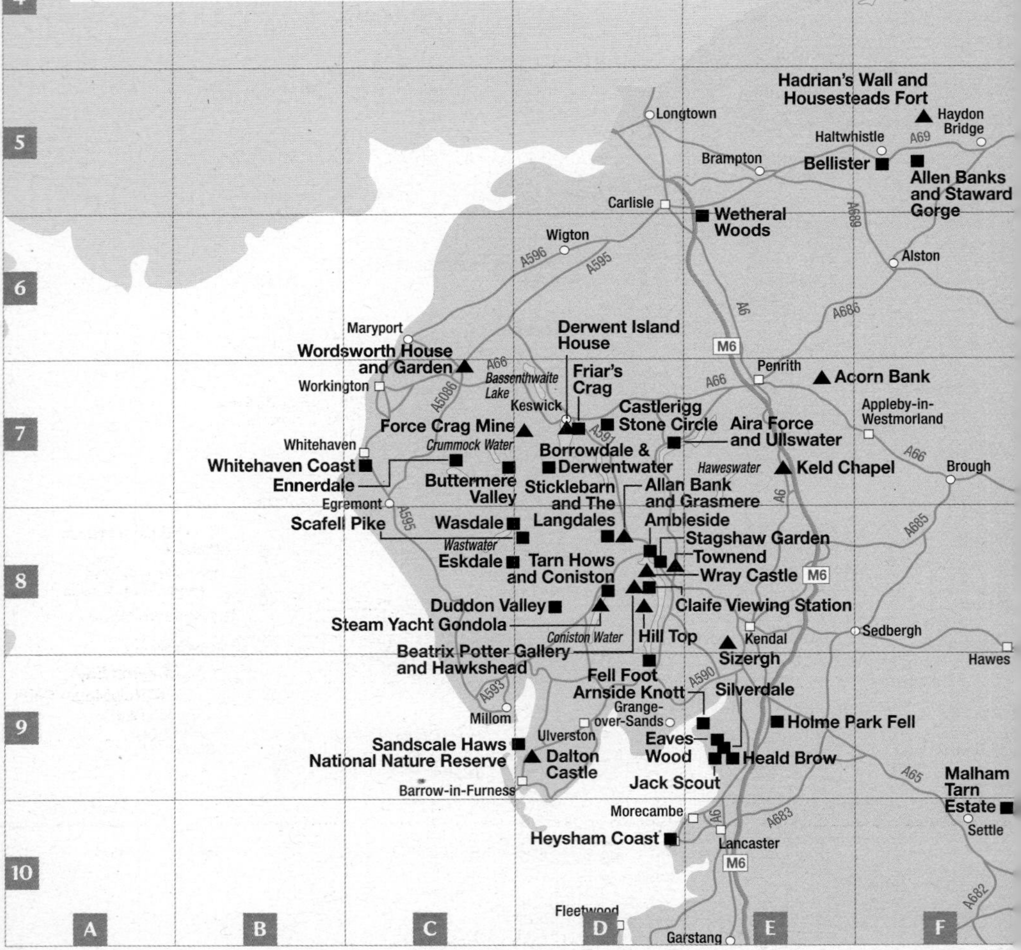

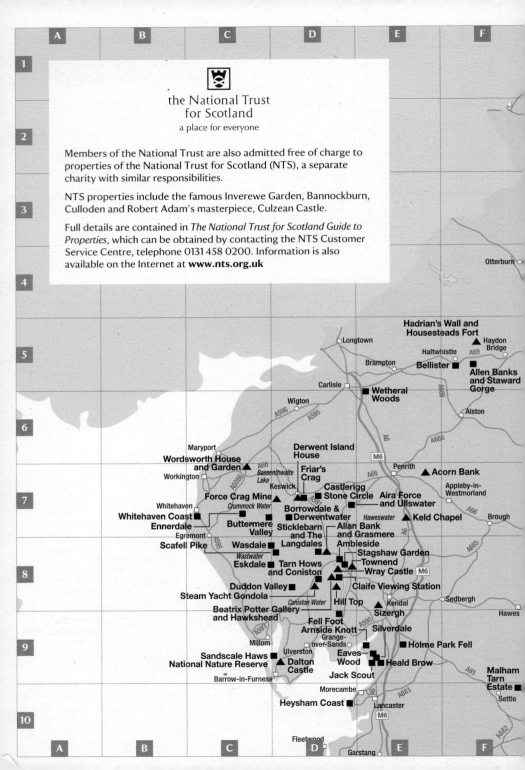

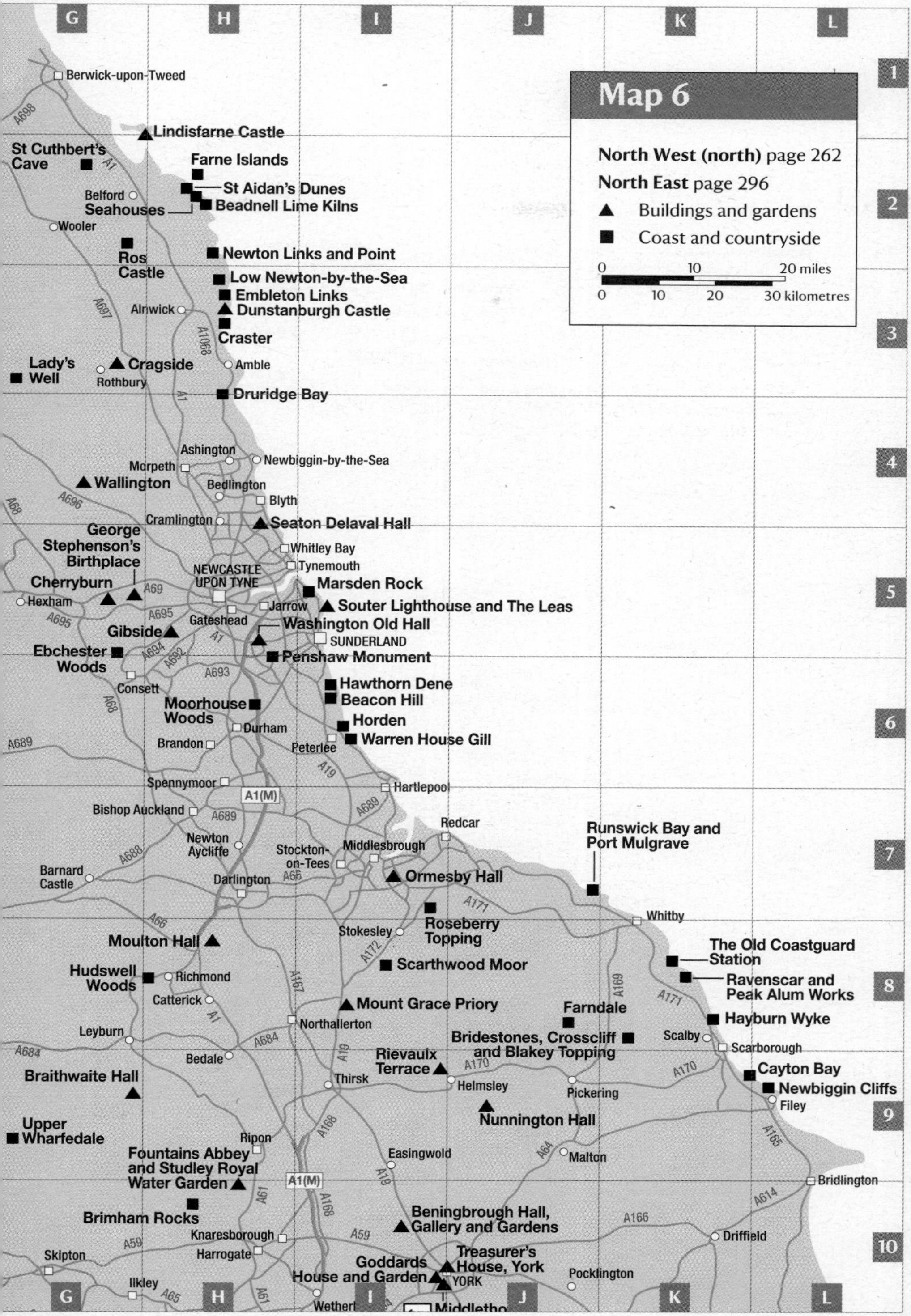
Map 6
North West (north) page 262
North East page 296
Buildings and gardens
Coast and countryside
0 10 20 miles
0 10 20 30 kilometres
G
H
I
J
K
L
1
2
3
4
5
6
7
8
9
10
Berwick-upon-Tweed
A698
Lindisfarne Castle
St Cuthbert's Cave
A1
Farne Islands
St Aidan's Dunes
Belford
Seahouses
Beadnell Lime Kilns
Wooler
Ros Castle
Newton Links and Point
Low Newton-by-the-Sea
Embleton Links
Dunstanburgh Castle
A697
Alnwick
A1068
Craster
Lady's Well
Cragside
Rothbury
Amble
Druridge Bay
Ashington
Morpeth
Newbiggin-by-the-Sea
Wallington
Bedlington
Blyth
A696
A68
Cramlington
Seaton Delaval Hall
George Stephenson's Birthplace
Whitley Bay
NEWCASTLE UPON TYNE
Tynemouth
Cherryburn
A69
Marsden Rock
Hexham
Jarrow
Souter Lighthouse and The Leas
A695
Gateshead
Washington Old Hall
Gibside
SUNDERLAND
Ebchester Woods
A694
A692
Penshaw Monument
A693
Consett
Hawthorn Dene
Beacon Hill
Moorhouse Woods
Horden
Durham
Warren House Gill
A689
Brandon
Peterlee
A19
Spennymoor
Hartlepool
A1(M)
Bishop Auckland
A689
Redcar
Newton Aycliffe
Stockton-on-Tees
Middlesbrough
Runswick Bay and Port Mulgrave
A688
Barnard Castle
Darlington
A66
Ormesby Hall
A171
Roseberry Topping
Whitby
A66
Stokesley
Moulton Hall
A172
The Old Coastguard Station
Hudswell Woods
Richmond
Scarthwood Moor
A167
Ravenscar and Peak Alum Works
A169
A171
Catterick
Mount Grace Priory
Farndale
A1
Northallerton
Hayburn Wyke
Leyburn
Bridestones, Crosscliff and Blakey Topping
Scalby
Scarborough
A684
A684
Bedale
A19
Rievaulx Terrace
A170
A170
Cayton Bay
Braithwaite Hall
Thirsk
Helmsley
Pickering
Newbiggin Cliffs
Filey
Nunnington Hall
Upper Wharfedale
Ripon
A168
A165
Fountains Abbey and Studley Royal Water Garden
Easingwold
A64
Malton
A19
A1(M)
Bridlington
A61
A168
A614
Brimham Rocks
Beningbrough Hall, Gallery and Gardens
A166
Knaresborough
A59
A59
Driffield
Skipton
Harrogate
Treasurer's House, York
Goddards House and Garden
YORK
Pocklington
Ilkley
A65
A61

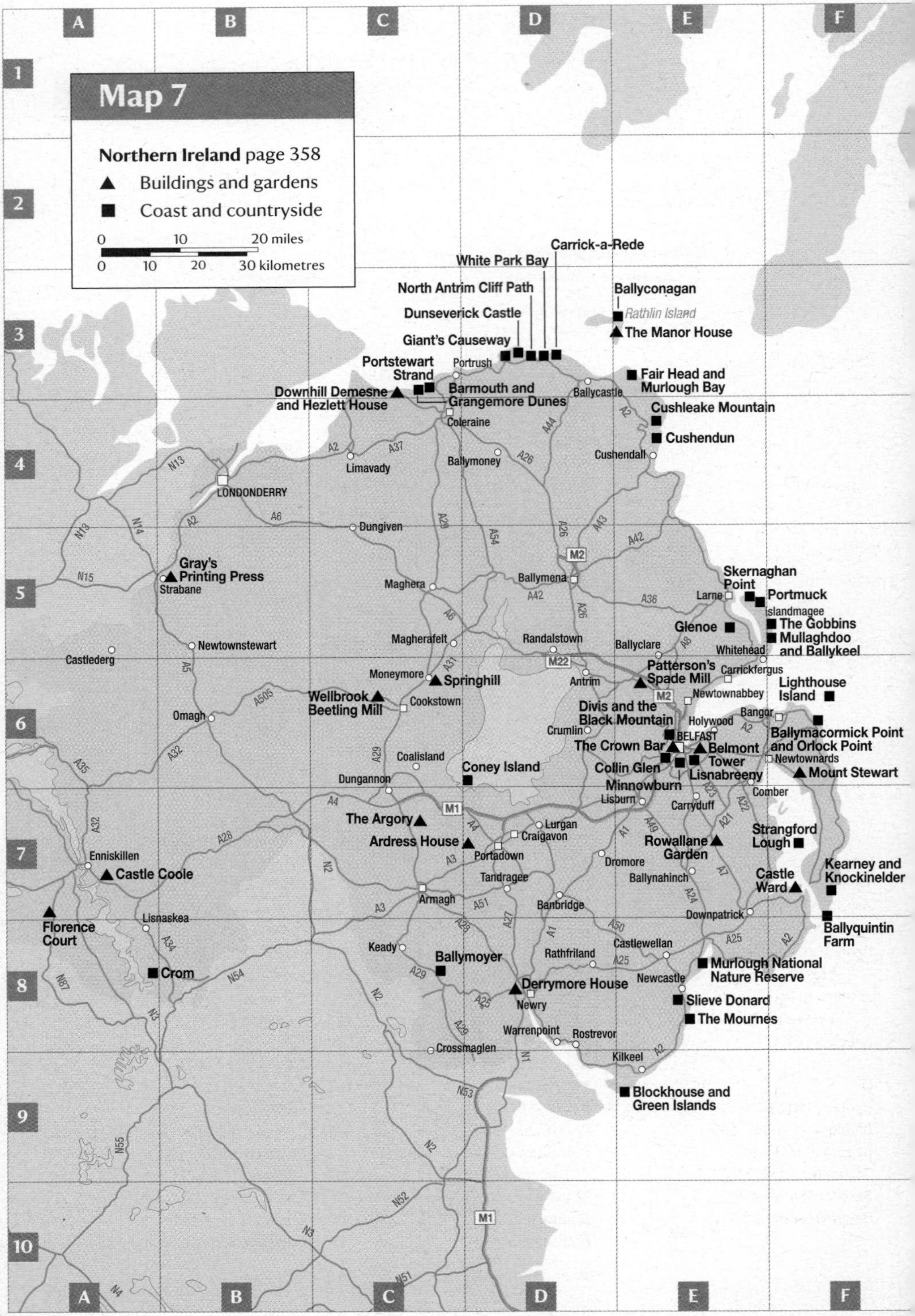
A B C D E F
1 2 3 4 5 6 7 8 9 10
Map 7
Northern Ireland page 358
Buildings and gardens
Coast and countryside
0 10 20 miles
0 10 20 30 kilometres
Carrick-a-Rede
White Park Bay
North Antrim Cliff Path
Dunseverick Castle
Giant's Causeway
Ballyconagan
Rathlin Island
The Manor House
Portstewart Strand
Portrush
Fair Head and Murlough Bay
Downhill Demesne and Hezlett House
Barmouth and Grangemore Dunes
Ballycastle
Cushleake Mountain
Coleraine
Cushendun
Cushendall
Limavady
Ballymoney
LONDONDERRY
Dungiven
Gray's Printing Press
Strabane
Maghera
Ballymena
Skernaghan Point
Larne
Portmuck
Islandmagee
The Gobbins
Mullaghdoo and Ballykeel
Glenoe
Whitehead
Castlederg
Newtownstewart
Magherafelt
Randalstown
Ballyclare
Moneymore
Springhill
Antrim
Patterson's Spade Mill
Carrickfergus
Lighthouse Island
Wellbrook Beetling Mill
Cookstown
Newtownabbey
Omagh
Divis and the Black Mountain
Holywood
Bangor
Crumlin
BELFAST
Ballymacormick Point and Orlock Point
The Crown Bar
Belmont Tower
Newtownards
Coalisland
Coney Island
Collin Glen
Lisnabreeny
Mount Stewart
Dungannon
Minnowburn
Lisburn
Comber
Carryduff
The Argory
Lurgan
Craigavon
Ardress House
Rowallane Garden
Strangford Lough
Enniskillen
Portadown
Dromore
Castle Coole
Tandragee
Ballynahinch
Castle Ward
Kearney and Knockinelder
Armagh
Banbridge
Florence Court
Downpatrick
Lisnaskea
Ballyquintin Farm
Keady
Castlewellan
Rathfriland
Ballymoyer
Murlough National Nature Reserve
Crom
Newcastle
Derrymore House
Newry
Slieve Donard
The Mournes
Warrenpoint
Rostrevor
Crossmaglen
Kilkeel
Blockhouse and Green Islands
M1 M2 M22
A2 A37 A26 A44 A29 A54 A43 A42 A6 A36 A8 A31 A505 A5 A32 A35 A4 A28 A3 A51 A27 A1 A49 A21 A22 A23 A24 A7 A50 A25 A34 A29
N13 N14 N15 N2 N54 N87 N3 N53 N1 N55 N52 N51 N4

Index

Places not in *italics* have an individual entry.

Getting in touch

The National Trust supports the National Code of Practice for Visitor Attractions. We are very willing to answer questions and keen to receive comments. Many National Trust places provide their own comment cards and boxes. All your comments will be read, considered and action taken where necessary, but it is not possible to answer every comment or suggestion individually.

Enquiries by telephone, email or in writing should be made to the Trust's Supporter Services Centre (see opposite), open seven days a week (9 to 5:30 weekdays, 9 to 4 weekends and Bank Holidays). You can also obtain information from **nationaltrust.org.uk**

National Trust Supporter Services Centre
PO Box 574, Manvers, Rotherham S63 3FH.
0344 800 1895, 0344 800 4410 (minicom)

Email **enquiries@nationaltrust.org.uk** for all general enquiries, including membership.

Central Office
The National Trust and National Trust (Enterprises) Ltd, Heelis, Kemble Drive, Swindon, Wiltshire SN2 2NA.
01793 817400, 01793 817401 (fax)

National Trust Holiday Cottages
0344 800 2072 (brochures)
0344 800 2070 (reservations)

To contact the Editor email
lucy.peel@nationaltrust.org.uk

NT LDS stock no:
73801/15

ISBN:
978-0-7078-0431-6

Sponsor
Louise McRae

Publisher
Katie Bond

Editor
Lucy Peel

Editorial assistance
Anthony Lambert
Trudi Marshall
Wendy Smith
Dee Maple

Production
Graham Prichard

Art direction
Craig Robson

Content management
Roger Shapland
Dave Buchanan

Design
LEVEL Partnership

Maps © **Blacker Design,** Maps in Minutes™/Collins Bartholomew 2014

Origination
Zebra

Printed
Wyndeham, Peterborough

If you'd like this information in an alternative format please telephone 01793 817858 or email customer.enquiries@nationaltrust.org.uk

Photography credits

National Trust Images' photographers and copyright holders:
Matthew Antrobus
Caroline Arber
Cristian Barnett
Andrew Besley
Mark Bolton
Jonathan Buckley
Andrew Butler
Michael Caldwell
Tony Cobley
Joe Cornish
Stuart Cox
Nick Daly
David Dixon
James Dobson
Rod Edwards
Andreas von Einsiedel
Phil Evans
Geoffrey Frosh
Dennis Gilbert
Nick Guttridge
John Hammond
Jerry Harpur
Paul Harris
Ross Hoddinott
Matthew Hollow
Tony Howell
Eddie Hyde
Tim Imrie
Jason Ingram
Laura Kennedy
Chris King
David Kirkham
Chris Lacey
David Levenson
Nadia Mackenzie
MMGI/Marianne Majerus
Leo Mason
Nick Meers
John Millar
John Miller
Paul Mogford
Andrew Montgomery
Robert Morris
James Mortimer
Clive Nichols
David Noton
Anthony Parkinson
Patrick Prendergast
Phil Ripley
Derry Robinson
Stephen Robson
David Sellman
Ben Selway
Arnhel de Serra
Neil Campbell-Sharp
Ian Shaw
Flo Smith
Timothy Smith
Solent News and Photography Agency
Mark Sunderland
Megan Taylor
Martin Trelawny
Rupert Truman
Angus Wainwright
Joe Wainwright
Jo Whitworth
Mike Williams
Derrick E. Witty

Additional images supplied by:
Bob Anderson
Richard Bryant/arcadiaimages.com
Stephen Ashworth
Rona Askew
Bailey Balloons
Steven Barber
Wyn Barnes
Rosemary Bird
Roger Bloxham
Peter Blyth
Heather Bradshaw
Andrew Brockbank
Paul Canning
Andrew Capell
Royal Borough of Kensington and Chelsea
Melanie Clarke
Natalie Cooper
Joshua Day
David Dixon
James Dobson
Jim Elliott
Simon Fraser
Jonathan Gardner
Jane Gosling
David Griffen
Susan Haimes
Marie-Louise Halpenny
Will Hawkins
Rob Hewer
Chris Hill
Jim Holden
George Kavanagh
David Kirkham
Robert Ledbury
Graham Lubbock
Sarah Mason
Eric McDonald
John Miller
Peter Muhly
Imperial War Museum
Philip Mynott
Nina Elliot-Newman
Martin Offer
John Parker
Ian Pearce
Josie Phillips
Parkway Photography
Evan Powell
Meleah Reardon
Tim Riley
Seamus Rogers
Norman Scott
David Sellman
Mike Simmonds
David Slade
David Slaviero
Claire Takacs
John Bigelow Taylor
Robert Thrift
Bexley Heritage Trust
John Faulkner
David Watson
Dave Wood